Asian Post-crisis Management

Also by Usha C. V. Haley

NEW ASIAN EMPERORS: THE OVERSEAS CHINESE, THEIR STRATEGIES AND COMPETITIVE ADVANTAGES
STRATEGIC MANAGEMENT IN THE ASIA PACIFIC: HARNESSING REGIONAL AND ORGANIZATIONAL CHANGE FOR COMPETITIVE ADVANTAGE
MULTINATIONAL CORPORATIONS IN POLITICAL ENVIRONMENTS: ETHICS, VALUES AND STRATEGIES
ASIA'S TAO OF BUSINESS: THE LOGIC OF CHINESE BUSINESS STRATEGY

Also by Frank Jürgen Richter

THE EAST ASIAN DEVELOPMENT MODEL
INTANGIBLES IN COMPETITION AND COOPERATION
ADVANCES IN HUMAN RESOURCE MANAGEMENT IN ASIA
MAXIMISING HUMAN INTELLIGENCE DEPLOYMENT IN ASIAN BUSINESS
THE DRAGON MILLENNIUM: CHINESE BUSINESS IN THE COMING WORLD ECONOMY
THE ASIAN ECONOMIC CATHARSIS: HOW ASIAN FIRMS BOUNCE BACK FROM CRISIS

Asian Post-crisis Management

Corporate and Governmental Strategies for Sustainable Competitive Advantage

Edited by

Usha C. V. Haley
University of Tennessee, Knoxville

and

Frank-Jürgen Richter
World Economic Forum, Geneva

palgrave

First published 2002 by
PALGRAVE
Houndmills, Basingstoke, Hampshire RG21 6XS and
175 Fifth Avenue, New York, N. Y. 10010
Companies and representatives throughout the world

PALGRAVE is the new global academic imprint of St. Martin's Press LLC Scholarly and Reference Division and Palgrave Publishers Ltd (formerly Macmillan Press Ltd).

ISBN 0–333–94964–1

This book is printed on paper suitable for recycling and made from fully managed and sustained forest sources.

A catalogue record for this book is available from the British Library.

Library of Congress Cataloging-in-Publication Data

Asian post-crisis management : corporate and governmental strategies for sustainable competitive advantage / edited by Usha C. V. Haley and Frank-Jürgen Richter.
p. cm.
Includes bibliographical references and index.
ISBN 0–333–94964–1 (cloth)
1. Industrial management—Asia. 2. Industrial policy—Asia. 3. Asia—Foreign economic relations. 4. Financial crises—Asia. I. Haley, Usha C. V. II. Richter, Frank-Jürgen.

HD70.A7 A768 2001
338.95—dc21

2001045867

10 9 8 7 6 5 4 3 2
11 10 09 08 07 06 05 04 03

Typeset by Integra Software Services Pvt. Ltd., Pondicherry, India
www.integra-india.com

Printed and bound in Great Britain by
Antony Rowe Ltd, Chippenham, Wiltshire

For our parents,
Dr. C. Venkatesan and Nandini Venkatesan
and
Bernhilde Richter and Ernst Richter

Contents

Part 3 Post-crisis Governmental Strategies

Part 4 Organizational Restructuring and Corporate Governance

Part 5 Post-crisis Business Environments

List of Tables

List of Figures

Notes on the Contributors

Yasuhiro Arikawa is a lecturer at the Faculty of Literature and Social Sciences, Yamagata University. He has been researching corporate finance and governance issues of contemporary Japan. He has written several articles on financial choice in collaboration with Hideaki Miyajima.

Caroline Benton was formerly a director of a Japanese subsidiary of a European manufacturer, and was chief consultant at a marketing consulting firm for foreign-affiliated companies in Japan over the last five years.

David M. Boje is Professor of Management, CBAE at New Mexico State University (NMSU); and a co-director of the NMSU Center for Strategic Decisions. He has published numerous articles and books. He serves on the board of directors of the International Academy of Business Disciplines and is a founding board member of the *Electronic Journal of Radical Organization Theory*. He is editor of the *Journal of Organizational Change Management* and also serves on the editorial boards of *Management Digest, Organization, Journal of Management Inquiry, Academy of Management Review* and *Management Communication Quarterly*.

Hock Beng Cheah is a senior lecturer at the School of Economics and Management, University College, University of New South Wales. In the field of economics, his research interests are focused on economic development in the Asia-Pacific region. In the management field, his teaching and research interests include Human Resource Management, Organizational Development and entrepreneurship. He has published in a variety of notable journals, including the *Journal of Business Venturing, Creativity and Innovation Management* and *Journal of Enterprising Culture*.

Melanie Cheah is a corporate lawyer at Allen, Allen and Hemsley in Sydney. She previously worked as an intern at the Capacity Building Unit (Africa Region) at the World Bank, Washington DC. She was a former President of the Golden Key National Honour Society (University of Tasmania chapter), and a former Executive Committee member of the

National Association of Australian University Colleges. She has a strong interest in entrepreneurship, risk management and development issues, and plans to undertake graduate studies with special focus on entrepreneurial strategies for sustainable development.

Baizhu Chen is Professor of Finance and Business Economics at the University of Southern California. His research covers a wide range of monetary economics, international finance and Chinese financial market reforms. He has published prolifically on the political economy of growth, private investment, foreign currency market, the Chinese financial market and monetary policy. He is a recipient of grants from the Washington Center for China Studies, the Chinese National Science Foundation and Eurasian Studies of Taiwan for his research on China's central bank monetary policies and the Chinese financial market.

Thomas Clarke is Professor of Management at the University of Technology, Sydney. He was previously DBM Professor of Corporate Governance at the Leeds Business School, UK, and Visiting Professor at the China Europe International Business School, Shanghai; FGV Business School, Sao Paulo, Brazil and UAM Business School, Mexico City. He has published five books. He has been consultant to the board of directors of international intellectual property rights companies, and is a member of the advisory board of the Strategic Partnership an international strategic management consultancy company.

Malcolm J. M. Cooper is currently Principal of the Wide Bay Campus of the University of Southern Queensland. He has also taught and researched at the Universities of Birmingham and Glasgow (United Kingdom), New England and Adelaide (Australia), and the Waiariki Institute of Technology (New Zealand). In addition to these academic positions he has held senior positions in State, Federal and Local Government in Australia, and has been a consultant to the governments of China and Vietnam in the development of tourism. His publications include more than 95 books, journal articles, book chapters, consultant's reports and research papers on a variety of topics, but specializing in environment and tourism management.

Birgit Ensslinger is an MBA student at the Department of Business Administration at the University of Erlangen-Nuremberg, Germany. Her research focuses on German direct investment in the People's Republic of China.

Yi Feng is Associate Professor at Claremont Graduate University. His areas of specialization include international political economy and methodology. He has published extensively and his papers have appeared in such journals as *British Journal of Political Science, European Journal of Political Economy, Journal of Peace Research, Journal of Conflict Resolution* and *International Interactions*.

Shruti Gupta is a doctoral student at the Fox School of Business and Management at Temple University, Philadelphia. Previously she was an adjunct professor with the Department of Geography and Urban Studies at Temple University. Her research interests are in the areas of international marketing strategy, corporate image and reputation, corporate philanthropy, corporate social responsibility, environmental consumerism and consumer behaviour in emerging markets.

George T. Haley is Associate Professor/Director of Marketing and International Business Programs at the University of New Haven. A frequent public speaker for corporate executives and government policy-makers worldwide, and an award-winning author, he has written over 75 books, book chapters, articles and research reports. His latest books include *New Asian Emperors: The Overseas Chinese, their Strategies and Competitive Advantages* (Butterworth-Heinemann, 1998), the top-selling book on Asian business strategies worldwide. He consults with Asian, Latin American and US companies on strategic management and industrial marketing issues and is on the review and advisory boards of several US and European journals where he lends his expertize on Asia and other emerging economies.

Usha C. V. Haley is currently Associate Professor of Management at the University of Tennessee, Knoxville (College of Business Administration). She has written more than 70 books, journal articles, book chapters and research presentations on international strategic management. She has taught in major corporate, governmental and universities' executive-development programmes internationally. She also serves as a consultant on issues concerning strategic management and foreign direct investment (FDI) for several multinational corporations and acts as Regional Editor (Asia Pacific) for two academic journals. She can be contacted through her WWW page at http://www.asia-pacific.com and e-mail uhaley@asia-pacific.com

John Kidd worked in industry for about ten years before he moved to Birmingham University, and later still, to his present position at the Aston Business School. His publications include essays upon Japanese management methods (funded by the Japan Foundation). This work has broadened to include all Asian managers following a period at the China Europe International Business School, Shanghai. He was a member of a UK Overseas Science and Technology Expert Mission evaluating manufacturing in Japan and Korea from a cultural and technical perspective.

Chang-Su Kim is a doctoral candidate in International Business at Rutgers University. His research interests include cross-border R&D Alliances, Culture and Learning in Interorganizational Cooperation, and Internationalization of Korean Firms.

Beverley Kitching currently lectures in International Business at Queensland University of Technology (QUT) in Brisbane, Australia. She has published on Chinese Science Policy, Sino-Australian Relations in Science and Technology and most recently on Women in Business in the PRC.

Masaaki 'Mike' Kotabe holds the Washburn Chair of International Business and Marketing, and is Director of Research at the Institute of Global Management Studies at the Fox School of Business and Management at Temple University. He has worked closely with leading companies such as AT&T, NEC, Philips, Sony and Ito-Yokado (parent of 7-Eleven stores), and currently serves as advisor to the United Nations' and World Trade Organization's Executive Forum on National Export Strategies. His research work has appeared in such journals as the *Journal of International Business Studies, Journal of Marketing* and *Strategic Management Journal*. He is the Associate Editor of the *Journal of International Business Studies* and the Co-editor of the *Journal of International Management*. He has been recently elected as a Fellow of the Academy of International Business for his lifetime contribution to international business research and education.

Brij Nino Kumar was Professor and Chair of Business Economics and International Management at the University of Erlangen-Nürnberg, Germany. He authored and co-authored over 100 publications on various subjects of international management in Germany, USA, UK, Japan and China. Besides his academic career he was consultant to companies and ministries and was acting member of the editorial boards of various professional management journals. The editors regret to inform you that Professor Kumar passed away in July 2000 prior to the publication of this book.

Nancy E. Landrum is Assistant Professor of Management at Morehead State University. Nancy was previously a mental health therapist and has over ten years of experience as a manager in non-profit social service organizations. Her teaching and research interests are in the areas of strategic management, organizational behaviour, human resources, entrepreneurship and non-profit management.

Keun Lee is Associate Professor of Economics at the Seoul National University. His research interests include corporate governance and growth, industrial policy, and innovation and technology policy in East Asia. In this field, he has published more than 20 articles in such journals as, *Journal of Comparative Economics, Economics of Planning, Cambridge Journal of Economics, World Development, Asian Economic Journal* and *China Economic Review*, as well as two monographs.

Xue Li is Professor in Management Sciences at Guanxi University, China and is currently a visiting scholar at Aston University, United Kingdom. She was in the first group of five persons to be authorized to tutor TOEFL and BEC courses in China; indeed she introduced BEC to China. She has first-hand knowledge of the issues facing managers who jointly wish to set-up ventures in China whist working as a 'go between', and also though working in import/export firms.

Yunshi Mao is a professor at the School of Management at Zhoughshau University in Guangzhou, of the People's Republic of China. He is a member of the Academic Committee of Management and Academic Degree Commission of the State Council of China.

Hideaki Miyajima is a professor in the School of Commerce, Waseda University. He has acted as a consultant to several institutions including The World Bank, Hawaii University, Hebrew University, Ministry of Trade and Industry, Ministry of Finance and others, and was also involved in the Joint project of TIT (Tokyo Institute of Technology) and IIASA (International Institute of Applied System Analysis). He has written several books and numerous papers both in Japanese and English.

Sek Hong Ng is Reader in Management in the School of Business, The University of Hong Kong. He is the author of many publications on Hong Kong and the People's Republic of China. He is an active consultant to several Hong Kong labour-management bodies, including trade unions.

Howard V. Perlmutter is Professor of Management and Social Architecture Emeritus at the Wharton School and one of the pioneers in the study of the multinational corporation and the globalization process. He currently serves as Secretary of the Faculty of Wharton School, Director of the Emerging Global Civilization project, and Academic Advisor for Wharton's Advanced Management Program. Over his career, he has been involved in educational and advisory roles in over 100 multinational corporations and international institutions including the World Health Organization, and the League of Red Cross societies. He is a Fellow of the Academy of International Business and of the Academy of International Management.

Frank-Jürgen Richter is Director for Asia, at the World Economic Forum, Geneva. He was educated in business administration and mechanical engineering in Germany, France, Mexico and Japan. Prior to joining the World Economic Forum, he gathered high-level management experience in Asia and Europe. He was based in Beijing for several years developing and managing a European multinational's China operations. An active scholar, he authored and edited several books on Asian economies and international business. He can be contacted through e-mail fj_r@yahoo.com

Fred Robins teaches and researches at The Graduate School of Management, University of Adelaide. He is a member of The University of South Australia's Marketing Science Center. Prior to his academic career he had public sector experience in Europe and Asia and, later, private sector experience in public relations and as a marketing manager. More recently he has researched the activities of Australian business in ASEAN markets and has published articles on Asian business in international academic journals. He has also written on the contrast between Asian and Australian trade and industry policies.

Michael A. Santoro is an assistant professor in the International Business and Business Environment Department at the Rutgers Graduate School of Management. His writings have appeared in *Business & the*

Contemporary World, The Wall Street Journal, the *International Herald Tribune, The Asian Wall Street Journal,* the *South China Morning Post* and the *Harvard Journal of World Affairs.* His book, *Profits and Principles: Global Capitalism and Human Rights in China,* was published in Spring 2000 by Cornell University Press. In the summers, he teaches an executive MBA course in Asian Business Strategies in Beijing to executives of Sinopec, the state-owned petrochemical company and one of the largest companies in China. He also teaches courses in professional ethics in law firms and in-house corporate legal departments.

Yoshiya Teramoto is Professor of Social System Design at the Graduate School of Knowledge Science, JAIST (Japan Advanced Institute of Science and Technology). He is also a Visiting Professor of Organization Theory at the Graduate School of Asia-Pacific Studies, Waseda University and a Visiting Researcher at the NISTEP (National Institute for Science and Technology Policy), The Science and Technology Agency, Japan. He has written and lectured widely on organizational learning and knowledge management.

Malcolm Warner is Professor and Fellow, Wolfson College, Cambridge and the Judge Institute of Management Studies, University of Cambridge. Formerly a Scholar, then later Research Scholar of Trinity College, Cambridge, he also took his doctorate at that university. He is the author and editor of a number of books on Chinese management and is the Editor-in-Chief, *The International Encyclopaedia of Business and Management*, London: Thomson Learning, 2nd edition.

Part 1
Introduction

1

Post-crisis Management Strategies in Asia: An Overview

Usha C. V. Haley

A decade ago, a writer from *Fortune* magazine, Louis Kraar, wrote in the preface to Kim Woo Chong's book, *Every Street is Paved with Gold*, that Kim, the Daewoo empire's founder, 'personifies the drive and imagination that makes East Asia a dynamic centre of economic growth'. Kim fled South Korea in late 1999, shortly after his empire crashed. From his initial exile post in Frankfurt, he submitted his resignation from all the Daewoo Group's companies. He has left no clue about his whereabouts since then.

Kim Woo Chong's meteoric rise as one of Asia's most powerful tycoons, and his equally spectacular fall, symbolize the Asian miracle and the prolonged crisis that threatened to destroy it in 1997 and that still hangs over the economic landscape. The system's flaws became apparent in mid-1999, when Kim acknowledged that his companies, which had acquired a global reach in a debt-fueled expansion binge, could not pay their creditors. By the time the banks that took over the Daewoo Group had calculated $80 billion in liabilities, Kim was changing addresses in Europe. For Asia, lessons from the crisis indicate that traditional methods of operation through debt financing and over investing will fail. This lesson and others will be explored in this book.

The new millennium appears a good time to reassess post-crisis strategies in Asia. Corporations and governments are still struggling to make sense of the tumultuous changes attending the financial crisis of 1997–98. A recent survey by the *Wall Street Journal* (Booth, 2001a) revealed that multinational corporations (hereafter referred to as 'multinationals') are delaying investments in Asia and focusing on curbing costs until the dust clears and the economic landscape becomes more hospitable. The multinationals also appear to be withholding investments from the higher-risk countries and companies most in need of liquidity (Booth,

2001a). Despite the turmoil in Asia, the *Wall Street Journal*'s survey indicated notable pockets of strength that corporations are striving to exploit, especially in the high-technology and Internet sectors. India's technology sector alone is seeing a torrent of venture capital flow in with a sevenfold increase in investment in 2000.

Governments in Asia, especially in Southeast Asia also have reasons to reassess strategies. All the economic news presently originating from Southeast Asia appears bad. The growth rates of the economies have fallen sharply to between 2.5 per cent and 5 per cent in 2000. The countries' financial systems, devastated by the crisis, still show fragility. The region's economies have historically recovered from economic downturns by exporting their way out of trouble. Now, the region's two biggest export markets, the USA and Japan, accounting for 46 per cent of the world output, are both teetering on the brink of recession. Conventional economic models that focus on trade links tend to understate the adverse impact of a US recession on Asia, especially in light of foreign direct investment (FDI) and financial contagion through stock markets. However, recession could also spread from the USA to Asia through the global Information Technology (IT) supply chain that links the USA, Japan and Asia. As the USA's IT spending bubble bursts, Asia's exports will slump and indeed, South Korea's gross domestic product (GDP) fell in the fourth quarter of 2000 affected by the USA's slump. Over the past couple of years, Japan's economic problems have also been getting worse (*Economist*, 2001a). Japan constitutes the only developed economy to have experienced true deflation since the 1930s. This means that although Japan's real GDP increased in each of the past two years, GDP in money terms shrank. Deflation has dragged the Japanese economy into a vicious circle, where falling prices encourage households to delay spending, thereby pushing prices lower still. Meanwhile, deflation increases the real burden of debt, further choking demand, and again necessitating a reassessment of strategies from both corporations and governments.

China, the most populous country in the world, and the largest potential market for several industrial sectors, also plans to join the World Trade Organization (WTO) soon. For the Southeast-Asian governments, China's rise ought to provide good news: China offers a large potential market for Southeast-Asian goods, and might even become the engine of regional growth. However, for the Southeast-Asian economies, China constitutes not just a market but also a ferocious rival in exports. Southeast-Asia's economies face direct competition from a growing range of cheap, well-made Chinese exports, such as labour-intensive textiles (China competes directly against Vietnam and Indonesia in this sector) and higher-value electronics (China challenges Thailand and Malaysia in these sectors). Governmental policy makers in Southeast Asia also suspect that the region once attracted lots of FDI because much of China's economy remained closed. If China opens wide, would FDI still seek out Southeast Asia, they wonder.

In FDI, a great shift in regional flows of capital highlights the challenges China poses to Southeast Asia. Not counting rich Japan, China presently gets nearly four-fifths of all Asia's FDI, whilst Southeast Asia scrambles for a share of the rest (*Economist*, 2000b; Prystay, 2001), roughly reversing the FDI trends of the mid-1990s. Figure 1.1 shows FDI flows into China and Southeast Asia. This swing of FDI hampers Southeast-Asia's recovery and deprives its economies of much-needed technology and outside skills. According to many analysts, this shift in FDI will last and should prompt new strategies from the Southeast-Asian governments. Although Singapore and Malaysia, in particular, offer attributes that China may take years to match, such as good infrastructure, skilled labour, stability and a relatively clear legal framework, China's sheer

SHEER WEIGHT OF NUMBERS

Net Flows of Foreign Direct Investment (US$ millions)

	1990	1991	1992	1993	1994	1995	1996	1997	1998	1999	2000[1]
China	2657	3453	7156	23115	31787	33849	38066	41674	41117	36978	35869
Indonesia	1093	1482	1777	1648	1500	3743	5594	4499	–400	–2817	225
Malaysia	2332	3998	5183	5006	4342	4178	5078	5137	2163	1553	2700
Phillippines	530	544	228	864	1289	1079	1335	1086	2127	632	781
Singapore	3541	4361	887	2534	3973	925	2050	–773	7018	3041	3600
Thailand	2303	1847	1966	1571	873	1182	1405	3315	7185	5867	3000
Vietnam	120	220	260	300	1048	2236	1838	2003	800	700	1000

[1]Data for 2000 are estimates by World Bank Staff

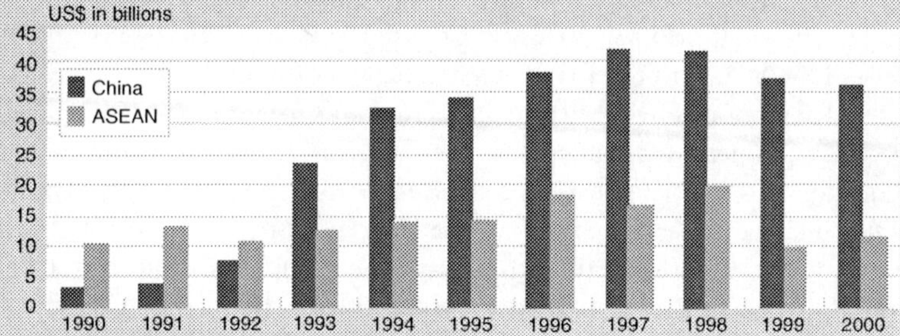

[1]Excludes Brunei

Figure 1.1 The FDI flows into China and Southeast Asia
Source: Japan Bank for International Cooperation.

market size and cost of labour offer key drivers. According to a 1999 JETRO (Government of Japan) survey, the cost of a factory worker in Shenzhen, China approximates about half that of one in Bangkok, Thailand and one-third of one in Kuala Lumpur, Malaysia; a middle manager in Cebu, Philippines, costs 47 per cent more than a middle manager in the relatively higher-priced Shanghai, one of China's most expensive cities.

However, China's advantages erode when analysts and managers weigh the enormous economic and business risks of operating there. The Southeast-Asian governments do have strategies they can follow to compete against the Chinese dragon including emphasizing clean governance, transparency and legal predictability; lowering regional trade barriers to allow integrated supply chains; and, upgrading financial institutions through reforms. However, these countries will have to quicken the pace of financial and corporate restructuring, and push their economies more quickly up the value-added chain. Hastening progress of the ASEAN Free Trade Agreement (AFTA) to make Southeast Asia a seamless market could also boost competitiveness against China.

Foreign multinationals and other investors have also noted that a lack of transparency still poses major problems in Asia. From Korea to Indonesia, scandals and irregularities have left investors severely burned. The countries have made some progress (see Haley, 2000a), but far less than optimists hoped. Peter Woicke, Executive Vice-president of International Finance Corporation (IFC), the private-sector lending arm of the World Bank said, 'The reform progress has been very slow. Part of the problem is that Asia has recovered too quickly, so (the countries) saw no need to put into place necessary reforms' (Booth, 2001b). Foreign institutional investors, including multinationals, form one of the groups most affected by lack of transparency: they have much less knowledge than local companies and businesses of local markets and conditions (Haley, 2000b). However, foreign investors can force countries to restructure by putting their money where their mouth is and investing in transparent and clean business environments; they are not doing so. China gets by far the most FDI in Asia despite consistently ranking near the bottom of executive surveys on transparency and corruption. In the most recent survey by the Berlin-based anti-corruption group Transparency International, China ranked as the eighth-most-corrupt nation in Asia, behind Thailand, and just ahead of India. In the Heritage Foundation's survey of economic freedom in Asia, China ranked ninth, behind the Philippines. China's inscrutability increases the risks of doing business there and requires novel, often improvised, strategies from multinationals.

Since the financial crisis, South Korea has also seen heavy foreign investment, particularly via the stock market, despite a mediocre record on corporate governance. 'A lot of fund managers get excited about the Korean market, but in terms of corporate governance it is one of the weaker markets', said Peter Hames at Aberdeen Asset Management Asia Ltd. in Singapore (Booth, 2000b). Irregularities in corporate governance have even undermined investors' confidence in Samsung Electronics, widely considered the leading blue chip company on the Korea Stock Exchange. In August 2000, South Korean Education Minister Song Ja, also an outside director of Samsung Electronics, resigned in part because of allegations that he accepted a 1.67 billion won ($1.3 million) interest-free loan from the corporation to buy its stock at discount prices. Some investors took the loan as a sign that the corporation was trying to influence unduly outside directors. Similarly, in November 2000, a group of foreign investors took legal action against Samsung Electronics' management over the corporation's decision to pay the bankrupt Samsung Motors' debts. Consequently, Samsung continued to trade at a discount to its global peers. 'If not for corporate governance, Samsung would have a price-earnings ratio of seven to ten times rather than five', said Teng Ngiek Lian, the Chief Executive Officer (CEO) of fund management firm, Value Partners Ltd. in Singapore.

Transparency and corruption problems loom larger in Southeast-Asia, especially in Indonesia where poor accounting standards and cronyism exist along with badly paid regulators themselves vulnerable to bribery (Haley, 2001a,b). For example, in Indonesia, the IFC is currently fighting a legal dispute over the bankruptcy of PT Panca Overseas Finance. The company was facing liquidation in early 2000, in which case IFC would have received part of the $13 million owed to it. However, a local court approved a controversial debt-restructuring plan requested by a minority of shareholders, many of whom IFC claims as bogus. Panca disputes this contention, and has won one of two cases involving the controversy in Indonesia's Supreme Court. IFC's Executive Vice-president Peter Woicke argued that such cases highlight how the independence of the judiciary, and indeed of all public officials, in Asia's less-developed nations remains in doubt. 'Unless they get paid a decent salary they are prone to bribery', he concluded (Booth, 2001b).

The inevitable forces of globalization may stem some of these tides and alter business environments even further. As Asian companies list their stocks in the USA, they are required to adopt US accounting standards, prompting other local competitors to improve their corporate governance to compete for investment. For example, Infosys Technologies

Ltd. of India trades in New York and follows US accounting standards. The corporation's popularity among US investors has persuaded other Indian technology firms to improve their accounting standards, boosting the image of the sector as a whole. 'At the end of the day there is only so much capital and that money will go to the companies that have the highest standards. The easy money is just not there any more', said Peter Hames at Aberdeen (Booth, 2001b).

'It is too bad if you lose money, but money is one of those things that is O.K. to lose since you can always make more,' Kim Woo Chong wrote in his book, *Every Street is Paved with Gold,* 'But you should never lose your reputation. You should treasure it as dearly as life.' This book is aimed at rebuilding lost corporate and national reputations and treasuring facets that still blaze strong: Several researchers, policy makers and managers attempt to shed light on old problems that linger and new opportunities that have resurfaced in post-crisis Asia. Many managers and analysts believe (as in the *Wall Street Journal* survey cited earlier) that austerity in Asia this year will set the stage for stable growth in the coming years when well-considered strategies should reap benefits. While Asia still gets low marks for corporate governance and corruption, the shortage of investment capital may prompt companies and governments to clean up their acts. On a broader scale, the shortage of capital is already forcing restructuring as corporations team up or buy each other out to cut costs. That trend has surfaced in the old economy, as steel companies in North Asia form strategic alliances to cope with overcapacity, and in the new, as China's dot-coms strive to consolidate because money is running out. The next section provides an overview of this book on post-crisis Asia including corporate strategies, governmental strategies, key issues such as transparency and corporate governance and finally, the business environments.

Overview and outline

Chapters 2–7 deal with post-crisis corporate strategies. In Chapter 2, Mike Kotabe and Shruti Gupta examine the Asian financial crisis and its ramifications on Asian corporations and consumers. The authors contend that until the mid-1990s, researchers and policy makers predicted that the Asian economy would grow at the fast pace of the previous 30 years. Many pundits had predicted the dawn of the Asian century in the new millennium. However, towards the end of 1998, the region's financial crisis brought the Asian economic miracle to a screeching halt, eliciting strategic reactions from corporations. The ramifications of the Asian financial crisis extend beyond Asian countries and their trading partners: Other emerging economies also suffered because of the ever-shifting international portfolio-investment flows at the whim of international investors. This new economic environment has necessitated new corporate strategies. Chapter 3 by Yasuhiro Arikawa and Hideaki Miyajima investigates recent changes in corporate finance and governance, and its impact on corporate behaviour, focusing on investments and Research and Development (R&D). Sweeping shifts in debt choices from bank borrowing to bond issuing occurred in the late 1980s in Japan. Although debt decreased since 1993, outstanding bonds have decreased at a much slower rate than outstanding borrowing. Given this drastic change in corporate finance, the main banking system that played an important role for corporate governance has been changing. The main bank is losing its disciplining role for management, and the market for corporate control is increasing with repercussions for corporate strategy. In Chapter 4, George Haley looks at the use of the Internet as a post-crisis strategy in Asia's emerging markets. Most emerging economies do not have the infrastructure or skill-base to permit the Internet to create large cost reductions and increases in productivity as in advanced economies. Consequently, the macroeconomic effects of the Internet on emerging economies produce a mixed bag of benefits, and in some cases, tremendous costs. However, countries that show ingenuity and perseverance in developing and employing Internet technologies can benefit substantially. Multinationals that show ingenuity and perseverance generally gain measurable competitive advantages over their competitors. In both instances however, they cannot simply mimic policies and strategies employed in advanced economies. In Chapter 5, Brij Kumar, Yunshi Mao and Birgit Ensslinger seek to uncover the patterns and determinants of global strategies in Asia and to isolate links to success and sustainable competitive advantage. The study draws on an investigation of global strategy and FDI of 36 German multinationals in China. Although the Asian crisis affected China less than other countries in Southeast and East Asia, many multinationals, including those from Germany, divested. When they could integrate Asian operations into their global strategies, German multinationals absorbed losses from declining local markets, and sometimes even boosted sales by harnessing lower factor costs and currency devaluations for more effective intra-corporate procurement and supplies. In these instances, global strategies cushioned the adversities of the Asian crisis through cross-subsidization. The potential of German multinationals to integrate and to coordinate Asian operations within their global strategies varied according to many factors explored in this chapter. Chapter 6 by Nancy Landrum and David Boje analyses the ways in which strategic narratives have changed in the footwear industry from before the Asian economic crisis to the present day. The authors examine the narrative contained in the 'Letters to Shareholders' of the top two footwear manufacturers in the world, Nike and Reebok, over the period 1990–99. The authors first examine the footwear industry in the USA and China before and after the financial crisis; a discussion of strategic management and narrative follows. Finally, the authors share their analysis and offer conclusions for corporate strategies and societies. Chapter 7 by Xue Li, John Kidd and Frank-Jürgen Richter explores the costs of hiring expatriates, including the psychological costs affecting the expatriates and their families, as well as their effects on multinationals and the countries in which the expatriates may work, especially on China. The authors argue that expatriates and their effects will assume more importance when China joins the WTO. Failure to effectively manage expatriates' assignments pose major hurdles for multinationals in Asia's post-crisis era because of internal corporate politics, cultural issues, family concerns about changes in employees' lifestyles, the rapid expansion of the global market place, and the escalation of expatriate costs. The authors examine the dominant issues in expatriate assignment and make recommendations for multinationals in the new post-crisis Asian environment.

Chapters 8–10 focus on post-crisis governmental strategies. Chapter 8 by Malcolm Cooper investigates the changing character of Vietnam's post-1997 economy, discussing the major themes and issues that have emerged since that watershed year of the Asian economic crisis. It outlines the economic, cultural and environmental dimensions of the Government's management of the economy of Vietnam, the approaches taken by the Government in responding to the twin problems of the crisis and the country's internal economic restructuring, and the likely economic future of Vietnam. The chapter concludes by commenting on the relevance of the policy of *doi moi* to the country in the post-crisis world of Asia. Chapter 9 by Yi Feng and Baizhu Chen analyses the tariff structure and its determinants in China, with research conducted under the rubric of endogenous policy theory. The authors studied the tariff rates for 95 industries in China in 1996. They collected the potential determinants of tariff rates from an array of variables characterizing industries in 1995 and used a principal component method to reduce these variables into four major dimensions. The first component comprises the information on the composition of employees broken down by age, education and job classification. The second component emphasizes the profitability of the industry. The third component captures variables with low salience in the first two components including gross product, foreign capital, inventory, sales revenue and total loss. Using variables identified by the principal component analysis and postulated by the variants of endogenous trade theory, regression analysis finds that trade policy in China rests on industrial policy favouring high-tech industries and a social policy minimizing social instability. The authors also discuss the implications for China's entry into the WTO. In Chapter 10, Howard Perlmutter formulates three scenarios for China for a longer term (30–50 years hence). The first scenario comprises a National Fortress China which retreats from the global economy and abandons reforms in the face of catastrophic unemployment and backlash from those not benefiting from free markets. A second scenario involves a Pragmatic Reformist China, a version of the current situation in which more privatization of industrial and business sectors occurs, but where the Internet does not play a major role because of the governmental fear of losing control. A third transformational scenario the author calls the Global Cyber Integration China involves a deep integration of China electronically into the primary domains of civilization: political, military, legal, economic, sociocultural, in science, technology and medicine, and ecology. The author argues that the third scenario has the best long-term prospects with the emerging global cyber-civilization and includes Taiwan and even the remotest villages of China. It requires that the Chinese leadership develop a new global mindset. Finally, the chapter discusses how an open China in the longer term will find that it needs to engage in a definable set of deepening, multilevel, interpersonal and interinstitutional dialogic interactions with people and institutions globally and in Asia.

Chapters 11–15 highlight key strategic issues in post-crisis Asia including corporate restructuring and corporate governance. Chapter 11 by Sek Hong Ng and Malcolm Warner explores the strategic implications of enterprise reform undertaken to implement the logic and practice of market socialism by two state-owned firms and one joint venture, Shougang, Founder and Beijing Jeep. The authors examine business restructuring and its attendant consequences on Human Resource Management practices, such as downsizing. Chapter 12 by Tom Clarke argues that as the painful process of restructuring and recapitalization proceeds, signs of economic recovery in the East Asian economies cannot disguise the severe dislocation and substantial output costs of the financial crisis, with the sacrifice of several years of economic growth. Progress towards reforms will follow different paths in the different countries concerned. Important objectives for the development of more robust modes of governance include clarifying and strengthening internal control structures within firms; and intensifying external monitoring and control through improvements in the legal framework and greater disclosure of information. Chapter 13 by Keun Lee discusses changes in corporate governance and finance in Korea before and after the 1997 crisis. Utilizing insights from Penrose's theory of the growth of firms, the author argues that changes in the external economic conditions since the mid-1980s contributed to increasing costs and reduced the benefits of the *chaebol*-type firms, as evidenced by their declining profitability and eventually the 1997 crisis. The chapter discusses economic changes after the crisis, focusing on the reform of corporate governance and financial systems. The Korean government followed the strategy of reforming the financial system first so that the banks and other financial organizations could pressure their corporate clients to change. The author elaborates on three aspects of the reform: financial sector reform, corporate governance reform and corporate restructuring to change capital and business structures. Chapter 14 by Caroline Benton and Yoshiya Teramoto analyses the co-evolution of corporate governance and business models. Since the burst of the Japanese economic bubble in the early 1990s, a series of socio-economic changes have occurred including a growing number of high-profile corporate corruption scandals, wide-ranging deregulation, and changes in investors' goals. These changes have had profound and far-reaching consequences on the way corporations conduct, manage and govern their businesses. The authors first give a synopsis of these major issues and changes in the Japanese market; second, they present how these changes have affected Japanese corporate governance using Sony as an example; and third, they present strategies for corporate governance in the twenty-first century.

Chapters 15–19 cover post-crisis business environments. In Chapter 15, Usha Haley argues that just as old maps carried the phrase 'Here there be dragons' to warn seafarers of potential dangers in uncharted territories, multinationals should be warned that the Chinese market poses enormous potential and horrendous obstacles. Effective strategizing by multinationals will need to consider both safe harbours and dragons in a reasoned light. The first section of this chapter analyses historical trends of FDI into China. The ensuing section estimates various risks associated with doing business in China including market potential, copyright violations, political manoeuvrings and corruption. The final section offers some suggestions for effective strategies by multinationals operating in China in the new millennium. Chapter 16 by Fred Robins examines how the crisis has influenced the Asian model of economic development sometimes referred to as Asian Capitalism. The author examines the business consequences of the crisis, successively, at three different levels: direct impact on daily business at the level of the firm; impact on business-relevant legislation and institutions; and, impact on the policy-making elite's economic-development thinking. Finally, the author speculates about the medium-term future of business–government relationships in the region. Chapter 17 by Michael Santoro and Chang-Su Kim offers an explanation of how political factors contributed to the Asian financial crisis. The authors show the lessons of the crisis for multinationals assessing the political risks of investing in Asia. Simply defined, political risk gauges the likelihood that political events will cause drastic changes in a country's business environment that in turn will affect adversely profits and other goals of a multinational. At first blush, the connection between financial crisis and political risk might not seem apparent: Political turmoil did not precede the financial crisis in Asia. On closer inspection, however, political factors did indeed play a significant though subtle role in the genesis of the crisis. The authors elaborate on these factors and their implications for the post-crisis environment in Asia. Chapter 18 by Beverly Kitching focuses on the position and experiences of women, people with disabilities and ethnic minorities in business in the new market system developing in China. The chapter raises and answers many issues about the position of women in China including greater opportunities for women to enhance their economic and social status; the proportion of new small businesses that they own and how these businesses are run; and, the career options open to women as well as the glass ceiling. This chapter also covers issues on people with disabilities and ethnic minorities in business. The author draws on ongoing research conducted in Yunnan Province in Southwestern China using literature search, questionnaire survey and structured interviews with women working in both state-owned and private businesses. Finally, in Chapter 19, Hock-Beng Cheah and Melanie Cheah argue that sustainable competitive advantage can be achieved principally through sustainable management. The authors examine the nature and the context of the concept of sustainable management, and its relationship to the concept of sustainable development in post-crisis Asia.

The epilogue briefly underscores some of the important themes in this book. In Chapter 20, Frank-Jürgen Richter offers some concluding thoughts on this book and its place in analyzing post-crisis strategies.

References

Booth, J. (2001a) 'Paying the price', *Wall Street Journal*, 12 March.
Booth, J. (2001b) 'Corruption takes its toll', *Wall Street Journal*, 12 March.
Economist (2001a) 'Can the world escape recession', 22 March.
Economist (2001b) 'The challenge from up north', 15 March.
Haley, U. C. V. (2000a) 'Corporate restructuring and governance in East Asia: an overview', *Seoul Journal of Economics* (Institute of Economics Research, Seoul National University), 13(3): 225–51.
Haley, U. C. V. (2000b) 'The hair of the dog that bit you: successful market strategies in post-crisis South-East Asia marketing' in Special issue on 'Strategic marketing in emerging economies', *Marketing Intelligence and Planning*, 18(5): 236–46.
Haley, U. C. V. (2001) *Multinational Corporations in Political Environments: Ethics, Values and Strategies*, World Scientific Publishing.
Prystay, C. (2001) 'China dragon hogs lion share', *Wall Street Journal*, 12 March.

Part 2
Post-crisis Corporate Strategies

2
Corporate Responses to the Asian Financial Crisis

Masaaki Kotabe and Shruti Gupta

The Asian financial crisis has escalated into the biggest threat to global prosperity since the oil crisis of the 1970s. The region's once booming economies are still fragile, liquidity problems are crippling regional trade, and losses from Asian investments are eroding profits for many Japanese companies. Similarly, among Western companies, quite a few US companies are reporting less than expected earnings because of their large investments in Asia. Others fear that the Asian crisis would wash ashore to the seemingly unrelated regions of the world, including the USA and Europe. For example, the unsettling ups and downs of the Dow Jones Industrial Average reflect the precarious nature of US investments in Asia. Economists blamed Asia for nipping the world's economic growth by one percentage point in 1998–99.

The US trade deficit consistently deteriorated from $96 billion in 1992 to $262 billion in 1998 (according to the latest official statistics at the time of this writing) and continues to do so. Since about 80 per cent of the US trade deficit is with Japan and other Asian countries, the Asian crisis has the potential to worsen US trade deficits, dampen corporate profits, weaken the US stock market, and reduce consumer confidence. Optimists hope that the surge in US production, employment, and exports will offset trade problems with Asia. If a second round of major currency depreciation were to occur in Asian countries, Latin American countries could be forced to devalue their currencies.

US exports, corporate profits, and stocks could suffer once again. Capital investment would drop and consumers would spend less. As a result, the USA could slip into an economic stagnation and Asia into an unprecedented depression. European companies could not be operating unscathed as they are heavily dependent on the US market for their livelihood as well.

Mass media tend to portray the message that this will be the end of the Asian, and particularly Japanese, corporate juggernaut. Indeed, our interest in Japan and Japanese competition has waned concomitantly in recent years. So has our learning from Japanese and other Asian competitors. This is a dangerously shortsighted viewpoint. The Asian financial crisis and its ramifications could not only have far-reaching economic consequences around the world but also force many companies to adopt new business views and practices for competing around the world at the dawn of the new century.

Although there is some commonality across the recent financial problems facing Asian countries, how they could affect businesses and consumers varies from country to country. Therefore, the Asian financial crisis can be better understood if its causal sequence is separated from reasons for various Asian countries' structural strengths and weaknesses. We see four discrete scenarios unique to Southeast Asia, Japan, Korea and China, respectively. A clearer understanding of the Asian crisis helps US and other foreign companies develop Asian strategies better suited to the climate and environment of the time.

The nature of the Asian financial crisis

Chronologically speaking, China's devaluation of its currency, yuan Renminbi (RMB), from R5.7/$ to R8.7/$ in 1994, triggered an on-going saga of the Asian financial crisis. The mechanism of how the Asian financial crisis occurred is summarized in Figure 2.1.

The currency devaluation made China's exports cheaper in Southeast Asia where most currencies were virtually pegged to the US dollar. According to Lawrence Klein, a Nobel laureate in economics, the Southeast-Asian countries' strict tie to the US dollar cost them between 10 and 20 per cent of export losses spread over three or four years (*Journal of International Management*, 1998).

Separately, Japan's post-bubble recession also caused its currency to depreciate from 99.7 yen/$ in 1994 to 126.1 yen/$ in 1997, resulting in two pronged problems for Southeast-Asian countries. First, recession-stricken Japan reduced imports from its Asian neighbours; second, the depreciated yen helped Japanese companies increase their exports to the rest of Asia. Consequently, Southeast-Asian countries' trade deficits with China and Japan increased abruptly in a relatively short period. Their trade deficits were paid for by their heavy borrowing from abroad, leaving their financial systems vulnerable and making it impossible to maintain their currency exchange rates vis-à-vis the US dollar. The end

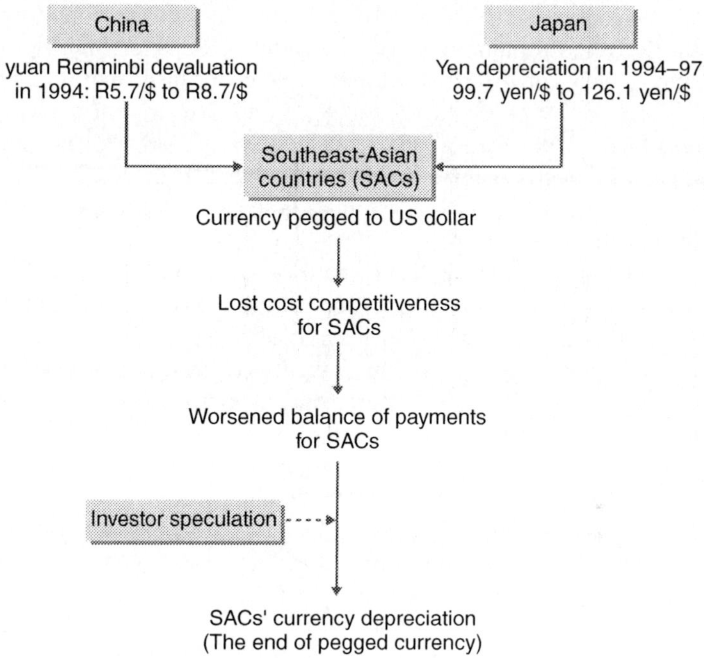

Figure 2.1 Mechanism of the Asian meltdown

result was the sudden currency depreciation by the end of 1997. For example, Thailand lost almost 60 per cent of its baht's purchasing power in dollar terms in 1997. The Malaysian ringgit lost some 40 per cent of its value in the same period. The Korean won was similarly hit toward the end of 1997 and depreciated 50 per cent against the US dollar in less than two months. The worst case was Indonesia whose rupiah lost a whopping 80 per cent of its value in the last quarter of 1997. In a way, it amounts to a US dollar bill becoming worth only 20 cents in three months! How could this unconscionable incident happen? Southeast-Asian countries' currency depreciation took on a whole new meaning for many countries around the world.

This financial crisis was further complicated not only by various structural problems unique to different Asian countries but also by their fundamental competitive strengths now shrouded in the shadow of the financial crisis itself. One could argue that the recent events show that there is no basis for the Asian model and the crisis marks the end of the competitive threat from Asian companies. To the contrary, another could argue that while the US economy is currently in a period of robust growth, nothing fundamental has changed over the years. Indeed, Paul Krugman, a well-known international trade economist, maintains that the US economy has been lucky enough to be in a cyclical upswing in the late 1990s while it was in a cyclical trough in the late 1980s when the end of the American century was widely believed (Krugman, 1998). The turnaround of the US economy in a decade suggests that Asian countries are not standing still, either.

First, we briefly summarize likely scenarios for each of the four regions/ countries that will shape the Asian economies for the next decade into the twenty-first century. The summary is also presented in Figure 2.2. Second, we offer likely changes in perspectives in marketing practices and strategy development to reflect on corporate responses to crisis management.

The Southeast-Asian countries' scenario

Thailand, which had borrowed money heavily from abroad, was the first to be hit hard. Foreign investors pulled their money out of the country in the second half of 1997. Investors and companies in neighbouring countries including the Philippines, Malaysia and Indonesia realized that these economies shared all or some of Thailand's problems with heavy foreign debt and wobbly banks. The same 'bank-on-the-run' phenomenon ensued with their currencies.

Relying heavily on inexpensive international credit line, many manufacturing companies in these Southeast-Asian countries expanded their production by increasing the use of unskilled and semi-skilled labour. The shortage of skilled labour could further thwart those companies' productivity improvement. Given the abundance of unskilled and semi-skilled labour, they are likely to increase labour-intensive exports as a primary way out of the recession.

While most of the East Asian economies like Hong Kong, South Korea and Malaysia are on the path of economic recovery, a series of economic reports indicate that the Philippine economy is declining even further. Compared to the other regional economies, even crisis-torn Indonesia posted a year-to-date growth of 59.6 per cent in local currency against Manila's rise of just 1.1 per cent. According to the Pacific Economic Cooperation Council (PECC), Philippines is lagging behind the other Southeast-Asian countries whose projected real GDP growth for 2000 and 2001 is predicted at 3.9 per cent and 4.2 per cent respectively. The US-based investment bank, Salomon Smith Barney, predicts the Philippine economy will grow at a rate of 3.3 per cent in 2000, which is below the

	Developed	Newly industrialized		Emerging	Communo-capitalistic
Country	Japan	Korea	Taiwan Singapore HongKong	Thailand Indonesia Malaysia Philippines	China
Trade balance	Surplus	Deficit	Generally balanced	Deficit/now surplus	Surplus
Debt obligation	Heavy internal debt	Heavy foreign debt	Low foreign debt	Heavy foreign debt	Low foreign debt
Currency	Likely to appreciate unless the central bank reflates the economy	Depreciate	Relatively stable, if no speculation	Depreciate	Possible devaluation
Highlights of technical resources	Increased R&D despite recession	*Chaebols'* dominance in skilled labour and capital	Highly skilled labour	Increased use of temporary unskilled/ semi-skilled workers	Classic labour-intensive operations
Competitive position	Formidable on technology side; but checked by low investment	Reeling from careless foreign investment and low ROI	Increasingly competent and technology-intensive	Decline in labour skills	Formidable low-cost producers
Strategy	Increased technology transfer; local procurement and production	Retreating from foreign expansion; operational consolidation	Increased domestic sales and exports	Try to export their way out of recession	Export-driven and mass production

Figure 2.2 Structure of Asian economies and corporate strategy
Note: Shaded areas represent the structural problems facing the four key Asian economies into the next millennium.

4–5 per cent forecast by the National Economic and Development Authority (NEDA), the government's economic planning agency (Mallari, 2000). According to analysts, this slump in economic recovery is on account of the country's sinking business image that it projects to its investors. A secondary explanation also lies in the concentration of wealth that rests in the hands of a few families. These families that control the top corporations of the country are unwilling to divest their shares and therefore are stifling the potential of the stock market by keeping liquidity low.

The Indonesian economy, on the other hand, is recovering rapidly from the Asian crisis. After the GDP had fallen by 13.21 per cent in 1998, it had bounced back to 0.23 per cent in 1999. In 2000, the GDP rate is expected to reach 3.8 per cent. Malaysia is also showing signs of economic recovery as its cheap ringgit has many of the multinationals pouring in money to upgrade their technology. According to the Malaysian Prime Minister, Koh Tsu Koon, Penang's good fortune is an outcome of the government's decision to peg the ringgit at 3.80 to the US dollar in September 1998. This peg allowed US companies to still continue making money on their FDI instead of losing it all in the other Asian countries where, their economies were rapidly losing currency value. As a result, FDI in Penang rose dramatically in 1999, jumping nearly 80 per cent from a year earlier to 4.8 billion ringgit ($1.25 billion). Thailand's economy also continued to grow in 1999 after its economy crashed in 1997–98. According to the National Economic Social and Development Board, Thailand's GDP rose by 4.2 per cent in 2000 and inflation was kept at a low of 0.3 per cent.

The Japanese scenario

Japan's financial problem, has been led not by foreign debt but rather by internal debt exposed by the burst of its asset-inflated bubble economy. Despite its internal debt problem, Japan remains the largest creditor nation in the world – a very different situation from the rest of Asia. Nevertheless, Japan's financial problem exposed its wobbly financial system. Like the US savings-and-loan crisis of the 1980s, Japanese banks are struggling to get a mountain of bad loans off their books (Aggarwal, 2000).

Until Japan's internal debt situation improves, Japanese companies' technological and marketing prowess, once touted to be invincible, will remain checked by low investment at home. However, while struggling in the post-bubble economy, many Japanese companies have accelerated their move toward their Pacific Rim global sourcing (i.e., product development and procurement) platform for marketing around the world. It is based on Japan's regional ties with the rest of Asia, Australia, and increasingly other parts of the Pacific Rim. Japanese companies' global sourcing platform builds on their famed target costing, target exchange rate, new product development style, and *keiretsu* (interfirm alliances) (Kotabe, 1998).

Japanese companies may have slowed the pace of their onslaught on the US market but have begun their geographical diversification into the emerging parts of the world market. Recently, according to the Japan External Trade Organization (JETRO), trade between China and Japan hit an all-time high in 1999, amounting to $66.18 billion. As a result, US and European companies are bound to face increasingly formidable Japanese competition around the world.

The Korean scenario

Korea is geographically too close to the rest of Asia to go unnoticed for different reasons. Korean conglomerates, known as *chaebols*, led by Samsung, Hyundai and Daewoo, had borrowed heavily abroad to invest in their rapid and sometimes careless foreign expansion. Most of their FDI has gone into mature industries characterized by overcapacity, such as automobile and semiconductor businesses. Similarly, investors started parting with the Korean currency, causing it to depreciate.

Korean companies are reeling both from heavy foreign debt and from lackluster corporate performance. The five largest *chaebols* that employ only 2.7 per cent of the nation's labour force shoulder as much as 30 per cent of the nation's debt. Worse yet, given their investment in mature industries, poor corporate performance may linger on for several years. As a result, Korean companies may retreat from aggressive foreign expansion and try to consolidate their operations by selling some of their under-performing units. The Daewoo *chaebol*'s attempt to sell its ailing car unit illustrates the point. However, after negotiating with Ford Motor Company to be one of the potential buyers, Ford, on 15 September 2000, decided to abandon its bid for the insolvent Daewoo Motor Company.

Despite the above problem, South Korea in the past 12 months has shown stunning economic recovery with a GDP growth of 10.7 per cent in 1999 and growth in 2000 projected at 6.0 per cent. In working toward a positive future, a great deal would depend on the success of corporate governance reforms initiated by the government. An example of such a corporate governance reform would be a requirement that a quarter of the board members of all listed companies to be independent. It is the failure of such corporate governance that has been frequently cited as the key reason behind the Korean financial crisis. An ultimate test of such reforms at the *chaebol* level will need them to undertake significant overseas acquisitions to be competitive.

Korea is perhaps the only economy in the world where decisions made by a small number of corporate groups overwhelmingly influence the overall economy. The 30 largest *chaebols* represent more than 40 per cent of the total value added in the economy with 20 per cent of direct employment.

The Chinese scenario

As stated earlier, the devaluation of the Chinese yuan Renminbi is generally considered to have caused the beginning of the Asian financial crisis, resulting in a disastrous competitive depreciation of the currencies of Thailand, the Philippines, Malaysia, Indonesia and Korea. However, now that other Asian currencies have depreciated – some even much more than China's – Chinese products have lost their cost-competitiveness vis-à-vis those from the Southeast-Asian countries in the markets around the world.

China keeps its foreign exchange controls, making its yuan Renminbi non-convertible. The black market rate of the yuan Renminbi has already been pushed down to R9.1/$ in Beijing and Shanghai, as opposed to the official rate of R8.3/$. Although the Chinese government has promised to defend its currency at all costs, there is some concern that China might devalue the Renminbi in an attempt to boost its enfeebled exports.

If the Renminbi did get devalued, Chinese companies would regain their status as export-driven low cost mass producers for the world market. Unfortunately, such government action might cause another round of competitive currency depreciation in Asia, further reducing the purchasing power of many Asian economies and even causing political instability in the region.

Today, China has recorded a GDP that grew 8.3 per cent on an annualized basis in the second quarter of 2000 bringing growth for the first half of the year to 8.1 per cent. The main driver behind this exceptional GDP figures is export, which increased by 38 per cent in the first six months of the year to $114.5 billion. Domestic demand also showed positive signs of economic recovery. Retail sales increased by 10 per cent in the first half of the year 2000 compared with the same period in 1999, while the consumer-price index rose 0.1 per cent. According to Huang Yiping, regional economist for Salomon Smith Barney in Hong Kong, people in China are more willing to spend as can be seen in an increase in power consumption in the first half of 2000 along with a shrinking factory inventory. It is predicted that China, rebounding from the crisis, could register an annual growth of 8–9 per cent for the next few years. This growth rate could be realized if the Chinese government decides to push systemic reforms such as privatizing more state enterprises and improving bank lending practices, among others.

So far, Singapore, Hong Kong and Taiwan have escaped from the full brunt of the Asian financial crisis. Singapore reported a 6 per cent growth for the second quarter of 1998, but analysts consider it artificial because the first quarter was unusually depressed. In 1998, Hong Kong's economy reported the first negative economic growth in 13 years, contracting 2 per cent in the first quarter of the year. However, by the third quarter of 1999, Hong Kong claims that its economy grew 4.5 per cent, so that the government upgraded its forecast of growth for the full year to 1.8 per cent from 0.5 per cent. Most recently, Hong Kong's economic output rose 14.3 per cent in the first three months of the year 2000 making it the territory's fastest quarter of growth since late 1987. Taiwan's GDP grew by 5.8 per cent in 1999. This growth was higher than the GDP increase of 5.3 per cent registered in 1998. Taiwan expects that the regional crisis will keep its growth rate lower for 2000 and beyond than prior to the crisis (*Asia Week*, 1998). However, overall, Asia's developing economies, including Singapore, South Korea and Hong Kong, are expected to grow by 4.4 per cent in 1999, and a more robust economic recovery is expected during 2000 and beyond.

Corporate responses to the Asian financial crisis

Reeling from the initial shock of Asia's financial crisis, corporate executives have begun to cope with the realities of marketing their products in a completely changed world – from the world that was once believed to keep growing with ever increasing prosperity to a world that has decimated the burgeoning middle class by snapping more than 50 per cent of the consumers' spending power. Those executives are facing two dire consequences of the crisis: namely, declining markets and increased competition from existing competitors. Their major task is to figure out how to keep current customers and gain new ones and maintain profitability in the long run. Hewlett-Packard in Thailand is working at retaining its customers by allowing them to pay for equipment over a period of two or three years and then to upgrade to new machines. Further, the company instead of enforcing a stringent 30-day collection period, is allowing its distributors in Bangkok to present bank guarantees, partial payments and promises of full payments eventually (Kroll et al., 1998).

Although Asia's current recession caused by its financial crisis is a serious one, other countries or regions have also experienced economic slumps over the years. Recession is usually defined as an economic situation in which the country's GDP has shrunk for two consecutive quarters. Based on this definition, the USA has experienced 28 recessions since 1894, approximately once every four to five years (Chadwick, 1998). We show different ways in which competing companies cope with the recession and the changed consumer needs.

Different companies have reacted differently to Asia's recession, based on their different corporate objectives. In general, there are short-term and long-term orientations in crisis management. Short-term orientations dictate that the corporate goal is to maximize year-to-year profit (or minimize loss), whereas long-term orientations tolerate some short-term loss for the benefit of future gains. Although any definitive value judgment should not be made of the two different orientations, short-term orientations tend to serve stockholders' speculative needs, while long-term orientations tend to cater to customer needs. A short-term oriented solution is to pull out of the market, at least temporarily, as long as the markets remain in a recession. Long-term oriented solutions are to modify marketing strategies in various ways to address the consumer needs completely changed during the recession (Tripathi, 1998). Most multinationals, with sufficient financial resources, have chosen the long-term option. Take for example, the German pharmaceutical company, Bayer, which has been hit hard by the crisis. Even though its Asian sales declined by 14 per cent, it continues to sustain its commitment in Asia. According to Dieter Becher, board member of Bayer, the company's policy is based on mid-term and long-term demand projections, which demonstrate the company's confidence in the region (Young, 1999).

Pull-out

Pulling out of the market is an easy way out, at least financially, in the short run. Immediately after Indonesia's rupiah depreciated by almost 80 per cent in a couple of months, J. C. Penny and Wal-Mart had no second thoughts but simply left the Indonesian market. Similarly, Daihatsu, a small Japanese automobile manufacturer, decided to pull out of Thailand. Likewise, Philadelphia-based Crown Cork and Seal Co. Inc. sold its ailing Carnaud Metal Box unit to Kian Joo, a Malaysian firm (Kroll et al., 1998).

While the pull-out strategy may be the least painful option in the short run, it could cause some irreparable consequences in the long run, and particularly so in many Asian countries where long-term, trustworthy, and loyal relationships are a vital part of doing business and short-term financial sacrifices are revered as an honourable act. It would be extremely difficult for foreign companies that once closed down their operations to come back to the market. A better strategy would be to cut the planned production volume and maintain corporate presence on the market as General Motors did in Thailand. For those considering the pull-out strategy, the argument is made on grounds of cutting immediate losses and concentrating on other markets (Martin, 1998). Hillenbrand Industries, Inc., a manufacturer of hospital beds based in Indiana, USA, changed its decision to invest in Asia and instead decided to build its manufacturing plant in Latin America.

It has also been suggested that companies do not have to lump all Southeast-Asian countries together into one market, when evaluating the market potential and can instead evaluate each subregion separately. Here, the Philippines and Thailand would rank higher on market appeal than Indonesia or Malaysia in terms of corporate investments (Martin, 1998).

Emphasize a product's value

Wary consumers become wiser consumers. In a prosperous time, middle-class consumers may have resorted to some impulse buying and conspicuous consumption. But during the current recession, they want to maintain their current lifestyle and standard of living. However, they also want to feel that the product or service they purchase is worth the money they pay for. Marketers will have to develop a promotion that emphasizes the value contained in the product. For example, Procter & Gamble's new Pantene shampoo line, which sells for $2.20 to $7.30, is one of the most expensive shampoos available in Hong Kong. Its advertising campaign promotes Pantene's extra moisturizers and other high-tech ingredients to tell clearly the benefits of Pantene over other less expensive brands.

Another way to add value is to enhance the perceived quality image of a product. For example, in Thailand, an advertising campaign for a relatively cheap Clan MacGregor scotch whiskey made locally under license emphasizes the product value: 'Even if you have to buy something cheap, you are getting something of real value.' This is stated in reference to three times more expensive imported Johnnie Walker Black Label whiskey. This advertisement helps to enhance Clan MacGregor's quality image in the minds of consumers.

Change the product mix

If a company has a wide array of product lines, it can shift the product mix by pushing relatively inexpensive product lines while de-emphasizing expensive lines. This strategy is suited to ride over a slump by generating sufficient cash flow not only to cover the fixed costs of business operations but also to maintain the corporate presence on the market. Particularly in Asia, the company's dedication to the market as perceived by local customers will win many favourable points in the long run. For example, Burberry's, a British fashion retailer, has replaced its expensive jackets in window displays with relatively inexpensive T-shirts, stressing that everyone can still afford some luxury even in hard times.

Narrow the product line

A company could also cut back on its product line to focus on its core products and customers that more closely match its core capabilities. Generally speaking, in developing countries, customers place more value on a dependable yet limited line of products rather than on a careless variety of products. By trimming its product line, a company can specialize in its planning, equipment, operations and marketing, thereby, simplifying the management's responsibilities and reducing the array of skills needed from the workforce (Chan and Timsawat, 2000).

Repackage the goods

As stated earlier, middle-class consumers want to maintain their lifestyles and quality of life as much as possible. It means that they will keep buying what they have been buying but consume less. Companies like Unilever are repackaging their products to suit consumers' declining purchasing power. Unilever has reduced the size of its Magnum brand ice-cream packs and made it cheaper, offers giveaways on its Lux soaps (you can now buy six, get one free), and markets its detergents in smaller and cheaper refillable packs.

Take control of distribution

The economic crisis found multinationals stepping in to take control of the distribution system so as to get closer to the Asian customers. This shift in vertical integration stems from the increased risks of leaving the critical interaction with customers to a third party. Additionally, in some situations, the financial crisis has driven the distributors out of business. The Asia division of BMW found itself taking charge of distribution because some of its partners did not have sufficient funds to maintain the company's standards. Keeping with the above trend, BMW plans to open a wholly-owned subsidiary in Thailand to manufacture cars, leaving its former Thai assembler and distributor, Yarnyon, in a dwarfed role as a parts supplier. When DaimlerChrysler found its Mercedes Benz dealers in Thailand engaged in a price war amongst themselves, it decided to set up a new distribution and marketing operation under company control. Some companies like Puma, the German sportswear company, have found out the hard way that they need to watch closely their distributors. Puma ran into trouble, when its Hong Kong based distributor, Hwa Kay Thai Holdings, stopped paying royalties. Similarly, Apple Computers in Thailand, Malaysia and South Korea has set up local offices staffed with Apple personnel to help distributors with marketing and promotion.

Maintain stricter inventory

Japanese companies have long taught us that their just-in-time inventory management practices not only reduce unnecessary inventory but also improve their product assortment by selling only what customers want at the moment. Even if companies were not practicing just-in-time inventory management, it would make a lot of sense to keep inventory low. Essentially, inventory is a tied-up capital of unsold merchandise that can be costly to the company. For example, the Kuala Lumpur store of Swedish furniture retailer, Ikea, has not restocked certain slow-selling items.

Look outside the region for expansion opportunities

Asia's recession is still a regional problem although there is some risk that it will bring down the rest of the world with it to cause a global economic crisis. Nevertheless, market opportunities can be found outside the recession-stricken part of Asia. This strategy is not only a part of geographical diversification to spread out the market risk but also an effective way to take advantage of cheaper Asian currencies which translate to lower prices in other foreign countries. For instance, Esprit, the Hong Kong based retailer, is now marketing very aggressively in Europe. Despite the Asian slump, its revenues increased 52 per cent during fiscal 1998 with most of the gain coming from the European market. Hewlett-Packard and Dell Computer, among others, who depend heavily on now less-expensive components made in Asia, have begun to trim the prices of their products.

Increase advertising in the region

It sounds somewhat antithetical to the strategy stated above. However, there is also a strong incentive to introduce new products now. It is a buyer's market for advertising space. Television stations are maintaining advertising rates but giving bonus airtime, effectively cutting advertising costs. As a result, Unilever can better afford to reach the large middle-class market segment in Hong Kong that its SunSilk shampoo targets. American Express is launching the Platinum card for the first time in Malaysia, and it is targeted at the highest-income consumers whose wealth has been cushioned by investment overseas.

Historical evidence also suggests that it is usually a mistake to cut advertising budgets during a recession (Chadwick, 1998). For example, Oxy, a South Korean household products manufacturer, like many other hard-hit companies, slashed its advertising budget by one-third, while its competitors halted their advertising completely. Before the slump, Oxy had commanded 81 per cent of the closet dehumidifier market with its Thirsty Hippo model. Now instead of losing sales, Oxy boosted its market share to 94 per cent at the expense of its rivals.

Increase local procurement

Many foreign companies operating in Asian countries tend to procure certain crucial components and equipment from their parent companies. Now that Asian currencies depreciated precipitously, those foreign companies are faced with those imported components and equipment whose prices have gone up enormously in local currencies. Companies that have localized procurement do not have to be affected easily by fluctuating exchange rates. As a result, many companies are scurrying to speed steps toward making their operations in Asian countries more local. Japanese companies seem to be one step ahead of US and European competitors in this localization strategy. Since the yen's sharp appreciation in the mid-1980s, Japanese manufacturers have moved to build an international production system less vulnerable to currency fluctuations by investing in local procurement (*Nikkei Weekly*, 1998).

Miscellaneous

All the above corporate responses point to the changes that a company can make in its marketing strategy to combat the crisis. However, in addition to practicing any one of the above strategies, a company can also practice prudent management (Kroll et al., 1998). For example, 3M is protecting itself against the aftermath of Asian currency devaluations by keeping current in collecting billings from its subsidiaries. The company asks for payments immediately instead of waiting for the end of the month to collect them. Additionally, 3M is also hedging the devaluation risk by both buying and selling materials in local currencies.

Similarly, Hewlett-Packard Co. in Bangkok is holding on to its best salespeople by offering new benefits and incentives, so that when the recovery time arrives, these salespeople instead of considering alternative employment opportunities will instead decide to stay with the company because of the new financial incentives. This strategy comes from the following realization: contradictory to common belief, the best time to hire people is not in times of crisis, because the people being laid off are not the best performers (Kroll et al., 1998).

Summary

Our assessment is based on facts, but no one could predict the future of the Asian economy with accuracy. We would strongly encourage you to evaluate the impact of the Asian crisis from various perspectives above and beyond our assessment. The bottom line is that we should not ignore either the importance of the Asian markets or the potential competitive threat from Asian companies for the twenty-first century.

This crisis has to be placed in proper perspective as the economic miracles of the East and Southeast-Asian countries have already shifted the pendulum of international trade from cross-Atlantic to cross-Pacific in the last decade. Companies from the USA and Japan, in particular, have been helping to shape the nature of cross-Pacific bilateral and multilateral trade and investment. Today, as a result, North America's trade with these five Asian countries alone exceeds its trade with the European Community by upwards of 20 per cent. The trend appears irreversible.

However, another opposing view held by economists is that US exports related to the Asian crisis did not suffer to the degree of prediction. Economists who support this view argue that foreign subsidiaries of US multinationals make the lion's share of their sales in Europe and not in Asia. Yet another set of evidence comes from the realization that while import prices fell, US domestic prices changed very little. This has been suggested to indicate that imports from Asian countries do not actually compete directly with US producers in most industries, with the exception of steel, where US prices were hit hard. Indeed, one could even argue that the Asian crisis was a 'free lunch' for the USA, where industries were mostly unaffected, while the consumers benefited from cheaper imports.

Although the recent stock market turmoil and the subsequent depreciation of the foreign exchange rates of many Asian countries may have set back their economic progress temporarily, the fundamental economic forces are likely to remain intact. Therefore, in order for these countries to sustain their strong economic performance, the importance of several necessary conditions needs to be stressed. These include: strong financial institutions – commercial and investment banks, stock exchanges; transparency in the way the institutions do business; financial reporting systems that are consistent with free markets where capital and goods flow competitively; and supply of a managerial pool to shepherd these economies through very difficult transitional periods. While the Asian countries remain strong and attractive with respect to their economic fundamentals, the recent events have demonstrated that the institutional environments of the countries need reforms. One of the key reasons that explains the post-crisis recovery is the improvement in political conditions in most of the countries. The banking system is undergoing significant restructuring and monumental changes are being made in law and order. In a recent poll of six Asian countries by Japan's Dentsu Institute, most respondents pointed to the failure of governmental policies as the key cause of the economic crisis (*Wall Street Journal*, 1999).

Today in 2000, the Asian financial crisis sounds like a bad dream, an event that has even strengthened the Asian economies beyond their pre-crisis potential. According to Goh Chok Tong, Singapore's Prime Minister, the crisis has produced four positive outcomes: First, it has speeded up the opening of economies. Second, it has forced the Asian region to be more aware of corporate governance issues and stipulations. Third, it forced the region to concentrate on its real competitive strengths. Lastly, it provided a lesson on globalization.

Today, positive GDP growth figures and rebounding demand for major commodities to pre-crisis levels in nearly every country of the region point to the end of the Asian economic crisis. We predict that companies from various Asian countries will eventually come out of the current crisis and become ever-leaner and more astute competitors in many different ways. It has been suggested that this crisis has heightened the notion and importance of cooperation among the Asian regional partners. Such regional cooperation could possibly lead to the emergence of a trading block with power to rival the USA and the European Union. It is for these reasons, among others, that US and other foreign companies doing business in Asia should not pull out of the Asian markets simply because it is very difficult to do business at present. Doing so will probably damage corporate reputation and customer trust – the two features that are considered sacrosanct throughout Asia. The US and other foreign companies should have longer-term orientation in dealing with Asian consumers and competitors by developing strategies that emphasize value and reducing operational costs.

References

Aggarwal, R. (ed.) (2000) *Restructuring Japanese Business for Growth: Strategy, Finance, Management, and Marketing Perspectives*, Norwell, MA: Kluwer Academic Publishers.

Asia Week (1998) 'Changes of direction, for better or worse', 9 October, p. 12.

Chadwick, J. (1998) 'Communicating through tough times in Asia', *Economic Bulletin*, August, pp. 25–9.

Chan, Peng S. and Pamela Timsawat (2000) 'Impact of the Asian economic crisis on US joint ventures', *American Business Review*, 18(1): 22–7.

Journal of International Management (1998) 'A special issue on the Asian financial crisis', 4(1).

Kotabe, Masaaki (1998) 'Efficiency vs. effectiveness orientation of global sourcing strategy: a comparison of US and Japanese multinational companies', *Academy of Management Executive*, 12 November, pp. 107–19.

Kroll, K. M., McClenahen, J. S. and W. Royal (1998) 'Like steering a boat in a storm', *Industry Week*, 18 May, pp. 24–32.

Krugman, P. (1998) 'America the boastful', *Foreign Affairs*, 77(May/June): 32–45.

Mallari, R. (2000) 'A game of chance', *Asian Business*, 36(8): 40–2.

Martin, J. (1998) 'If not Asia, where'? *Management Review*, 87(8): 16–20.

Nikkei Weekly (1998) 'Manufacturers reshape Asian strategies', 12 January, pp. 1, 5.

Tripathi, S. (1998) 'Asia's sinking middle class', *Far Eastern Economic Review*, 9 April, p. 12.

Wall Street Journal (1999) 'Markets, not architects, will solve economic crisis', A22, 20 July.

Young, Ian (1999) 'Bayer shrugs off the Asian crisis', *Chemical Week*, 17 March.

3

Corporate Finance and its Impact on Corporate Strategy after the Bubble: Is the Long-term Strategy of Japanese Firms Really Changing?

Yasuhiro Arikawa and Hideaki Miyajima

Introduction

Entering into the 1990s, the Japanese economy has suffered from a long recession. The GDP growth rate of the Japanese economy in the 1990s was quite low, and even fell into negative realms in 1997 and 1998 after the Asian economic crisis. The high investment ratio, which used to be a conspicuous feature of the Japanese economy, dramatically decreased since 1992. On the other hand, the institutional characteristics of the Japanese financial system have begun to change in the 1990s. The main-bank relationship has been weakening under the drastic change of corporate financial practices through the liberalization of the capital market. Intercorporate shareholding strategy has reportedly been revised due to the decade-long sluggish stock market after the collapse of the bubble economy in the mid-1990s, and according to NLI Research Institute (2000), the percentage of intercorporate shareholdings decreased from 21.5 per cent in 1987 to 10.9 per cent in 1999.

How have changes in the institutional characteristics of the Japanese financial system affected long-term management strategy, which used to be acknowledged as one of the noticeable features of Japanese firms (Abegglen and Stalk, 1985; Porter, 1992; Sheard, 1994)? According to conventional understanding, the characteristics of Japanese financial systems could encourage long-term investments through mitigating asymmetric information problems emanating from main banks and solving the problem of managerial myopia through intercorporate shareholdings.

In the line of this thought, the decline of the main-bank relationship and intercorporate shareholding may have led to the long stagnation of investment by Japanese firms.

A contrary understanding of the Japanese financial system is recently getting more popular among researchers: here, institutional characteristics have played a less significant role (Weinstein and Yafeh, 1998; Hall and Weinstein, 1996; Hayashi, 2000), or rather played a negative role for inducing the excess investment problem by protecting managers from appropriate monitors in the late 1980s. From this perspective, portfolio investors such as foreign investors might provide an appropriate disciplinary role for Japanese corporate governance.

The purpose of this study is to investigate recent changes in Japanese corporate finance and governance, and its impact on the long-term oriented strategy of Japanese firms. The remainder of the chapter is organized as follows: the section 'The Japanese financial system' briefly summarizes the unique features of the Japanese financial system. The section 'The changing strategy of Japanese firms on corporate finance' focuses on corporate finance in Japanese firms, mainly focusing on the choice of financial resources. The emphasis is on the point that, along with the deregulation of financial markets, Japanese large firms with less default risk and higher profitability tend to reduce their reliance on borrowings from the main bank. The section 'Changing bank-centred corporate governance' addresses the changes of corporate governance structure in the Japanese firms. We would emphasise the fact that the role of main banks has been decreasing, showing the empirical result that the frequency of interventions by the main bank is less sensitive to corporate performance compared to the 1980s, while that intervention has contributed less to improve the firm's performance. Further, we examine the rapid restructuring of the banking sector after the financial crisis in 1997. Especially, we consider the reason and the effect of that restructuring on the main-bank system. The section 'The effect of changing the corporate governance system on corporate investment strategy' highlights the effect of changes in corporate finance and governance on corporate behaviour. We test the hypothesis that physical investment and R&D expenditures are constrained by internal funds, and the constraint is mitigated by a certain governance structure. Some of the results are discussed in the section 'Conclusions and discussion'.

The Japanese financial system

The J-Type firm system is a typical depiction of the corporate organization in the Japanese big-business sector since the 1950s. The J-Type firm system is composed of several subsystems, such as cooperative industrial relations based on 'life-time' employment, etc.[1] The focus in this chapter, however, is on the Japanese financial system, the essence of which can be generalized as follows:

Main-bank relationships

The so-called 'main bank', which engages in ex ante, interim, and ex post monitoring of client firms, plays an active role not only in supplying funds to a firm, but also in disciplining the firm's top management team. Borrowing from main banks is characterized as a debt with long-term, bilateral relationships between banks and borrowers, and sometimes called as relationship banking (Boot and Thakor, 2000). Under this system a main bank is charged with the task of supplying new money for the investment projects of client firms, mitigating the asymmetric information problem between lender and borrower through intensive monitoring. Main banks do not themselves intervene in the management of well-performing borrowers. In times of financial distress, however, main banks dispatch representatives to client firms, at times take over the boards of the firms, and take the initiative in restructuring the firms. This disciplinary mechanism differs from the Anglo-American system based on takeovers and bankruptcy procedures.

As Aoki and Dinc (2000) explain, these behaviours by main banks are induced by the expectation of future rents, which include information rents, monopolistic rents and so on. Having bilateral and long-term relationships with their borrowers, main banks can get the specific information about those borrowers, and that information brings rent opportunities to main banks. Further, financial regulation, especially entrance regulation, brings the incumbent banks some market power and monopolistic rents. In fact, until the 1990s, the Japanese financial market was heavily regulated, and it was prohibitively difficult for new-comers to enter into the banking market. This monopolistic rent might provide incentives to take a long-term strategy for banks, because, as Petersen and Rajan (1995) explain, in a monopolistic market, banks can bail out the distressed firms with the expectation that they can impose higher interest rates in the future on that firm.

Intercorporate shareholdings

Thanks to stable cross-shareholding among the members of corporate groups or *keiretsu*, the top managers of the J-Type firm are mutually insulated from the myopic pressures of the stock market. This relationship between top managers and the capital market is quite different from the Anglo-American model in which the capital market functions as an effective device for monitoring and disciplining firms' managements. It is often argued that the growth-oriented behaviour and long-term time horizons of the J-Type firm were encouraged by this institutional setting (Abegglen and Stalk, 1985; Porter, 1992).[2]

Board of directors composed of insiders

The board of directors of a J-Type firm is composed mainly of corporate managers promoted within the company, and the membership of this board overlaps with the membership of the top management team. It is quite common, in fact, for large firms to have boards that do not contain any outsiders. The one exception to this general rule is that the firm's main bank is represented on the board. This structure is quite different from the Anglo-American model, where boards of directors regularly include outsiders who represent large shareholders, and closely monitor the activities of the top management team. Furthermore, the size of the board in J-Type firm is relatively larger than that of the Anglo-American firm.

Summary

These features of J-Type firms briefly described above evolved since the post-war period, and were established during the latter half of the high-growth era (1965–71) (Aoki and Patrick, 1994; Miyajima, 1998). They functioned well in the high-growth era and the period after the oil crisis. In the high-growth era, these features enabled the banking sector to supply the funds for satisfying large investment demand, and encouraged long-term investment. Further, the rapid adjustment of Japanese firms after the oil crisis was often attributed to these characteristics.

The changing strategy of Japanese firms on corporate finance

Along with the deregulation in the financial market since 1970s, the Japanese firm's strategy on corporate finance has been changing. Large Japanese firms actively reduced their reliance on banks and began to diversify their financial resources. The total amount of bonds issued from 1985 to 1989 increased by more than 140 per cent from the ones issued between 1980 and 1984 (see Table 3.1). Bank borrowing was decreased dramatically in the same period. In the 1990s, although total raised debt decreased, the bond issuance did not decline as drastically as bank borrowing did.

Table 3.1 Issued financial instruments by large Japanese manufacturing firms in each period (in 1000 million yen)

	Total debt	Bank borrowing	Bond	Equity
1980–84	3 241 682	2 071 125	1 170 557	210 397
1985–89	3 769 320	951 935	2 817 386	708 772
1990–94	3 424 088	1 604 373	1 819 715	151 769
1995–98	736 472	–532 982	1 269 454	133 832

Note: Data is averaged for each period.
Source: Compiled from the Kigyo Keiei no Bunseki by Mitusbishi Research Institute.

Financial deregulation in the 1980s and 1990s

First of all, let us check the deregulation process of the Japanese financial market in the 1980s and 1990s. Importantly, the bond market became available for many borrowers. Until the end of the 1970s, Japanese firms did not have any financial options except bank borrowing because of the strict regulation on bond issuance. Due to collateral requirements for bond issuance, it was prohibitively difficult for firms to issue bonds. Furthermore, the Bond Issuance Committee (the *kisaikai*) decided which firms should issue bonds and how many bonds should be issued. It was in 1979 that the issuance of unsecured straight bonds was permitted for the first time by introducing the accounting index and profitability index criteria as the Bond Issue Criteria. At this time, there were just two companies eligible for issuing unsecured bonds. Thereafter, the deregulation proceeded step by step, increasing the number of firms eligible to issue unsecured bonds as well as secured bonds. This relaxation of the Bond Issue Criteria was one of the conditions, besides other favourable macroeconomic factors, that made it possible for Japanese firms to raise money through equity-related bonds in either domestic or foreign markets. By the end of 1989, the number of firms that had any financial options increased to approximately 500.[3]

The deregulation of bond issuance reached its final stage in the 1990s. In November 1990, every criterion except the rating criterion was lifted from the Bond Issue Criteria. In April 1993, the lowest bound of the rating criteria for issuing unsecured straight bond was lowered to BBB from A. This is important because the main form of bond issuance drastically changed, from equity-related bonds in the late 1980s to straight bonds in the early 1990s. As a result of this relaxation, 184 listed firms became eligible to issue unsecured straight bonds. Finally, in January 1996, bond issuing criteria and some other covenants were finally removed, freeing Japanese firms from regulation with regard to debt choice.

The strategy on debt choice by Japanese large firms

Under the deregulation of the bond market, what factor determined the strategy of debt choice between bond and bank borrowing by Japanese firms? Instead of immediately responding to this question, we discuss some theoretical differences about bond and bank borrowing from main banks.

As explained above, borrowing from the main bank is characterized as a debt with long-term, bilateral relationships between banks and borrowers. Aoki (1994) denotes this relationship as contingent corporate governance, and clarifies the rescue operation mechanism by the main bank. As there exists a borrower's output level where the main bank rescues and restructures the borrower in financial distress, in this arrangement, a manager who borrows from the main bank expects a rescue operation in cases of financial distress.

Although borrowing from the main bank has the benefit of implicit rescue for borrowers, there exist costs that prevent firms from borrowing exclusively from banks. In general, bank borrowing is associated with strict monitoring, which mitigates agency problems. This monitoring behaviour, on the other hand, might reduce the manager's own non-pecuniary benefit created by having discretion over management. When a manager acknowledges that the costs of bank borrowing exceed the benefits of having an implicit rescue-insurance, she chooses to issue bonds.

Based on these hypotheses, Miyajima and Arikawa (2000) present the empirical evidence of what determines the Japanese firm's choice between unsecured bond and bank borrowing in the 1980s and 1990s. They test the hypotheses that the firm does not use bank borrowing with an implicit rescue-insurance when the default risk is low or future profitability is high enough. They treat, therefore, debt choice as one between debt without implicit rescue-insurances (NRI debt) and debt with implicit rescue-insurances (RI debt), rather than the choice between public and private debt. Here, NRI debts include unsecured convertible bonds, unsecured straight bonds, and non-bank-guaranteed warrant bonds, whereas RI debt is composed of bank borrowings, secured convertible and straight bonds, and bank-guaranteed warrant bonds. The main reason for classifying secured and bank-guaranteed bonds as RI bonds, similar to bank borrowing, is that defaulted corporate bonds with collateral were bought back by the trustee banks without any exception from 1955 to 1997, while bank-guaranteed warrant bonds are, by definition, guaranteed by banks.[4]

Following their result, in the late 1980s, a firm's choice between unsecured bond and bank borrowing was basically determined by default risk and future profitability. For the firms that could choose either unsecured bonds or other debt (secured bonds or borrowing), the debt choice was significantly correlated with default risk and future profitability. Even among the firms that could fully choose their financial methods, firms with high default risk and low future profitability still continued to borrow to keep implicit rescue-insurance, in spite of the fact that bank borrowings might lead to hold-up problems and high interest rates.

For the firms eligible for only secured bonds and bank guaranteed bonds, the choice of bond was also sensitive to default risk. Further, this choice was sensitive to future profitability only among firms having strong main-bank ties. This result provides the evidence that the managers with their non-pecuniary benefit created by having discretion over management tend to avoid borrowings from main banks. Since the deregulation of financial markets made it possible for firms with strong main-bank ties to have new financial options for the first time, bank monitoring reduced bank borrowing for firms with less default risk and higher future profitability.

It is worth emphasizing that these facts imply the deterioration of client firms in the banking sector in the latter half of the 1980s. As firms with low default risks depend on bond issuance, and firms with high risks still remain to raise external funds through bank borrowing, this rational self-selection will lead banks to the deterioration of clients. Given this deterioration, it was an inevitable consequence that the financially distressed firms would become a larger proportion of bank clients when the negative macro shock in the 1990s attacked the Japanese economy.[5]

On 1 April 1993, the Financial System Reform Act became effective. This new law allowed banks (securities) to set up their securities firm (trust bank) subsidiaries. Furthermore, in 1996, the Japanese government announced the financial system reform programme known as the Japanese 'Big Bang'. When this programme is completed in 2001, bank, security firm and insurance company will compete directly with each other. Then, even the firm having a strong relationship with a main bank might put more value not only on the bank's lending but also on other financial services like security underwriting.

Changing bank-centred corporate governance

The decline of the main-bank system

As we mentioned in the section 'The Japanese financial system', a main bank played a disciplinary role in the Japanese financial system. Then, along with the scaling down of bank borrowing in the 1990s, does the bank-centred financial system transform into a market-based one?

One of the symptoms, which implies the transformation of the Japanese financial system, is the decrease of the intervention by main banks to rescue their client firms from financial distress. According to Miyajima et al. (1999), it is clear that the frequencies of dispatching bank members to client firms with poor performance significantly decreased in the 1990s compared with previous periods. Similar results are confirmed by Hirota and Miyajima (2000), who picked up as a sample only firms facing financial distress. Compared with the 1970s and 1980s, they show that the probability of dispatching managers from main banks to firms with financial distress significantly decreased in the 1990s (Table 3.2). Here, financial distress means that a firm's operating income is below the interest payment for two years.

The effect of dispatching managers on improving the borrower's performance has also been declining in the 1990s. When the manager from a main bank was dispatched to the firm in financial distress, the performance of that firm relatively improved until the 1980s. However, in the 1990s, this positive relationship became unclear.

These results show that in the 1990s, fewer benefits accrued to borrowers having long-term bilateral relationships with a main bank. One of the possible reasons for the fading of the positive effects of the main bank's intervention is that, as many Japanese banks have suffered from bad-loan problems after the bubble, they have had to take conservative lending policies to pick up their capital base. These conservative policies might have led to the decrease of intervention rescuing borrowers in financial distress. In addition, the capital adequacy requirements by Bank of International Settlements (BIS) urged Japanese banks to reduce the total amount of lending. Due to the fall of asset prices, the unrealized

Table 3.2 Intervention by main banks in financial distressed firms

			1970s	1980s	1990s	Whole period
Frequency of intervention	(a)	The number of firms in financial distress	132	70	99	301
	(b)	The number of firms intervened by banks	45	16	16	77
	(b)/(a)		34.1%	22.9%	16.2%	25.6%

Source: Hirota and Miyajima (2000).

gains from shares banks contracted. As banks counted this gain as capital base to comply with the BIS banking regulations, the fall of share prices automatically reduced the capital bases and banks could not help reducing the loans they made. The disappearance of a long-term strategy taken by main banks might provide large Japanese firms with many financial options and more opportunity to be independent from main banks.

The merger-mania in the Japanese banking sector and its effect on corporate strategy

The Japanese financial system had gone into turmoil in November 1997, when Hokkaido Takushoku bank, one of the city banks, and Yamaichi Securities, one of the 'Big-Four' security companies in Japan, were forced into bankruptcy. The common feature of these bankruptcies is that the evaluation of capital markets incurred this turbulence. As for Hokkaido Takushoku bank, no participant at the interbank market supplied funds for required reserves after its failure to merge with Hokkaido Bank, while the collapse of Yamaichi Securities was triggered by the downgrading of Moody's rating because of the huge hidden losses.

Thereafter, in late 1998, Long-Term Credit Bank of Japan (LTCB) and Nippon Credit Bank (NCB) were nationalized, followed by the introduction of the Financial Reconstruction Act. The government also injected 74 592 trillion yen of public funds into the undercapitalized 15 large banks based on the Prompt Recapitalization Act in March 1999, and required these banks to carry out strict restructuring plans that would aim at increasing profits by 50 per cent over the next four years.

Following this financial turmoil, the Japanese banking sector has rapidly plunged into merger-mania. In August 1999, Fuji Bank, Dai-Ichi Kangyo Bank and Industrial Bank of Japan announced the comprehensive consolidation of three banks under the Mizuho Holdings. In October, Sumitomo Bank and Sakura Bank announced a merger in spite of the fact that each bank is in the centre of their Japanese *keiretsu* groups, Sumitomo and Mitsui. Furthermore, Sanwa and Tokai bank announced their integration under UFJ (United Financial of Japan) Group in March 2000.[6] In April 2000, Bank of Tokyo-Mitsubishi announced the establishment of their holding company, Mitsubishi Tokyo Financial Group with Mitsubishi Trust Bank. In April 1999, there were nine big city banks in Japan. In 2001, only four big bank groups and two other city banks will remain as a result of this merger-mania.

One of the major forces of this rapid restructuring of the Japanese banking sector is the Japanese 'Big-Bang' Plan that aims at thorough deregulation of the Japanese financial system. This plan was announced in November 1996 as the last step of a deregulation process since the late 1970s (Hoshi and Kashyap, 2000). Following this plan, the restrictions that separated banking, the securities business, and insurance business will be lifted. Japanese banks have now started looking for partners to survive the fierce competition in the domestic and international financial market.

Another driving force of this merger-mania is the public funds injected into large banks and the restructuring plan submitted to the government (see Table 3.3). The government has injected public funds mainly by preferred stocks, which can be converted into ordinary stocks after certain periods. That means the government might exert stronger control on each bank's management if a bank with public funds does not fulfil the restructuring plan. Then, to return the public funds as soon as possible, each bank will try to be more profitable by merging with other banks and restructuring the whole organization. For example, Mizuho Holdings plans about a 90 billion yen reduction in annual expense by reducing 170 domestic branches and 54 overseas branches and so on.

Is this merger-mania undermining the bank-centred and long-term oriented financial system in Japan further? As explained above, the main-bank system is sustained by each bank's expectation of future rents. Being more competitive in the Japanese financial market reduces

Table 3.3 Public funds injected into big banks (in billion yen)

	Preferred stock	Subordinated bond, Subordinated loan	Total
Mizuho Group	1940	850	2799
IBJ	350	350	700
Daiich	799	200	999
Fuji	800	300	1100
MistuiSumitomo	1301	200	1501
Sumitomo	501	100	601
Sakura	800	100	900
UFJ Group	1400	350	1750
Sanwa	600	200	800
Tokai	600	100	700
Toyo Trust	200	50	250
Mitubishi Tokyo Group	200	150	350
TokyoMitsubishi	0	0	0
Mitsubishi Trust	200	150	350

Source: *Diamond Weekly*, 21 October 2000.

the monopolistic rent for banks, and for that reason, the long-term strategy taken by Japanese banks would more or less transform into a more arm's-length one.

However, this does not necessarily mean that the rapid restructuring of the Japanese banking sector itself leads the bank-based financial system into the market-based and arm's-length one, because, it is not clear whether the information rent created by the long-term bilateral relationship between a bank and its borrower disappears along with a bank merger or not. Certainly, as Hanazaki and Horiuchi (2000) say, the mergers between the big city banks might blur the current Japanese corporate groups. But, that is not the same as the bank merger also blurring each bank's organization that generates the borrower-specific information. As long as the borrower-specific information created by the pre-merger bank is saved, as Aoki and Dinc (2000) explain, the post-merger bank might also take a long-term strategy toward its borrowers. In other words, whether the Japanese banking sector becomes more arm's length or not by recent merger-mania would depend on how the merger proceeds without breaking up the established relationship between lender and borrower.

The emergence of another corporate governance system after the financial system crisis

While the significance of a main bank for corporate governance has been decreasing, alternative corporate governance mechanisms are appearing in the 1990s. As mentioned above, the characteristics of the board of directors in Japanese firms are: (1) the board is composed mainly of corporate insiders; (2) there are a very limited number of outside directors; (3) the firm's insiders have the power to determine the candidate for director. Therefore, shareholders could not effectively control the management through its board of directors.

In the 1990s, however, these less disciplinary boards of directors are rapidly changing their appearance into one of the major devices for corporate governance. The results of inquiries done by Ministry of Finance (MOF) (2000) show that more than 50 per cent of the directors are considering the introduction of outside directors (Table 3.4). This means Japanese firms are considering making the board of directors into a more independent organization for efficiently monitoring the firm's behaviour.

According to the same research, 48 per cent of the sample Japanese firms have already introduced or are considering introducing stock options as an executive compensation. Provided share prices contain

Table 3.4 Result of MOF Inquiries

Panel 1 Outside directors		
Already introduced	343	30.1%
Going to introduce	13	1.1%
Considering on introducing	311	27.3%
No intention to introduce	471	41.4%
Total	1138	
Panel 2 Stock options		
Already introduced	115	10%
Going to introduce	27	2%
Considering on introduction	339	26%
No intention to introduce	528	44%
No idea	229	19%
Total	1238	

MOF, Inquiries on MB system.

enough information about future profitability, stock options are effective ways to ensure that managers pursue the interests of shareholders. These results of inquiries suggest, therefore, that many Japanese firms are becoming more sensitive to shareholder's interest especially in the post-crisis period.

Another remarkable change in terms of Japanese corporate governance is the increase of the portfolio investor, especially of the foreign investor. We estimated the share held by portfolio investors increased more than 6 per cent, mainly caused by the increasing shares held by foreign investors.[7] For example, Sony's shares held by foreign investors increased from 15.3 per cent in 1989 to 33.4 per cent in 1995 and even in Mitsubishi Heavy Industries Co., one of the core firms in Mitsubishi Groups, foreign investors' shares increased from 7.5 per cent to 15.7 per cent during the same period.

This changing ownership structure might perform a complementary role, with the strengthening of the board of directors, for the transformation of Japanese corporate strategy into one more conscious of the interest of shareholders. Portfolio investors are more likely to require transparency of decision-making from management, and also require that managers pursue the maximization of shareholders' interest. Furthermore, the introduction of stock options and outside directors helps provide managers with the incentive to act in the interests of shareholders. Then, as the share held by the portfolio investors increases, it is far more possible for the board of directors to run the company in the shareholders' interests.

Table 3.5 The effects of ownership structure on the sensitivity of dividends to profits estimated using the method, OLS, for 1992–98 period

Variable	**1**		**2**	
	Coefficient	***p*-value**	**Coefficient**	***p*-value**
π: profit	–0.025	.000	0.011	.001
MB	–166.383	.775	1178.390	.084
γ	–		–	
ε	–94.953	.340	–	
SHFOR	–		–66.595	.504
π*MB	0.023	.000	0.019	.001
π*ε	0.099	.000	–	
π*SHFOR	–		0.047	.010
Adjusted R^2	0.940		0.927	

Notes: Div: dividend; π: profit; MB: main bank dummy; ε: the share held by portfolio investor; SHFOR: the share held by foreign investor; π*MB: profit times main bank dummy; π*ε: profit times portfolio investor dummy; π*SHFOR: profit times foreign investor dummy. The main bank dummy equals one if a main bank identified by a firm itself was its largest shareholder among banks and dispatched a director to the firm.
Source: Accounting data are obtained from JDB Corporate Finance Database.

Increasing the share held by portfolio investors introduced substantial change in Japanese firms' corporate strategy and performance. First, increasing the share of foreign investors raised the responsiveness of dividends to profits among Japanese firms. By the end of the 1980s, the dividend-payout ratio of Japanese firms was far less responsive to profits. As is often pointed out, constant dividend-payout policy was a characteristic of the J-Type firm. However, according to our simple regressions in Table 3.5, portfolio investors accelerated the responsiveness of dividends to profits in the 1990s. Although it should be noted that the responsiveness of dividends to profits was originally low and the magnitude of this effect is still quite small, it is certain that the firm's dividend-payout policy changed from the former constant policy to a more responsive one.[8]

Second, the increasing share held by foreign investors could have improved firm performance. According to the empirical results shown by Yonezawa and Miyazaki (1996), firm's performance measured by Total Factor Productivity is positively correlated with the share held by portfolio investors and foreign investors, while the main-bank relationship and intercorporate shareholdings does not have any significant influence on performance. This seems to show that the change of corporate governance structure plays a positive role for the Japanese economy without collapsing the long-term oriented strategy by Japanese firms.[9]

The effect of changing the corporate governance system on corporate investment strategy

In the previous sections, we saw the decline of the main-bank system and the increasing role of portfolio investors in terms of both corporate finance and corporate governance. We also confirmed the burgeoning of the alternative Anglo-American type of corporate governance system in the 1990s. Then, does the increasing role of capital markets in corporate finance and corporate governance have any effect on corporate investment strategy? In fact, entering into the 1990s, the physical investment of Japanese firms dramatically decreased, while their R&D expenditure still stayed relatively high (Figure 3.1).

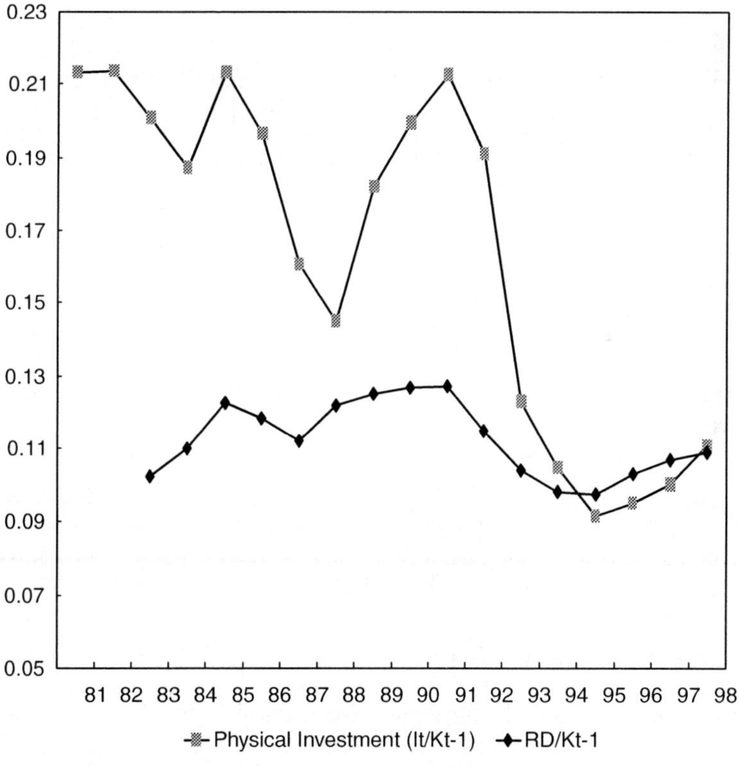

Figure 3.1 R&D and physical investment (353 large Japanese firms)
Sources: The data of physical investment is taken from JDB data base. The R&D expenditure is taken from Toyo Keizai Shinposha, Japan Corporate Handbook.

According to the conventional understanding discussed in the section 'The Japanese financial system', the Japanese financial system encouraged long-term investment of Japanese firms through mitigating asymmetric information problems from main banks and solving the market-myopia problem through intercorporate shareholdings, although the recent literature about the Japanese financial system claims that the main-bank system has played a less significant role for encouraging investment in the Japanese economy (Hayashi, 2000).

To confirm which story is plausible, Miyajima, et al. (2000) examined the responsiveness of corporate investment to its cash flow, and then tested whether governance structures (main-bank relationships, intercorporate shareholdings, presence of portfolio investors) could mitigate or accelerate the sensitivity of investment to cash flow.

According to their tentative estimation results, it might be possible that the role of main banks for mitigating cash flow constraints on R&D expenditure still remained in the 1990s. We interpret that, since a main bank has access to insider information in a firm and the net present value of R&D is harder to evaluate than physical investment for outside investors, it could play an important role in financing R&D expenditure. Furthermore, this effect is more evident for younger firms with high growth opportunities. Younger firms should face more serious asymmetric information problems between a manager and outside investors because of the lack of reputation, and a firm with high growth opportunity is also likely to face asymmetric information problems, as Anderson and Makhija (1999) explained, because the realization of business chance depends mainly on the manager's discretion.

On the other hand, in the 1990s, the sensitivity of R&D expenditure to cash flow was accelerated by the share held by portfolio investors, especially by foreign investors. This result is consistent with the managerial myopia hypothesis, which predicts that portfolio investors urge managers to pay higher dividends as a signal of good performance for getting better evaluation when there is asymmetric information between portfolio investors and managers.[10, 11]

Conclusions and discussion

As outlined in the preceding sections, economic institutions that were unique to the Japanese economic system substantially changed in the 1990s. The choice by Japanese large firms between bond and bank borrowing is now based on the capital market. As for the governance structure of firms, the main bank has stepped back, while the portfolio investor has been getting influential. The financing for corporate investment by large firms also has become reliant on the capital market.

Does this mean that the Japanese bank-based financial system, which enabled long-term oriented corporate strategy, has been totally transformed into a more market-based one? Some researchers insist that there has been a convergence of the Japanese financial firm system toward the Anglo-American style market-based system. However, it might not be appropriate to conclude that the Japanese financial system is totally converging toward the Anglo-American system, because there are some evidences to suggest that some part of the Japanese financial system is still in place.

As we have already mentioned, R&D expenditure still faces liquidity constraints due to the asymmetric information problem, and main-bank relationships seem to mitigate that problem. This constraint is especially the case for relatively young and small firms. Consequently, for those with enough growth opportunity but likely to face asymmetric information problems, the main-bank system might still play a significant role for their long-term investment strategy.[12]

On the other hand, for larger firms which can raise their necessary financial resources from the capital market, the board of directors, or portfolio investors would work well as a major corporate governance device for implementing innovative management strategy, replacing the main-bank system. Among those firms, the issue would be the long-term employment system. The market pressure for keeping higher stock prices might let managers in financial distress reduce employment more easily than before as is often pointed out. As long as the stock price contains enough information about expected profitability of the firm, the lay-offs induced by shareholders lead to improvements in the efficiency of the firm. However, if capital market suffered from the asymmetric information problem, the increase of liquidity in labour market induced by shareholders' pressures might incur the destruction of the long-term formation of firm-specific skills, which was one of the primary factors for sustaining the high productivity of the Japanese manufacturing sector. Thus far, there has been no evidence that firms changed their long-term employment system in the manufacturing sector except for a few firms that faced financial distress. This fact may be complimentary to the fact that the cross-shareholdings among firms are still kept at a certain level.

Furthermore, there is some evidence that in the 1990s the reforms initiated by insiders was implemented, which shows a kind of internal governance mechanism in Japanese firms. Boards' reforms referred to in the section 'The changing strategy of Japanese firms on corporate finance' were not directly initiated by foreign investors, but by corporate insiders who realized the pressure of capital market. In our estimation, the presidential managerial turnover initiated by insiders became much more sensitive to corporate performance in the 1990s, which is different from former periods when insider presidential turnover was mainly based on seniority rules. Therefore, one of the possible and hopeful scenarios is that the increased shares held by portfolio investors improve the efficiency of Japanese firms, while the proper cross-shareholdings among firms prevents managers from engaging in myopic behaviours in the labour market.

Acknowledgement

We received research support from Waseda University Grant for Special Research Projects.

Notes

1 See Aoki (1990) and Aoki and Dore (1994) for the detail of J-Type firm system.
2 As Sheard (1994) pointed out, there has been no rigorous quantitative research on this point. Only exceptional work is Hall and Weinstein (1996) that find evidence to the contrary.
3 See Hoshi et al. (1993) and Hoshi and Kashyap (2000) for further detail of the deregulation process of Japanese capital market.
4 In 1997, for the first time after WWII, the publicly issued unsecured convertible bond of *Yaohan* was defaulted and not bought back by the trustee bank.
5 This understanding is partly contrary to conventional understanding on the causes of bad debt problems in the 1990s. See, Horiuchi (1995), Miyajima and Arikawa (2000).
6 In July 2000, Toyo Trust Bank was also announced to join UFJ Group.
7 The share of portfolio investors, is defined as percentage share of individual shareholder plus percentage share held by trust banks plus foreign investors minus individual block-shareholder minus foreign block-shareholder.
8 This result might suggest that firms with more portfolio investors as shareholders tend to forgive more frequently implementing some projects for paying current dividend.
9 It should be noted that it is possible to interpret this result as a portfolio investor just investing in firms with better performance.
10 See Stein (1988) for the details of the managerial-myopia problem.
11 Nonetheless, these estimation results on R&D expenditure might also be consistent with the idea that a firm's managers were under a soft budget constraint due to the Japanese corporate governance system. Assuming that portfolio investors can properly evaluate an investment project, while the R&D expenditure is determined by managerial discretion for private benefit to

some degree, portfolio investors tend to play a disciplinary role through voice or exit. This implies that if the R&D expenditure determined by manager would be upward from optimal due to managerial discretion, the portfolio investors play a positive role by disciplining a manager.

12 This point is close to what Aoki and Dinc (2000) explained.

References

Abegglen, J. C. and G. Stalk (1985) *Kaisya, the Japanese Corporation*, Basic Books, New York.

Anderson, C. W. and A. K. Makhija (1999) 'Deregulation, disintermediation, and agency costs of debt: evidence from Japan', *Journal of Financial Economics*, 51: 309–39.

Aoki, M. (1990) 'Toward an economic model of the Japanese firm', *Journal of Economic Literature*, 28: 1–27.

Aoki, M. (1994) 'The contingent governance of teams: an analysis of institutional complementarity', *International Economic Review*, 35: 657–76.

Aoki, M. and R. Dore (1994) *The Japanese Firm: Sources of Competitive Strength*, Oxford University Press.

Aoki, M. and S. Dinc (2000) 'Relational financing as an institution and its viability under competition', in M. Aoki and G. R. Saxonhouse (eds) *Finance, Governance, and Competitiveness in Japan*, Oxford University Press.

Aoki, M. and H. Patrick (eds)(1994) *The Japanese Main Bank System: Its Relevancy for Developing and Transforming Economies*, Oxford, UK: Oxford University Press.

Boot, A. and V. A. Thakor (2000) 'Can relationship banking survive competition'? *Journal of Finance*, pp. 679–713.

Hall, B. and D. E. Weinstein (1996) 'The myth of the patient Japanese: investment horizons in Japan and the US', NBER working paper 5818.

Hanazaki, M. and A. Horiuchi (2000) 'Have banks contributed to efficient management in Japan's manufacturing', Centre for International Research on the Japanese Economy, Discussion paper series F-76, Faculty of Economics, The University of Tokyo.

Hayashi, F. (2000) 'The main bank system and corporate investment: an empirical reassessment', in M. Aoki and G. R. Saxonhouse (eds) *Finance, Governance, and Competitiveness in Japan*, Oxford University Press.

Hirota, S. and H. Miyajima (2000) 'Ginko kainyu gata Gabanansu ha Henka shitaka' ('Is the bank based governance really changing?: empirical test for 1970s to 1990s'), mimeo. Waseda University.

Horiuchi, A. (1995) 'Financial structure and managerial discretion in the Japanese firm: an implication of the surge of equity-related band', in M. Okabe (ed.) *The Structure of the Japanese Economy*, Macmillan.

Hoshi, T. and A. Kashyap (2000) 'The Japanese banking crisis: where did it come from and how will it end'? *NBER Macroeconomic Annual 1999*.

Hoshi, T., Kashyap, A. and D. Sharfstein (1993) 'The choice between public and private debt: an analysis of post deregulation corporate financing in Japan', NBER working paper 4421.

Miyajima, H. (1998) 'Will the deregulation change J-type capitalism?: the impact of deregulation on corporate governance and finance in J-type firm', in L. Carlile and M. Tilton (eds) *Regulation and regulatory Reform in Japan: Are Things Changing*? Blookings Institute.

Miyajima, H. and Y. Arikawa (2000) 'Relationship banking and debt choice: evidence from the liberalization in Japan', IFMP discussion paper series 00A-07, Institute of Fiscal and Monetary Policy, Ministry of Finance.

Miyajima, H., Arikawa, Y. and A. Kato (2000) 'Corporate governance, relational banking and R&D investment: evidence from Japanese large firms in the 1980s and 1990s', Forthcoming in *International Journal of Technological Management.*

Miyajima, H., Yamamoto, K. and Y. Kondo (1999) 'Nihon Kigyo System no Keisei to Henyo' (The formation and metamorphoses of Japanese firm system), Discussion paper 99A-03, Institute of Fiscal and Monetary Policy, Ministry of Finance.

NLI Research Institute (2000) *Kabushiki Mochiai Jyoukyo Chousa (The Investigation on Inter-Corporate Shareholdings).*

Petersen, M. and R. G. Rajan (1995) 'The effect of credit market competition on lending relationships', *Quarterly Journal of Economics*, 110: 407–44.

Porter, M. E. (1992) 'Capital disadvantage: America's failing capital investment system', *Harvard Business Review*, 70: 65–82.

Sheard, P. (1994) 'Long-termism and the Japanese firm', in M. Okabe (ed.) *The Structure of the Japanese Economy*, Macmillan.

Stein, J. C. (1988) 'Takeover threads and managerial myopia', *Journal of Political Economy*, 96(1): 61–80.

Weinstein, D. and Y. Yafeh (1998) 'On the costs of a bank-centred financial system: evidence from the changing main bank relations in Japan', *Journal of Finance*, 53: 635–72.

Yonezawa, Y. and M. Miyazaki (1996) 'Nihonkigyo no Corporate Governance to Seisansei', (The corporate governance and productivity in Japanese firm), in: T. Tachibanaki and Y. Tsutsui (eds) *Nihon no Sihon Sijyo*, Nihon Hyoronsya.

4
Internet-based Strategies in Asia's Post-crisis Emerging Economies

George T. Haley

Introduction

The Internet and other new-economy technologies have provided tremendous sources of economic growth for the more advanced industrialized economies of North America, Europe and Asia. These technologies have also provided significant strategic tools for those companies adroit enough to discern their advantages, and capable of both adapting the technologies to their own purposes, and themselves to the new realities of their changed competitive environments. However, in more developed economies, advanced communications and computer technologies are pervasive, distribution and warehousing networks are generally extensive, fast and reliable, and though there are exceptions such as Japan, financial/credit networks are readily available and efficient. These technologies and the skilled work forces necessary to employ them provide the infrastructure needed to make the new-economy technologies so powerful. Unfortunately, these infrastructural elements do not exist in most emerging economies.

The pre-existing infrastructure of the developed economies is what permits the Internet and its related web-based technologies to create the fantastic cost reductions and increases in productivity that it has in advanced economies. The established infrastructure is also what permits the private sector to take the fullest possible advantage of the new-economy technologies. Thus the question becomes, when discussing less-developed economies where the heretofore-available infrastructure is not available, what are the true effects and benefits of the Internet to emerging economies? If the answer to this first question determined that significant benefits would still flow from the Internet and other web-based technologies, a related question arises: how can Internet-generated benefits be maximized? These questions must be asked, and answered, from both the public and private sectors' perspectives.

The Internet's macroeconomic effects on emerging economies can be a mixed bag of benefits and costs, but countries that show ingenuity and perseverance in developing and employing web-based technologies can benefit substantially. Companies that show ingenuity and perseverance generally gain measurable competitive advantages over their competitors. In both instances, however, they cannot simply mimic policies and strategies employed in advanced economies. This chapter discusses some of the problems and successful Internet strategies that have been developed in Asia's post-crisis emerging markets.

The problems

The public sectors' problems

Asia's emerging economies, along with virtually all other emerging economies, face two substantial problems. First, they seldom have sufficient Internet-capable communications infrastructure and skilled personnel that the more advanced economies have (Barnert et al., 2000; Cheskin Research, 2000; Jeffrey, 2000a; Lee et al., 2000). Second, they rarely have the supporting service-industry infrastructure to maximize the benefits of Internet tools (*ChinaOnline*, 1999; Barnert et al., 2000; Cheskin Research, 2000; Jeffrey, 2000a; Lee et al., 2000). For example, Internet-based vendors in China can accept credit-card payments only if the credit card was issued by a bank located in the same city as the vendor (Jeffrey, 2000a). Additionally, many emerging economies, such as those in Asia, include business cultures that have difficulties with some of the Internet's impersonal characteristics (*ChinaOnline*, 2000a). Additionally, countries have confronted recently the imbalances in development caused by the fascination investors have had for Internet-based investments and start-ups. Entire countries that failed to develop a strong, perceived presence on the dot-com horizon were, for a time, starved of funds needed for their economic development. Some countries such as China, initial darlings of the dot-com investors, later suffered as investors funneled funds into Internet start-ups and ignored other sectors of the Chinese economy that badly needed investment. Finally, one tremendous problem for some countries' governments includes acquiring the benefits of the Internet and its related technologies without surrendering much power or influence over the nation's economic, political and social environments (*ChinaOnline*, 2000a; Jeffrey,

2000a,b). *ChinaOnline* (2000a) noted that five significant threats exist to a successful web-based presence in China:

1 *Commercial* – the government owns many of the players and could interfere with private parties' access.
2 *Corruption* – this increases operating expenses for all businesses, Internet-based or brick-and-mortar.
3 *Security concerns* – especially dealing with encryption, where government regulators at one time insisted that businesses hand over copies of all encryption codes and their projected uses to government regulators.
4 *Ideology* – will content providers have freedom to operate?
5 *Enforcement* – the lack of an adequate tradition of rule-of-law.

As the list indicates, at least to some extent, the government forms a major element in each one of the five threats to the Internet's success in China. To varying degrees, most of the five threats to the Internet apply to most Asian countries.

The private sectors' problems

Established, successful companies frequently have significant difficulty, making changes in their operating procedures during difficult periods, and usually much greater difficulty when making changes during successful periods. Yet, many companies overcame these difficulties to implement changes to their strategies required by the new Internet environments. Though the changes in strategy have been successful in their home markets and other advanced economies, in emerging markets, the companies frequently find that the infrastructure that made their success possible in advanced economies simply does not exist, and they have to develop entirely new ways of doing things all over again (Jeffrey, 2000a; *The Economist*, 2001). The end effect is like having to reinvent the wheel all over again, something that is always a source of frustration.

Other problems companies face include the uncertainty that frequently surrounds governmental attitudes and regulatory environments dealing with e-commerce in many developing economies (Jeffrey, 2000b); the local business cultures' resistance to adopting practices desirable in Internet (Cheskin Research, 2000) and technology-based (Haley et al., 1998) business environments; a scarcity of qualified personnel; the tremendous increase in competition that the Internet makes possible (*MeetChina.com*, 2000); and the huge amount of information, and even worse, disinformation, that spreads like wildfire over the Internet (Varian, 1995). To make his point Varian (1995) quoted Herbert Simon's well known statement, 'What information consumes is rather obvious: it consumes the attention of its recipients. Hence, a wealth of information creates a poverty of attention and a need to allocate that attention efficiently among the overabundance of information sources that might consume it.' When the recipient receives both information and disinformation, some of the latter appearing quite credible, the demands on the recipient's time are even more cumbersome as he or she must first discern information from disinformation. Bob Berkman (1997), editor of *The Information Advisor*, even questioned whether the masses of information and disinformation found on the web might eventually lead to information's demise as a critical resource in decision-making. Most of these problems exist in the industrialized economies also.

Strategic solutions

Though I have dissected the problems facing the Internet and its users into those facing public and private sectors, this classification system is a matter of concern. To resolve effectively the issues, policy-makers and managers must address the problems jointly, from a combined public and private sector perspective. Hence, the strategic solutions in this chapter will address the problems from both public and private sectors' perspectives.

Solutions tackling the scarcity of skilled personnel

The first general problem involves the lack of people with sufficient Internet-related skills. The two basic methods of handling this include training and recruiting. China has thrown itself wholeheartedly into the training and certification of its present working population. The government has developed a program whereby people who, through training or through proof by examination, will receive certification as an e-commerce capable business or businessperson (*ChinaOnline*, 2000b). The necessary talent can also be recruited. Schmit (2000) reported of tremendous offers being made to attract Internet-capable personnel away from their present employers and to Internet-based companies; and Haley and Low (1998) commented on the Singapore government's efforts to attract people with talents desirable for Singapore's continuing economic development to the island nation. The scarcity of skilled personnel constitutes a long-term problem that will continue to plague both emerging and industrialized economies for the near future. Hence,

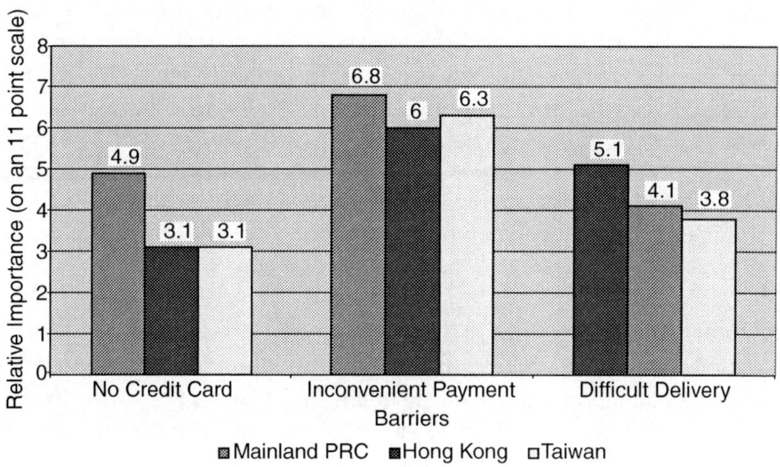

Figure 4.1 Barriers to e-commerce in Greater China
Source: Cheskin Research (2000).

emerging economies will have to live with this problem, and minimize damages either through high wages or improved technologies.

Solutions tackling insufficient service-industry infrastructure

These include solutions aimed at transportation, payments, the wireless applications protocol (WAP) factor and the general business environment.

Transportation

The second, general, long-term problem revolves around insufficient service-industry infrastructure. No Federal Express of the People's Republic or nationally accepted credit card exists, and few nationally/regionally accepted local brands prevail. Most Internet vendors depend on the Chinese postal service to send their products out to their customers. The slow and costly results, though reliable by emerging markets' standards, contribute in large part to customers' complaints about purchasing on-line. The other major complaint involves payments. Figure 4.1 presents the results of a survey taken by Cheskin Research and *China.com*. Though this problem occurs commonly in consumer markets, business-to-business marketers have overcome it with a little ingenuity and hard work. Jeffrey (2000a) reported of a commercial food caterer that takes orders for food deliveries to commercial sites and uses contracted taxis to deliver his food, hot and fresh, to the work sites that ordered the food. A bottled-water company takes orders over the Internet from companies it serves, e-mails the orders to the appropriate regional communication centres and warehouses within the major cities it serves, and delivers the bottles through traditional means including bicycle and human carriers. In both the above instances, a little ingenuity and compromise has allowed a company to take advantage of at least some of the efficiencies provided by Internet-based communications and order processing.

Payments

Issues of payment also pose difficulties. Though some Asian countries have highly developed financial-payment infrastructures – some do not. With some countries, such as Japan, it is by choice. In others, such as China and Indonesia, the infrastructure has yet to be completely built.

One severe problem occurring in China, where Internet growth has doubled every six months (Richardson, 2000), is that credit cards are only useable in the city where the issuing bank is located. As noted in Figure 4.1, not having a credit card and difficulties with payment constitute two of the most important reasons for not purchasing on-line. Web portals and Internet vendors can tackle this problem through maintaining offices in each of their major markets so that credit-card orders can be processed through the office in each market. This solution generates obvious inefficiencies, but when financially practical, it allows vendors to build semi-national market shares today rather than wait until business environments catch up with Western standards. Though this problem primarily concerns consumer markets, it helps explain why the Chinese preference for face-to-face negotiations and personal relationships extends to the Internet. Cheskin Research (2000), among countless others, indicated that even businesses purchasing Internet services insist on personally meeting with the service provider's representatives for negotiating and signing of a contract.

An example that brings all of the above-mentioned problems into focus concerns China's most successful Internet auction site. It holds its position because it not only provides a site where people can exhibit their wares for sale in an efficient and user-friendly environment, but also provides physical locations for the buyers and sellers to meet, and to arrange for payments and physical transfers of the goods being sold (Jeffrey, 2000a). This cautionary attitude may appear ludicrous in the West where E-Bays' reach crosses international boundaries; but, in China, where credit cards are good only within the city in which they were issued, and transportation constitutes a major issue affecting customer satisfaction and the desirability of conducting business over the Internet, this uniquely Chinese personal touch has been the site's key to success.

Wireless application protocols (WAPs)

One last factor that is helping to overcome China's lagging infrastructure and limited penetration of PC-based Internet is the WAP. The WAPs should also help many other emerging economies overcome their infrastructural problems. Though limited, private PC connections exist in the more prosperous and economically developed urban areas, cellular phones are so ubiquitous that they no longer correspond to conspicuous consumption (Cheskin Research, 2000). The number of cellular phone subscriptions in China is growing by 1 000 000 a month, and is projected to grow by 37 per cent compounded annual growth rate through 2006 (Snyder, 2001). Some believe that the WAP's limitations and currently poor reception by customers will limit its importance to e-commerce (*China.com*, 2001); however, it should prove useful to businesses in China and other emerging markets. Due to the shortage of telephone lines in China, most PCs have multiple users even in businesses. Additionally, for all the fantastic growth in cellular-phone subscriptions, surveys of Chinese cellular phone users indicate that 70 per cent of the owners see cellular phones primarily or exclusively as business tools. Consequently, the WAP's current unpopularity among consumers should not affect its importance to the development of wireless e-commerce in the business-to-business (B2B) markets, which have been projected to represent 90 per cent of the growth in Asia's e-commerce. Other factors favouring the development of B2B e-commerce in China include the long-term relationships that businesses generally build, the established channels of distribution for their products, and their established credit lines with financial institutions, which minimize many of the problems associated with B2C (business-to-consumer) e-commerce.

Business environment

As noted earlier, the Chinese government dominates the business environment surrounding the Internet. Of the five factors in the business environment that this section identifies, the government has already launched a withering attack on three, despite being seriously divided within its ranks on the desirability of freeing the Chinese economy and of accepting the Internet. Despite significant opposition with the Chinese government, the privatization of Chinese industry is progressing. Unfortunately, despite reductions, the huge presence of the Chinese government still exists in Chinese industry, and will continue to exist for the near future. The government continues to dominate not just the means of production, but also business services such as distribution. In many of the more remote and rural parts of China, the military remains the sole transportation and distribution source for any company serving those areas. Huge conflicts of interest emerge, especially as the military remains the largest industrial concern in China, including many companies that produce consumer goods.

Though enforcement of contracts and intellectual property rights in China remains a problem, the government is making strides in improving this aspect of business (Haley, 2000); unfortunately, the government is not the all-powerful monolith that many envision. The central government has only partial control over matters not pertaining to foreign affairs and the military. Provincial governments in recent years have openly ignored the centre in many commercial and economic matters, such as enforcing China's intellectual property rights laws, which in actuality, are quite strict (Haley, 2000). To push forward here, companies must actively pursue and protect their own interests and work to convince the local provincial and municipal governments that it is in their best interests to enforce intellectual property rights. They must also decide what technology they can afford to risk, and what technology is so central to their competitive position that it must be protected at all costs, and simply not to risk (Haley, 2000). As China's economy and legal system develop, protecting one's technology should become easier; however one must remember that China's development is not uniform. Though China's economic growth is quite strong, average income in urban centres is thrice that of rural areas (Cheskin Research, 2000); in some rural areas and areas dominated by the old government-owned heavy industries, average per capita income levels have fallen over the last decade. Hence, until intellectual property rights become an economic good throughout China rather than a perceived hindrance to local entrepreneurs and economic development, significant difficulties will continue for businesses. It is not just a matter of what laws are on the books, but of how well those laws are enforced.

The government is also dealing with corruption, although as yet, the effects of governmental efforts are difficult to discern. Some of these governmental efforts may also be politically motivated by the struggle between China's economic reformers and the Old Guard. Nevertheless, anti-corruption efforts are being made. Businesspersons doing business in China should support the government's efforts for two reasons. First, controlling corruption will greatly enhance the business environment and profitability for all. Second, opposing the government can lead to highly undesirable results: In 1997, 50 per cent of all Australian businessmen of Chinese origin doing business in China were languishing in prison on corruption-related charges. Sometimes the businessmen were guilty, but many claim to have been set up. At times, competitors filed the charges, but usually the charged businessmen exhibited some appearance of wrongdoing.

Two items that will represent continuing areas of difficulty include issues of ideology and security concerns. Members of the Chinese government, whether reform oriented or anti-reform, are first and always loyal members of China's communist party. They will not willingly do anything that they perceive are threatening the party's dominant position in Chinese governance and society. Many members of the government fear that Microsoft's programs, and all other programs produced by US companies, come equipped with backdoors that the US government can access (Cheskin Research, 2000). Hence, the government initially demanded that copies of all encryption programs be deposited with government regulators so that it could more easily track encrypted communications. This distrust of business is not reserved for US-based and other foreign-based companies, but has been practiced by Chinese governments against their own businesses for centuries (Haley et al., 1998). Unfortunately, it is likely to remain as one of the basic tenets of Chinese policy for a substantial time in the future. Thus wherever and whenever ideological and security issues arise, business interests must fight for their own interests through any legal available channels. They should prepare for these events by keeping scrupulous records and data to prove the basic honesty and straightforwardness of their intentions in any and all business dealings, develop the strongest relationships possible with both central and provincial governments to argue their cases when the time comes, and remember that, regardless of China's laws, it remains a public-law system of justice rather than the rights-based system of a Western industrialized country. In public-law systems, an individual's rights stem entirely from the governing authority's willingness to recognize those rights, and not on an inherent possession of rights (Carver, 1996; Haley, 2000).

Concluding remarks

The future for e-commerce looms very bright in Asia, and in particular, in China. Present growth rates have the potential to continue for a good number of years due to the low penetration levels of e-commerce related technologies. Even where market penetration appears relatively high, such as in cellular phones, potential growth opportunities exist because of the total population size. Hence, investing in Asia's e-commerce related businesses is a necessity for any company in these sectors that hopes to remain a global force. Motorola has made itself the largest single investor in China, moving into China in every business sector the company operates in, from cellular phones to silicon chips to broadband net products (*ChinaOnline*, 2001; Snyder, 2001), and has no intention of slowing its rate of investment. Though many problems exist in the market, they are not insurmountable if managements apply effort and ingenuity to adapt where necessary to the infrastructural, business and political situations that exist.

References

Berkman, B. (1997) 'Information losing value/impeding decision-making', posted Friday, 21 February.

Barnert, R., Gupta, R., Lee, J. B., Schroepfer, A. M., Gould, G. M. and S. Tan (2000) *B2B Commerce/Internet Asia Pacific: B2B@sia Powered by E-frastructure*, Goldman Sachs Global Equity Research, New York.

Carver, A. (1996) 'Open and secret regulations in China and their implication for foreign investment', in J. Child and Y. Lu (eds) *Management Issues in China, International Enterprises*, London: Routledge.

Cheskin Research (2000) *Greater E-China Insights*, prepared in cooperation with China.com Corp., Redwood Shores, US, October.

China.com (2001) 'Chinese mobile users give thumbs down to WAP', 10 January.

ChinaOnline News (1999) 'E-commerce in China: horse drawn Buggies on the information highway?', 29 December.

ChinaOnline News (2000a) 'State of the internet in China', 31 July.

ChinaOnline News (2000b) 'New program to train China companies in e-commerce', 12 June.

ChinaOnline News (2001) 'Motorola becomes largest foreign investor in China', 6 February.

Economist, The (2001) 'From bamboo to bits and bytes', Survey of Asian Business, 7–13 April, p. 8.

Haley, G. T. (2000) 'Intellectual property rights and foreign direct investment in emerging markets', *Marketing Intelligence & Planning*, Special issue on 'Strategic marketing in emerging economies', 18(5): 273–80.

Haley, U. C. V. and L. Low (1998) 'Crafted culture: governmental sculpting of modern Singapore and effects on business environments', *Journal of Organizational Change Management*, 11(6): 530–53.

Haley, G. T., Tan, C. T. and U. C. V. Haley (1998) *New Asian Emperors: The Overseas Chinese, their Strategies and Competitive Advantages*, Oxford, UK: Butterworth-Heinemann, 164 pp.

Jeffrey, L. (2000a) *China's Wired*, Toronto: Stonecutter Communications.
Jeffrey, L. (2000b) 'New Internet rules: red tape or money grab', *China's Wired* (Newsletter), 4(11), November.
Lee, J. B., Barnert, R., Murray, C., Yamashina, H., Gupta, R., Berquist, T. P. and Friedman, J. (2000) *B2B Commerce/Internet Asia Pacific: B2B@sia: E-volution or E-xtinction*, Goldman Sachs Global Equity Research, New York.
MeetChina.com (2000) 'MeetChina.com expands to Korea with nation's most popular trade portal', Business to business section, 6 December.
Richardson, M. (2000) 'Internet gap is widening for Asians: experts seeking ways to narrow digital divide', *International Herald Tribune*, 14 September.
Schmit, J. (2000) 'Internet revolution rolls through Asia', *USA Today*, 11 February.
Snyder, C. (2001) 'Motorola (China) plans move into broadband, net products', *ChinaOnline News*, 5 February.
Varian, H. R. (1995) 'The information economy', *Scientific American*, September, pp. 200–1.

5

Global Strategic Management of German MNCs in China: Patterns and Determinants of Sustainable Competitive Advantage in the Aftermath of the Asian Crisis

Brij N. Kumar, Yunshi Mao and Birgit Ensslinger

Introduction

In general, FDI in Asia was not hit by the Asian crisis as hard as were portfolio investments and bank lendings. Still, there is evidence that the investment behaviour of Western and particularly German multinational corporations (MNCs) in the critical period went through some changes (Kumar and Mohr, 1999). On one hand, market-oriented FDI slackened due to rapid decline of market potential. On the other hand, FDI for re-exports remained stable or even picked up because of steep depreciation of local currencies, the fall of local wages or other factor costs. In the same vein, some MNCs could cope with the crisis in terms of keeping FDI stable and continuing their corporate activity in a better way than others. They were able to compensate the negative effects of unfavourable developments by using their strategic advantages (Kumar and Mohr, 1999).

As shown by Kumar and Mohr (1999), one of the success factors, even during the crisis, was their capability to include Asian subsidiaries in worldwide activities. To the effect that Asian operations could be integrated in global strategy, MNCs were able to balance losses and – in some cases – even boost up sales if they could harness sinking factor costs and currency devaluation for more effective intracorporate procurement and supplies. Thus, global strategies of MNCs proved to be a competitive advantage in cushioning the adversities of the Asian crisis through cross-subsidization. Obviously, the potential of the MNCs to integrate and to coordinate Asian operations within global strategies varied according to many factors, and this chapter explores them.

This study picks up the issue left open in the study by Kumar and Mohr (1999) and explores the actual dimensions of the global strategy pursued in Asia by MNCs. We seek to uncover the pattern and determinants of global strategy and to answer the question whether it has any relationship to success and the consequences that can be drawn for sustainable competitive advantage. The study is based on an investigation of global strategy and FDI of 36 German MNCs in China. Although the People's Republic was not affected by the Asian crisis as hard as other countries in Southeast and East Asia, the developments are nevertheless comparable. After reaching an all time high of US$45.5 billion in 1998, FDI in China dropped to US$33 billion in the following year. Investment flows slowed down considerably, many companies divested. German FDI flows followed the general trend as they fell from approximately US$1 billion in 1997 to US$736 million in 1998 (*China Statistical Yearbook*, 1999).

Global strategy framework

General overview

The purpose of this study is to carry out an assessment of global strategy as employed by German MNCs with reference to their activitities in China. In order to pursue this objective, it is necessary to envisage the general framework of global strategy.

The building blocks of the Fayerweather (1969) model of unification – fragmentation and innovation – conformity through which he claimed to capture a meaningful managerial method of defining the key characteristics of MNCs' strategy were picked up by several authors in later years for developing a number of theoretical approaches to global strategy. Fayerweather's model underlies Porter's (1986) configuration/coordination paradigm, as it does Prahalad and Doz's (1987) concept of global integration/coordination and local responsiveness, developed later also by Bartlett and Ghoshal (1989) for construction of their multinational–global–international–transnational typology.

Hedlund (1981) was among the first to recognize the key role of integration for achieving worldwide corporate synergies through coordinating inputs, for example, of innovative capabilities, know-how, knowledge and flows of resources within the network (Kobrin, 1991). On the other hand Bartlett (1981) emphasized the importance of national

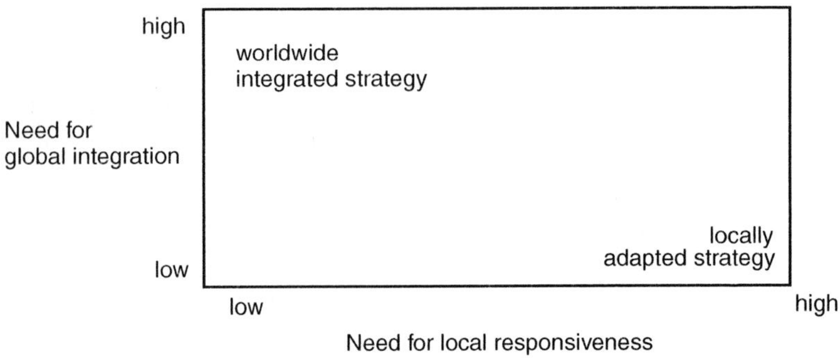

Figure 5.1 Concept of global strategy

responsiveness in a situation of rapid international growth, and this has been confirmed repeatedly in literature (White and Poynter, 1984; Agthe, 1990; Taylor, 1991), stressing the need and effectiveness of differentiation. Bartlett and Ghoshal (1989) made clear the same point by emphasizing that in certain cases even corporate survival may depend on proactive development of such differentiating local responsiveness in specific functional areas, for example international R&D, especially in the pharmaceutical or consumer goods industry, where product specifications and consumer tastes vary widely by country.

Taggart (1997) evaluated the integration–responsiveness framework extensively which has been subjected to supportive empirical testing, notably by Roth and Morrison (1990) and by Johnson (1995). Both confirmed the original concept proposed by Prahalad and Doz (1987) by identifying strategies along the integration–responsiveness grid (Figure 5.1).

Propositions and research questions

From the discussion above, it is clear that the global strategy of German MNCs with reference to their operations in China must be investigated within the integration–responsiveness management grid. The resulting proposition (P) can be formulated as follows:

P1 The global strategy of German MNC with respect to their Chinese operations can be formulated within the integration–responsiveness framework.

The connected research question (RQ) then can be summarized:

RQ1 Where is the global strategy of German MNCs with regards to their operations in China located within the integration–responsiveness grid? How is it defined?

As suggested previously, there seems to be a relationship between global strategy and success, since corporations capable of integrating their Asian subsidiaries within their worldwide operations survived the Asian crisis generally with fewer problems than others (Kumar and Mohr, 1999). As Taggart (1997) has shown, Leontiades (1986) identified coordination of global resources as essential to MNC success, as also did Porter (1986) who defined coordination in terms of the linkages between similar activities in different countries/and or different parts of the MNC's international network. He recognized that coordination allows for accumulation and sharing of knowledge across the network, it helps the MNC to gain international economies of scale, and – as in the case of German MNC-operations in Asia – also allows it to shift comparative advantage between countries where it is located. On the other hand, local responsiveness cannot be neglected, and successful global strategy should therefore be balanced between the two generic dimensions. The resulting proposition and research question are:

P2 There is a relationship between the global strategy of German MNCs with respect to the Chinese operations and their performance.

RQ2 How is successful global strategy of German MNCs with respect to their operations in China balanced between integration and responsiveness? What is the relationship to subsidiary performance?

As suggested above, the degree to which MNCs opt for integration and/or responsiveness depends on several factors. For instance Hedlund (1981) related integration to the degree of subsidiary autonomy and Bartlett and Ghoshal (1989) found a positive relationship between corporate innovative capabilities and integration. An overview of the literature shows that several influencing variables have been identified independent of each other (Taggart, 1997). Based on the view that global strategy basically is instrumental for achieving the strategic goals pursued by establishing foreign operations, Kumar (1993) suggested relating it (global strategy) to the determinants of FDI. That is, the degree to which global integration or/and local responsiveness are practical will depend on the variables underlying the corporate decision to invest and set up operations abroad.

The corporate foreign investment decision has been conceptualized in the framework of the theory of direct investment in several ways (Aharoni, 1969; Buckley and Casson, 1976). For our study, the Eclectic paradigm (Dunning, 1989) offers a purposeful approach especially because the three categories of determinants, ownership advantages, location-specific factors and internalization advantages also fit into the general strategy framework (Hofer and Schendel, 1978; Quinn, 1980; Fredrickson, 1983) which defines corporate characteristics and environmental factors as the main influencing blocks of (global) strategy formulation (Kumar, 1993).

The influence of ownership advantages on global strategy can be assumed to the extent that their effective use worldwide can be facilitated by integrating important aspects of operations across borders. On the other hand, the implementation of intended integration can be made easier when local entities in the worldwide network are convinced by the competitive edge that can be achieved by adhering to underlying ownership advantages. This relationship can be summarized in the following proposition:

P3 There will be a positive relationship between the ownership advantages of German MNCs in their Chinese operations and integration strategy (and vice versa).

MNCs invest abroad in order to avail location-specific advantages which can be seen in the local market, low production costs and so on. On the other hand, certain location factors like bureaucracy of the local government can be an impediment to effective operations. It can be assumed that relatively difficult host-country environments will lead foreign companies to develop specific adapted solutions to handle the corresponding problems, whereas congenial conditions can favour the application of standardized resources and know-how. In the same vein, the divergence of host-country environment from the home country will require shift in the balance of global strategy from unification towards more fragmentation (Fayerweather, 1969) if management is to be functional in the alien location. Obviously, the global strategy balance between integration and responsiveness that is finally adopted will depend on how the MNCs can actually handle environmental divergence and the connected problems. These arguments lead to the following proposition:

P4 There will be a positive relationship between the German MNCs' perception of environmental difficulties for their Chinese operations and the local responsiveness strategy (and vice versa).

Finally, it can be argued that achieving internalization advantage in foreign operations as conceptualized by the transaction cost theory

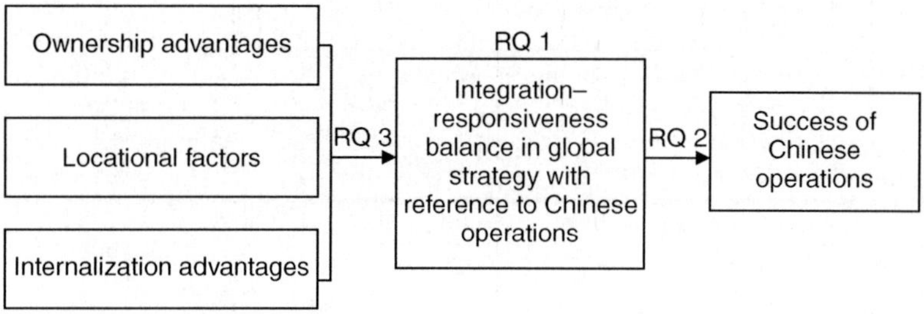

Figure 5.2 Research design

with the help of hierarchies (Buckley and Casson, 1976), requires keeping down the incurred coordinating costs within internal markets. This presumes that standardized functions can be integrated more easily than diverse activities.

P5 There will be a positive relationship between the degree of internalization achieved in Chinese operations of German MNCs and integration strategy (and vice versa).

On the basis of propositions P3–P5 the research question can be defined as follows:

RQ3 What are the determinants of the global strategy of German MNCs with reference to their operations in China? Which factors in alignment with the Eclectic paradigm influence integration and responsiveness in the Chinese operations of German MNCs?

Figure 5.2 summarizes the research design and questions.

Methodology

Sample

In this study, the sample of German MNCs with their own manufacturing and sales subsidiaries and joint ventures in China was generated from the database of the Chamber of Industry and Commerce Nürnberg. From May to August 1998, questionnaires were mailed to 294 German parent companies addressed to the CEO. The profiles of the 36 companies which responded are indicated in Table 5.1. Whereas the German parent companies are on the average big to large organizations, their Chinese operations are generally small- to medium-sized which on the average contribute with sales under 20 per cent of total turnover.

Table 5.1 Sample

Annual sales of German parent company	
Under 500 million DM	41%
500–1000 million DM	15%
Over 1000 million DM	44%
Total employees in Chinese subsidiary	
Under 500	74%
500–1000	14%
Over 1000	12%
Branches of industry (3 largest)	
Electrical/electronic	42%
Automobile	17%
Med. engineering	14%

Measures

Integration–responsiveness

The integration and responsiveness dimensions were operationalized by two main variables:

1 Degree of adaptation of management in Chinese operations to German parent-company global standards – this measure has been used in previous studies (Porter, 1986; Kumar, 1993) and proved to be a robust indicator for integration–responsiveness. Standardization of management functions on a global scale notably facilitates coordination and integration (Martinez and Jarillo, 1991; Rosenzweig and Singh, 1991) and vice versa a lack of consistency favours differentiation and local responsiveness.

2 Degree of decision-making autonomy in the Chinese subsidiary – Hedlund (1981) was among the first to relate integration with the degree of decision-making discretion of foreign subsidiaries. The general assumption is thereby that autonomy usually encourages differentiation and adaptation of management to local conditions and vice versa. Several studies prove that MNCs tend to centralize decision-making in management, that is in the R&D function, when the thrust in strategy is towards integration and vice versa.

Determinants

The three blocks of influencing factors based on the Eclectic paradigm (Dunning, 1989) were operationalized as follows:

1 *Ownership advantages* – According to the theory of oligopolistic advantage (Hymer, 1976; Kindleberger, 1969), foreign operations must possess a competitive edge over locally operating companies to ward off their home country privileges like better information, standing relations with indigenous partners and so on. These competitive advantages can be manifested in several ways. Indicators used in this study are: perceived competitive advantages in the Chinese operations of German MNCs vis-à-vis competitors in China (local and foreign) in the field of product programme, technology, financial standing, cultural competence and personnel training.
2 *Locational factors* – As discussed earlier, the environment in the host country can pose threats or opportunities for the foreign companies. The extent to which the locational factors are perceived by the MNCs as such will influence the global strategy. The environment is a complex configuration, and what count are the relevant location factors. These can be operationalized according to the concept of investment climate as proposed in literature for evaluating host-country risks and opportunities (Dülfer, 1997). In this study, 18 locational factors were enlisted for evaluation by the German MNCs with reference to the environment in China: bureaucracy, investment laws for foreign companies, public attitude towards foreign companies, availability of services, corruption, overheads for foreign companies, production costs, licencing procedures, qualification of employees, currency and repatriation policy, contract loyalty, availability of short-term capital, taxation, environmental laws, infrastructure, political stability, economic policy and incentives of local government.
3 *Internalization factors* – As mentioned earlier, achieving competitive advantages also depends on the extent to which internal markets can be built and coordinated. A robust indicator is the intracorporate or intersubsidiary exchange of goods, resources and information (Kobrin, 1991). Effectively, the proportion of sales and procurement of the Chinese operations in conjunction with the German parent company can be delineated as a proxy for internalization.

Success and performance

Organization success and performance can be measured in many ways. Usually a range of financial variables are used which include profits, growth and market share (Miller and Cardinal, 1994). However, particular problems inherent in this study of German MNC-operation in China invalidate this approach. Changes in profitability, growth or market share of the Chinese operation maybe constrained by the parent-company strategy; thus simple profit measures take no account of differences in German head office management, transfer of payments and royalties. The intracorporative transfers are used to maximize group profits at the expense of the Chinese operations. Also, changes with performance of the Chinese operations may be determined by German corporate marketing policy within global strategy rather than the success of the individual Chinese operation.

In order to overcome these problems, the measure used in this study is based on the perceived success of the Chinese operations by the German parent companies. Two indicators are thereby used: perceived goal attainment and repetition of decision to set up operations in China. This measure has the advantage of evaluating success of the Chinese operations relative to the original motivation and expectations of the German MNCs to start operations in China. Such subjective indicators have proved to be appropriate for reflecting performance of foreign subsidiaries in previous studies (Geringer and Herbert, 1989; Millington and Bayliss, 1997).

Results

The main results are put together in the correlation table (Table 5.2) and described below.

Performance

Table 5.2 does not indicate the results regarding the opinion of the respondents whether they would repeat their investment decision in China: however, 80 per cent would and 20 per cent would not or only under other circumstances. The mean value pertaining to perceived goal attainment (on a 5-point Likert scale: 1 = all goals achieved; 5 = none achieved) as indicated is 2.89, which can be considered mediocre. There is a significant correlation between the two performance variables ($p \leq 0.01$): the group of companies which would repeat their investment decision showed better goal attainment value (2.68) than the non-repeat group (3.71). The results are plausible and prove that the large majority of German MNCs in China do not repent their decision to start operations there since most of them see their expectations fulfilled to a fair amount.

Global strategy: the integration–responsiveness practice

According to the measures developed, global strategy of German MNCs in China was ascertained on two indicators:

Table 5.2 Correlation table: dimensions and determinants of global strategy and performance

	Mean	SD	1	2	3	4	5	6	7	8	9	10	11	12	13	14	15
1	2.89	1.12	1.00														
2	2.86	1.13	0.260†	1.00													
3	1.81	0.92	0.528†	0.004**	1.00												
4	1.69	0.67	0.561	0.756	0.797	1.00											
5	1.71	0.89	0.050	0.140	0.373	0.017*	1.00										
6	1.72	0.66	0.599	0.474	0.599	0.124	0.077	1.00									
7	2.67	1.04	0.261	0.251	0.038*	0.725	0.690	0.704	1.00								
8	2.74	1.11	0.259	0.124	0.081	0.653	0.706	0.490	0.181	1.00							
9	2.88	0.86	0.390	0.738	0.611	0.600	0.795	0.760	0.006**	0.256	1.00						
10	1.57	0.70	0.905	0.638	0.851	0.145	0.987	0.318	0.444	0.577	0.178	1.00					
11	2.03	0.76	0.064	0.338	0.716	0.019*	0.009**	0.480	0.796	0.449	0.610	0.109	1.00				
12	1.97	1.03	0.173	0.016*	0.921	0.338	0.616	0.543	0.846	0.855	0.619	0.447	0.426	1.00			
13	3.14	0.81	0.117	0.357	0.828	0.881	0.116	0.220	0.062	0.637	0.145	0.842	0.069	0.030*	1.00		
14	1.21	0.86	0.632	0.805	0.124	0.416	0.523	0.592	0.853	0.584	0.746	0.874	0.348	0.261	0.824	1.00	
15	2.48	1.68	0.219	0.678	0.429	0.977	0.327	0.027*	0.427	0.605	0.679	0.177	0.053	0.423	0.035*	0.769	1.00

† Negative correlation; * $p \leq .05$; ** $p \leq .01$.

1 Goal attainment
2 Adaptation to German/Chinese conditions
3 Influence of German MNC on decision-making in China
4 Perceived strength: product programme
5 Perceived strength: technology
6 Perceived strength: cultural experience
7 Perceived strength: financial power
8 Perceived strength: personnel training
9 Technology vs. global competition
10 Technology vs. Chinese competition
11 Competitive position vs. global competition
12 Competitive position vs. Chinese competition
13 General investment climate (mean of 18 locational factors)
14 Proportion of sales to German parent company
15 Proportion of procurement from German parent company

1 Degree of adaptation of management in Chinese operations to local conditions or to German parent-company practice – The respondents were asked to estimate this on a 5-point Likert scale: 1 = strongly adapted to German practice; 5 = strongly adapted to local Chinese practice. As Table 5.2 shows, the mean score is 2.86 which means that on the whole there seems to be quite an even balance of both management practices present in the Chinese operations. In this study, the details as to which specific aspects and functions of management were adapted to German or Chinese practices could not be established.
2 The second measure of global strategy is the degree of decision-making autonomy in the Chinese operations – The respondents were asked to indicate on a 5-point Likert scale the amount of influence the German parent company exercised on strategic decisions (e.g., product programme, staffing key-positions, etc.) in the Chinese operations: 1 = very big influence; 5 = no influence at all.

The mean score is 1.81 which clearly indicates that the main locus of control lies with the German parent company which suggests a higher thrust of integration in the global strategy (see Table 5.2). This is confirmed by the correlation between the two variables at a high level of significance: $p \leq .004$ (Table 5.1). In accordance with P1 and RQ1, we can state that global strategy of German MNCs with respect to their operations in China can be established on the integration–responsiveness scale, and thereby the integration dimension is the dominant strategy element.

Global strategy and performance

P2 and RQ2 presumed a relationship between global strategy and performance. Our results are very clear in this respect. Firstly, Table 5.2 shows a negative correlation between perceived goal attainment and adaptation of management to German company practice as well as between perceived goal attainment and parent-company control. The performance falls with increasing German orientation in management and also with parent-company control and vice versa.

Secondly, our results show (not in Table 5.2) that the group of companies that would repeat their investment in China indicated lower parent-company control (mean 1.86) than the group that would not repeat the investment decision (mean 1.71) (significant $p \leq .05$). Furthermore, the group of companies that would repeat their investment in China indicated a higher degree of adaptation of management to

Table 5.3 Perceived ownership advantages of German MNCs with reference to their Chinese operations ($N = 36$)

Dimensions of competitive advantage	**Mean of a 5-point Likert scale indicating degree of possession of strengths and advantages (1 = very high; 5 = very low)**
Perceived strengths in general	
• Product programme	1.69
• Technology	1.71
• Cultural experience	1.72
• Financial resources	2.67*
• Personnel training	2.74
Perceived advantages vs. main competitor	
• Technology vs. global competitor	2.88
• Technology vs. Chinese competitor	1.57
• General competitive position vis-à-vis other global players	2.03
• General competitive position vis-à-vis Chinese companies	1.97*

* $p \leq .05–0.01$.

Chinese conditions (mean 3.00) as opposed to the group that would not repeat (mean 2.57) (significant $p \leq .05$).

The results indicate very clearly that although German MNCs tend to lay more importance on the integration strategy in China, local responsiveness in terms of lesser adaptation of German management and lesser German parent, control seems to be the more effective strategy for achieving better performance.

Determinants

According to our research design (P3–P5 and RQ3), the determinants of global strategy are assumed to be found in the ownership advantages of the MNCs, their capabilities of tackling the local environmental factors and their presumptive internalization advantages. Tables 5.3 and 5.4 show through descriptive statistics, how the responding German MNCs evaluate their capabilities with respect to their Chinese operations.

Our results (Table 5.3) show that German MNCs with operations in China can count on substantial strengths and competitive advantages, the greatest being in the area of product programme and technology as compared to local competitors. These results are in line with the general theory of FDI that MNCs are characterized by such factors that enable them to face the risks of operations abroad. The capabilities required also refer to overcoming locational restrictions or availing of the opportunities host country environments offer. This is especially important in host countries like China where culture and institutions are completely different from those of the home country. Table 5.4 shows where German MNCs see problems and where they perceive opportunities in the business environment in China.

German MNCs perceive the Chinese environment as being rather difficult for business (average mean 3.14). The biggest problem perceived

Table 5.4 Problems and opportunities in Chinese business environment as perceived by German MNCs for their indigenous operations ($N = 36$)

Locational factors in China	Mean of a 5-point Likert scale indicating degree of perceived locational opportunities/difficulties (1 = big opportunities; 5 = big difficulties)
• Bureaucracy and efficiency in government offices	3.74
• Laws for foreign investors	3.28
• Attitudes of local authorities and public vis-à-vis foreign investors	2.72
• Availability of services (banks, consultants, etc.)	3.44
• Corruption/integrity in local authority	3.76
• Overheads for foreign investors (rents, transportation)	3.72
• Production costs, wages	2.00
• Licencing procedures	3.42
• Qualification of employees	3.36
• Currency stability/foreign exchange policy	3.03
• Attitudes towards honouring contracts	3.44
• Availability of short-term capital	3.59
• Taxation of foreign companies	2.86
• Environmental laws	2.69
• Incentives from government	2.86
• Infrastructure	3.31
• Political stability	2.75
• Economic policy	2.61

Note: Average mean: 3.14.

is corruption and lack of integrity, followed by bureaucracy in Chinese authorities and government offices. The biggest opportunities for doing business in China are seen in the low production costs and wages and then in the economic policy. Also the environmental laws are seen as favourable, especially as compared with the very restrictive policies in Germany which companies have to face.

Finally, the internalization advantages were measured by the exchange of goods between the Chinese operations and the German parent company. Two indicators were taken as proxy, intracorporate sales and intracorporate procurement. Our results show the following:

- In 86 per cent of the responding MNCs, intracorporate sales account for only up to 20 per cent of total turnover; only 5 or 6 per cent achieve more than 60 per cent of their sales in the German parent company.
- In 42 per cent of the responding MNCs up to 20 per cent of total procurement is intracorporate; 48 per cent import more than 60 per cent of their inputs from the German parent.

On the whole, the internalization of German MNCs with respect to the Chinese operations is largely restricted to intracorporate procurement. This is explainable on one side with the large domestic market which absorbs most of the subsidiary sales, and on the other side with the problems of securing quality inputs indigenously. Looking now at the relationships between the determinants on one side and global strategy on the other, we see only two significant results (see Table 5.2). First, a positive correlation between the German MNCs' financial strength and adaptation of management to German practice, and second, a positive relationship between perceived general competitive position vis-à-vis local Chinese companies and control of Chinese operations by the German parent company. All together, this suggests that with rising ownership advantages, also the degree of integration in global strategy becomes stronger. This is in line with P3. On the other hand, we can establish no other significant relationships so that P4 and P5 and the strategy forming role of locational and internalization advantages with respect to the Chinese operations of German MNCs could not be reliably testified in our sample.

Discussion and implications

Based on previous studies by Kumar and Mohr (1999), we had initially suggested that German MNCs could ward off the adversities of the

Asian crisis by integrating their Asian operations intensively within their global strategy. In other words, the dominance of the integration dimension in global strategy was presumed to be a success factor for operations in Asia.

The results of this study contradict this initial assumption. Although the integration dimension appears to be the dominant strategy, these MNCs were less successful than those which gave local responsiveness more importance. The presumptive explanation can be seen in the fact that German MNCs in Asia during the crisis had resorted to absorbing a higher proportion of production from the Asian operations in the form of reimports than what this study established for the Chinese operations. Higher reimports at that time helped to ward off the risks of the collapsed local markets, but also made integration easier, because of required standardization of products sold to the parent company.

The present study relates to Chinese operations after the crisis. As the results showed, German MNCs achieved the major part of their subsidiary sales on the Chinese local market which deviates to a great extent from the German market. Hence local responsiveness is required to a greater extent and is more appropriate for higher performance.

The tentative conclusion which can be drawn from these findings for Chinese operations of German and other foreign MNCs is that the dominant element in global strategy extended to China should be local responsiveness like the adaptation of management functions to Chinese local conditions or decision-making autonomy of the local management. To be competitive in China, MNCs need to stress more on local responsiveness than on integration strategies.

The findings for the determinants supported the argument that ownership advantages of the German MNC favoured integration strategy. Especially their financial strength and the general competitive advantage in the Chinese market seemed to be the decisive determinants. Obviously the MNCs feel that their financial strength could be used best when management in the Chinese operations is adapted to German standards. Financial cross-subsidization is considered effective when management in the Chinese operations is standardized. Moreover, in order to retain the competitive position in the local market, control of the German parent is considered necessary. Although the other presumptive determinants within the ownership advantages, location factors and internalization advantages did not prove to be significant, their empirical evidence is interesting in itself.

Finally, it should be noted that generalizations from our findings need to recognize certain limitations of the study. First, our sample is of moderate size. Second, the model and the statistical evaluation concentrated only on singular influences on global strategy. It is possible that a more holistic approach, requiring a much larger sample would have changed some of our findings (Bagozzi and Phillips, 1982). Third, our model cannot prove causation, but merely infer it from plausible arguments from FDI and global strategy theory. Nevertheless, the research did uncover some elements of successful global strategy with reference to MNC operations in China. Further research could connect at this point to substantiate the findings.

References

Agthe, K. E. (1990) 'Managing the mixed marriage', in *Business Horizons*, January/February, pp. 37–43.

Aharoni, Y. (1969) *The Foreign Investment Decision Process*, Boston: Harvard Business School Press.

Bartlett, C. A. (1981) 'Multinational structural change: evolution versus reorganization', in L. Otterbeck (ed.) *The Management of Headquarters-Subsidiary Relationships in Multinational Corporations*, Aldershot, Hants: Gower, pp. 121–45.

Bagozzi, R. and L. Phillips (1982) 'Representing and testing organizational theories. A holistic construct', in *Administrative Science Quarterly*, 27: 459–89.

Bartlett, C. and S. Ghoshal (1989) *Managing Across Borders. A Transnational Solution*, Boston: Harvard Business School Press.

Buckley, P. and M. Casson (1976) *The Future of the Multinational Enterprise*, New York: Holmes & Meier.

China Statistics Press (1999), *China Statistical Yearbook*, Peking.

Dunning, J. (1989) 'The theory of international production', in F. Khosrow (ed.) *International Trade*, New York: Taylor & Francis.

Dülfer, E. (1997) *Internationales Management*, München: Oldenbourg.

Fayerweather, J. (1969) *International Management. A Conceptual Framework*, New York: McGraw Hill.

Fredrickson, J. W. (1983) 'Strategic process: questions and recommendations', *Academy of Management Review*, 8: 565–75.

Geringer, J. and L. Herbert (1989) 'Control and performance of international joint ventures', *Journal of International Business Studies*, Summer, pp. 235–54.

Hedlund, G. (1981) 'The hypermodern MNC: a heterarchies: new approaches?', *Human Resource Management*, 25: 9–36.

Hofer, C. and D. Schendel (1978) *Strategy Formulation: Analytical Concepts*, St Paul, MI: West.

Hymer, S. (1976) *The International Operations of National Firms*, Cambridge: MIT Press.

Johnson, J. H., Jr. (1995) 'An empirical analysis of the integration–responsiveness framework: US construction equipment industry firms in global competition', *Journal of International Business Studies*, 26(3): 621–35.

Kindleberger, C. (1969) *American Business Abroad*, New Haven: Yale University Press.

Kobrin, S. (1991) 'An empirical analysis of the determinants of global integration', *Strategic Management Journal*, 12: 17–31.

Kumar, B. (1993) 'Globale Wettbewerbsstrategien für den europäischen Markt', in M. Haller, K. Bleicher, E. Breuchlin, M. Haller, H. J. Pleitner, R. Wunderer, A. Zünd (eds) *Globalisierung der Wirtschaft*, Bern: Hauptverlag, pp. 49–76.

Kumar, B. and A. Mohr (1999) *'Strategies of Western firms for transformation in Asia – some preliminary considerations and prospositions'*, in H.-C. de Bettignies (ed.) *Crisis and Transformation in Asia: Implications for Western Corporations, Insead Euro-Asia Centre, Fontainebleau*, 14th LVMH conference, February.

Leontiades, J. (1986) 'Going global – global vs national strategies', *Long Range Planning*, 19(6): 96–104.

Martinez, J. I. and J. C. Jarillo (1991) 'Co-ordination demands of international strategies', *Journal of International Business Studies*, 22(3): 429–44.

Miller, C. and L. Cardinal (1994) 'Strategic planning and firm performances', *Academy of Management Journal*, 37(6): 1649–65.

Millington, A. and B. Bayliss (1997) 'Internationalization and the success of UK transnational manufacturing operations', *Management International Review*, 37(3): 199–221.

Porter, M. (1986) 'Changing patterns of international competition', *California Management Review*, 28: 9–40.

Prahalad, C. K. and Y. L. Doz (1987) *The Multinational Mission: Balancing Local Demands and Global Vision*, New York: The Free Press.

Quinn, J. B. (1980) *Strategies for Change: Logical Incrementalism*, Homewood, IL: Irwin.

Rosenzweig, P. M. and J. V. Singh (1991) 'Organisational environments and the multinational enterprise', *Academy of Management Review*, 16(2): 340–61.

Roth, K. and A. J. Morrison (1990) 'An empirical analysis of the integration–responsiveness framework in global industries, *Journal of International Business Studies*, 21(4): 541–64.

Taggart, J. (1997) 'An evaluation of the integration–responsiveness framework: MNC manufacturing subsidiaries in the UK', *Management International Review*, 37(4): 295–318.

Taylor, W. (1991) 'The logic of global business', *Harvard Business Review*, March/April, pp. 91–105.

White, R. E. and T. A. Poynter (1984) 'Strategies for foreign-owned subsidiaries in Canada', *Business Quarterly*, Summer, pp. 59–69.

6
Kairos: Strategies Just in Time in the Asian Athletic Footwear Industry

Nancy E. Landrum and David M. Boje

This chapter explores the ways in which strategic narratives have changed in the footwear industry from before the Asian economic crisis to the present. We examine the narrative contained in the letters to shareholders of the top two footwear producers in the world, Nike and Reebok, over the period 1990–99.

An examination of archival documents of firms can reveal patterns of behaviour of corporations. Letters to stockholders included in annual reports serve as the archival documents for this study to trace storytelling narratives. The stories told from 1990 to 1999 in letters to stockholders are a rich source of data for storytelling. 'Narrators indicate the terms on which they request to be interpreted by the styles of telling they choose' (Riessman, 1993: 19). Thus, each style follows its own unique path of telling and evokes a series of emotions; the selection is at the discretion of the narrator.

This chapter first examines the footwear industry in the USA and China. We look at the industry in China both before the financial crisis and since the crisis; a discussion of strategic management and narrative follows. In the discussion of narrative, the genres of Frye (1957) and White (1973) are introduced and used as a model for evaluating the narrative styles found in Nike and Reebok's letters to shareholders. We then share our analysis of the letters and offer our conclusions.

Footwear industry in the United States

Footwear is a mature industry in the USA (Choe, 1999). Mature industries are typically characterized by slow or no growth, intense competition for market share, for profits, and for product innovation to rejuvenate sales, increased international competition, declining profitability, and consolidation of the industry (Thompson and Strickland, 1999). Companies rely more and more on new styles and new technology to increase sales (Choe, 1999) as well as manufacturing process improvements (Thompson and Strickland, 1999). Research and design takes place in the USA while manufacturing takes place in low-wage countries (Shetty, 1996). Footwear is a highly labour-intensive process, resulting in the shift to offshore production and the continuing movement to countries with lower wages (Shetty, 1996; International Child Labor Program, 1998). Thus, footwear is primarily an imported product.

The USA is the largest importer of footwear in the world (Shetty, 1996). Estimates of the amount of all types of footwear imported to the USA range from 86 per cent (Shetty, 1996) to 98 per cent (Institutional Investor Americas, 2000).

Athletic footwear segment in the United States

Athletic footwear (Standard Industrial Classification 3149 and North American Industrial Classification System 316211) makes up the largest segment of the US footwear industry. Women's athletic shoes account for more retail sales (46 per cent of retail sales) than men's athletic shoes (41 per cent) in the US market (Choe, 1999). Sales of athletic footwear declined in 1998 in the USA for the first time in five years (Choe, 1999). For this reason, companies are looking for growth in international markets.

In the USA, Nike and Reebok are the two top athletic shoe companies in terms of market share and retail sales (Figure 6.1). Nike's market share ranged from 28.24 per cent in 1990 to 51.1 per cent in 1998 (Sporting Goods Intelligence, 1999). Reebok's market share ranged from

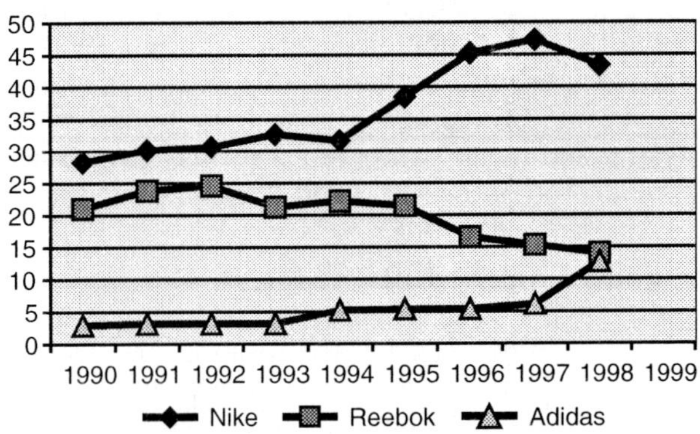

Figure 6.1 The US market share, 1990–98

21.03 per cent in 1990 to 16.5 per cent in 1998 and is challenging Nike's slim lead (Sporting Goods Intelligence, 1999).

Since the industry in the USA is mature, recent trends have seen mergers in manufacturing and restructuring of corporate operations in an attempt to become more efficient (Choe, 1999; Sporting Goods Manufacturers Association, 2000). The industry also has an overabundance of inventory and excess retail space (Choe, 1999; Sporting Goods Manufacturers Association, 2000), causing several retailers to close stores or go out of business. Sales of athletic footwear are expected to remain flat in the USA (Sporting Goods Manufacturers Association, 2000). Both Nike and Reebok appear to be trying to create an on-line presence through sales of footwear and apparel on their websites.

Footwear as an industry worldwide is 'driven by economic conditions, demographic trends, and pricing' (Choe, 1999). In the USA, the economy has been strong and sales have remained stable. Economic conditions in international markets also drive sales.

The baby boomer fitness craze of the 1980s saw athletic shoe sales jump from 185 million pairs in 1982 to 381 million pairs in 1991, which translates to US$3.5 billion in 1982 and to $12 billion in 1991 (Fried, 1992). Athletic shoe sales in the USA averaged around 15 per cent growth per year in the 1980s but sales of athletic footwear declined in 1998 in the USA for the first time in five years and the industry is considered a mature market (Choe, 1999). Sales within the industry were at $11.7 billion in 1997, virtually unchanged from 1991 (Baglole, 1999).

'Consumer and industry analysts agree the flat sales are the result of changing demographics' (Baglole, 1999). Changing consumer preferences for outdoor shoes in early 1990s and to brown shoes (brown leather casual shoes) in the mid- to late 1990s have contributed to the decline in athletic shoe sales (Choe, 1999). Sales were once targeted to baby boomers, then to generation X, and now to generation Y (Choe, 1999). Generation Y individuals do not want to be considered 'mainstream' (Choe, 1999). Nike believes they have oversaturated the market with their products and they are now producing products noticeably lacking the swoosh logo and Nike name. In the mid- to late 1980s, prices climbed to $100 or more for a pair of athletic shoes for the first time. Throughout the 1990s, prices consistently exceeded $100 per pair.

Nike not only dominates the US market, but also dominates the worldwide athletic footwear industry with 22.51 per cent market share in 1991 increasing to 33 per cent by 1999 (Figure 6.2). Reebok maintains its second place position with 18.82 per cent worldwide market share in 1991 falling to 16 per cent by 1999. Adidas-Salomon is third

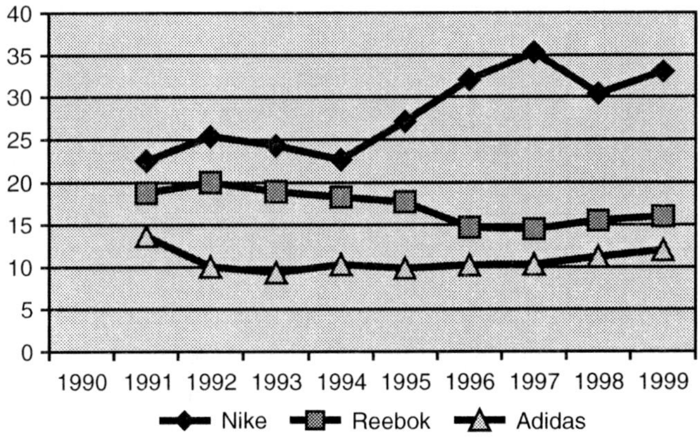

Figure 6.2 Worldwide market share, 1990–99

with 13.63 per cent world market share in 1991 and falling to 12 per cent in 1999 (Sporting Goods Intelligence, 1999). Future growth in the athletic footwear industry is expected to come from international sales, particularly Europe and Asia (Choe, 1999). The greatest growth is expected in the Asian markets as the economy grows and consumer spending increases (Shetty, 1996; Choe, 1999). For this reason, events in Asia, particularly the Asian economic crisis, are critical to the future of the athletic shoe industry.

Athletic footwear industry in Asia and China

Asia produced between 60 and 70 per cent of all sports footwear (International Standard Industrial Classification 3240) for the world in the 1990s (Darnay, 1998). Of the Asian countries, China consistently produced the most sports footwear, as shown in Table 6.1 (Darnay, 1998).

Table 6.1 Country of manufacture of athletic footwear, 1999

	Nike	Reebok
People's Republic of China	40%	44%
Indonesia	30	29
Vietnam	12	
Thailand	11	16
Italy	2	
The Philippines	2	
Taiwan	2	
South Korea	1	

Due to the importance of Asia, specifically China, to the footwear industry, information will be provided relevant to these markets.

Pre-Asian economic crisis

Management style

The overseas Chinese are a diverse group of individuals of Chinese origin who have migrated to Southeast Asia. They are most populous in Taiwan, Singapore, Malaysia, Thailand, Myanmar and Indonesia. According to Haley et al. (1998), overseas Chinese executives 'craft' strategy, consistent with the theories of Mintzberg (1987; 1994) and Mintzberg and Waters (1985). Mintzberg and his colleagues suggest that strategy can be emergent and crafted as employees respond to the environment and, over time, those responses form patterns of responses. Haley et al. (1998) argue that this accurately describes the strategic planning processes of the overseas Chinese companies. Overseas Chinese executives frequently act on intuition and in response to their environment, based upon their intimate knowledge of their company and industry (Haley et al., 1998). This emergent strategy contradicts the rational planning process emphasized in US companies. That is, in the USA, companies are encouraged to engage in exhaustive detailed planning and to create a priori plans, rather than to allow strategy to emerge and be defined post hoc.

Hamlin (2000) states 'Like Collins and Porras, Moore invokes the environmental metaphor to explain that strategy evolves as a result of many factors, and cannot be clinically devised. But it can be scientifically explained – in hindsight' (p. 157).

Haley et al. (1998) argue that as a group, the overseas Chinese typically share a common pattern of core competencies. These competencies include their speed of decision-making, their dominant control over information, and their influential networks of familial, ethnic and governmental contacts. We argue, however, that a core competency is unique to a company and is the source of one company's edge over competitors. If all companies engage in a pattern of behaviours, as suggested by Haley et al. (1998), this actually creates a situation of competitive parity, or behaviours necessary by all companies to compete effectively. We would, then, state that Haley et al. (1998) have identified key success factors or behaviours needed for competitive parity, rather than core competencies.

Pre-crisis corporations relied heavily on *guanxi*, or connections, for business success. Sixty-six per cent of business executives surveyed agreed with the statement 'connections are more important than strategy for a company to succeed in Asia' (Hamlin, 2000: 105). Explaining why he was not concerned with strategy during the booming Asian miracle years, the businessman said in effect that he could do anything and make money – even by mistake – in that heady development environment. All it took was a few friends (Hamlin, 2000: 156). Specifically, 79 per cent of Malaysian executives, 78 per cent of Indonesian, 74 per cent of Taiwanese, 73 per cent of Singapore and 73 per cent of South Korean executives agreed with this statement (Hamlin, 2000). Michael Porter visited pre-crisis Asia and in a conversation with a business executive it became apparent how important *guanxi* was to Asian business.

Footwear industry

Prior to the economic and financial crisis, Asia had seen rapid economic development over the last several decades, dubbed 'the Asian miracle'. However, accompanying this economic boom had been a parallel boom in the exploitation and abuse of workers in factories throughout Asian countries. Reports of abuses and harsh discipline first began to surface in the late 1980s (Chan and Xiaoyang, 1999). Most of the footwear factories are owned and managed by Taiwanese and Hong Kong firms but they subcontract and manufacture for footwear designers like Nike and Reebok (Chan and Xiaoyang, 1999).

In a 1996 survey of 54 footwear factories across China, it was found that management practices were authoritarian and punitive, incorporated rigid hierarchies, encouraged domination of workers, and relied on institutional discipline, including excessive working hours, discipline for going to the bathroom or taking water breaks, monetary penalties and corporal punishment (Chan and Xiaoyang, 1999).

Many of the workers in China's factories, and all Asian factories, migrate from rural areas in search of employment in the factories. One study offers a unique glimpse into the personal lives of migrant factory workers in China. In 1993, Chan (1999) examined 65 personal letters written to Chinese factory workers from friends and family. She found that issues most discussed in the letters were references to trying to find other jobs, discussions of work hours and overtime, and discussions of physical conditions. Twenty-three letters made specific mention of wages paid at the factory, and it was discovered that 19 of those letters, or 83 per cent, indicated pay below the government-mandated minimum wage. Furthermore, the minimum wage was paid as a day's wage and she found that the average workday for that daily minimum wage was 11.8 hours, which exceeds the 8-hour workday upon which the minimum wage is based. Workdays typically started early in the morning, allowed a break for lunch, worked several hours in the afternoon, allowed another break for dinner, and then worked several more hours into the night. These long hours lead to exhaustion and also prevent workers from seeking other employment, although virtually all letters spoke of the desire for better employment.

Eleven, or 48 per cent, of the 23 letters discussing wages mentioned difficulty in obtaining these wages due to factory withholdings, irregular payments by the factory, and sporadic availability of work. While other letters did not state specific pay rates, they did mention these same difficulties in obtaining wages. In fact, it seemed that the norm was to be owed wages rather than to be paid wages. The problem was so prevalent that workers didn't know how much they were supposed to be earning and lost track of how much they were owed. If employees quit the factory they would forfeit the owed wages. This management tactic effectively prevented workers from leaving for other jobs.

In all, 46 of the 65 letters, or 71 per cent, complained about some aspect of wages. These letters suggest low wages and long hours for the workers.

> Wages were merely management's arbitrary manipulation of figures. Irregular small sums of money known as 'wages' were being doled out now and then to the workers. The function was not to provide a predetermined, calculable award for the worker's labor. Its purpose was to ensure that at least the workers could physically stay alive, and that they did not become so desperate as to stage protests or run away (Chan, 1999: 6).

Many factories provide housing and meals for workers and deduct the costs from the workers' wages. Housing varies from eight persons in bunk beds sharing one room to up to 100 persons in bunk beds sharing a single hall in a warehouse. Factories usually provide 2–3 meals per day for workers. They generally have a lunch break and a dinner break.

Workers are also exposed to dangerous and unsafe working conditions. 'The toy-making and footwear industries are particularly hazardous because of toxic solvents in the spray paints and glues that are commonly used' (Chan, 1999: 9). In 1994, it was found that over half of the factories in Shenzhen City were classified as hazardous according to occupational health and safety standards. Benzene is considered such a dangerous substance, causing anemia and leukemia, that it has been banned in USA and European countries (Asia Monitor Resource Centre, 1997).

Identification cards are required for employment at factories. It was not uncommon for factories to take an employee's ID card upon hire and to refuse to return to workers their ID cards. The Chinese household registration system requires individuals to show their ID card to authorities when approached. If an individual does not have their ID card, they risk being sent back home. Thus, withholding an employee's ID card effectively prevents them from leaving the factory or seeking work elsewhere. Once inside the factory, the employee is trapped and unable to leave the factory. In some instances, it was even reported that security guards bar workers from leaving the factory.

Factory conditions appear to be similar across Asia. The problems which exist in the Chinese footwear factories have also been documented in Indonesian (Ballinger and Olsson, 1997) and Vietnamese (Manning, 1997a–g) footwear factories. On a positive note, although child labour is of concern in the worldwide footwear manufacturing industry, this has not been a concern raised in Chinese factories (International Child Labor Program, 1998).

In June 1997, Andrew Young released his report of 12 manufacturers of Nike shoes (Young, 1997). Young concluded that Nike was doing a good job with its Code of Conduct. He found factories to be favourable, and he could not document reports of abuse. He did, however, state that Nike could do better. This report has been criticized for its methodology (Asia Monitor Resource Centre, 1997) and contradicts the findings of many other reports on working conditions in Asian footwear factories, such as those findings by Chan discussed above and the findings of the Asia Monitor Resource Centre and the Hong Kong Christian Industrial Committee.

In 1995 and again in June and July of 1997, the Asia Monitor Resource Centre and the Hong Kong Christian Industrial Committee conducted research on workers' rights and working conditions within athletic shoe factories operated by five major subcontractors in Southern China. The factories manufacture shoes for both Nike and Reebok. Their research concludes that in the two-year period between their research visits, factory conditions deteriorated. 'All categories of the companies' Code of Conduct – health and safety, freedom of association, wages and benefits, hours of working, overtime compensation, non-discrimination, harassment and child labour – are being violated' (Asia Monitor Resource Centre, 1997: 2).

Asian economic crisis

On 2 July 1997, the floating of the Thai baht triggered a currency turmoil first in Southeast Asia and then in South Korea. The whole

Asian region and even the rest of the world have felt the severe impact of the crisis since then (*China Daily*, 1998). The crisis was caused by poor banking practices and weak financial regulations and supervision throughout Asia during periods of rapid economic growth (*China Daily*, 21 June 1999).

The result of the crisis was a drop in the stock market, a decrease in GDP growth, a high number of layoffs and unemployment, currency depreciation and reduced exports. The severity of the crisis varied for each Asian country. For example, in Thailand, as many as 300 000 men and women lost their factory jobs since the economic crisis began in July 1997 (Star, 1999). Yet in Singapore, it is estimated that only 28 300 people lost their jobs and unemployment increased from 1.8 per cent to only 3.2 per cent (Freeman, 1999). Star (1999) states that 'women are more vulnerable in times of recession'. This is particularly germane since more than 80 per cent of the Nike factory workers in Asia are female (Shaw, 1999).

The crisis also affected the USA, in that exports to Asian countries decreased, tourism from Asian visitors decreased, and the US economy slowed its growth (Li, 1998). In China, the government did not devalue currency but continued efforts to grow the economy, thus resulting in a milder impact of the crisis in China (Li, 1998). Economists finally announced the end of the Asian financial crisis in November 1999 (*China Daily*, 29 November 1999).

Post-Asian economic crisis

How are Nike and Reebok changing their strategies in response to the economic crisis? Three forces are defining the new face of business in post-crisis Asia: the financial crisis, globalization and liberalization (Hamlin, 2000). The financial crisis brought a restructuring of the economy, globalization brought new standards for business, and liberalization brought more competition (Hamlin, 2000). The results of these forces are that organizations must restructure to seek out new profit zones; create new business models focused on profitable customers and based on profitability, efficiency, productivity and quality; and begin strategic planning to increase competitiveness (Hamlin, 2000). Following traditional US strategy, Asian businesses must build upon core competencies.

Nike's core competencies seem to be R&D (innovation), marketing and globalization. Reebok doesn't seem to have well-developed core competencies. Reebok speaks of innovation and globalization, but their efforts do not seem to be effective. In 1997, Nike spent 13 per cent of net revenues on R&D compared to Reebok's 6 per cent. In both 1998 and 1999, Nike spent 9 per cent compared to Reebok's 5 per cent. Reebok consistently spent 2 per cent of net revenues on advertising from 1997 to 1998 and spent 3 per cent in 1999. No figures are available on Nike's advertising budget.

Increasing competition between the exporters in Asian countries will lead to improved efficiency and quality, thus allowing Asian companies to charge a premium for their products (Hamlin, 2000). Will this force Nike and Reebok to move to other low-wage countries? 'Transnational companies (TNC's) move production to countries where the cheapest labour and least worker protection is promised. As standards rise, over time, the companies move their production to a more "attractive country"' (Ballinger and Olsson, 1997: 4). For example, a majority of Nike shoes had been manufactured in South Korea and Taiwan since the early 1970s (Ballinger and Olsson, 1997). In 1988, production began in Indonesia and by 1995, exports from Indonesia totaled nearly $3 billion (Ballinger and Olsson, 1997).

In response to criticisms that Nike flees higher wage countries (Ballinger and Olsson, 1997; Klein, 1999) Nike argues that it remains in Taiwan, South Korea, the Philippines and Italy, despite higher wages and unionized labour rights (Nike, 2000a). It points to this as evidence that it does not flee higher wage countries in constant search of lower wage countries. However, if you look at the country of origin of their shoes (see Table 6.1), it becomes evident that in 1999 the manufacturing operations in Taiwan, South Korea, the Philippines and Italy are negligible in the overall volume of shoes manufactured for Nike and has, in fact, diminished over time. Furthermore, we see that Reebok has no manufacturing in these countries. When we track the manufacturing operations of Nike and Reebok from 1990 to 1999, it becomes evident that production in higher wage unionized countries has decreased while production in lower wage non-unionized countries has increased (Figures 6.3 and 6.4). Both companies show a decline in manufacturing in South Korea and an increase in manufacturing in China and Indonesia during the 1990s.

Currencies from Thailand and Korea have strengthened in value since the economic crisis, causing products imported from those countries to be more expensive (Choe, 1999). This may add further understanding to the declining manufacturing operations of Nike and Reebok in Thailand and Korea. Currency value from China has remained fixed and, therefore, China remains an inexpensive source for importing

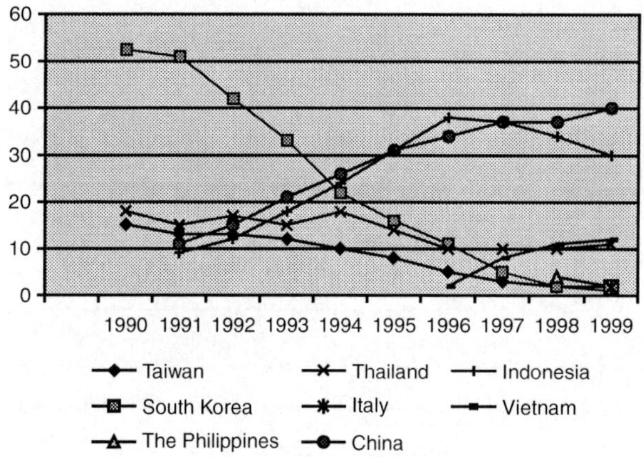

Figure 6.3 Nike manufacturing, 1990–99

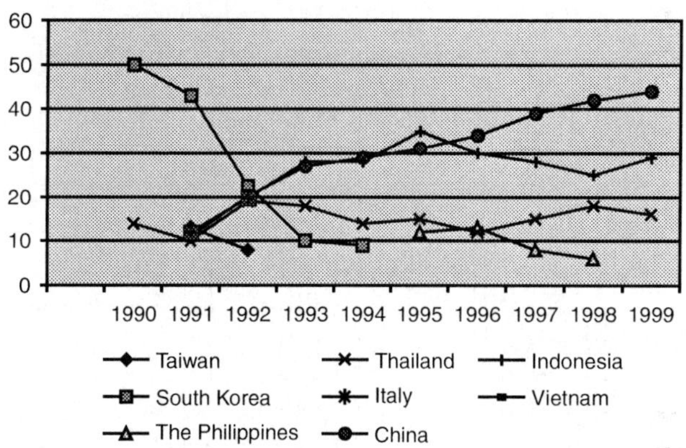

Figure 6.4 Reebok manufacturing, 1990–99

products to the USA (Choe, 1999). Thus, manufacturing in China still remains cost efficient for both Nike and Reebok.

There appears to be no change in labour practices, however, since the economic crisis. On 18 October 1999, Reebok released a report of independent monitoring of abuses in its factories in Indonesia (Fireman, 1999; Insan Hitawasana Sejahtera, 1999; Kirchofer, 1999; Reebok, 1999). Although the problems were serious, Reebok was applauded for not trying to hide the problem (Krupa, 1999). Reebok issued a statement of the improvements made in its Indonesian factories but there was no mention of improvements in Chinese factories (Students for Informed Career Decisions, 1999).

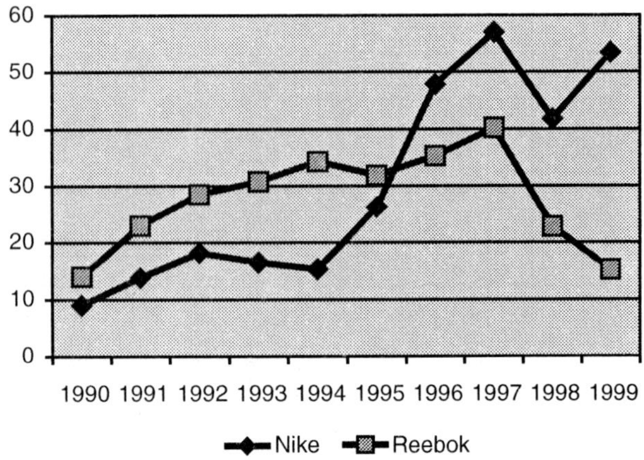

Figure 6.5 Average US stock prices for Nike and Reebok, 1990–99

We can see that the stock prices of both companies fell following the start of the Asian economic crisis in 1997 (Figure 6.5). Since 1995, there has been a noticeable change in both Nike and Reebok. Nike has increased and Reebok has decreased in market share, stock value and annual revenues. Nike is listed as number 490 in the Fortune Global 500 (Hoover's Handbook of World Business, 1999).

Interplay of narrative and strategy

Numerous individuals have discussed the use of storytelling as a management tool and the integration of storytelling with strategy (Breuer, 1998; Holden, 1999; Lieber, 1997; Neuhauser, 1999; Shaw et al., 1998; Solovy, 1999; Turner, 1998). Strategy can be viewed as a narrative form of fiction; something created to persuade others (Barry and Elmes, 1997). Since executives serve as figureheads or spokespersons for the whole organization (Mintzberg, 1973), they are responsible for crafting and communicating the strategy.

If strategy is a story, Barry and Elmes (1997) suggest that 'strategy must rank as one of the most prominent, influential, and costly stories told in organizations' (p. 429). Since stories are likely to be remembered, 'cognitive science argues strongly for strategic planning through storytelling' (*Harvard Business Review*, 1998: 42).

The historical tracing of Nike and Reebok text is important in discerning their strategy, or strategic posturing. Strategy is usually viewed as a meticulous process of planning, design and implementation. However, strategy can also be viewed retrospectively and defined as a pattern of actions that combine to create a path; strategy can be emergent (Mintzberg and Waters, 1985; Mintzberg and McHugh, 1985). It is in this vein that we will view the historical storytelling of Nike, Inc. and Reebok International Ltd. to discern their strategy. Through tracing Nike and Reebok stories in their letters to stockholders, we can view the patterns as indicative of their emergent strategy.

Previous research using annual reports

Previous research has used annual reports for data. Preston et al. (1996) note that annual reports are a 'visual medium through which corporations may seek to create and manage their images' (p. 114). 'Indeed, in the design and advertising literature, annual reports are frequently referred to as marketing tools and as a means of communicating a particular image or message' (Preston et al., 1996: 114). The images and texts within annual statements will suggest an image or message that they seek to convey to stakeholders. Their website is another text that seeks to project an image for organizations. As Riessman (1993) points out, authors of text choose the way in which they wish to be perceived by the way in which they decide to convey their image. This is why the study of text and visual images is a revealing approach to understanding and interpreting organizations. Rumelt (1974) used information found in company annual reports as one data source for his dissertation and subsequent book on diversification strategy and organizational structure.

Analysis

This study used letters to shareholders from 1990 to 1999 found in the Nike and Reebok annual reports. In viewing the Nike and Reebok letters to shareholders, we were able to trace both companies' narratives on Asia and China. Table 6.2 shows the frequency with which each company mentions Asia or China in their letters from 1990 to 1999.

Nike letters

During the decade of the 1990s, Nike mentions Asia or China 20 times in its letters to shareholders (Table 6.2). In 1991, lines 80–83, Nike states that it is finally becoming a major player in the Asian market (Table

Table 6.2 Frequency of Asia or China in letters, 1990–99

	Nike	Reebok
1990	1	0
1991	2	0
1992	1	0
1993	0	0
1994	1	0
1995	2	0
1996	3	1
1997	0	0
1998	8	0
1999	2	0

6.3). In 1995, lines 124–125, Nike recognized that Asia offers great growth potential for the industry and for the company and is positioning itself to be ready for this opportunity, lines 118–122. In 1996, lines 105–107, Nike noted the increased sales in China and reflected on its skill in capturing opportunities, lines 108–113. In 1998, lines 24–26, lines 79–103, Nike recognized the impact that the Asian financial crisis has had on the company's profitability. In 1999, lines 46–47, Nike foresees the comeback of the Asian market and continues to rely on Asia for growth in sales.

Table 6.3 Excerpts of Nike letters

Year	Excerpt
1991	80: The payoff from overcoming all these challenges can be seen in our
	81: international growth of 80% to $862 million in revenues. We are at
	82: last, after many sometimes comical fits and starts, after 10 years of
	83: hard work, a serious threat not only in Europe, but in Asia as well.
1995	118: Four years ago, when I talked about two Americans, a Swede and a
	119: Frenchman who had gone to climb the Matterhorn before opening our new
	120: European Headquarters, we had nary a national as a country manager in
	121: Europe. Today, every major country is headed by a citizen of that
	122: country. In the process sales have turned back up in Europe, a
	123: contribution far more significant than anyone has noted in writing to
	124: date. Asia is on the threshold of the greatest regional growth in
	125: industry history. And Latin America has positioned itself where Asia
	126: was two years ago.

1996 105: Also in that part of the world is a unique country called the People's
106: Republic of China. Sales there were $13 million, up from $7.9 million
107: the year before. It doesn't mean much in the harsh voice of
108: arithmetic, but it screams with the kind of potential NIKE is
109: especially good at developing. China is perhaps the most complicated
110: of all the markets. But we are making progress, one step at a time,
111: just like we used to say about Japan and Germany. There are a lot of
112: unusual forces that exist in China that do not exist in other markets.
113: But at the end of that enormous maze are two billion feet.

1998 24: So, what knocked us down in 1998?
25:
26: Asia . . . brown shoes . . . labor practices . . . resignations . . . layoffs . . .
27: boring ads. Also, we have been criticized for our headquarters
28: expansion. But understand this: We need a much bigger place to house
29: all our troubles.

72: One drag earnings that even an improved management group cannot affect
73: is Asia. This is the area we were looking to for our strongest growth,
74: over the next couple years. We will not get over $2.68 per share, our
75: 1997 number until Asia comes back for us. To come back does not mean
76: Asia has to be booming again, but it does mean we need to see the
77: bottom of the slide, so that retailers are again confident enough to
78: order several months in advance. Asia is a big part of this company's
79: heritage, and it remains a big part of our future.
80:
81:
82:
83: This is one of the things that is keeping operating expenses at an
84: abnormally high percentage of sales in the region. Still it is a great
85: long run play. But, how long is long? Well, I'm confident I will
86: personally predict the exact date of the Asia turnaround. Its just a
87: matter of how many predictions that will take. For now, I believe
88: we'll see the changes we need in two years, not five. We're a company
89: founded by distance runners – some of them pretty slow – so we have a
90: certain amount of patience. Nonetheless, we prefer to be timed by a
91: stop watch, not a calendar.
92:
93: On our labor practices: Our friends in the media are slowly becoming
94: more knowledgeable. This is good. It means that consumers are

Table 6.3 (*continued*)

Year	Excerpt
	95: actually getting informed rather than just alarmed. This, too, will
	96: take time. Meanwhile, the contrasts between us and our competitors and
	97: other companies in the needle trade will show more each year.
	98:
	99: There is an interesting relationship going on between the Asia economic
	100: crisis and the labor practices issue, which would take many chairman's
	101: letters to cover. Instead, let me cut straight to the moral of the
	102: story: It is simply not acceptable for America to continue to be
	103: "moated"
1998	129: Above all else stands the global passion for sports. Just as NIKE
	130: cannot affect the resurgence of Asian economies, nations and exchange
	131: rates cannot derail the competitive spirit. Athletes and the world of
	132: sports they create continue to enhance the quality of life, and
	133: business, for all of us.
1999	46: Asia is coming back. Despite the recent volatility, we continue to believe
	47: that the Asia Pacific region offers us our best opportunities for growth.

Reebok letters

In 1996, lines 113–121, Reebok makes the only mention of Asia in the ten-year period covered by this research (Table 6.4). Reebok expects that Asian and international growth will be key to growth in sales. The company never again makes mention of Asia or the Asian economic crisis.

In a similar analysis of strategic narratives (Landrum, 2000), Nike showed an increased usage of Epic/Design genres (Mintzberg, 1990; Barry and Elmes, 1997) in 1998 and 1999 following the start of the Asian financial crisis. This type of strategic narrative speaks of coming out of a time of change and entering into a new period of stability, as discussed above in the passages from the Nike 1998 and 1999 letters.

In 1998, Reebok peaked in usage of the Purist/Positioning genre of strategic narrative (Mintzberg, 1990; Barry and Elmes, 1997). This narrative style speaks of the personas or characterizations the company uses to describe itself and assumes the ready-made identity. Specifically,

Table 6.4 Excerpts of Reebok Letters

Year	Excerpt
1996	113: Internationally, the growth potential for the Reebok brand is 114: significant. In 1996, Reebok's international revenues rose nearly 6 115: percent, with strong double-digit growth in the key regions of northern 116: Europe, Asia Pacific and new market territories. Compared to the 117: U.S., the international per capita consumption of athletic footwear 118: remains substantially lower. Continued growth of the international 119: athletic footwear industry, along with anticipated progress in Reebok's 120: business over the long run, should bode well for our Company's global 121: prospects.

in 1998, Reebok makes frequent mention that the company stands for diversity and human values.

Discussion

Nike appears to be much more tuned in to what is happening outside the USA and particularly in the Asian market. This is evidenced in a review of letters from 1990 to 1999. Nike is fairly consistent in mentioning Asia or China throughout the years, particularly in 1998 following the start of the economic crisis. In 1991, Nike mentions the sales growth in the Asian market, in 1995 it acknowledges that Asia is on the verge of great growth for the industry, and in 1996 it again mentions the sales growth in the Asian market. In 1998, Nike recognizes that the Asian economic crisis impacted the bottom line and that the recovery of this market is key to financial improvements. In 1999, Nike is optimistic that the Asian market is recovering. In another analysis of the strategic narrative of the letters (Landrum, 2000), Nike notes that it is coming out of a time of change following the beginning of the Asian economic crisis and entering a new period of stability.

Reebok, conversely, is fairly consistent in failing to mention Asia or China even though this is where the majority of its shoes are manufactured (Reebok International Ltd., Annual reports) and this is the market where the greatest growth is expected (Shetty, 1996; Choe, 1999). Following the start of the Asian financial crisis, Reebok never mentions the crisis or its impact on the company. Reebok's only mention of the Asian market or China is in 1996. In this year, it mentions that Asia was a strong growth market for them. Asia and China are not mentioned again, despite the importance of this market to the company. In fact, the letters following the crisis primarily focus on the humanitarian values of the company.

Nike has consistently outspent Reebok in research and development and in advertising. Both appear to be key success factors for this industry and both appear to be core competencies of Nike. Reebok's lack of strength in these areas is taking its toll on the company's market share and sales.

Nike also continues to move production to lower wage countries in an effort to become more cost efficient in this mature industry. Reebok has also followed this industry trend. However, we must conclude that Reebok's lack of focus on economic events in international arenas critical to the future has had a negative impact.

Conclusion

This chapter has discussed the mature footwear industry in the USA and the growth potential of the industry in international markets, particularly in Asia and China where athletic footwear is primarily manufactured. This market is viewed as the future of the athletic footwear industry (Shetty, 1996; Choe, 1999).

The Asian financial crisis began in 1997 and in late 1999 was finally declared to be over. In a review of letters to shareholders from annual reports of Nike, Inc. and Reebok International Ltd. from 1990 to 1999, we have looked for indications of changes in the strategic narrative of the two companies in the Asian market as indicative of their emergent strategy. Our review suggests that Nike is astute in monitoring the Asian market and its relationship to its growth and that Reebok is unperceptive in monitoring global issues.

Nike's primary response to the Asian financial crisis was to view this as a time of change and to seek subsequent stability. Reebok had no response to the crisis in its letters and instead focused on the humanitarian values of the company. It is reasonable to expect that Nike will continue to monitor the Asian market and strategically respond to changes in this market. Nike views the Asian market as critical to its future growth as a global company. Reebok is less attuned to international events although it recognizes that international growth is key to its future success.

We would also predict that both Nike and Reebok will continue moving production to low-wage countries. If Asia becomes more competitive and wages rise, as Hamlin (2000) predicts, this could become a trigger for Nike and Reebok to search for lower wage areas of production.

We conclude that historical documents of a company, such as letters to shareholders found in annual reports, can give us a glimpse into the emergent strategy of a company. We have used the letters to shareholders from Nike, Inc. and Reebok International Ltd. annual reports from 1990 to 1999 to trace their strategic narratives related to the Asian economic crisis and to discern their emergent strategy within the Asian market.

References

Asia Monitor Resource Centre and Hong Kong Christian Industrial Committee (1997) 'Working conditions in sports shoe factories in China making shoes for Nike and Reebok', September. See http://www.saigon.com/nike/NikeChina.html [28 May 2000].

Baglole, J. (1999) 'Footwear giants hope NBA shoe fits', *The Toronto Star*, 8 January.

Ballinger, J. and C. Olsson (1997) *Behind the Swoosh: The Struggle of Indonesians making Nike shoes*, Uppsala Sweden: Global Publications Foundation and International Coalition for Development Action.

Barry, D. and M. Elmes (1997) 'Strategy retold: Toward a narrative view of strategic discourse', *Academy of Management Review*, 22: 429–452.

Breuer, N. L. (1998) 'The power of storytelling', *Workforce*, 77(12): 36–41.

Chan, A. (1999) 'The culture of survival and Chinese migrant workers: through the prism of private letters' (Draft), Paper presented at *Popular Culture in China* conference, Princeton University, 7–10 October 1999, in P. Link, R. Madsen and P. Pickowicz (eds) (2000) *Popular Thought in Post-socialist China*. Boulder, CO: Rowman & Littlefield.

Chan, A. and Z. Xiaoyang (1999) 'From a critique of Confucian culture to a model of disciplinary labor regime: a survey of Chinese footwear workers', Unpublished manuscript.

Asia to fix structural weakness (1999a) *China Daily*, 21 June, http://www.chinadaily.com.cn/cndydb/1999/06/d4-4fix.f2l.html

Asian financial crisis likely to persist (1998) *China Daily*, 4 July, http://www.chinadaily.com.cn/cndydb/1998/07/d4-598.g04.html

Asian financial crisis 'over' (1999b) *China Daily*, 29 November, http://www.chinadaily.com.cn/cndydb/1999/11/d6-lasia.b29.html

Choe, H. (1999) 'Apparel & footwear: Standard & Poor's industry surveys.' See http://www.netadvantage.standardpoor.com/netahtml/IndSur/apf/apf_0999.htm [28 May 2000].

Darnay, A. J. (1998) *Manufacturing Worldwide: Industry Analyses, Statistics, Products, and Leading Companies and Countries*, Detroit, MI: Gale Research.

Fireman, P. (1999) 'Steps we must take on third-world labor', *The Washington Post*, 17 October, p. B7.

Freeman, N. J. (1999) 'Commentary: Singapore's strategy for economic recovery in the post-"Asian crisis" period'. See http://www.nira.go.jp/publ/review/99summer/free.html [28 May 2000].

Fried, J. (1992) 'Profits grow by leaps and bounds', *Calgary Herald*, 29 September, p. B8.

Frye, N. (1957) *Anatomy of Criticism: Four Essays*. Princeton, NJ: Princeton University Press.

Haley, G. T., Tan, C. T. and U. C. V. Haley (1998). *New Asian Emperors: The Overseas Chinese, Their Strategies, and Competitive Advantages*, Woburn, MA: Butterworth-Heinemann.

Hamlin, M. A. (2000) *The New Asian Corporation: Managing for the Future in Post-crisis Asia*, San Francisco, CA: Jossey-Bass Inc. Publishers.

Harvard Business Review (1998) 'The science of stories', 76(3): 42.

Holden, B. A. (1999) 'Winning strategies: Tell me a story', *Incentive*, 173(2): 65–66.

Hoover's Handbook of World Business (1999) Austin, TX: Hoover's, Inc.

Insan Hitawasana Sejahtera (1999) 'Peduli Hak: Caring for Rights', Jakarta, Indonesia, October. See http://reebok.com/pindex.html [28 May 2000].

Institutional Investor Americas (2000) *Philip Knight of Nike: Just do it!* 34(1): 22.

International Child Labor Program (1998) US Department of Labor, Bureau of International Labor Affairs.

Kirchofer, T. (1999) 19 October 'Reebok points to substandard conditions at 2 of its factories', *The Oregonian*, See http://www.oregonlive.com/business/99/10/bz101902.html [28 May 2000].

Klein, N. (1999) *No Logos: Taking Aim at the Brand Bullies*, St Martin's Press, Inc.

Krupa, G. (1999) 'Reebok hailed for releasing study of factory abuses: Reebok releases study detailing abuses at factories in Indonesia', *Boston Globe*, 19 October, C1.

Landrum, N. (2000) 'A qualitative and quantitative analysis of the dynamics of Nike and Reebok storytelling as strategy from 1990–99', Unpublished doctoral dissertation, New Mexico State University.

Li, G. (1998) 'Economists laud China's role in combating crisis', *China Daily*, 27 November, http://www.chinadaily.com.cn/cndydb/1998/11/d4-lkan.k27.html

Lieber, R. B. (1997) 'Storytelling: A new way to get close to your customer', *Fortune*, 135(2): 102–108.

Manning, J. (1997a) 'Nike's Asian machine goes on trial', *The Oregonian*, 9 November. See http://www.oregonlive.com/series/nike11091.html [28 May 2000].

Manning, J. (1997b) 'Huge subcontractors find they must dance the tune Nike calls', *The Oregonian*, 9 November. See http://www.oregonlive.com/series/nikeside.html [28 May 2000].

Manning, J. (1997c) 'Poverty's legions flock to Nike', *The Oregonian*, 10 November. See http://www.oregonlive.com/series/nike11101.html [28 May 2000].

Manning, J. (1997d) 'Nike battles back, but activists hold the high ground', *The Oregonian*, 10 November. See http://www.oregonlive.com/series/nikeside 2.html [28 May 2000].

Manning, J. (1997e) 'Nike steps into political minefield', *The Oregonian*, 11 November. See http://www.oregonlive.com/series/nike11111.html [28 May 2000].

Manning, J. (1997f) 'Modern veneer conceals simmering stew of troubles', *The Oregonian*, 11 November. See http://www.oregonlive.com/series/nikesidei.html [28 May 2000].

Manning, J. (1997g) 'Vietnam's open door led to problems', *The Oregonian*, 11 November. See http://www.oregonlive.com/series/nikesidev.html [28 May 2000].

Mintzberg, H. (1973) *The Nature of Managerial Work*, New York: Harper & Row.
Mintzberg, H. (1987) 'Crafting strategy', *Harvard Business Review*, 65(4): 66–75.
Mintzberg, H. (1990) 'Strategy formation: Schools of thought', in J. W. Fredrickson (ed.) *Perspectives on Strategic Management*, Boston: Balling, pp. 105–235.
Mintzberg, H. (1994) 'The fall and rise of strategic planning', *Harvard Business Review*, January/February, 107–14.
Mintzberg, H. and A. McHugh (1985) 'Strategy formation in an adhocracy', *Administrative Science Quarterly*, 30(2): 160–97.
Mintzberg, H. and J. A. Waters (1985) 'Of strategies, deliberate and emergent', *Harvard Business Review*, 6(3): 257–72.
Neuhauser, P. (1999) *Corporate Legends and Lore: The Power of Storytelling as a Management Tool*, New York: McGraw-Hill.
Nike, Inc. (1990–99) *Annual Reports to Shareholders*.
Nike, Inc. (2000) 'Nike's response to No Logo'. See http://www.nikebiz.com/labor/nologo_let.shtml [28 May 2000].
Preston, A. M., Wright, C. and J. J. Young (1996) 'Img(in)ing annual, reports', *Accounting, Organizations and Society*, 21(1): 113–137.
Reebok International Ltd. (1990–99) *Annual Reports to Shareholders*.
Reebok International Ltd. (1999) 'Peduli Hak report'. See http://www.reebok.com/pindex.html [28 May 2000].
Riessman, C. K. (1993) *Narrative Analysis*, Thousand Oaks, CA: Sage Publications.
Rumelt, R. (1974) *Strategy, Structure, and Economic Performance*, Boston: Harvard University.
Shaw, R. (1999) *Reclaiming America: Nike, Clean Air, and the New National Activism*, Berkeley, CA: University of California Press.
Shaw, G., Brown, R. and P. Bromiley (1998) 'Strategic stories: How 3M is rewriting business planning', *Harvard Business Review*, 76(3): 41–44+.
Shetty, S. (1996) 'Structural changes and competitive strategies of the US footwear industry in the 1990s', in *US International Trade Commission: Industry Trade and Technology Review*. http://www.stat-usa.gov [28 May 2000].
Solovy, A. (1999) 'Once upon a culture', *Hospitals & Health Networks*, 73(5): 26.
Sporting Goods Intelligence (1999) http://www.sginews.com [28 May 2000].
Sporting Goods Manufacturers Association press release (2000) 'US sporting goods market outlook for 2000', 11 February. See http://www.sportlink.com/pressroom/2000releases/m2000-001.html [28 May 2000].
Star, K. L. (1999) *'Asian Crisis and Women Workers'*. See http://www.globalpolicy.org/socecon/global/women99.htm [28 May 2000].
Students for Informed Career Decisions (1999). Stanford University. See http://www.stanford.edu/groups/SICD/ Reebok/reebok.html [28 May 2000].
Thompson, A. A. and A. J. Strickland III (1999) *Strategic Management: Concepts and Cases*, 11th edn, Boston: Irwin/McGraw-Hill.
Turner, I. (1998) 'Strategy and meaning', *Manager Update*, 10(1): 1–8.
White, H. (1973) *Metahistory: The Historial Imagination in Nineteenth-Century Europe*. Baltimore, MD: The Johns Hopkins University Press.
Young, A. (1997) *The NIKE Code of Conduct*, Atlanta, GA: GoodWorks International LLC.

7

The Realization of Meanings: Understanding Expatriates' Needs in the Asian Post-crisis Environment

Xue Li, John B. Kidd and Frank-Jürgen Richter

Introduction

Throughout Asia, many firms have been worrying about the external factors of the economic crisis. Such external factors like the foundations of economic policy and the efficiency of the finance sector are almost beyond their own control. Internal factors, on the other hand, such as their mode of management in general and their ways of human resource management in particular are well within their power to change (Richter, 2000).

In pre-crisis Asia, human resource management often secured socialization, mutual loyalty, and emotional commitment to the employer. People working for Matsushita, Hyundai or Legend agreed to live in a community in which they would not exploit each other, but rather co-evolve jointly. Such an attitude was grounded on shared commitment to visions and values. Labour mobility became relatively low, especially if compared to the USA, where the new economy even increased labour mobility in recent years. Japan, in particular, celebrated the practice of life-time employment which provided a rationale for huge investments in employees – such as training – confident in the belief that employees will improve in capability and ability, and that an employee will not be hired away by a competitor.

The post-crisis environment is driving Asian firms to adapt to the globalization of the economy, to reconsider traditional intercompany relations like the *keiretsu* in Japan, the *chaebol* in Korea, and the overseas

Chinese networks in Southeast Asia, and to proactively adjust employment practices. It is now thought that lifetime employment may have hindered flexible adjustments necessary to make changes in demand and competition. And there may have been less creativity from the people involved in these life-time jobs as compared with the honeybee approach of Silicon Valley where talent easily moves between employers, leading to cross-fertilization. Change agents throughout the whole of East Asia are now demanding a more diverse workforce and the promotion of intellectual elites and high performers in order to enable creative problem solving.

In post-crisis Asia, international firms have to change their approach towards human resource management as well. Asia seems now to be poised for great growth in the future leaving big opportunities for international firms in terms of merger and acquisitions (M&A), but also for greenfield ventures. Business laws and practices have changed greatly leading to the need to adapt management techniques. Formerly, it was a prerequisite to apply the Asian rules of *guanxi* (Chinese: connection) and *konne* (Japanese: derived from the English 'connection'). Even so, international firms still have to bear in mind all cultural antecedents and psychometric profiles when choosing the right expatriates to be seconded to Asia. But they may apply standard elements of a modern human resource policy as well, for example, promotion by performance (and not by seniority) as well as transparent decision-making (and not pure *guanxi*). In many cases, human resource (HR) systems with hybrid characteristics are emerging.

Amongst the myriad of difficulties facing international firms in the post Asia-crisis era, several come from within. Their greatest threat being their failure to manage effectively their expatriates' assignments (Haley, 2000). The reasons for these problems are plentiful: internal corporate politics, cultural issues, family concerns about changes in employee lifestyle, the rapid expansion of the global market place, and the escalation of expatriate costs. There are a number of quite specific aspects: dual-career issues of the expatriate and his/her partner, the assignment duration, reassignment preparation (or lack of it), foreign service incentives, shipping restrictions, home sale, home leave, risks in assignment location, tax treatment, and more. These problems reflect the fact that in most organizations the HR function has had a limited role in expatriate selection, management, and repatriation: but they were in charge of this task. Formerly, HR's role was primarily administrative support, but now the opinion is that HR has a powerful opportunity now, and in the future, to make a real impact on their business success abroad.

In this chapter we will explore the costs of the expatriation process, the psychological aspects affecting the expatriate and his or her family, and the nature of the Asian world (often specifically the Chinese world) in which the expatriates find themselves. These aspects are all interwoven and will become more critical given the new investiture of China into the WTO, as firms inside and outside of China commence even more vigorous partner searching. We understand of course that China is not the only target country to which staff are assigned. For instance, the UK, USA and Hong Kong are said to be the most targeted destinations, with China, Brazil and Mexico as emergent destinations. It is said also that China, Russia and India are the locations where it is most difficult to perform adequately as an expatriate.

Economic imperatives

FDI activity

In the ministries of many developed nations, there is agreement on the merits of acquiring inward FDI. Some countries go so far as to have their regional development bodies competing against each other for this inward investment, rather than let market forces play their natural part. Provided that new investment actually arrives in the country, any other game yields inefficiencies when compared with allowing the firm to invest wherever it will under natural market forces. Cantwell and Janne (1999), Driffield and Munday (2000) show that there are benefits accruing from FDI investments which stimulate the indigenous firms, but all is not rosy. They suggest that local adverse effects can occur, namely that inefficient firms may be bankrupted under the new competition from outsider firms.

It is clear that quite massive FDI flows continue; and they are reaching record highs (see UNCTAD, 1999). These flows further indicate that many projects will occur worldwide, as new alliances are established between existing firms, or other forms of new joint ventures are established. Herein we predict there will be many complexities that arrive predicated upon culture, power, and other national differences. Such conflicts are not considered in the statistical analyses of FDI noted above (Cantwell and Janne, 1999; Driffield and Munday, 2000), but they may be severe enough to cause a firm to pull out of its commitment – especially if it finds the culture gap too large, overcoming its capacity to cope.

The globalized market place

In a sense different from the FDI flows noted above (and not included as FDI) are cash flows involved with M&A (see Table 7.1). They are

Table 7.1 Global indicators of M&A activity

Topic	**1996 (US$ billion)**	**1997 (US$ billion)**	**1998 (US$ billion)**	**% Growth rate (1997–1998)**
M&A activity				
FDI inflows	359	464	644	38.7
FDI outflows	380	475	649	36.6
FDI inward stock	3086	3437	4088	19.0
FDI outward stock	3145	3423	4117	20.3
Cross-border M&A[a]	163	236	411	73.9

Source: UNCTAD – Press release TAD/INF/2821, 27 September 1999.

Topic	**1991**	**1992**	**1993**	**1994**	**1995**	**1996**	**1997**	**1998**
Regulation changes								
Number of countries introducing investment regime changes	35	43	57	49	64	65	76	60
Number of regulatory changes	82	79	102	110	112	114	151	145
Of which								
More favourable to FDI[a]	80	79	101	108	106	98	135	136
Less favourable to FDI[b]	2	–	1	2	6	16	16	9

[a] Including liberalizing changes aimed at strengthening market functions as well as increased incentives.
[b] Including changes aimed at increasing control as well as reducing incentives.
Source: UNCTAD – Press release TAD/INF/2820, 27 September 1999.

excluded strictly from the aggregate FDI figures, as the cost of a merger or the acquisition of another firm is not direct (inwards, thus foreign) investment per se. The M&A have continued unabated through the Asian financial crisis, and may be seen to have increased greatly in later years. In part, this is due to the opening up of national regimes shown as Regulation Changes and noted by the United Nations Conference on Trade and Development (UNCTAD).

As countries open up their regimes by reducing regulatory hurdles, there will be a greater awareness of the benefits of creating an alliance or an M&A activity – for a variety of reasons. These may be to develop further one firm's market power and reach, to achieve economies of scale or scope, or to formalize existing specific symbiotic relationships that in themselves may be perceived as fragile and open to abuse. Typically the high-technology sector sees high growth in M&A with De George (1993) stating there was a 25 per cent increase in merger activity in the IT sector over 1998–99. There were, he says, over 4000 transactions globally as smaller firms consolidated with each other to achieve viability, or were absorbed into larger firms.

Strategic alliances, on the other hand, have been described as 'relatively enduring interfirm cooperative arrangements, involving flows and linkages that use resources and/or governance structures from autonomous organizations, for their joint accomplishment of individual goals linked to the corporate mission of each sponsoring firm' (Parkhe, 1991). Clearly one of the obvious difficulties for the individual actors, be they senior managers or shop-floor operatives, is to come to an understanding of how their individual goals and aspirations can be merged and aligned effectively with those of 'the other side', as partner firms' staff are often perceived. Given the research from UNCTAD and elsewhere, there is no dearth of research into strategic alliances – for instance see Richter (1999), or Lu (1998) who noted the Japanese were pursuing over 2000 alliances in China.

The People's Republic of China (PRC) is quickly developing into a major economic power and is likely to develop into a huge economy, some might say it will be the world's largest market by 2020. With a population that makes up approximately one-fifth of the world's consumers, it has already attracted US$ 300 billion of FDI over the past 20 years (and has been seen to be the world's second largest inwards FDI nation). This inwards FDI has resulted in a substantial number of foreign business people, and thus expatriates, being placed in Sino-foreign joint ventures, in foreign representative offices, in foreign-owned subsidiaries, and in branches of foreign firms. Note a selection of sales volume statistics on national Chinese firms in Table 7.2.

We suggest many mergers, acquisitions, consolidations – whatever – will soon take place in the Chinese economy over all sectors given that their emergence into the world market accelerates. Put in perspective, however, the top Chinese firm – China Petrochemical Corp. – ranks only twenty-seventh in the Asia 1000 list (with sales of US$ 26 000 million). Top in the Asia 1000 is Mitsui which has sales of US$ 109 000 millions, and at this level, ranks fifth in the global Fortune list. But these all fall below General Motors (US$ 161 315 million in sales) which ranks number one globally: '1999 Global 500', *Fortune*, August 1999.

Table 7.2 Chinese firms in the *Asia Week* 'Top-1000'

Rank	Company name	Sales US$million
27	China Petrochemical Corp.	26 339
43	Sinochem	17 880
63	Jiangsu Sup. & Mktg. Co-Op.	13 981
67	Cofco	13 526
126	Shanghai Automotive	8 848
163	East China Electric Power	6 813
181	Daqing Oil Mgt. Bur.	6 123
211	China State Const. Eng.	5 380
259	Baoshan Iron & Steel	4 636
291	Central China Power	4 133
292	China Faw Group	4 111
339	Citic	3 563
376	Shanghai Volkswagen	3 175
402	Shougang Corp.	2 976
444	China Huaneng Group	2 643
535	Sichuan Changhong Elect.	2 268
630	Fushun Petrochemical	1 973
631	Motorola Electronic (China)	1 966
668	China Telecom (HK)	1 868
694	China National Offshore Oil	1 798
701	Qilu Petrochemical	1 786
737	China National Agri.	1 690
756	Haier Group	1 646
805	China Southern Airlines	1 547
839	Beijing Yanshan Petrochem.	1 471
857	Shanghai Petrochemical	1 427
861	Sinopec Daqing Petrochem.	1 419
880	Air China	1 377
904	Dong Feng Motor Corp.	1 327
907	China Harbour Engineering	1 321

Source: See *Asia Week* 'Asian Top-1000' for a current list – at http://cnn.com/ASIANOW

Success and failure of IJVs

The UNCTAD figures tracking FDI show there is an increasing volume of investment flowing between the developed nations, and the analysts note that recently more FDI is flowing into newly developed nations and undeveloped nations. Even newly developed nations have significant outward investment. Although much of the M&A and the associated FDI are across borders, these flows often result in a significant form of strategic alliance between two or more firms with their roots often spanning the globe. But all is not generally rosy – many developing nations' M&A activity results in strong fund flows to a neighbouring cheaper labour economy thereby worsening the home economy.

Frequently we may imagine that M&A will take place to achieve economies, and thus in general terms one might expect the firm's share price to rise through its merger, due to it operating in a more efficient market (Oster, 1994). But recently the consultants, KPMG, have found that 83 per cent of mergers did not produce any increased shareholder value, and indeed half of the merged firms generated a reduction in the company's share price (Kelly and Cook, 1999). Often the main reason for failure is in the 'us and them' mentality of the staff involved. The merged CEOs may not have resolved their own personal hostilities and these are communicated downwards in the new organization. Hence a feeling of mutual hostility develops between individuals who are supposed to be colleagues.

There are alternatives to M&A. The firm might be able to develop its own in-house expertise directly (though this is a slow and fragile process, especially when related to new technology breakthroughs). It may take up a licensing agreement (but too often the licensor is reluctant to divulge too deeply its secrets, so would offer second-class products, last years' models as it were), or it may consider a strategic alliance (to overcome the above problems). The alliance process is much cheaper than an M&A and it is an arrangement that may be terminated when one or both sides consider they have gained enough. Such alliances can be seen to be a quick and flexible way to cope in the fast-moving globalized high-technology world, whereas an M&A inclines to stability and a more slow-moving scenario. But, in being quick and flexible, alliances are also highly disturbing to the staff therein – many individuals in the subsidiary partnership are often made redundant given the existence of a similar set of functions (and people) in the dominant partner firm.

Issues of corporate governance

As may be imagined, some of the anticipated benefits of an international joint venture (IJV) are tangible, such as reduced transaction costs or having better access to new markets. But others are less tangible, such as access to knowledge or some aspects of raising entry barriers. The stated (and unstated) reasons for entering into the IJV may differ between partners in the same venture. A Chinese firm, for example, may be looking for the inward transfer of Western technology while at one time the Chinese Finance Ministry was looking to acquire hard (dollar) currency from the alliances. Alternatively, the European or global partner might be seeking entry into a new (Chinese) market simply to expand global reach. If the espoused reasons are achieved the globalized joint venture may be said to be a success. However there is often a large asymmetry, leading to one or the other side complaining about being a victim. If this culture gap is too great a burden, the IJV will break up; or instead, if regulations allow, it may become a wholly owned venture so easing the confusing issues that may have been pulling this way and that way.

Localization issues

We noted above that FDI and the financial cross-border flows have significant effects on a local economy – sometimes by stimulating growth, other times by forcing inefficient firms out of business. In some strong regional economies – the US (NAFTA), and in Europe (the EU) – there are statutes which ensure that after a period of initiation, there must be a high percentage of locally produced subassemblies in what ostensibly is a foreign import, for instance, a Japanese car. But localization goes further than this – deep inside a firm and its governance. We note that as a firm becomes more mature in its host country, it also uses more of the other local resources, for instance, using local manpower throughout its organization, and even fully localizing its investment and capital portfolio.

For firms operating in developing economies, there is less pressure to localize – the quality of the host life-style may be variable, its general infrastructure fragile, and its local personnel may not have had the right training so there may be few suitably trained local staff to fill key positions (Kanter, 1995). Furthermore, its financial markets and institutions may not be well-developed so precluding localizing investment. Additionally, we may find in these circumstances a rich pasture for bribery and corruption.

There are many issues to be faced when engaging in cross-cultural ventures. Not only do we have differing personal habits and inclinations in an organizational and social sense as indicated by Hofstede (1980; 1991), but we find also a growing pressure upon Asian firms to conform to Western models of business probity and governance which is not easy. Kishi (1998) notes that cross-border transfers are not only of goods but also of know-how, people and culture, which confounds the interpersonal exchange of simple organizational models. More broadly, there is the need to develop trust between venture partners at an organizational level (we will discuss this aspect later). We observe here that trust is developed first at a personal level, between individuals who have the same needs – they eat, drink, socialize, have families to support; and second, at the level of each need to meet business goals. How each individual deals with these factors differs (see Lovett et al. 1999).

Garelli (1992) intriguingly presents a trend, stating that as societies mature they have shown more of a tendency towards individualism, moving away from the collective values they supported in their immature societies. He bases this notion upon changes observed in Europe from the 1900s to the present day. He comments further on the way in which Asian countries are now moving from an earlier reverence of hard work to wealth acquisition, and from social participation to personal self-achievement.

Sociometrics as grounded theory

It may be said that the seminal work of Hofstede (op cit) is grounded theory insofar as it offers some opportunity for induction in novel situations. But it also suffers from being overworked and it is a little dated now – though there are several replications which support his main findings: see, for instance, Smith and Peterson (1994), Yang (1988), and Hoppe (1993), Schwartz (1990), Smith and Bond (1993), Trompenaars (1993), Darlington (1996), Smith (1996). One of the interesting links between Hofstede's work and this chapter is the research of Kogut and Singh (1988) who discuss 'cultural distance'.

In Hofstede's data, a sample of which is in Table 7.3, we see four factors, and in addition Kogut and Singh's data (which is based on these factors):

1 power distance (PDI: the willingness generally to accept organizational hierarchy);
2 uncertainty avoidance (UAI: the pressure to reduce ambiguity);
3 individuality (IDV); and
4 masculinity (MAS).

The first two factors are seen as the drivers of organizational culture, the other two as indices that are more indicative of social skills. Later, Hofstede developed a fifth index that he called Confucianism relating to a propensity to have a long-term orientation (this too is in Table 7.3).

Shown in Table 7.3 is the Kogut and Singh (1988) measure of cultural differences (CUL). This is, in effect, a weighted sum of the differences between a target profile (here the UK) and the profile of another country. It provides a single comprehensible number with which to rank all countries. In this table, we compare the UK with other countries on this measure. We see from the data that the USA is reasonably similar to the

Table 7.3 A sample of culture measurements and indicators

Country	PDI	UAI	IDV	MAS	CUL	Long-termism
Great Britain	35	35	89	66	0	25
USA	40	46	91	62	0.08	29
Australia	36	51	90	61	0.12	31
Ireland	28	35	70	68	0.16	
W Germany	35	65	67	66	0.55	31
Italy	50	75	76	70	0.85	
Belgium	65	94	75	54	2.07	
Denmark	18	23	74	16	2.09	
Netherlands	38	53	80	14	2.11	44
France	68	86	71	43	2.13	
Hong Kong	68	29	25	57	2.17	96
Japan	54	92	46	95	2.82	80
Pakistan	55	70	14	50	3.00	0
Taiwan	58	69	17	45	3.01	87
Philippines	94	44	32	64	3.05	19
Singapore	74	8	20	48	3.10	48
China	80	60	20	50	3.27	118
Indonesia	78	48	14	46	3.42	
South Korea	60	85	18	39	3.76	75
Malaysia	104	36	26	50	4.13	

Note: Cultural Difference – CUL (due to Kogut and Singh) is displayed relative to the UK; long-termism is not measured on all countries.
Sources: Hofstede (1980; 1991), Kogut and Singh (1988).

UK on all Hofstede measures – though perhaps the UK is a little more individualistic (higher IDV) and a little less materialistic (lower MAS): thus the Kogut and Singh difference between the UK and the USA is negligible. Other countries are increasingly different from the UK. France, though of continental Europe, is notable in having a cultural difference of 2.13 against the UK. In the full data set, the countries with an even larger cultural difference (from the UK) are mainly those of the Orient, or South of the equator, (but note Greece has a cultural difference score of 3.91 – well into the range expressed by Oriental countries).

For comparison, we repeat a sample of Hofstede's data in Table 7.4 to note the cultural differences between China (as a target) and several of its Asian and non-Asian neighbours. We can see immediately, if Kogut and Singh are correct, there will be some facility in the way Chinese expatriates work in Indonesia or Taiwan, but they will have most difficulty in working in Japan, the USA, or in the worst case, in Denmark. As noted elsewhere in this chapter, the Japanese represent the greatest group of Asian expatriates, but surely soon China will begin to exert its

Table 7.4 A second sample of culture measurements and indicators

Country	PDI	UAI	IDV	MAS	CUL
China	80	60	20	50	0
Indonesia	78	48	14	46	0.08
Taiwan	58	69	17	45	0.31
Thailand	64	64	20	34	0.33
Philippines	94	44	32	64	0.40
India	77	40	48	56	0.50
Hong Kong	68	29	25	57	0.49
Malaysia	104	36	26	50	0.54
South Korea	60	85	18	39	0.54
Singapore	74	8	20	48	1.06
France	68	86	71	43	1.40
Germany (West)	35	65	67	66	2.14
Canada	39	48	80	52	2.37
Japan	54	92	46	95	2.53
USA	40	46	91	62	3.02
Australia	36	51	90	61	3.08
Denmark	18	23	74	16	4.56

Note: Cultural difference – CUL (due to Kogut and Singh) is displayed relative to China.
Sources: Hofstede (1980; 1991), Kogut and Singh (1989).

economic power and begin to engage increasingly in FDI on its own account throughout the globe. This table thus has some significance with respect to Chinese expatriates' management.

Western ways/Asian ways

Transparency and opacity of the other culture

What comes over quite clearly as Occidental persons work more closely with Asian persons (holding radically different cultural norms) is the problematic notion of truth – or of Asians being what the Westerners might call economical with the truth. Much of Confucian learning pivots on personal relationships and the consequent necessity of maintaining the face of one's opponents – even if they are losing the battle. So, while one should not lie, one may by omission commit a type-2 error, and thus lead the opposition and even one's own IJV partners to believe what may be seen (in the West) to be an untruth. In these circumstances, it is necessary for both groups in the IJV to hold self-therapy sessions in order to learn about the other and so become more confident in telling the truth. We note that there is some difficulty in following this line of argument, as many Asian persons are fatalistic, whereas the Westerner is happy to play the odds and attempts to influence the outcome by acquiring more information and by canvassing decision makers.

We can see in an IJV that managers need to exert subtle influence to get their staff to think in a coherent way. The Western worker has to be made more aware of the benefit of being more open towards his fellows with respect to data garnered for personal use. If the data is gathered during the pursuit of organizational goals, it might be argued the data should be openly accessible to all. We suggest it has to be treated in the way in which we are led to believe Japanese middle management assess data. That is, talked through openly many times so its nuances can be understood, both intrinsically of itself and with respect to its relationships with the wider interactions as perceived by other managers (i.e., *nemawashi*). If the data is dealt with out of context, one may infer the wrong action; thus the intangible has to be made tangible to a degree, the tacit made explicit but under advice of the majority of the decision-makers, in the correct context for such openness.

Similarly, we have to ensure the Asian managers become more at ease with the concept of transparency, especially in their accounting function. At the moment they often treat this activity as similar to a household economy, even having a respected family member running the function – thus it is an inside job, opaque to outsiders, especially to Western outsiders, even if they are in the same IJV. It is pertinent to note the Western pressure to conform globally to published accounting standards, for example, the US GAAP (Generally Acceptable Accounting Principles), so that all business units of the IJV can be compared unequivocally. But we have to ponder the meaning of generally acceptable – acceptable to whom? We raise this question since it has been shown that accounting disclosure, at least historically, is strongly correlated with cultural measures, such as the measures of Hofstede (op cit), Gray (1996), Gray and Vint (1995), Salter and Niswander (1995) and Zarzeski (1996), state that the Oriental cultures are biased towards secrecy (non-transparency). Even so, we should note that opaqueness is not uniquely an East/West issue, since the Channel Islands, Belgium, Spain and Switzerland all have low levels of disclosure (Gray, op cit).

Further, research on the Oriental concept of probability and risk has shown that persons from that region are fate-oriented and are less willing to take a probabilistic view of the world (Phillips and Wright, 1977). This might suggest that sophisticated accounting is not needed in Asia since what will be, (to use a phrase translated from the Spanish!) and no subtle provisioning will hide poor performance. On the other hand, the collective spirit will carry an ailing firm without loss of face, whilst in the West the clarity of accounting might well show-up a technical failure and thus the firm is forced to liquidate, notwithstanding any mitigating circumstances.

Corruption

As we noted above, the Asians deploy opaque accounting practices and they also practice gift giving on a scale that seems to an American nothing short of bribery. In China there is the universal practice of *guanxi*, the maintenance of which will involve gift giving (note: the same word and social process is endemic in Japan). But there is the darker practice of bribery which has come under considerable public scrutiny in the recent years in China. In Chinese society the exchanges of favour involving *guanxi* are not strictly commercial, they are also social – involving *renqing* (social or humanized obligation), and the giving of *mianzi* (the notion of face – see Lou, 1997). More recently, as China opens up, *guanxi* has become known as social capital, which, taking a Western view, is used to make tidy commercial contracts between corporations, thus leading the innocent Westerner towards an over reliance on gift giving and banqueting as a means of conducting business in China. These activities are both normal facets of Chinese *guanxi*, but many Western firms' operations go too far, and operate too close to bribery. Following this, Western individuals can become known as meat and wine friends defeating the object of true *guanxi* – which is really the offering of favours during the development of a personal relationship, naturally promoting business in China, between the Chinese. Sometimes, therefore, Confucianism is accused of promoting corruption in East Asia given that its teachings called for individuals to improve and maintain the relationships among relatives and friends through their influence and contacts. It is here that the Confucian concept of reciprocity plays a strong role leading to an exchange of gifts that may escalate in value.

The World Bank and the International Monetary Fund (IMF) are now ready to be whistle blowers when they detect funding diversions: and other organizations now more publicly claim they resist bribery. For instance, the USA has had laws from 1977 which declared acts as criminal if commercial payoffs were offered to public servants abroad by national personnel; and the Royal Dutch/Shell Group in its April 1998 annual report said it fired 23 of its staff on ethical grounds, and that it had terminated contracts with 95 firms, also on ethical grounds (Walsh, 1998). We note too that Japan has been paralysed for years in being unable to disentangle its opaque systems resting on bribery and extortion.

In China there is a strong history of *guandao*, or official corruption, which according to Walsh is more pervasive than it is in Japan. As an example, President Jiang Zemin declared war on this evil when it became obvious that a $2.2 billion scandal had involved Chen Xitong (who was a former party chief and politburo member) and his deputy Wang Baosen (who later committed suicide). Altogether some 500 000 persons in China in recent years have been reprimanded or punished for taking kickbacks, but the use of extortion is still rife in China (Walsh, op cit).

Organizational ethics

We have to state that we find the concept of ethics somewhat relative – it is in the eyes of the beholder, when in Rome and so on. It is wrong, as De George (1993) says, to assume that American righteousness is the uniquely correct approach to define ethical forms of governance and behaviour. Herein we have a dilemma: as Yang (1994) finds, there is a difference (in China) between the popular interpretation of *guanxi* as maybe having some benefit, and the Communist Party's partial interpretation that it is anti-socialist. The same broad reasoning can be applied from the US perspective – first, that there is no universal global definition of *guanxi*, and second, that it is tied to the practice of bribery and so is ethically reprehensible. We have to agree with Yang that while there is an element of bribery in *guanxi*, it is a concept which is strictly Eastern in its origin, and thus only fully understandable when contextualized in Asia. So, accepting that in the East aspects of bribery are present, Yang says this is firstly not only part of a gain/loss calculation [of bribery operations] but also that this [bribery] is much less strong in *guanxi* operations. Secondly, the development of *guanxi* is for the long-term future, while bribery is immediate and for short-term gain. Thirdly, *guanxi* has an emotional content, while bribery does not.

The reason we bring ethics into focus is that, in Western literature we find two academic movements drawing attention to the concept. One comes from the Business Ethics school which links economics and ethics (as in Transaction Cost Theory or in Agency Theory) and thus puts the value of a project or object into an assessment of the utility of the value to the individual. The other movement comes from decision theorists who, from the days of Blaise Pascale, have studied the laws of probabilities. This has led to expected value theory, and thence to expected utility theory, where again the individual decision-maker puts his/her personal value judgements to outcomes so informing the decision process. But it is only after the 1970s that a consideration of ethical values gained prominence in the West, since academicians had taken one reading of Adam Smith which suggested there was no need for ethical values as they did not make business sense (Sen, 1993). In China, however, we find there has always been a debate about *yi* and *li* – since the times of Confucius, where *yi* is ethical value (justice), and *li* is economic value (profit).

In Chinese Confucianism both *yi* and *li* have been central concepts. It is said, when one can not have both fish and bear's paw at the same time, one will favour *yi* and discard *li*, and thus it is to be understood that *xiao-ren* (a mean person) is pushed by *li* (profit), whereas *jun-zi* (a gentleman) is delighted by *yi* (justice). Nowadays this attitude has been changed in the age of globalism as the world is reduced to only one market economy. As Wang Keqian (1992) has noted, ethical value has two dimensions: one is of utility, the other of non-utility. The former indicates that ethical norms are in need of certain material resources and political support. The latter suggests that ethical norms must lead to a satisfying human life – of feeling, self-consciousness, willingness, spiritual creativity and so on. Thus ethical value can be affirmed as having public utility, supporting ethical value but not supplanting it. Efficient economic behaviour itself has ethical value. Many instances of economic value growth are supported and reinforced by ethical value, so this points to a way of resolving the problem of the blending of ethical and economic values without having to establish some hierarchy of values.

We note that for the Chinese, at least, their ethical value structure is related to utility through moral norms. They will connect *yi* and *li* in the manner of a publicly declared *li*. Before the reforms in China, the people inclined only toward political ethical values and divorced these from economic values: they accepted a public *yi* without questioning the relevant *li*. At that time, the economy was undeveloped and people could not enjoy any profit they had made. But from the beginning of the Reform process, economic value (*li*) was seen to surpass all other values: a report from the Zero Point Company said 97 per cent of respondents now put the God of Wealth above all other Gods (Jing and Xu, 1996). As a result, bribery, bankruptcy, corruption and *guandao* grow constantly. Although bribes are not explicitly accepted in many Asian countries, they are a norm of business life, which, from a Western ethical perspective, should be resisted both in the giving and the taking.

An ethical vacuum left by Confucius?

Confucius' five cardinal relationships and their accompanying moral code established the importance of hierarchy that survives across Asia to this day. But there is one relationship that he missed – that between the individual and the outsider (Haley et al., 1998). Outsiders do not fit readily into the Confucian hierarchy; indeed, they represent a challenge to it. It is this missing sixth relationship that is of most interest to Western business people, because in Asia they, the Western outsiders, are one of the most extreme forms of outside. Effectively, Confucius left an ethical vacuum: how to deal with outsiders and strangers – those who are the expatriates of today? He did not address this issue which is not surprising, since, in his day, there would be very few outsiders and so he did not establish a further rule of behaviour. Thus the modern Chinese person, who is normally a rule-follower, is confused when there is no internalized rule to be followed, or broken, as the case may be.

One of the observable effects is akin to that seen in Catastrophe Theory (originally proposed by Réné Thom (1923)). Herein, the subject when pushed hard in a situation often smoothly responds. But sometimes, seemingly in absolutely the same circumstances, he or she responds violently. Thus, instead of passing gently along the response surface the subject apparently falls over a cliff as a cusp is encountered in the response surface. Thus, in the case of the Western outsider meeting the insider Chinese person, who as a nation have refined their (Confucian) response surface over thousands of years, the reaction may be smooth: but it may not, with the Chinese person reacting strongly, even violently, to some slight nuance unobserved, and maybe unintended, by the outsider. In these circumstances, the outsider finds it difficult to develop trust. This is so for insiders also, as they are not guided by their internalized (Confucian) rules of behaviour, as these do not cover the rules of engagement with outsiders. We could say they miss the sixth sense.

We suggest this loss of sense-making is perhaps more deeply felt in China than in some other, but younger, Asian societies – for instance, a similar concept is used in Japan where behaviour regarding the *uchi* (in-group) is collectivist. Further afield we recognize that Latin American *simpatia* works very much like the Chinese *guanxi* where out-group members are often treated with hostility.

In Chinese business culture, initiative is associated with company leaders. Employees must avoid mistakes at all cost and they know, for all workers and staff alike, that relationship maintenance is crucial to completing a job (we mentioned *mianzi* above – the notion of face). In the global economy, having a workforce that is fluent in the ways of the world is a competitive necessity. But when building a staff development strategy in China, Western corporations must begin with the underlying characteristics of the PRC workforce, particularly the fact that the skills necessary to be successful in a Chinese firm are often at odds with those accepted to be successful in a Western company. Young Chinese professionals who do not go along with their (native) unwritten rules quickly isolate themselves from their peers and superiors. For large Western companies in China, with Chinese staff ranging from young to old, and from labourer to executive, cultural dichotomies can disrupt staff development. Any effort to improve long-term staff quality and to localize senior positions must first address this cultural divide noted by Frazer (1998). Efforts at consistency can be more complicated in joint ventures, as the many business units may have cultures separate from and perhaps even clashing with that of the parent company. Companies with offices spread across China, and staffed by people who speak different dialects, may also find consistency especially hard to attain. We accept that striving for consistent corporate cultures is almost as daunting as attempting to cope with international cultural differences. It must be the prime aim for Human Resource Management (HRM) managers in the multinationals to hold many group briefings to help align procedures, objectives, and staff attitudes across their multiple offices.

The emergent role of the HRM function

At one stage in the natural development of Western firms, the HRM function was quite a low level function – dealing with hiring and firing of staff who had roles defined by senior managers, there were rigid job descriptions. The HRM staff gradually acquired new skills – in negotiating in particular. Insofar as they helped senior managers in their discussions with the labour unions, they also showed they could work at an abstract and strategic level – as per the senior managers themselves. Thus it came to pass that the HRM function became strengthened to absorb new forms of organizational design. As well as dealing with Employment Law (the old hiring and firing) they have to now address the role of the expatriate, and to aid these individuals who will have to deal with the complexities of working far from home territory handling the many strange aspects mentioned above.

Managerial and cultural predicates

Expatriates have to thus come to grips with the ways of others, their norms and their psychology. We must state clearly that in this chapter we are not considering the view of expatriates as those US or European persons who are placed to work briefly in a distant developing nation. Rather, we are considering persons who are moved by their employer to work with others over a longer term, maybe a year or so, and to work with others who often have a radically different view of business and private ethics. In general we focus on the Occidental entering the Orient but note the largest expatriate group spreading outwards from Asia is that of Japanese managers who are deployed through their global subsidiaries. There are many other Asian managers who are quite widely deployed as expatriates throughout Asia and who suffer in ways we will discuss below. We suggest that the overseas Chinese are not generally expatriates in this sense – of course they have an affinity for their homeland, but their life and business is located outside the PRC, in Hong Kong, Malaysia and elsewhere. Their enterprises may not in fact have any need for expatriates as such.

In an early article on expatriates, Hays (1974) categorizes expatriate managers into four types:

1 The structure reproducer who is responsible for reproducing in the foreign subsidiary a structure similar to that of another part of the company, often a copy of the firm back home.
2 The technical troubleshooter who is sent to analyse and solve a technical problem in a foreign affiliate firm.
3 The operational expatriate is the individual who carries out a well-defined position in an ongoing foreign business.
4 The CEO overseas who directs the entire foreign operation.

It is clear that the roles defined above imply different skills and very likely that they will not be found in one person. However, the experienced expatriate may have progressed through role learning in a form of apprenticeship while he (more usually) or she was groomed to be a CEO working in a foreign land on a near-permanent basis.

Similarly, Derr and Oddou (1991) identify two types of expatriates:

1 Those who are assigned abroad to fix a problem, including those assigned to line management and/or specialized functional positions; and
2 Those who go abroad as high-potential persons to broaden their development.

Also in this context, Pucik (1992) differentiates between demand-driven and learning-driven international assignments.

Are agents cheaper than expatriates?

At the time of the Industrial Revolution in Europe and America, it was possible for significant transfers of technological knowledge to take place through the migration of skilled individuals (Scoville, 1951). However, the complexity of modern technology and the highly specialized role played now by individuals in the production process (even in service-type industries) indicate that most useful knowledge today is held corporately, rather than in the mind of individuals (Gabriel, 1967). Even so, some sort of technology transfer can be achieved by hiring skilled and knowledgeable individuals. But before this process of rent-a-body takes place in China, we suggest that agents be considered since the fully-fledged expatriate is a costly item.

Creating and generating trust in the agent by the employer, by the agent of the host firm, and between each other openly accepting their mutual trust in their joint future is necessary. The generation of trust will not come about through simple reliance on Agency Theory (Baiman, 1982; 1996) nor through Transactional Cost Theories (Williamson, 1975; Rugman and Verbeke, 1992; Parkhe, 1993). In the case of China, it will develop through the realization and observation of the historical cultural predicates that continue to act as drivers while accepting these necessary changes under modern economic conditions. For instance, early in Confucius' times, both *yi* (justice) and *li* (profit) were central concepts in China: as he said, 'wealth and rank by injustice and dishonesty are as floating clouds to me' (Confucius, 551–479 BC, Analects). This saying has become a motto for Oriental businessmen. Historically, the mutual relationship between *li* and *yi* has been clearly understood, but now business people have to realize that there is not an either/or situation, and merging of economic and ethical values have to be in a single harmonious process. Such a movement will redraw the interdependence of *yi* and *li* and the associated Chinese values in Business Ethics (Jing Ji) which itself could be described as governing the world in harmony to bring about the well-being of its people. So *yi* may be thought of as *li* in conformance with morality.

Thus, principals and agents have to be in tune with these facts. The latter, while accepting a contract for what is a peanut fee (in terms of the expatriates' fees generally) have nevertheless to deliver the results demanded in these contracts which then may lead to new business. Agents should thus work in the fashion that expatriates work, but much more cheaply.

A unique way to construct an agent being a hybrid of expatriate knowledge and local national behaviour is by hiring foreign national students or equivalent who are studying or undertaking research in the home-base country of the enterprise. These agents would have achieved their master's degree or equivalent in the host country and many students in host countries want to work for foreign companies and live/ work back in their native country. It would be natural for the home-country office to take care of all necessary legal documentation and manage visas. In this way the foreign company starts out ahead, with employees who not only know both local languages, but who also know the target culture and the ways of working in that region which is their native country. They could be agents set to look diligently at the broad picture – being paid less than true expatriates, but receiving more than the usual low local salary from their native firms.

The selection of expatriates

Is a short-term assignment the solution to high cost?

With the continuing high cost of expatriate assignments, there are increasing concerns about dual-career issues: that is, families comprising career wives and career husbands. Many who would be expatriates today refuse to uproot their families or forgo a critical second income. With dual-income families fast becoming the norm in many countries, short-term assignments provide what might be an acceptable alternative for the key employee who might otherwise decline a long-term position abroad. Recently it has been found that 73 per cent of Europe-headquartered companies, 65 per cent of North American companies, and 44 per cent of Asia-based companies use short-term assignments to overcome the above employee resistance (McMorrow, 1998). Within these programmes which have a reduced time abroad, 82 per cent of the international assignees' family remain at home. But, as the short-term assignments vary from about two months to a year, they could ultimately have an adverse effect on the achievement of company goals and cost-containment efforts in the long-term since there may not be enough dwell time to develop a good and effective transfer of knowledge.

It is possible to meet certain corporate objectives through the use of short-term assignments such as market exploration or development, start-up operations, troubleshooting assignments, critical-shortage filling, technology transfer, and training of personnel at the foreign headquarters. We find 78 per cent of all participants replied that their companies' terms and conditions for short-term assignments were different from those for business trips, and also for fully-fledged expatriate assignments. Interestingly, only 59 per cent of Asia-based companies make this distinction (McMorrow, op cit). It is seen that the differences between standard and short-term assignments are evident in the levels and quality of housing, goods and services received, incentives, home trips and home-country expenses. It seems, the major attraction of short-term assignments is the mutual satisfaction that both employers and employees, and their families can enjoy. If such an assignment is suitable, the company can effect cost savings while the employee can avoid uprooting family members from jobs, schools and friendships. This is an excellent example of what Pucik (op cit) termed a demand-driven process.

It is desirable that companies focus on alternatives to costly long-term overseas positions – we mentioned above that using an agent is one possibility; another possibility is the short-term assignment. Even so, it is accepted that due to the high cost of moving expatriates to and from a foreign assignment, it is generally more economical to keep them overseas for a few years rather than to rotate several people through the position to gain experience.

Why not rely on local staff?

The duration of stay is dependent upon the continuation of the perceived need to have an expatriate in the overseas firm, and the fulfilment of the training and transition plans for the local staff. The employment of local staff throughout the overseas firm brings its own set of benefits since they understand the local business environment and know-how to transact their business most effectively. They are from the local culture and know the nuances that are important in the country, and they thus provide valid insight into local marketing, sales and product development. 'Local people knew the local situation better than foreigners and were therefore better placed to handle marketing', said Jacob Varghese, Deputy Managing Director of Communications Concept, '...expatriates were not worth the hefty salaries and allied perks given to them when in many Third World countries' (quoted in Gachamba, 1999).

But using local staff also has its challenges. Local talented people may be few and far between, and they need training to understand the corporate culture of the home office. This applies particularly to the acquisition of good Chinese staff. Furthermore, there are few HR managers of outside MNCs who are experts in these lands: as a consequence, very few foreign companies in China have their act together. When they started-up in China most of the foreign companies would leave HRM of the locals to their Chinese partners, because the outsiders thought the insiders could handle it. But oddly the Chinese partners did not know how to fulfil this function in the IJV. It was found that the Chinese partners had little practice in this function generally, as there were many other persons who traditionally exerted their influence upon the deployment of staff in the original Chinese firm. The party member in the Chinese firm, for instance, could assign a friend to the workplace without consulting his Chinese HRM staff (Warner et al., 1999). Now this attitude is changing slowly.

According to the round table conference on Human Resources in China (1999), we learn that most of the big foreign companies aim at young Chinese graduates for both marketing and engineering jobs. They do not pay too well, but they do give them chances of being trained and the further possibility of a career both in Asia and Europe. These firms seldom use headhunters, for new people approach them knowing the name of the company. Some of the foreign companies use headhunters only for highly specialized qualified people. On the other hand, the situation in small foreign companies is somewhat different. They cannot afford to offer detailed training or a deep career plan, so the Chinese staff would come only if they were offered much more money. Essentially this is the situation in Shanghai and other large metropolitan areas where there is much aggressive competition for qualified staff. Small firms state, 'if no bonus is given – once, perhaps twice per year – then there is no work done': sometimes the bonus is in non-pay benefits like subsidized housing. Retention of local staff is going to be the big issue – and ever-higher salaries will not be the answer, hence the need for other forms of bonus payments. A 1997 survey of 49 Foreign Invested Enterprises (FIEs) in five major Chinese cities reported average staff turnover rates of 13 per cent for both managers and non-managerial staff, happily down from an overall average of 16 per cent in the previous year (cited in Goodhall and Burgers, 1999). The highest level of managerial turnover at 17.5 per cent was found in Shenzhen. In general, surveys of Chinese companies have consistently positioned staff retention among their top three problems.

What are the factors that aggravate staff turnover in China? Goodhall and Burgers (op cit) on a survey of 80 MBA graduates from the China Europe Management Institute (CEMI) in Beijing (the original location of what is now the China Europe International Business School (CEIBS), Shanghai) reported that almost half the reasons given by their MBA graduates for leaving jobs related to their lack of perceived development opportunities and dissatisfaction with their interpersonal relationships compared to less than 15 per cent who mentioned poor salaries.

One of the most surprising findings, given the traditional importance in China of opportunities for personal growth and development, is the low level of attention paid by companies to career planning. Only a quarter of those who were going to leave knew the company career plan, and even for those who were planning to stay, only just over half knew the career plan. There will be companies that have a career plan, but have failed to communicate it; and if it is not communicated, then in the employees' perception, it does not exist. Kidd and Teramoto (1995) found exactly the same phenomenon in the UK. Here it was the Japanese CEOs (being the expatriates in the UK in this case) who were not communicating company plans to their UK line managers so causing them anxiety as to the future of their personal and business lifestyle projections in continuing working for the Japanese firm.

It is very difficult to picture an effective personnel retention plan in Chinese firms without embracing the strategic focus of their highly qualified top managers – both local and (if appropriate) expatriate. They have to prepare their forecast of the future of the company, especially to link within the plans of the MNC as one of its IJVs. This planning need, for both the operations of the firm as well as its human stock, is further confirmed in a study published by the Asian Business Consortium (Tung, 1999). Of course, an effective personnel retention plan should consider proper levels of responsibility and the related supervisory methods that empower this. The latter aspect, however, becomes confusingly many-sided in a cross-cultural environment. Both Chinese and expatriate managers would need to know how their specific and diffuse cultures might clash, and the implications of high and low power distance of boss ⇔ subordinate relations (Hofstede, op cit).

The demand for managers in Asia

It is easy to say that there will be no decrease in the demand for good quality indigenous executives in China – ever. China continues to see annual GDP growth of at least 6 per cent; and China's economy is one of the least affected in Asia by the recent regional currency crisis. Demand for good quality managers and executives have at the moment vastly exceeded supply.

Nanjing University conducted a survey recently which showed that though China has a huge labour force, there is a shortage of skilled managers (cited by Wong, 1998). Their Universities produce fewer than 1000 MBA graduates per year (and sometimes Western academics doubt the calibre of many of the awarding institutions). Many senior Western managers in China estimate that 20 000 well-trained managers are needed to meet their growing business demands – they note that of the 44.65 million Chinese people who have either a technical secondary education or professional certificates, only 8.85 million can bring proven management qualifications to a multinational company. But their qualifications are well below the crucial MBA level.

The extremely rapid pace of FDI in China has contributed to the current shortage of local skilled labour, and the resulting problem of staff retention. Meanwhile, 'localizing will take 10–15 years', says an expatriate. 'It will need time', agrees headhunter Helen Tantau . . . 'now you just don't have enough local people with experience. You need expatriates, but [the need is] lesser and lesser. Many companies now cannot function without them, but you have to show local people that they have a potential for growth. If foreign management always occupies the first line, good people will leave your company, because they see there is no real chance for them. You have to show them, there is a future for them' (Round Table Conference, op cit). However, one of us suggests that as information flows more openly into and out of China relating to its customs, culture and business needs the localizing time will decrease quite rapidly (Kidd, 1994). Although his research related to Japanese manufacturing firms in Europe, it was noted that the acclimatization period of local staff to working with the Japanese expatriates, which may have been up to 10 years in the late 1970s, became four to five years by the 1990s. Allegedly this is through a fuller awareness of each of the others needs, by word of mouth, by the media and by business education programmes.

A particularly worrying phenomenon is observable in modern Japan. Many young persons are opting to be jobless, to not have any long-term plans, and certainly to not join the cadres in the major firms who enjoy a job-for-life. They are called *freeter*[1] – and they earn enough money for their lifestyle in temporary jobs: they are a growing cause for concern, and features upon them are written even in the popular press – note a reprint from the *Asahi Shimbun* in the *Asahi Evening News* (Tuesday, 4 January 2000: 5). What concerns us in this study is that breakdown of the traditional 'apprenticeship' of the Japanese firms which ensured a well-trained and learned workforce able to confer deeply while at home or abroad. This was the bedrock upon which Nonaka and Takeuchi (1995) based their seminal work on the knowledge creating company. The Japanese firms depend, as do all firms, on the quality of their workers – and now their youth across the country seemingly do not wish to work and acquire the skills traditionally associated with Japanese staff. It follows, that if this breakdown continues, it will certainly affect the ability of outside firms operating in Japan to enrol suitably qualified staff (either male or female) and it may cripple the advance of technological development of the local Japanese firms as well.

Will expatriates become a thing of the past?

The lower-than-expected reward from the business environment in China generally is making overseas companies look very closely at their investment costs. In many cases, after a decade of intensive capital injections, multinationals are expecting better profits. Now they are imposing careful cost controls. This aspect becomes a great challenge to executives hired in China since they assume the outside firm to be rich. Further, the growing costs of both compensation and fringe benefits offered to their expatriates greatly concern the parent companies.

Sending an employee from USA to work in China has always carried a big price tag. There are plenty of expatriate-related costs, for instance:

1 Direct labour cost

- employee benefits, based upon salary in dollars; and
- foreign tax payments to the PRC.

2 Hardship premiums

- foreign service salary premiums;
- lost spouse income needs to have compensation;
- moving expenses for the household goods;
- home maintenance, if the original house is retained by the expatriate; or, home-selling price guarantees if that house is sold;
- travel allowance to provide the expatriate and family one or more return visits to home; and
- other vacation, 'rest and recuperation' allowances.

3 Housing costs

- home security-systems installation and associated monthly charges;
- limousine and driver's cost in country;
- maid service in country;
- country club and other in-country benefits; and
- private schooling for children, usually back home, incurring holiday flight costs.

On average, the total cost of an expatriate will range from US$250 000 to 500 000 – a rule of thumb being three to four times the expatriate's salary. Others suggest international assignments can cost up to $2 million each (Gregersen and Black, 1999). They went on to say that 10–20 per cent of managers returned home early at a cost of $300 000 each comprising costs that were both personal direct costs, and which also included opportunity losses due to forgone business. Further, they said, of those expatriates staying the course only one-third performed up to expectations.

Relocating cost is generally the main cost item. For instance, the cities of Shanghai, Beijing, Guangzhou and Shenzhen are setting the trends for demand in human resources in China and these cities are intrinsically quite costly. Further, these cities are becoming particularly important for the financial services industry, and are attractive centres for consumer-based industries like health care, retailing and insurance. All such rapid development helps inflate housing costs. Interestingly, in addition to local executives, developing local businesses are creating a new and strong demand for qualified expatriates in addition to their demand for highly qualified local staff (needing their high bonus levels). One example is quoted by the French Chamber of Commerce and Industry in Beijing. They say that there are around 500 French expatriates based in China, about 50 per cent are stationed in Shanghai, 40 per cent in Beijing, and the remaining 10 per cent spread across the country.

Why hire these expensive expatriates? 'Expatriates are here to protect the interest of the foreign partner', says a businessman, 'you need a foreigner to do this. For instance, you can't ask the Chinese staff of your bank to make a risk analysis as they are unfamiliar with the need for this technique' (Round Table Conference, op cit).

Final notes

Some parent companies move all expatriate-related costs on to their subsidiaries, but not all expenses billed to the subsidiaries may be considered tax deductible; in the PRC such expenses are within the tax laws. This approach causes angst in the subsidiaries, as they have to cover these costs before being able to declare a profit to the group account – and, as we have seen earlier, some Asian accounting is not transparent so further confounding harmony.

The low return on international human resource investment and the high opportunity costs associated with international assignments have far reaching impact on the global strategy of multinational companies. It is reported that 20 per cent of all repatriated managers and executives who performed well overseas leave their employers within two years of return to their home base. This is due to many anxieties, one of which is their uncertain job status, coupled with personal issues related to resuming life at home. As Tung shows, expatriates not only participate in international assignments in order to manage overseas projects, but also to advance their overall career development (Tung, 1999). Essentially, these global assignments are seen as a means by which they develop their core competencies and their skills. They are individuals with highly developed interpersonal, intercultural and managerial human resources, and in effect they become world class individuals who are in high demand by all multinationals. Moreover, they possess the attributes of the potential CEO for the twenty-first century. From this point on, global companies know they need to increase the support they offer to the returning expatriates to ensure their retention – and these offers need to be across a spectrum of salary and non-salary benefits to foster the integration of the returnee.

Indeed, we accept that these individuals are not of the common mould. They have a strong ability to work in quite isolated situations taking sweeping decisions that obviously affect their local venture, but which have repercussions round their MNC. Psychologically they have to be strong individuals. They have to have confidence in their ability to progress upwards in their chosen firm, notwithstanding their remote placement. In their outposts they will be out of touch with the gossip and the chat in the corridors of power, they will not have the proximity to meet their superiors on a casual basis so they will have to believe that their job – well done – will be reflected in future benefits. We noted above that a part of the expatriate package contains trips back home, and it has been noted that the Japanese managers in their joint ventures in the USA and Europe had frequent trips, often monthly, to their Japanese Head Quarters (HQ) (Kidd and Teramoto, op cit). These trips were partly to help embed the expatriates' data in the HQ data set. But partly they were to maintain interpersonal networking associations thereby remaining in touch with the subtleties of senior managerial review and appraisal. In China, we have noted above, this mechanism is the maintenance of *guanxi*. So, to be removed from this touchy-feely management mechanism, to be outposted, and to remain confident of his or her promotion prospects, the expatriate must have outstanding capabilities.

Summary

It has to be agreed that we are ill prepared for life! We are usually trained only in technical subjects, math, languages and science in schools, and later if we get to colleges and universities, we become more and more specialized and focused upon minute details in our research. We are not generally trained in how to live life, to behave interpersonally, or to manage in our workplace. This is learned via a 'kick it and see' process, which is hardly a purposeful method. Of course, we also have academic research upon psychology, organizational behaviour and sociology and we study how expatriates have evolved in their jobs. Hopefully in this chapter we would have added a little to the appraisal of how the expatriate and his or her employer can be better joined in their joint venture. And in turn, we hope their learning also will benefit their joint venture partners.

We conclude that the needs of the expatriates have to be understood as the realization of the needs of both parties (organizations and organizational systems), not just as a means of better processing high-cost individuals as expatriates. These persons are indeed needed in many circumstances, but we must also use the lower-cost host-country staff to act as agents for their paymasters, and we must develop the trust of both sides.

Organizations just entering the global marketplace will have to find their own best combination of expatriates and locals. The time it takes to localize an operation, integrating expatriates and host-country individuals is as unique as is each company. Regardless of each firm's strategy, choosing, managing and compensating employees around the globe is no small issue.

Note

1 *Freeter* – is coined from two words. The English word *free*, and the German word *arbeiter* (part-time worker) (*Asahi Evening News*, op cit).

References

Baiman, S. (1982) 'Agency theory in management accounting: a survey', *Journal of Accounting Literature*, pp. 154–213.

Baiman, S. (1996) 'Agency theory in managerial accounting: a second look', *Accounting, Organisations and Society*, 15(4): 341–71.

Cantwell, J. A. and O. Janne (1999) 'Technological globalisation and innovative centres: the role of corporate technological leadership and location hierarchy', *Research Policy*, 28: 119–44.

Darlington, G. (1996) 'National cultures and the values of organisational employees', in P. Joynt and M. Warner (eds) *Managing Across Cultures: Issues and Perspectives*, London: International Thompson, pp. 92–104.

De George, R. T. (1993) *Competing with Integrity in International Business*, New York: Oxford University Press.

Derr, B. C. and G. R. Oddou (1991) 'Are US multinationals adequately preparing future American leaders for global competition?', *International Journal of Human Resource Management*, 2(2): 227–44.

Driffield, N. L. and M. C. Munday (2000) 'Industrial performance, agglomeration, and foreign investment in the UK', *Journal of International Business Studies*, forthcoming.

Frazer, A. J. (1998) 'A scouting report on training options', *The China Business Review*. See http://www.uschina.org/cbr/990/fraz er.htm

Gabriel, P. (1967) *The international transfer of corporate skills*, Boston: Harvard University Press.

Gachamba, C. W. (1999) Marketing Society Divided over Expatriate. *Africa News*, 26 February, p. 1.

Garelli, S. (1992) 'The competitive impact of values', *The World Competitiveness Report 1992*, Presented at the 12th World Economic Forum, Laussane, Switzerland, pp. 4–7.

Goodhall, K. and W. Burgers (1999) 'Frequent fliers? Chinese managers in a turbulent job market', China European International Business School, Shanghai. Internal paper. See http://www.ceibs.edu/business_in_china/human_resources/ff2.htm

Gray, S. J. (1996) 'International comparisons of business performance: measurement and disclosure issues', *International Review of Business*, 1(1): 1–15.

Gray, S. J. and H. M. Vint (1995) 'The impact of culture on accounting disclosures: some international evidence', *Asia-Pacific Journal of Accounting*, 2: 33–43.

Gregersen, H. B. and J. S. Black (1999) 'The right way to manage expatriates', *Harvard Business Review* (Mar/Apr): 52–60.

Haley, G. T., Tan, C. T. and U. C. V. Haley (1998) *New Asian Emperors: The Overseas Chinese, their Strategies and Competitive Advantages*, Oxford, Butterworth-Heinemann.

Haley, U. C. V. (2000) 'Family support for expatriate employees', in U. C. V. Haley (ed.) *Strategic Management in the Asia Pacific. Harnessing Regional and Organizational Change for Competitive Advantage*, Oxford, Butterworth-Heinemann, pp. 346–47.

Hays, R. (1994) 'Expatriate selection: insuring success and avoiding failure', *Journal of International Business Studies*, 5(1): 25–37.

Hofstede, G. (1980) *Culture's Consequences: International Differences in Work-related Values*, London: Sage Publications.

Hofstede, G. (1991) *Cultures and Organisations: Software of the Mind*, London: McGraw-Hill.

Hoppe, H. M. (1993) 'The effects of national culture on the theory and practice of managing R&D professionals abroad', *R&D Management*, 23(4): 313–25.

Jing, H. and S. Xu (1996) 'Empirical interpretation on several theoretical issues in culture research', *Philosophy Development*, 3. Reprinted in *Xinhua Wenzhai*, 6: 158–60 (in Chinese).

Kanter, R. M. (1995) 'Thriving locally in the global environment', *Harvard Business Review* (Sep/Oct): 151–61.

Kelly, J. and C. Cook (1999) *Mergers and Acquisition Integration*, Available in the 'Virtual Library'. See http://www.kpmg.co.uk

Kidd, J. B. (1994) 'Globalisation through localisation: reflections on the Japanese production subsidiaries in the United Kingdom', in H. Schütte (ed.) *The Global Competitiveness of the Asian Firm*, New York: St Martins Press, pp. 265–88.

Kidd, J. B. and Y. Teramoto (1995) 'Can the Japanese localise? – a study of Japanese production subsidiaries in the UK', in S.-J. Park and M. Jovanovic (eds) *What is Behind the Japanese miracle*? London: Megatrends IEC, pp. 136–52.

Kishi, M. (1998) 'The establishment of international standards: focus on the financial aspects of Japanese foreign direct investment in Asian countries', in Y. Takahashi, M. Murata and K. M. Rahman (eds) *Management Strategies of Multinational Corporations in Asian Markets*, Tokyo: Chuo University Press, pp. 199–210.

Kogut, B. and H. Singh (1988) 'The effect of national culture on choice of entry mode', *Journal of International Business Studies*, 19(3): 411–32.

Lou, Y. (1997) 'Guanxi: principles, philosophies and implications', *Human Systems Management*, 9: 1–9.

Lovett, S., Simmons, L. C. and R. Kali (1999) 'Guanxi versus the market: ethics and efficiency', *Journal of International Business Studies*, 30(2): 231–48.

Lu, J. (1998) 'Characteristics and performance of Japanese FDI in China', in *Proceedings of the 13th LVMH Conference, INSEAD* on *Asian Foreign Investment in Asia*, 6–7 February, pp. 168–90.

McMorrow, V. G. (1998) 'Short-term assignees: when to use them, how to pay them', *1997–98 World-wide Survey of International Assignment Policies and Practices*, Organisation Resources Counselors (ORC).

Nonaka, I. and H. Takeuchi (1995) *The Knowledge-Creating Company*, Oxford: Oxford University Press.

Oster, S. M. (1994) *Modern Competitive Analysis*, New York: Oxford University Press.

Parkhe, A. (1991) 'Interfirm diversity, organisational learning, and longevity in global strategic alliances', *Journal of International Business Studies*, 22: 579–601.

Parkhe, A. (1993) 'Strategic alliance structuring: a game theoretic and transaction cost examination of interfirm cooperation', *Academy of Management Journal*, 36(4): 794–829.

Phillips, L. D. and C. N. Wright (1977) 'Cultural differences in viewing uncertainty and assessing probabilities', in H. Jungermann and G. de Zeeuw (eds) *Decision Making and Change in Human Affairs*, Dordrecht: D Reidel Publishing.

Pucik, V. (1992) 'Globalisation and human resource management', in V. Pucik, N. Tichy and C. Barnett (eds) *Globalising Management: Creating and Leading the Competitive Organisation*, New York: Wiley.

Richter, F.-J. (1999) *Strategic Networks: The Art of Japanese Interfirm Co-operation*, Binghamton, NY: International Business Press.

Richter, F.-J. (2000) 'A perspective on Asian management', in F.-J. Richter (ed.) *The Asian Economic Catharsis. How Asian Firms Bounce Back from Crisis*, New York: Quorum, pp. 1–7.

Round Table Conference (1999) *Human Resources in China*. Organized by the Dutch Business Association, Shanghai, 27 November. See http://www.ceibs.edu/businessinchina/humanresources/hrdba1.htm

Rugman, A. M. and A. Verbeke (1992) 'A note on the transnational solution and the transaction cost theory of multinational strategic management', *Journal of International Business Studies*, 23(4): 761–72.

Salter, S. B. and F. Niswander (1995) 'Cultural influences on the development of accounting systems internationally', *Journal of Inemational Business Studies*, 26(2): 379–98.

Schwartz, S. H. (1990) 'Individualism-collectivism: critique and proposed refinements', *Journal of Cross-Cultural Psychology*, 21: 139–57.

Scoville, W. (1951) 'Minority migrations and the diffusion of technology', *Journal of Economic History*, pp. 15–38.

Sen, M. (1993) 'Does business ethics make economic sense?', in P. M. Minus (ed.) *The Ethics of Business in Global Economics*, Eindhoven: Kluwer Academic Press, pp. 51–56.

Smith, P. (1996) 'National cultures and the values of organisational employees', in P. Joynt and M. Warner (eds) *Managing Across Cultures: Issues and perspectives*, London: International Thompson, pp. 92–104.

Smith, P. B. and M. H. Bond (1993) *Social Psychology across Cultures: Analyses and Perspectives*, Hemel Hempstead: Harvester-Wheatsheaf.

Smith, P. B. and M. F. Peterson (1994) *Leadership as Event Management: A Cross-country Survey based upon Middle Managers from 25 Countries*, A symposium of the International Congress of Applied Psychology, Madrid.

Thom, R. (1923) *Logos et Theories des Catastrophes*, Paris: Patino.

Trompenaars, F. (1993) *Riding the Waves of Culture: Understanding Cultural Diversity in Business*, London: The Economist Books.

Tung, R. (1999) *The Expatriate Employee: Who, What and Why*, ABC Bulletin. See http://www.canasiaweb.com

UNCTAD (1999) *World Investment Report 1999: Trends and Determinants*, Geneva, United Nations.

Walsh, J. (1998) 'A World War on bribery', *Time*, 22 June.

Wang, K. (1992) *What is Value*? Zhangshan University Press, pp. 134–35.

Warner, M. Goodhall, K. and D. Z. Ding (1999) 'The 'myth' of human resource management in China', in M. Warner (ed.) *China's Managerial Revolution*, London: Frank Cass, pp. 223–37.

Williamson, O. (1975) *Markets and Hierarchies: Analysis and Antitrust Implications*, New York, NY: Free Press.

Wong, V. (1998) 'The needs for executives in the "Paris of the Orient"', in the French Business Associations' journal *The Hong Kong Echo*, Hong Kong, July.

Yang, K. S. (1988) 'Will societal modernisation eventually eliminate cross-cultural psychological differences?', in M. H. Bond (ed.) *The Cross-Cultural Challenge to Social Psychology*, Newbury: Sage.

Yang, M. (1994) *Gifts, Favors and Banquets: The Art of Social Relations in China*. Ithica, NY: Cornell University Press.

Zarzeski, M. T. (1996) 'Spontaneous harmonisation effects of culture and market forces on accounting disclosure practices', *Accounting Horizons*, 10 March, pp. 18–37.

Part 3

Post-crisis Governmental Strategies

8

Vietnam: Is *Doi Moi* the Way Forward in Post-crisis Asia?

Malcolm Cooper

Introduction

In the Vietnam of the 1970s and 1980s, government-policy discussions focused around the development of a liberalized market-oriented economy (through *doi moi*, or renovation) that would bring the country greater prosperity and higher standards of living (Beresford, 1988; 1997; Cooper, 1997; 2000; Le Dang Doanh and McCarty, 1997). From 1986, restrictions on private investment were gradually lifted and foreign investment and ownership encouraged in line with similar trends that were occurring throughout Asia. However, opening up the economy was not easy in the beginning as Vietnam lacked capital, experience, infrastructure and a trained labour force. Moreover, at that time Vietnam was virtually isolated from the outside world as a result of an American embargo on trade. Despite these constraints, so effective was the *doi moi* strategy that the country had by 1992 passed into a stage of rapid economic development. At the end of 1994 the American embargo was lifted, and in 1995 Vietnam was accepted as full member of Association of Southeast Asian Nations (ASEAN).

Real GDP per capita continued to rise in Vietnam even during the Asian economic crisis of 1997–99. While down from an 8.8 per cent expansion in 1997 to 4.0 per cent in 1999, growth in Real GDP nevertheless remained ahead of population growth during this period, meaning that the Vietnamese economy overall performed relatively well during the economic downturn experienced by the more developed nations of Asia. This positive trend has continued in the post-crisis period but does disguise the fact that Vietnam's economic development started from an extremely low base, so that once it began, high rates of growth would be expected for some time while it caught up with the rest of the world. At the latter point, growth in the economy under the conditions favoured by *doi moi* would begin to depend more on the relative efficiency of local industries vis-à-vis international competitors than on unmet local demand.

At this point also, governmental responses to the efficiency question become critical. In the post-crisis period, for example, the pace of structural reform has remained slow, and the country's business sector is denied both financing and access to markets through slow reform of the banking sector. Administrative and legal barriers are also causing costly delays for foreign investors and are raising doubts about Vietnam's ability to maintain the flow of foreign investment capital previously used to offset rapid increases in imports.

This chapter investigates the changing character of Vietnam's post-crisis economy from the point of view of governmental responses to the problems facing it, discussing the major themes and issues that have emerged since the watershed years of the Asian economic crisis. It outlines the economic, cultural and environmental dimensions of the government's management of the economy of Vietnam, the approaches taken in responding to the twin problems of the crisis and the needs of the country's internal economic restructuring, and the likely short- to medium-term future of Vietnam on the Asian and world economic stages. The chapter concludes by commenting on the relevance of the policy of *doi moi* to the country in the post-crisis world of Asia.

The Asian crisis and its aftermath

While it is not the province of this chapter to analyse in detail the antecedents and development of the Asian economic crisis and its aftermath, some comments are appropriate in order to set the scene for a discussion of the response of the Vietnamese economy and government. Causes for the crisis can be classified into long- and short-term (Chong, 1998), and even the name of the crisis has changed over time – from the Asian currency crisis at the time of the Thai IMF rescue package in 1997, to the Asian financial crisis in early 1998, and finally to the Asian economic crisis by mid-1998. Nevertheless, it is generally accepted that the crisis had its beginnings in an attack on the value of the Thai baht and its decoupling from the US dollar and devaluation in July 1997, an attack which quickly spread to other regional foreign exchange markets, and the subsequent fall-out experienced by the region's banks, especially those of Indonesia, Japan and South Korea (Morgan, 1988).

Much of the crisis can be attributed to weak financial sectors, reliance on overseas borrowings to fund public infrastructure, export dependence on a narrow range of products, weak domestic markets, overcapacity amongst the region's manufacturers (e.g., South Korean *chaebol*), cronyism and deflation in the Japanese economy. Other factors, such as the growing ability of international money markets to shift enormous amounts of capital on a 24-hour basis, led regional politicians such as Dr Mahathir Mohammed to pin some blame on currency speculators. While the judgement of history will determine the relative importance of these factors, it is likely that significance must be given to an ongoing financial weakness in the Japanese economy as perhaps the central cause, coupled with unsound financial practices throughout the Asian region.

Solutions to the crisis were found in IMF-brokered assistance (although not without significant criticism of the Fund's rigidity and arrogance), the official floating of currencies, new fiscal disciplines and the creation of reserves, and (fortuitously) rising commodity prices. Demand for Asian products in America, especially in the hi-tech electronics area, also rapidly grew and has fuelled the recovery of South Korea and Malaysia especially. The remedies chosen have been successful in the main, in fact so much so that Asia's economic turnaround has been spectacular in the six months to March 2000. South Korea's GDP for example, rose by almost 11 per cent during 1999, and its output is now above pre-crisis levels. By the end of 2000, Malaysia and Thailand look to be in the same position, and portfolio capital flows to these economies have once again begun to grow rapidly (*The Economist*, 14 April 2000).

The answer to the question of whether or not the region has removed all of its underlying economic weaknesses, and which methods (if any) have been most successful, is left to other commentators in this volume. Suffice to say here that governments have embarked on financial restructuring that will assist regional economies to resist the pressures of 1997–98 in the longer term, and demand for the products of Asia in the American market continues to underpin the region's recovery. That recovery will assist the government and people of Vietnam in their quest for continuing economic development.

Vietnam – the nation

Vietnam, situated in the eastern part of Southeast Asia, is a country of some 78 million people at a point of convergence for many ethnic groups, and a crossroads of different civilizations (Cooper, 1997). Its rugged topography adds another factor to ethnic complexity, in that many minority groups now inhabit the highlands, having been displaced from more favourable areas by the dominant Viet population. Fifty-four ethnic groups inhabit Vietnam; the Kinh or Viet, the most numerous, accounting for 87 per cent (68 million) of the total population. Other major groups such as the Tay, Thai, Muong, Hoa and Khmer number in excess of 1 million each, but others are much smaller. To the North, the country has an 1150 km border with China, a 2600 km border to the West with Laos and Cambodia, and a total land area of 329 560 km^2. About the size of Italy, the country is divided into 58 provinces and three independent municipalities, Greater Ha Noi, Greater Ho Chi Minh City and Greater Hai Phong. With a significant degree of local autonomy, these local authorities can and do vary in their approach to economic development, political reform, foreign investment, and the attraction of foreign tourists. Since July 1995, Vietnam has been a member of the ASEAN.

One of the strengths of the country lies in its very high degree of literacy, despite over 70 per cent of the workforce still being employed in rural areas. A reported literacy rate of 94 per cent puts Vietnam above most neighbouring countries, and health indicators are also better. One of the reasons for this is that the reforms of the *doi moi* programme from 1986 included the lifting of restrictions on private investment and long-term land leases, which in turn led to substantial rises in the standard of living of the rural population. On the down side, budget deficits have also meant a rapid decline in state-employee salaries, and a consequent large rise in underemployment and unemployment in the cities. Pressure from a young population reaching employable age will exacerbate this for some time to come.

Vietnam's economic development has been gradual since reunification in 1975. The collapse of the Soviet Bloc and partial market development prior to 1986 saw rapid inflation and brought realization that comprehensive reforms were necessary. The year 1986 saw the introduction of reforms (*doi moi*) that were intended to eventually lead to a liberalized market-oriented economy that would bring the country greater prosperity and higher standards of living (Cooper, 1997; 2000). From 1986, restrictions on private investment were gradually lifted and foreign investment and ownership encouraged in line with similar experiments that were occurring throughout Asia. A variety of institutional reforms have been introduced since that time which have produced a supply-side response in the economy, and rapid growth. Substantial movement towards trade liberalization laid the foundation for further growth prior to 1997 and the onset of the so-called Asian economic crisis (Le Dang Doanh and McCarty, 1997). So, how did these changes benefit the Vietnamese economy during and after that crisis?

The Vietnamese economy in recent times

Although little statistical information is available for the post-1997 period, it is possible to sketch the development of the Vietnamese economy during the three years to 2000, in preparation for a discussion of the continuing debate on its direction. This debate remains hotly contested in both the popular media within Vietnam, and in Asian regional economic journals and meetings. Indeed, as late as the beginning of April 2000 no less a person than General Vo Nguyen Giap called for a stronger commitment to the economic reforms first introduced in 1986 (Watkin, 8 April 2000).

There is no doubt that the Vietnamese economy performed at an annual growth rate of Real GDP similar to that recorded in the so-called Asian Tigers throughout the 1990s (Barnes, 2000). Combined with a slowly falling rate of population increase, this growth led to continuously rising Real GDP per capita during the decade (Table 8.1). This combination of circumstances led the international community to label Vietnam as the next Tiger (*The Economist*, 8 January 2000). Throughout the recent decline and resurgence in Asia's economic fortunes that growth has continued, with the latest budget figures for 1999 indicating a growth in nominal GDP (in Dong) of 27 per cent since 1997 (Haughton, 2000). If accurate, this level of performance indicates an underlying strength in the economy and quite a sharp rise in GDP per capita since the fall in the growth rate of GDP during 1998–99.

The market-oriented economic reforms implemented under *doi moi* assisted in the generation of a high rate of growth by shifting resources out of agriculture and into industry and services, and by influencing industry towards producing for export. So much so that agriculture's share of GDP fell from around 55 per cent in 1981 to 23 per cent in

Table 8.1 Real GDP per capita (purchasing power parity)

	1994	1995	1996	1997	1998	1999
Real GDP increase	8.8	9.5	9.3	8.2	3.5	4.0
Total population (millions)	71.62	72.81	73.98	75.12	76.24	77.31(e)
Real GDP per capita (1990 USD, purchasing parity)	1151	1240	1334	1429	1458	1770

Note: (e) stands for estimated.
Sources: CIA World Factbook, IMF World Outlook, UN Statistical Yearbook, various years.

1998. Simultaneously, the contribution of the industrial and services sectors rose from 20 and 25 per cent of GDP in 1981, to 34 and 43 per cent respectively by 1998 (IMF, 1999). New enterprises in clothing and textiles, tourism, retailing and trade services initially spurred these changes, with transport, marketing, and professional services also adding strength in recent years.

In addition to high economic growth rates and rapid industrialization, *doi moi* has achieved a strong measure of macroeconomic stability. Restrictions imposed on domestic credit expansion and the financing of the government's budget deficit through bond issues helped to reduce domestic inflation, as did heavy FDI, largely from East Asia, and reform of state-owned enterprises (SOEs) (Dung, 1996). Indeed, the latter were reduced from some 12 000 in 1990 to about 6000 in 1996, without loss of production (EAAU, 1997). Large military-run companies are also emerging, including those run purely for profit. These companies are operating in the mining, power generation, infrastructure and building construction, textiles, fishing and tourism sectors, alongside those engaged in national defence enterprises and economic activities by local defence forces (as a subsidiary task). Large military enterprises are also involved in joint ventures with foreign companies. These enterprises contribute to the reduction of the government's fiscal burden by returning profits to help pay for the armed forces.

The main government reforms assisting the economic system were liberalizing trade, promoting foreign investment, and recognizing private ownership of the means of production. By eliminating internal trade barriers, private transport could develop, and by recognizing private ownership the private retail sector could expand. Increased foreign trade and investment has promoted the development of financial services within the country. Finally, reform of SOE ownership and productivity has meant the creation of large state corporations theoretically able to compete internationally, in priority industries like steel, coal, power and textiles.

Many major American firms operating in Vietnam (Coca-Cola, Ford, Pepsi, Proctor & Gamble) have been forced to target the limited domestic market, however, by the slow breakdown of the restrictive regulatory framework in Vietnam and the lack of normal trading relations with the USA. Others, for example, Nike and its Korean/Taiwanese subsidiaries, have been able to operate through Asian subcontractors and have been able to export much of the products they produce.

Macroeconomic stability and diversification has assisted Vietnam to 'ride out' the worst of the Asian economic crisis, certainly with respect to the rapid decline in FDI, the country has not appeared to have suffered unduly. These achievements, however, mask to some extent the fact that Vietnam remains one of the world's least developed economies, with significant infrastructure and financial problems and a very high concentration of population in rural industries within a small land area. Also, due to a lack of political consensus and the fact that the economy is still basically a state-run enterprise, these reform measures have not been pursued to their logical conclusion. The SOEs in priority sectors, for example, still receive substantial state support through land, credit and regulatory protection, and their full privatization is not seen as desirable. The increases in production that resulted from the amalgamation of SOEs occurred because they benefited from increased market power without having to become more efficient or innovative (Gates, 1996). Furthermore, SOEs control most of the important sectors of the economy and are heavily protected from import competition, while foreign investors wanting to participate in these sectors are restricted to joint ventures with the SOEs in that sector.

Financial markets

Chief amongst the problems faced by the government in implementing further change are the country's underdeveloped financial markets. With a non-convertible currency, a rudimentary banking system and no stock market, Vietnam faces considerable difficulties in financing further growth from either internal savings or foreign capital investment. While a private sector has emerged during the past five years, its development remains both politically contentious and difficult to finance. The development of the sector is not centrally encouraged, which results in hoarding rather than declaration of profits, and the banks deem such firms to be less creditworthy while they do not use the system to deposit profits. In addition, while the formal company tax rate on private sector firms is lower by some 10 per cent than that imposed on SOEs, the tax system as a whole is ambiguous and local authorities have the power to impose ad hoc taxes.

Consequently, the unofficial (shadow or black market) financial system is often the only source of funds for small firms and individuals. Recent estimates have put the size of the unofficial economy at 60 per cent of the total economy (Grant, 1996). Even the advent of foreign banks, in the limited numbers currently allowed, has made little difference. A combination of reserve requirements, turnover tax and profit tax make financial operations very unprofitable for foreign banks, and the rudimentary nature of the financial sector infrastructure referred to above has resulted in appropriate financial instruments and payments systems being too underdeveloped to assist. The bulk of private sector savings goes into the shadow economy, and fewer than 10 per cent of Vietnamese have bank accounts as a result.

In trying to offset these problems, and as part of necessary reforms to the financial system designed to bring the informal economy into the formal system, the government has allowed the formation of Credit Cooperatives and Circles. These operate outside the formal system and are often the only source of funds for private sector businesses and individuals. Collateral remains a problem though, as land cannot be used owing to restricted use rights. This means that interest rates are high in the informal sector, but also that the ability of the formal sector to lend and to provide a real alternative to this shadow economy is severely constrained. Having to lend on the basis of estimated future cash flows is a risky business at any time, made doubly so by the impact on Vietnam's FDI inflows and external trade of the Asian Crisis.

In recognition of these problems, the government moved to further deregulate the financial sector in 1997, just before the Asian economic crisis occurred. Financial institutions were given the ability to trade the Dong at rates 5 per cent above or below the official rate, thus counteracting appreciation pressures resulting from earlier high foreign investment and loan inflows, and the 1996 reforms allowing commercial banks to open foreign currency accounts. By doing this, the government sought to stabilize the currency to avoid dollarization of the economy (EAAU, 1997), and in hindsight this was probably an effective move in relation to the crisis as experienced by other Asian countries, as internal exposure to external currency fluctuations was lessened somewhat and protection was afforded to the commercial banks by increasing their ability to hedge to some extent on foreign currency transactions.

Government debt servicing requirements, while much reduced since restructuring in 1996, remain between 10 and 15 per cent of total spending. Of more concern is management of the rising deficit in net factor services, including interest payments, profit repatriation and dividends on capital (commercial debt) to overseas. In order to contain this, the government has restricted the foreign borrowing power of SOEs, and has sought to raise the economic profile of tourism and the *Viet Kieu* (overseas Vietnamese), both sources of positive balances in the services sector.

Trade, foreign aid and investment

Even with the patchy reforms under *doi moi*, external trade remains one of Vietnam's major difficulties. The import framework is non-transparent, the rules change often, and imports are subject to formal tariffs, reference prices, excise taxes, import licences, quotas and other restrictive practices (Kokko and Zejan, 1996). Exports have been constrained until now by the country's inability to achieve across-the-board Normal Trade Relations status with the USA, potentially a major market, and its historical enmity with China. The USA now takes agro-products at zero-tariff, but textiles, machinery and tourism remain difficult areas, and the rapidly growing Chinese market touchy. As a result, unprocessed primary products, rice, oil, raw materials and minerals dominate exports, while machinery and intermediate goods to build up productive capacity (mainly from East Asia) dominate imports.

One of the consequences of this low-value export and high-value import regime has been increasing pressure on budget deficits and subsidization of imports by FDI and aid dollars, a situation that is reminiscent of the pre-*doi moi* economy and of major concern to central planners. By allowing imports to be financed by deferred letters of credit and by debt financing the country's joint venture investment contributions, Vietnam is building up future debt servicing obligations while not significantly increasing its economic capacity (EAAU, 1997) and is certainly risking renewed inflationary pressures. In addition, although FDI approvals were relatively strong throughout the 1990s, actual disbursements and therefore economic development have been slow in materializing. Only 30 per cent of approved investment has actually occurred, while almost half of all projects approved since 1988 have been withdrawn (EAAU, 1997), largely due to Vietnam's inability to absorb investment. The prevailing pattern of infrastructure problems, lack of construction materials and counterpart budget funds, and complex administrative and legal procedures strongly inhibit aid and FDI contributions to future economic growth.

On the other hand, *doi moi* has persuaded the approximately 2.5 million overseas Vietnamese (*Viet Kieu*) to consider investing in the mother country. Special incentives are offered under the 1996 Foreign Investment Law, and the *Viet Kieu* made most of the US$900 million yearly private transfers to Vietnam in the mid-1990s. By 1999 this had risen to US$1.1 billion, plus about US$200 million in some 50 investment projects (AFP, Ha Noi, 9 March 2000). Government endorsement of this connection is rising despite, perhaps as much again, being sent into Vietnam through non-government channels. Such connections are important for the economic growth of the country, not the least in their potential to aid foreign partnership arrangements with domestic business through common language, contacts and culture.

The overall picture of a bright start followed by disillusionment is noticeable also with respect to the government's attempts to create more favourable conditions for domestic and foreign companies by approving special industrial and export-processing zones. For investors locating in these zones, Vietnam provides in theory at least tax breaks and holidays, duty-free imports and exports, simplified licensing procedures, utilities and preferential dividend remittances. However, the reality is somewhat different. Most of the 60-odd zones have failed to attract large-scale investment, as basic utility infrastructure is not available or insolvent local partners cannot fulfil contractual obligations, while foreign firms find that they are charged a premium for all services, and arbitrary taxes and tariff barriers may be imposed by local bureaucracies at any time (*The Economist*, 8 January 2000).

Perhaps no clearer indication of the real problem with investment in Vietnam comes from a comparison of the Nomura Export Production Zone (EPZ) in Hai Phong with the highly successful zones in Dong Nai and neighbouring provinces (Dapice, 2000). In spite of excellent location and infrastructure, the Nomura EPZ has only six investors not associated with the running of the zone itself, and no new investors were attracted in 1999. Only 800 workers are employed in the zone, which has been operating for two and a half years. The Port of Hai Phong has developed a bad reputation among investors for its cumbersome customs and aggressive tax authorities, and other unhelpful regulatory procedures, and investors avoid it. In contrast, Dong Nai's foreign investment assisted industry grew 25 per cent in the first half of 1999 to $320 million, accounting for 60 per cent of total industrial production in that province, while employing tens of thousands of local workers in clothing and footwear companies (Dapice, 2000). Dong Nai has a good reputation among investors as a place where the authorities want to help solve problems, not create them. Rather than aim for a small number of large, costly and inefficient projects with few jobs, Dong Nai has concentrated on attracting smaller, low-cost producers that can tap export markets. An ability to export means that capital is used carefully and labour is used more intensively. It also means that sales are limited by the efficiency of the producer, not the size of the small local market. The Dong Nai model is therefore more like Taiwan's, which has continued to perform well throughout the Asian crisis.

The US–Vietnam Bilateral Trade Agreement

Besides Vietnam, only five countries did not enjoy Normal Trading Relations status (NTR) with the USA prior to July 2000 – North Korea,

Cuba, Iraq, Yugoslavia and Libya. With the signing of a Bilateral Trade Agreement (BTA) between the two countries will come both NTR and lower tariffs on Vietnamese exports to the USA once the agreement comes into effect in 2001. Commentators suggest that duty on Vietnamese goods will drop from an average of 40 per cent to an average of 3 per cent (Reed Irvine, 2000). So what will be the net effect of this change in policy by both governments on the Vietnamese economy?

When Cambodia began trading with the USA on NTR terms in 1997–98, that country's textile exports to the American market increased by over 2000 per cent. Vietnam has also proven that it can produce quality textile products for developed markets (exports to Japan in 1998 exceeded US$300 million), and stands ready to absorb export demand in excess of quota from Asian countries, including China. A marked growth in textile exports could be expected during the first year of NTR status, before quotas are placed on Vietnam's textile exports in line with those of other Asian countries. Footwear producers should also see marked gains, especially makers like Nike whose existing output from Vietnam has been restricted by prohibitively high duties in the American market. In all, the World Bank estimates that Vietnam's export earnings will rise by some US$800 million in the first year of NTR status alone (Reed Irvine, 2000: 3).

However, while there will be short-term benefits for Vietnamese and foreign invested exporters, the BTA is much more historic and important for the reason that it will force the government to make long overdue changes to the way it manages the economy. For the first time, the government's freedom of action will be constrained by a detailed system of commitments on the liberalization of its economy. Indeed, to improve transparency, Vietnam must provide advance notice of all laws and regulations relating to matters covered in the agreement. If a particular ministry or provincial government fails to abide by the agreement's provisions, there are mechanisms for review that could ultimately see NTR status revoked. This will have a profound effect on the progress of promised legal and economic reforms.

Relations between the central government and the provinces

Nowhere is this more apparent than in the relationships between central and local authorities. The capacity of the central government to manage the economy is affected by uneven regional development and semi-autonomous regional administrations. Regional autarchy is an acknowledged problem, exacerbated by the low revenue raising ability of the centre, and a tendency to the formation of local networks based on family, party and business connections in a protected local economy. Similarly, central government attempts to equalize income differentials resulting from the emergence of wide regional disparities has led to resentment over cross-subsidization and privilege (Beresford, 1997). The central government will have to address the extension of market-oriented reforms in regional markets if it is to ensure success in modernizing the national economy sufficiently to achieve membership of the WTO in due course.

The environment

The economy also suffers from inadequate attention to environmental concerns, although these are now receiving greater attention. As the economy's growth rate accelerated during the 1990s, the country's legacy of overloaded colonial-period water supply and drainage systems, narrow roads, and heavily polluted industrial zones threw up not only infrastructure problems for new investors, but also environmental problems. But while the country's institutional frameworks for dealing with environmental problems remain underdeveloped, pollution and congestion are only dealt with when they become obvious bottlenecks to further economic growth (Beresford, 1997). This could cause problems with respect to aid donors and investment, as increasingly, aid programmes are being tied to effective environmental protection outcomes.

Hi-tech industries

One measure of the likely ability of any economy to grow strongly in the twenty-first century is the emphasis put on developing an industrial base in modern technology. The Vietnamese government has plans to establish a hi-tech park outside Ha Noi, by 2010, but like many of Vietnam's plans, it is a reality only on paper. The necessary infrastructure will take years to acquire, aid in this area is limited, thus limiting available capital, and the government has a monopoly on Internet access. Extremely high telecommunications costs and numerous firewalls – set up to make much of the Internet inaccessible – make the development of a significant software industry problematic. Nevertheless, there are many Vietnamese subcontracting software development tasks from foreign programmers, and a number of Silicon Valley and Indian software development companies have a presence in the country.

Recently, Vice-Minister Chu Hao, in charge of science, technology and the environment, proposed the formation of a hi-tech venture capital fund to assist the growth of Vietnam's technology industry (Keenan, 1999). However, the deficiencies in the country's legal and financial structure outlined above mean that the required regulations are not in place, and this proposal looks likely to be as slow in coming to maturity as many others have been. For hi-tech venture capitalists, especially in today's volatile markets, tax breaks, the formation of a stock market, and ownership/management control are all prerequisites for investment. Currently, Vietnam is not in a position to offer these enticements.

Tourism

For the first time since Vietnam reopened itself to international tourism, official figures in 1998 showed that the number of foreign visitors to Vietnam had declined from the previous year. The total number of international arrivals fell by 11 per cent; arrivals from Taiwan, Japan and France, Vietnam's three main sources of tourists, declined by between 10 and 22 per cent. However, arrivals from both China and the USA grew, by 4 and 436 per cent respectively. Hotels reported a decline in occupancy rates, such that Vietnam's two major tourist destinations, Ho Chi Minh City and Hanoi, were experiencing for the first time an oversupply of hotel rooms. Occupancy rates fell to 52 per cent in Hanoi and 48 per cent in Ho Chi Minh City, forcing a dramatic cut in room tariffs in large state-owned and joint-venture hotels, and bankruptcies for many smaller private minihotels.

A serious decline in tourism would clearly be problematic for Vietnam since the Vietnamese government throughout the 1990s has perceived the industry as being something of a panacea for the country's economic problems. International tourism brings with it the promise of foreign exchange and investment, economic diversification and employment. It is reported that the industry accounted for 3.5 per cent of Vietnam's GDP in 1997, a figure the government was hoping to triple by 2000, and it employed 120 000 Vietnamese directly and an additional 260 000 indirectly (Cooper, 2000). The slump led the Vietnam National Administration of Tourism (VNAT) to ask for government action to arrest and even reverse the trend. The actions suggested include an easing of some visa restrictions, an overseas advertising campaign and corresponding rise in advertising budget, lower land rent, expansion of tax exemptions and tariff reductions for the import of cars and other hotel facilities. All of these were clearly within the ambit of *doi moi*, and the government moved to ease visa restrictions and advertise. It is not known if the other recommendations have yet been taken up.

To an extent the causes of this decline can be attributed to a too-rapid expansion of tourism in Vietnam, rather than the Asian economic crisis per se. Indeed, the tourism industry itself appears to attribute the decline principally to poor tourism infrastructure and inferior services, inflated airfares, visa restrictions and increased security concerns. Certainly, the hotel glut is in part the result of a building boom initiated by Western and Asian investors in 1992–93, when Vietnam was a newly opened destination and predictions of tourist arrivals were highly optimistic.

However, it also appears that the international tourist market is changing in character and perhaps also in size. An issue that will need to be resolved is the balance to be struck between the top and lower levels of the international tourist market. Will the luxury and backpacker tourist markets remain segregated – one actively encouraged and one barely tolerated? There is some sign of a softening of official attitudes towards the lower end. Opinion remains divided: a deputy manager of Vietnam tourism is quoted as saying 'The cheap tourists don't bring too much benefit to our country...They don't spend money. They sit on the streets. They never use guides or cars', while others disagree, arguing that at least the backpackers' contribution to the economy goes directly to the people who need it most – the local family or food vendor, rather than to a hotel chain based in France (Cooper, 2000).

The Asian economic crisis has had lesser but nonetheless important effects on Vietnam's tourist development. A decline in the number of Asian and other foreign business personnel visiting Vietnam has impacted on tourism figures, hotel occupancy rates, restaurant patronage and other tourist activities. As business-related tourism has faltered, Vietnam has been forced to depend more heavily on leisure tourism, especially that based on the country's rich cultural heritage.

Industry officials and foreign tour operators now recognize that Vietnam will not achieve its target of 3.8 million visitors in 2000, and efforts are being made to offset a number of the adverse criticisms made about the tourism experience in Vietnam. The Ho Chi Minh City Department of Tourism, for instance, has called for staff training programmes to improve service and for increased security for visitors. Other proposals would curtail the growth in hotel-bed numbers at both the luxury and the very lowest ends of the market.

Equally, a shift in emphasis from business and luxury to economy tourism seems warranted, especially until the economic crisis is resolved and interregional business activity revives. The more progressive voices in the government and VNAT have begun to urge a shift in policy towards economy class tourists, including the once-feared backpackers, and towards special interest tourism, including cultural tourism. Second generation Americans, Australians and Canadians of Vietnamese origin represent another market that requires investigation.

The common prediction that improved regional exchange rates will attract increasing numbers of Westerners to Vietnamese tourist destinations may well be wrong, given the infrastructure and other problems outlined above; instead, static or declining international tourism may contribute to overall economic instability. The hard evidence to evaluate either prediction is not yet to hand although initial impressions are that these problems have turned potential tourists away from Vietnam. Whether the country can reposition its tourism industry remains to be seen.

Conclusions: the future of *doi moi* and the Vietnamese economy

The major impact that the Asian economic crisis of 1997–99 actually had in Vietnam, apart from causing some problems for exports and tourism and drastically reducing the level of foreign investment, was to intensify the ongoing debate about the best economic path to take. While there is a general agreement in Vietnam that a greater level of economic integration with the rest of the world is necessary, even inevitable, there is definite disagreement and uncertainty about the best way to pursue this and the Asian crisis exacerbated those disagreements (Corben, 2000). It is not just a matter of slow or fast, or whether it should be externally or internally financed, but fundamentally it is a question of how much economic control by the state is compatible with opening the economy to the world enough to ensure continuing stability and economic growth.

While leaders such as General Giap assert that the speed of reform should be increased, they might be better asking why there was a slowdown in some regional economies between 1997 and 1999, and not (or much less so) in others. Dong Nai Province exports for example rose to US$1.15 billion in 1999, an increase of 25 per cent over the previous year, making the province Vietnam's largest export earner. Even Ho Chi Minh City, concerned about a slowdown, saw its exports grow by over 20 per cent during that year. In comparison, Ha Noi's exports grew by only 8.2 per cent while Hai Phong's exports dropped. It also appears that areas in the south that export manufactured goods avoided all or most of the downturn and that, overall, the trade deficit narrowed appreciably. While export performance is by no means the only criterion the government should be cognisant of, or take as reflecting the health of the economy, it does need to recognize the structural reasons for these differences and, at least, support further reforms necessary for the better performing regions to grow and diversify further.

Foreign investors have become increasingly impatient over the past few years with the lack of real progress being made with promised legal and economic reforms. While post-crisis government reforms have included implementing a new Law on Foreign Investment (June 2000), the transparent legal framework and generous incentives that would bring back FDI to its earlier levels remained elusive until the advent of the BTA with the USA, signed in July 2000. The BTA is crucial to post-crisis governmental responses in that it is easily the most detailed and far-reaching trade agreement that the Vietnamese have ever signed. Operating on two fronts, that of ensuring NTR status and obliging Vietnam to phase in the reforms hitherto only sporadically achieved, the BTA should also bring Vietnam closer to receiving additional trade benefits offered by the USA to developing countries under its Generalized System of Preferences, and to receive US support in joining the WTO.

It would seem then that the message is clear: continue *doi moi* across the economy and society, seeking always to promote a balance between social, environmental and economic pressures at both a regional and national level. One of the positive reforms that could be carried out across the country as a whole would be to let the nascent private sector in Vietnam assume a more normal, and larger, role in the nation's economic and industrial affairs. Outside of the agricultural and service sectors, for example, private businesses (larger than family level) accounted for only 7.1 per cent of GDP in 1998, while the non-state sector in industry as a whole contributed just 17.1 per cent. The alternative in many regions is reliance on a weak and stagnating state sector.

And this, clearly, is still the major problem facing post-crisis government policymakers. Even if the BTA with the USA is an outstanding success, it can only assist, not guarantee, economic growth. The structural problems in Vietnam are deeper than this. In post-crisis Vietnam, foreign investors still face severe bureaucratic restrictions, weak local markets and infrastructure problems, and find they cannot make money. The systemic frustrations of recent years explain why actual inflows of FDI have been so low, but it is not only FDI that is likely to decline further, even aid is likely to shrink as projected growth rates and capacity requirements plunge. The two contracting together are likely to have a strong and interacting effect, effectively creating the preconditions for a further economic crisis.

Any further decline in the economy is however likely to present a sharper and more immediate problem. A lack of decent jobs and rising dissatisfaction will exacerbate tensions within the community. Neither agriculture, nor the state sector, nor FDI/AID sources can currently provide relief for this eventuality. A continuation of low savings and poor capital allocation will result in further economic stagnation and pressure on employment in the cities. Compared to this prospect, the risks of the world market look to be mild. Even though an export-oriented, open-economy strategy does face risks from fluctuations in Vietnam's export markets, these are likely to be far less than those that could be caused by not trying to open up the country's isolated and small domestic markets.

Vietnam really has little choice if it wants to sustain reasonable rates of economic growth. It requires foreign capital goods and technology, and these have to be paid for. While some measure of debt relief can assist (as in 1998 – US$413 million, London Club rescheduling), in reality an export surplus is needed to earn hard currencies to pay for them. At present raw material exports are limited, leaving manufactured exports and service sector exports such as tourism as the only way to earn foreign currency. However, manufactured exports' growth will require the government to allow foreign and domestic private firms to play a larger role in the economy, and tourism requires further reforms to banking and border control systems to allow tourists to gain easy access to money as they can in other destination markets. Some government members regard these changes as unwelcome as they would mean a lesser role for the state sector, at least relatively. They would also favour the southern, more developed regions unless there is intensified administrative reform in other parts of the country.

There is also the more immediate concern that rapid reform of inefficient SOEs would create social instability if not handled well. This was evident in the recent decision to instruct the managers of coal mines in Quang Ninh Province to re-employ over 50 000 laid off miners, even though the company had 4 million tons of stockpiled coal, to avoid social instability in that province (Dapice, 2000). Such decisions to subsidize a sunset industry in reality though only draw resources away from those sunrise industries that could create sustainable growth. And, the unrest of 50 000 miners is nothing compared to the problems that prolonged stagnation of the economy will create. With 1.2 million workers joining the labour force each year, no job growth in the state sector, and limited development prospects for agriculture, any restriction of manufactured or service exports from a lack of progress on trade agreements or the restructuring of state enterprises would remove the one and only path out of poverty that Vietnam has so far found. Fortunately, since 1998 exports have been rising faster than imports, shrinking the trade gap and, along with an increase in private capital inflows, creating room for the government to move with respect to greater financial reforms. In February 2000, the MOF introduced further tax reforms and investment guarantees for new and foreign businesses, aimed at streamlining and simplifying foreign investment procedures (Corben, 2000).

The government of Vietnam has traditionally shown an ability to recognize and act upon economic problems. *Doi moi* is a programme and a style of response that can deliver the necessary change. While it will be slow and cautious, there is no sign that the government wishes to turn the clock back to a command-style economy, even if it could. The dilemma for Vietnam's economic managers is that there is a very high internal resistance to further reforms, and even if these can be agreed upon, success is not certain due to the continuing risks in the world and Asian regional economy. Yet if a bold reform strategy looks risky, the alternative of maintaining the status quo could be disastrous. It is certain that there will be fewer jobs, and the debts being accumulated in non-producing investments will become a crippling burden in a few years that will further reduce any scope for progress, unless there is continued reform.

References

Agencie France Presse/Reuters (2000) *Vietnam eases taxes on Viet Kieu funds*, Ha Noi, 9 March.

Barnes, K. (2000) *Capital Flows to Emerging Market Economies*, Institute of International Finance, 24 January.

Beresford, M. (1988) *Vietnam: Politics, Economy and Society*, London: Pinter.

Beresford, M. (1997) 'Vietnam: the transition from central planning', in G. Rodan, K. Hewison and R. Robinson (eds) *The Political Economy of South-East Asia*, Oxford: Oxford University Press.

Chong, Frank (1998) *Finally, Japan is on the Right Track*, Sydney: The Australian, 15 October, p. 24.

Cooper, M. (1997) 'Tourism planning and education in Vietnam: a profile 1995–2010', *Pacific Tourism Review*, 1(1): 57–65.

Cooper, M. (2000) 'Destination Vietnam', in C. M. Hall and S. Page (eds) *Tourism In South East Asia: Issues And Cases*, Sydney and London: Butterworth-Heinemann (Forthcoming).

Corben, R. (2000) 'Slide demands a brake', in *Inside Asia: The Business Experience*, Sydney: The Australian, 17 April, p. 38.

Countrywatch (1999) 'Vietnam', 11 November. See http://excite.countrywatch.com

Dapice, D. (2000) 'Point of no return', *Vietnam Business Journal*, 15 February.

Dung, N. T. (1996) 'Foreign direct investment in Vietnam', in S. Leung (ed.) *Vietnam Assessment: Creating a Sound Investment Climate*, Singapore: Institute of Southeast Asian Studies.

East Asia Analytic Unit (1997) *The New Aseans*, Canberra: Department of Foreign Affairs and Trade.

Economist, The (2000) *Foreign Direct Investment – Goodnight Vietnam*, Ha Noi, 8 January.

Economist, The (2000) *Let the Good Times Roll*, Washington DC, 14 April.

Gates, C. L. (1996) 'Enterprise reform and Vietnam's transformation to a market-oriented economy', *ASEAN Economic Bulletin*, 12(1): 29–52.

Grant, J. (1996) 'Vietnam diaspore ponders links with home', *Financial Times*, 22 July.

Haughton, J. (2000) 'Opening the books', February. See http://www.viam.com/02–2000/budget.htm

International Monetary Fund (1999) *Vietnam Statistical Appendix*, Washington DC: IMF.

Irvine, R. (2000) 'Reason to cheer'. See http://www.viam.com/archive/2000/08/rtc.htm

Keenan, F. (1999) 'What's the rush?', *Far Eastern Economic Review*, 15 July.

Kokko, A. and M. Zejan (1996) *Vietnam at the Next Stage of Reforms*, Stockholm: Stockholm School of Economics.

Le Dang Doanh and A. McCarty (1997) 'Economic reform in Vietnam: achievements and prospects', in S. F. Naya and J. Tan (eds) *Asian Transitional Economies*, Singapore: Institute of Southeast Asian Studies, pp. 99–153.

Morgan, J. (1988) *The Downward Spiral of the Asian Tigers*, London: BBC News, 31 March.

Watkin, H. (2000) *Reform the New Battle Front for Vietnam's War Hero*, Sydney: The Weekend Australian, 8 April.

9

Trade Policy Management, Industrial Characteristics and WTO: A Case Study of China*

Yi Feng and Baizhu Chen

Introduction

Joining the WTO has now become a paramount policy decision in China. Integration in the world economy provides an organizing theme for the country. The over two decades of economic reform have brought profound changes in the Chinese economy and meanwhile, have seen shifts of China's policy paradigms. Now the nation needs a new central strategic policy that will mobilize the people. The major policy shift in the Chinese reform agenda happens to be full integration with the world economy, which is likely to become the leading issue for China in the future.

Like every policy change, this one will create losers and winners. The upside of China joining the WTO is that China will improve its competitiveness in the world market through absorbing advanced technology and management while exporting the products over which it has comparative advantage. The downside is that many of China's own industries will flounder under international competition.

Joining the WTO has also been perceived as a political move. It will provide an intended constraint on the personnel system as well as efficiency standards. There have been leaders who cannot compete under the market principle, but it has been impossible to remove them. There have been enterprises that have been losing money, but it has been difficult to shut them down. The WTO can be used as a guideline to remove those leaders and to shut those factories. It is like an equation, if one plus one does not equal two, then it must be wrong and axed.

To predict the success of this strategy is difficult, as it involves not only a multitude of political, economic, international and domestic factors. In this essay, we try to focus on the relationship between government tariff policy and industrial characteristics. We maintain that protectionism will determine the degree of China's integration into the world economy, though ironically, such integration implies the removal of protectionism.

Analyzing the tariff structure and its determinants in China in the context of industrial characteristics, this research is conducted under the rubric of endogenous policy theory. This theory presupposes that government policy is an outcome of the engagement between the government – which maximizes its likelihood to remain in office or its legitimacy to rule – and various interest groups seeking to affect government policy in their favour.

We find that trade policy in China is fundamentally determined by two concerns of the government. The first has to do with the protection of high-value added and high-tech industries. This industrial policy may be inconsistent with China's open-door policy, but such an industrial policy may help develop the country's high-value added industry in the long run if it can overcome the inefficient problem ensuing from the lack of international competition. The second concern stems from the government's need to protect industries that incur financial losses. Such industries are typical SOEs. Removing protections for these industries implies that massive lay-offs will occur in inefficiently run factories, leading to social chaos and political unrest. Therefore, trade policy in China is mainly defined by an industrial policy favouring high-tech industries and a social policy minimizing social instability.

China's re-entry into the WTO requires its opening many high-value added industries to foreign competition. These industries including telecommunications, finance, distributions and many others, are the ones in which China does not have a comparative advantage. Opening up these industries to foreign competitions implies that the Chinese government has to stand up against strong domestic protectionist pressure.

Our study shows that China's trade policy during the mid-1990s was largely shaped by its intention to protect its high-value added industries. It thus explains why it has been so difficult to reach an agreement with China during the WTO negotiation. Even though China has pledged to open its high-value added industries after its re-entering the WTO, many observers believe that China may still find other non-tariff barriers, such as administrative controls, to restrict foreign competition in finance, telecommunications, distributions and others.

We have also found that China's trade policy to a large degree is determined by its concern over political stability caused by firms facing financial losses and massive lay-offs. These are likely the inefficient SOEs. As foreign competition intensifies after China's re-entry into the WTO, the losses in the SOEs will accumulate and the pressure on the government will mount. What will be put to test will be the political will of the Chinese government to allow foreign firms to compete with the inefficient SOEs. It is reasonable to conjecture that as China opens its market to foreign competition, trade conflict between China and the USA and other industrial nations may increase.

The next section of the essay reviews variants of endogenous trade policy, followed by their implications in the context of China. The section 'Endogenous trade policy and the Chinese context' offers an overview of the major changes in Chinese tariff policy since 1949. The section 'Tariff reductions in China' looks into the data that may account for the country's tariff policy and discusses the causal structure of China's industrial tariffs based upon regression analysis. The last section concludes the essay with some policy implications with regard to the WTO.

Endogenous trade policy and the Chinese context

How a tariff level is determined in a nation has been under empirical scrutiny since the 1970s, which has led to the emergence of endogenous policy theory. Such a theory assumes that trade policies are endogenously determined by the interaction between private agents and politicians. Baldwin (1985) discusses five models of trade protection.

In the common-interest group model, the key argument is that an industry's success in achieving protection by exerting political pressure on elected officials depends upon its ability to organize itself into an effective political pressure group. The ability to overcome the free-rider problem and organize effectively depends on the size of the firms within the industry and the degree of their concentration in terms of output and geography. Other factors considered in the model include low or negative growth rates of employment and output, low or declining profit rates, rising import penetration ratios and low-value added share of output.

By contrast, the adding-machine model assumes that an industry's workers and management vote as a bloc to promote their short-run economic interests, and considers the size of an industry to be the key factor in influencing public officials' decisions to protect it. The number of employees in the industry has a positive effect on the protection of the industry by the government through tariffs. Other factors include labour-output ratio and dispersion of small firms.

The status-quo model postulates that voters and government officials have a conservative respect for the status quo and oppose any significant reductions in real incomes of any significant groups. Thus the government tries to minimize the short-run adjustment costs of workers. This model implies relatively high tariffs to protect the industry when adjustment costs are large, which is typically true of unskilled labour, older employees, rural areas and industries with low growth rates.

Similarly, the social-change model postulates that government officials and voters seek to promote social goals that go beyond the maintenance of the status quo. They try to bring change to the distribution of income and other socioeconomic relationships. For example, even if there are no differences among the workers in their ability to find new jobs, voters and the government would still want to shield low-income, unskilled workers from job displacement in order to promote equity and social justice.

Finally, the foreign-policy model assumes that government officials and voters view the state as an entity whose collective economic welfare they wish to promote. They adopt a mercantilist attitude, and do not reduce US tariffs on items of special export interest to other countries if those countries do not cut duties on items of special interest to US exporters. Such a model implies high tariffs for developing countries, since they tend to compete with low-skilled workers in the USA, and low tariffs for countries where there is direct foreign investment from the USA.

Similarly, Caves (1976) puts forth three models. His adding-machine model posits that the party in power acts to maximize its chance of re-election by protecting the industries that have the largest numbers of voters. The interest-group model argues that a tariff level is a function of pressure imposed by interest groups, in that they calculate their benefits and loss from a tariff and consequently lobby the political party to raise a tariff. In the national-policy model, the government sets a tariff for nationalistic (collective) preferences.

Pincus (1975) assumes that the levels of the different duties passed by Congress are the result of pressure coming from interest groups, with the amount of pressure depending on the anticipated effects of the tariffs. The foundation of the chapter lies in the public-good and free-rider problems. The geographic and structural concentration of an industry, as well as a substantial presence in Congress that represents the industry's constituency, lead to a rise in tariffs.

Cassing et al. (1986) examine the political economy of a tariff cycle. They assume that labour is immobile because of industry-specific skills and place-specific assets such as land and housing. Their theory predicts that during economic downturns, the old import-competing sector benefits from tariff increases and the old export sector benefits from tariff reductions. During economic upturns, the new import-competing sector gains from tariff increases and the new export sector gains from tariff reductions. As a result, the old region import-competing industry has more incentive for protection at the downturn than at the peak compared to the new region import-competing industry, with the underlying reason that it suffers from economic hardship, which reduces the organization cost. During the peak of economy, the old industry cannot produce more to make more profits (beyond their production limits); therefore, there is a lack of incentive for protection at the peak of the economy. The result is that protection is more likely at economic busts than booms.

McKeown (1989) studies the causes of the repeal of the British corn laws. The substantial change in voting in the House of Commons leading to the repeal of the corn laws in 1842–46 was viewed as a victory of the constituents' political and economic interests as well as the result of Parliament members' private economic gains. In a somewhat different perspective, James and Lake (1989) posit that the capital and labour interests in Britain formed a coalition to push through the repeal of corn laws. These interest groups wanted to open the US market, and the price they were willing to pay was to open the grain market to the USA. Before taking action on corn laws, they knew that if they opened their grain market to the USA, they would win over the farmers in the mid-West. A new coalition would form between the planters in the South and farmers in the West, and both sectors would promote trade with Britain. This is exactly what happened. The South and the West united themselves against the Eastern protectionists, and won free trade.

Kaempfer and Willett (1989) try to answer why quotas are used in lieu of tariffs even though quotas create more deadweight loss than tariffs do. Their argument is that foreign lobby, foreign relations and concerns for retaliation all determine rent allocation. For instance, domestic producers can benefit from an increased ability to collude with foreign producers after the introduction of a quota. Also, it is in domestic leaders' self-interest to have good relations with foreign leaders. Furthermore, tariffs invite counter-tariffs from foreign countries. Leaders would therefore opt for quotas, which are less confrontational than tariffs.

Hillman (1982) studies the political mechanisms of protecting declining industries. He challenges the notion that a government provides protection for the sake of social insurance, fairness and altruism. He alternatively argues that government protection is based upon its calculation of the political support it can generate by protecting declining industries in the face of world competition. Through various levels of tariff rates, a government may retard or accelerate the decline of an inefficient industry, depending upon the marginal support the government garners from society through the chosen level of protection.

In much the same vein, Magee et al. (1989) explain tariff levels as a result of a political party's desire to secure office through strategizing a tariff level to maximize votes. The strategy of the protectionist lobby is to maximize its revenue by its choice of contributions to political parties. The strategy of the protectionist party is to choose its tariff so as to maximize its probability of winning the election. The decision to contribute to the political process and the announcement of policy positions are assumed to occur before elections. Thus, the lobbies maximize their expected returns from contributing to the political parties while the parties maximize their expected probability of winning the election.

In sum, endogenous trade theory examines trade and protection as an outcome of the relationship between government and interest groups. It stipulates that government policy maximizes the net support it can obtain from the populace by adopting a certain level of protection, and that interest groups lobby for protection or export promotion, only when the marginal benefit from the policy they lobby for, equals the marginal cost incurred in lobbying activities. The various models discussed above have been tested on the data for the USA, Britain and Canada – but have never been tested on countries not in the Western Hemisphere.

This study proposes to test these models on data in the PRC. Since the open-door policy was initiated in 1978, the Chinese economy has been moving in the direction of marketization and integration with the world market. Various interest groups have emerged in the process of economic decentralization. Some of them have gained from the export-oriented economic regime while others have had to seek government protection. The proposed project argues that various Chinese industries function as rational private economic agents trying to seek economic rents through political influence. The difficulty of applying endogenous trade theory in China lies in the lack of political competition among parties in the country. The incumbent government officials do not face a serious threat of being pressured out of office, and new political entrepreneurs do not have to seek popular support to gain political office to the degree that their Western counterparts do.

However, it is possible to examine China's trade policy in the endogenous context for at least three reasons. First, the Chinese government tries to legitimize its power through normative social goals. One such goal is economic growth. The high-performance record of China's economic reform has strengthened the legitimacy of the government as it endeavours to adopt a national policy to accelerate growth. Trade policy is an important tool that the government can use strategically to ensure the success of economic reforms and, therefore, its own legitimacy.

Second, China's economic reform creates both winners and losers. A large presence of losers certainly will cause social unrest and political instability. While the government may want to maximize economic growth through marketization and privatization, massive layoffs and inflation that ensue from rapid transformation may break out. When it comes to trade policy, the government may have to consider the factors emphasized by the status-quo/social-change model in order to preserve political stability and economic equity.

Third, some recent works have found government policy in China to be the outcome of compromise between subgovernmental or intergovernmental players. The political centralization of the party and the political capacity of the government have weakened and the power of the local governments has escalated (Shirk, 1993; Montinola et al., 1995; Feng, 1997). As economic and political decentralization continues, interest groups will gain financial and political power over the central government.

This chapter attempts to identify patterns of influence of various industrial groups on government trade policies. The findings of the determinants of protection will confirm or discredit the endogenous policy theory in the Chinese context. As this will be one of the first empirical analyses in terms of endogenous trade policies that has ever been conducted on a developing or non-democratic nation, it will provide important nuances for model construction and refinement under the rubric of endogenous policy theory.

Tariff reduction in China[1]

This section provides an overview of major changes in China's tariff policy over the years. Tariffs in China have been determined largely by the priorities in the nation's political and economic agenda, which have differed substantially over time. After the founding of the PRC in 1949, the nation adopted an import-substitution strategy. The purpose of the tariffs was to protect the infant industries in China. The Agreement on Tariff Policies and Customs, passed in the seventeenth council meeting of the government in January 1950, stipulated that 'tariffs must be used to protect our nation's production and our products in competition with those made in other countries.' It also required that the tariff levels for products manufactured on a large scale or with a potential for mass production be set above the difference between the cost of imported products and the cost of domestic products so that domestic industries could be shielded.

The tariff policy in favour of an autarchy gradually was transformed into one oriented toward an outward-looking, open economy after economic reform was initiated in 1978. In 1984, the State Council of China laid the foundation for a new tariff policy that would be consistent with its open-door policy. A State Council working group on tariff reforms reformulated the objective of tariffs from that of protecting national industries into one that 'conforms to the new open-door policy of the nation, promotes exports, ensures daily necessities, enhances economic development and guarantees government revenue'. The protection of national industries was no longer considered the predominant goal of tariffs.

China significantly reduced its tariff rates in 1992 and 1996 (see Figure 9.1). By the early 1990s, the reform of China's export sectors was far ahead of its reform for its import-competing industries. For instance,

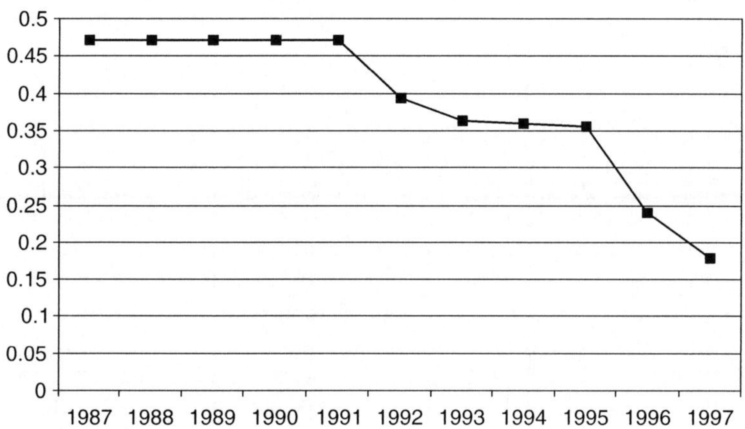

Figure 9.1 Mean tariff rates in China, 1987–97

export subsidies had been suspended and the extent to which permits were required for exported goods had been reduced, but imports remained largely state-controlled. In addition to high tariffs, severe non-tariff barriers existed, such as import quotas, exchange control and permit authorization. The imports subject to quotas, permits and import control numbered 1247, or about 20 per cent of total imported items. The enterprises' losses due to imports were also subsidized by the state (Yang, 1997). The inconsistency between the deregulation of the exporting and the protection of importing industries ran counter to the establishment of price mechanisms. In this context, the reduction of tariffs in 1992 and 1996 marked a turning point in China's trade liberalization.

By 1992, China reduced tariffs for 3371 items, with an average tariff reduction of 7.6 per cent. By 1993, China cut tariffs on another 2898 items, with an average reduction of 8.8 per cent. In 1994, the tariffs for automobiles were significantly reduced, and tariffs on cigarettes, liquors, videotapes and buses all decreased in 1995. On 1 April 1996, China launched a major tariff reduction that involved 4900 items, or 76.3 per cent of all existing tariff items. The average reduction in tariff levels reached 35 per cent, the largest by that time. The following provides some highlights of the 1996 tariff reduction in China.

Tariffs for industrial raw materials were reduced significantly. For instance, tariffs for metal materials decreased on average by 47.7 per cent, to the level of 8.15 per cent, on 161 non-ferrous metals and 179 ferrous metals. The tariffs for textile materials were reduced by 50.7 per cent, leading to an average tariff level of 18.8 per cent. Raw materials for mineral and forestry products were reduced to below 3 per cent. Raw materials for inorganic chemical products were reduced by 52.7 per cent to an average level of 9.5 per cent, and for organic products by 44.1 per cent to 10.5 per cent.

One reason that China significantly reduced tariffs on raw materials was that it intended to protect its own natural resources, particularly those that were non-generative or lacking in reproductive capabilities such as raw materials used in mineral and forestry products. It is also plausible that China reduced these tariff rates to lower the cost of the finished products (e.g., textile products) so as to increase their competitiveness in the international market.

In 1996, China also reduced tariff levels for electrical machinery by 36.5 per cent to the level of 13.65 per cent. The reduction in the tariffs for electrical machinery was supposed to lower the cost of technological innovation in China. Consumer electrical products experienced a tariff reduction by 43.5 per cent to the 28.2 per cent level. Tariffs on automobiles also decreased. The reduction in tariffs for passenger cars ranged from 150 per cent to 90 per cent and 100 per cent to 90 per cent for vans. For motorcycles, the reduction was from 120 per cent to 70 per cent. No reduction was given to buses, specialized vehicles and tractors, which stood at 55 per cent, 3–20 per cent, and 15 per cent, respectively.

China enjoyed a large international market for textile products. In 1996, the tariff level for cotton apparels was reduced from 60 per cent to 40 per cent, and from 45 per cent to 20 per cent for other cotton products. Similarly, China was competitive in light-industry products and tariffs were reduced on those products by 31.6 per cent to the level of 41.8 per cent. In tandem with the gradual openness of its current account, China has reduced its mean tariff rate from 47.2 per cent in 1991 to 17.8 per cent in 1997, with an annual average reduction rate of 5 per cent.

It has been projected that China will reduce its average tariff rate to 15 per cent by 2000 and to 10 per cent by 2005. The effort to reduce protection also extends to non-tariff barriers (NTBs). For instance, about 2000 items were subject to import permits in 1992. By contrast, only 300 items were required to have permits in 1998 (Yang, 1999).

From these examples, it can be seen that China changed the goal of its tariff policy from protectionism to coordination with its open economy. Tariff reduction in China, particularly in 1996, was conducive to technological transformation by importing advanced machinery and equipment from abroad. It also decreased the cost of production by lowering the tariffs for raw materials, thus increasing the competitiveness of these products in the world market. Natural resources in China also stood a better chance of being preserved since the tariffs on these products were reduced to close to zero. Besides, tariff reductions also benefited consumers by increasing possible purchases of international products or by lowering the price of domestic products. More importantly, tariff reductions increased the competitive pressure on Chinese industries and therefore improved their efficiency. As implied by Hillman (1982), a government may accelerate the decline of certain industries by reducing protection. In China's context, such industries may include those inefficiently run and insolvent – particularly SOEs.

Some SOEs are large heavy industries, characterized by obsolete or obsolescent technology, raw-material processing and a long production cycle. For years, technological innovations have been lacking. Because of low-skilled labour, a single product-line and obsolescent technology and equipment, it is difficult for SOEs to develop and to manufacture new profit-earning products. SOE inventories have been on the rise, causing a slow turnover of capital. Also, some SOEs owe debts to each other, causing a severe shortage of capital. Furthermore, SOEs' employees are redundant; a massive layoff will cause very serious social and political problems. Finally, SOEs have a substantial number of retirees drawing pension, further dragging down the SOEs' profits.

In contrast to the economic downside of the SOEs, these enterprises have some intrinsic values in keeping social and political stability. They used to be both the political and economic pillars of the nation. They carry social insurance for hundreds of millions of employees and their families. Their non-profit appendages include day-care centres, elementary schools, middle schools, vocational schools, universities, grocery stores, housing provisions, medical centres, social clubs and so on. These grassroots institutions have helped to stabilize the society, although they also demand a great deal of financial resources. Further reform may produce some serious negative consequences on SOE employees' welfare, as many of them would lose jobs (the status-quo model). Furthermore, the employees tend to be low-skilled industry-specific labour, making it even harder for them to find other jobs (the social-change model). A tariff reduction for the products of the failing SOEs will further provoke the problems mentioned above and accelerate the enterprises' continued decline. If the endogenous tariff theory is correct, we could find China's evidence consistent with the status-quo, social-change and interest-group models.

Data analysis

In this section, we introduce the data analysis of the factors that may affect tariffs in China in light of the endogenous trade policy. In an effort to identify the underlying factors that account for the variation of tariffs across the economy, we collected information on 95 industries. These industries include excavation, food, textile, clothing, building materials, furniture and household goods, energy, chemical, transportation, metallurgy, machinery equipment, communications, electronics, electrical equipment, retail, wholesale and material supply, paper, publishing and stationary supply and so on.[2] While the sample is not random, it certainly reflects the main components of Chinese industries. Tables 9.1–9.6 summarize the methodology and results of the data analysis.

As discussed previously, 1996 marks a major transformation of the tariff structure in China. In the next section, we use the tariff rates for these 95 industries in the year 1996 as our dependent variable in cross-section regression. In terms of the predetermined variables, we examine a wide array of variables measured in 1995 to reduce endogeneity problems. The sources for these variables are *The Data of the Third National Industrial Census of the PRC in 1995 by Ownership Type* and *The Data of the Third National Industrial Census of the PRC in 1995 by Industry*. From

Table 9.1 Eigenvalues of the correlation matrix

Factor	Eigenvalue	Difference	Proportion	Cumulative
1	21.4899	16.9378	0.6512	0.6512
2	4.5521	2.1929	0.1379	0.7892
3	2.3592	1.045	0.0715	0.8606
4	1.3142	0.4425	0.0398	0.9005
5	0.8717	0.2541	0.0264	0.9269
6	0.6176	0.2321	0.0187	0.9456
7	0.3855	0.0476	0.0117	0.9573
8	0.3379	0.0694	0.0102	0.9675
9	0.2685	0.0628	0.0081	0.9757
10	0.2056	0.0673	0.0062	0.9819
11	0.1383	0.0443	0.0042	0.9861
12	0.094	0.0235	0.0028	0.9889
13	0.0705	0.0068	0.0021	0.9911
14	0.0637	0.0163	0.0019	0.993
15	0.0473	0.0051	0.0014	0.9944
16	0.0422	0.0099	0.0013	0.9957
17	0.0323	0.0086	0.001	0.9967
18	0.0237	0.0025	0.0007	0.9974
19	0.0211	0.0048	0.0006	0.998
20	0.0164	0.0025	0.0005	0.9985
21	0.0139	0.0027	0.0004	0.999
22	0.0112	0.0046	0.0003	0.9993
23	0.0065	0.0021	0.0002	0.9995
24	0.0044	0.0013	0.0001	0.9996
25	0.0031	0.0002	0.0001	0.9997
26	0.003	0.0009	0.0001	0.9998
27	0.0021	0.0007	0.0001	0.9999
28	0.0014	0.0003	0	0.9999
29	0.0011	0.0003	0	1
30	0.0008	0.0004	0	1
31	0.0004	0.0002	0	1
32	0.0003	0.0003	0	1
33	0		0	1

Note: Total = 33; average = 1.

Table 9.2 Rotated factor pattern

Variable	Factor			
	1	2	3	4
Number of firms	31	0	17	88*
Number of firms in the red	30	–7	43	81*
Gross product	37	39	78*	19
Value added	55	75*	30	2
Gross capital	69*	45	47	14
Foreign capital	2	3	82*	38
Total assets	65*	53	53	–3
Inventory	41	44	74*	6
Net fixed capital	76*	49	33	–7
Total debt	64*	47	59	–2
Long-term debt	71*	49	31	–15
Sales revenue	48	52	65*	6
Sales taxes	–9	80*	–9	14
Sales profits	58	63*	46	–3
Investment return	24	65*	47	–4
Total loss	49	3	76*	22
Total profits	1	68*	14	–1
Income taxes	22	93*	21	–4
Net profit	14	93*	2	–6
Number of full-time employees	87*	6	29	36
Number of technical staff	76*	29	43	19
Number of managers	85*	16	33	34
Employees age 36–50	92*	9	18	30
Employees age 51 and above	93*	12	6	25
Employees with college education	81*	40	30	–15
Employees with professional education	93*	25	20	3
Number of technicians	89*	33	23	–3
Employees with secondary education	81*	6	42	34
Employees with primary education	80*	4	–5	54
Total workforce	87*	7	29	36
Total wages	90*	22	28	19
Number of retirees	91*	1	26	16
Retirement pension and welfare	84*	5	10	0

Note: Rotation Method: Varimax.
* represents factor values greater than 60.

a multitude of variables and based upon a principal component analysis, we selected several variables as regressors as outlined in Table 9.5:

- the number of firms in the industry;
- the number of firms that incur losses in the industry;

Table 9.3 Component contents

Component 1: employees and assets	Gross fixed capital Net fixed capital Total assets Total debt Long-term debt Total work force Total wages Number of full time employees Number of technical staff Number of managers Employees age 36–50 Employees age 51 and above Employees with college education Employees with professional education Number of technicians Employees with secondary education Employees with primary education Number of retirees Retirement pension and welfare
Component 2: profit and taxes	Value added Sales taxes Sales profits Investment return Total profit Income taxes Net profit
Component 3: product and foreign capital	Gross product Foreign capital Inventory Sales revenue Total loss
Component 4: firms and bad firms	Number of firms Firms in the red

- the amount of total losses;
- value added per worker;
- the number of employees;
- foreign direct investment as a percentage of total capital;
- inventory;
- percentage of employees with primary education or lower;
- sales taxes; and
- average industry wages.

Table 9.4 Regression using factor scores as regressors

Variable	Parameter	*T*-statistic	*P*-value
Intercept	62.948	15.124	0.0001
Factor1	–12.416	–2.966	0.004
Factor2	5.574	1.331	0.1868
Factor3	11.901	2.843	0.0057
Factor4	11.891	2.84	0.0057

$R^2 = 0.211$; $\sigma = 38.598$.
Note: Dependent variable: industrial tariff rates, 1996.

Table 9.5 Variables and models

	Interest group	Adding machine	Status-quo/ social change	Foreign/ national policy
Number of firms	–	+		
Number of losing firms	+		+	
Total loss	+		+	
Value added per worker	–			+
Number of employees		+		
FDI share of capital				+
Inventory			+	
Percentage of employees with primary education or lower			+	
Sales taxes				+
Average industry wages			–	

Table 9.6 Regression analysis: dependent variable – industrial tariff rates, 1996

	1	2	3	4
Intercept				
	40.66	61.6	40.53	53.58
	(2.00**)	(2.93*)	(2.00**)	(2.82*)
	[a]	[a]	[a]	[a]
	.	.	.	.
	0[b]	0[b]	0[b]	0[b]
Number of firms				
	0.001	0.001	–	0.001
	(0.39)	(0.17)		(0.31)
	0.1[a]	0.1[a]		0.53[a]
	9.67[b]	9.64[b]		1.9[b]

Number of losing firms				
	–0.003	–0.001	0.001	–
	(–.24)	(–.04)	(0.25)	
	0.08[a]	0.08[a]	0.4[a]	
	12.7[b]	12.7[b]	2.51[b]	
Total loss				
	1.987	1.408	1.825	1.73
	(2.19**)	(1.47)	(2.27**)	(2.17**)
	0.15[a]	0.16[a]	0.19[a]	0.2[a]
	6.55[b]	6.36[b]	5.2[b]	4.97[b]
Value added/worker				
	–10.1	8.054	–9.93	–
	(–1.9***)	(3.49*)	(–1.9***)	
	0.08[a]	0.5[a]	0.08[a]	
	12.3[b]	1.99[b]	12.3[b]	
Number of workers				
	–0.197	–0.134	–0.189	–0.158
	(–2.7*)	(–1.8***)	(–2.7*)	(–2.2**)
	0.28[a]	0.29[a]	0.3[a]	0.3[a]
	3.63[b]	3.43[b]	3.34[b]	3.32[b]
FDI				
	139.9	125.9	137.7	133.9
	(5.32*)	(4.51*)	(5.40*)	(5.28*)
	0.78[a]	0.79[a]	0.82[a]	0.85[a]
	1.29[b]	1.26[b]	1.22[b]	1.17[b]
Inventory				
	0.041	0.082	0.043	0.047
	(0.59)	(1.11)	(0.62)	(0.67)
	0.21[a]	0.22[a]	0.21[a]	0.21[a]
	4.73[b]	4.61[b]	4.71[b]	4.72[b]
Primary education				
	45.63	53.75	49.93	48.45
	(0.85)	(0.94)	(0.96)	(0.91)
	0.78[a]	0.78[a]	0.82[a]	0.81[a]
	1.28[b]	1.27[b]	1.22[b]	1.24[b]
Sales tax				
	0.825	–	0.82	0.44
	(3.70*)		(3.70*)	(4.87*)
	0.12[a]		0.12[a]	0.76[a]
	8.2[b]		8.18[b]	1.32[b]
Wages				
	–14.4	–116	–14.7	–74.2
	(–.32)	(–3.0*)	(–.33)	(–2.3**)
	0.25[a]	0.4[a]	0.25[a]	0.53[a]
	3.93[b]	2.49[b]	3.93[b]	1.87[b]

Table 9.6 (*continued*)

	1	2	3	4
Adj. R^2	44.0	35.4	44.6	43.0
σ	31.9	34.3	31.8	32.2

[a] Tolerance index.
[b] Variance inflation factor.
* Statistically significant at the 0.01 error level in a two-tailed test.
** Statistically significant at the 0.05 error level in a two-tailed test.
*** Statistically significant at the 0.10 error level in a two-tailed test.

The use of these variables presents an approach toward a parsimonious statistical model. Many variables are highly correlated with each other – for instance, sales revenue, sales taxes, and total and net profits. The selection of variables is made with a view to reduce the number of variables that significantly overlap with others.

The regression results (Table 9.6) support variants of all the models presented at the beginning of the chapter. The national and foreign policy model comes out strongly. The firms that have a large presence of foreign capital are better protected than other firms, keeping everything else constant. Some previous studies (e.g., Feng and Zhang, 1999) find that an open economy is conducive to the acquisition of direct foreign investment. The contrary result here provides new evidence at the level of the industry, rather than at the level of the economy. In order to attract foreign capital, the government may set up a protective tariff for a particular industry to ensure the profitability of foreign investment.

Additionally, the government tends to protect those industries that have generated larger tax income for the government. The tax base of the central government in China has been weakened as a result of political and economic decentralization. Setting a higher tariff for an industry that is able to generate higher taxable income is a win–win game for the central government and the industry. The government benefits from both the tariffs on imported goods and the excise taxes on domestic products; the industry enjoys the rent from protection.

It is also found that those industries with a higher level of per-worker value added tend to enjoy a higher level of protection. While exercising an open-door policy, the government still has an incentive to protect high-value added industries. Such an industrial policy may benefit the long-run development of these high-tech industries. In the short-run, the government benefits from tariff revenues and excise taxes generated by these products.

Further examination of the data shows that value added, together with several other variables – sales taxes, the number of firms and the number of firms that incur losses – potentially suffers from multicollinearity. It can be speculated that value added and sales taxes are interrelated; higher value added leads to higher taxes. As it turns out, the correlation between the two is 0.88. After sales taxes are removed from the regressors, value added takes the positive sign and remains highly significant, which is consistent with our inference.

Among the three other models – the interest-group, the adding-machine and the status-quo/social-change models – the regression result seems to confirm the last one. All the relevant variables have signs consistent with the status-quo/social-change perspective. Losses of the industry, inventory of products and the lack of education among employees are all positively related to tariff levels, although only loss is statistically significant. The government does appear to protect those industries that suffer from losses. Such industries, as discussed in the section 'Tariff reduction in China', are likely to be SOEs. While it will prove futile to protect inefficient industries in the long run, the rationale to extend protection to them is that it provides political stability. Such policy is consistent with the gradual approach China's reform has undertaken.

One variable that does not agree with the status-quo/social-change model is wages, which are found to have a negative effect on tariffs. The government tends to impose a lower tariff for those industries in which the average salary is higher. This may be another version of the evidence in favour of the national-policy model, which says that government tend to support those industries that have high levels of value added and yield large tax receipts. More importantly, China has a comparative advantage in labour-intensive products and, therefore, may not need to protect its industries that use intensively low-skilled, low-wage earning labour.

Finally, the evidence favouring the interest-group model or the adding-machine model is not strong. The multicollinearity problem appears to exist for the number of firms and the number of firms that have losses. The removal of one of them does not, however, improve the statistical significance of the other. Our findings seem to confirm the national/foreign-policy model and the status-quo/social-change model.

Policy implications and conclusions

This study finds evidence of some variants of an endogenous tariff policy in China's context. The level of tariffs has been found to be related to some variables prescribed by the national/foreign-policy model and the status-quo/social-change model. The direction and trajectory of China's economic reform are between these two models. The government launched a far-reaching reform that transformed the political and economic life of the nation, ushering in a protracted economic boom. Such transformation has had disrupting effects on the social status quo, and the inefficiency of SOEs has worsened the social aspects of the economic reforms. It has been and will continue to be a great challenge for the government to strike a balance between a national policy positing economic transformation and the destabilizing forces released from such a policy. The litmus test for the success of the two-decade long period of reform now focuses on the transformation of the failing SOEs.

These findings are relevant to China's strategy to join the WTO. China has been persistently negotiating its membership for the past four years, and our findings should shed light on China's negotiation strategy with its Western counterparts. The identification of winners and losers in China's trade policy has directly affected our understanding of the next-phase economic reform in the country, particularly regarding the restructuring of SOEs. Our findings regarding the relationship between government and interest groups have provided an insight into the progression of political liberalization in the country. It has been argued that new forces released by marketization will seek political representation, thus weakening government control.

Since China's initiation of its open-door policy, international trade has become an integral part of its modernization drive. The percentage of its exports in GDP increased from below 5 per cent in 1979 to 19 per cent in 1997. Sustained growth requires that China join the WTO. However, China has been very reluctant to accept the terms demanded by Western nations. The ramifications of China's entry in the WTO involve both positive and negative consequences in light of our findings in this chapter.

The following discussions of some selected sectors and their relevance for the WTO are provided based on the results in this chapter as well as a recent analysis by Yu et al. (2000).

Textile has been China's mature industry. China terminated subsidies for textile products in 1991 (Yu et al., 2000). Abroad, China's textile products suffer from quotas. The WTO will benefit China's textile products and after joining the WTO, China's textile exports will no longer be subjected to quotas. China's joining WTO will improve China's competition in the world textile market.[3]

China is the largest steel producer, but is also a net-importer of steel. It imported high-value added steel products, and exported low-value added products (Yu et al., 2000). Therefore, the impacts on the high-tech and high-value added products will be affected. The cost of producing steel in China is also high compared to advanced countries. According to our analysis, the steel industry is typical of SOEs in China. It can be foreseen that some protection measure will be meted out for this sector.

China relied on tariffs to protect its petrochemical industry. A drop in the tariff level from 17 per cent to 9 per cent will result in a reduction of the domestic market share of the Chinese industry by 50 per cent (Yu et al., 2000). Therefore, the profit for Chinese petrochemicals will be seriously reduced under the WTO. The production cost in this sector in China is also very high. Most firms in this sector are run by the state. Like the high-value added steel industry, the petrochemical industry should be a favourite of state protection.

In China's machinery industry, metal processing, instruments, wiring and cables have been competitive. Three sectors within this industry will be likely to suffer: the high-tech and high-value added sectors that are still in infancy, those that lack the economy of scale and, those at the low end, but cost more to produce than in other countries (Yu et al., 2000). Consistent with our finding here, clearly these sectors will require state protection.

China's automobile industry is the most protected industry. Due to the huge market in China, the competition will be intense in this area. Multinational corporations will move into this market quickly after China joins the WTO, but competition will benefit China's automobile industry in the sense that efficiency will have to be improved and technology upgraded in order to survive. However, it is expected that non-tariff barriers will step in to take the place of tariffs.

China's telecommunication faces serious challenge. The WTO requires that member states open their telecommunications market to other member states. For developing countries, the last year of restriction will be 2005. Most member states are able to control the majority share in the telecommunication market. The Chinese government agreed that in joint ventures, foreign capital can own 49 per cent of shares and can reach 50 per cent one year later. Foreign Internet service providers are also allowed to participate in the Chinese market. Foreign companies can also join China in its satellite communications market.

Our finding shows that China's national policy is to extend protection to those industries with relatively high average wages and high-value added per worker. However, if China did not join the WTO, most of China's industries will lose competitive advantage in the world economy. The trade off is between losing market share to foreign companies in the short run and losing competition entirely in the long run. China's tariff policy reflects a balance of an industrial policy that favours high-tech industries and a social policy that protects firms in debt – a combination which offers some explanation for China's strenuous dilemma to embrace the Western terms for its membership in the WTO. This policy combination can work to the best interest of the Chinese government and industries only if the protected industries can improve their efficiency without competition, which is almost an oxymoron.

Notes

*Earlier versions of this chapter were presented at the American Political Science Association annual meeting, Atlanta, 2–5 September 1999, and an international conference on Development through Globalization in Pudong, China, 5–7 July 2000. The analysis was also published earlier in 'Openness and Trade Policy in China: An Industrial Analysis', by Baizhu Chen and Yi Feng in *China Economic Review* (2001), 11(4): 323–41. The analysis, including all tables and the figure are reprinted with permission from Elsevier Science.

1 Data and discussions from Yang (1997), unless noted.

2 The complete list includes coal, petroleum, natural gas, oil shale, stone, nonmetal, timber, sugar, meat processing, aquatic product, bakery, dairy product, canned food, yeast product, spice, alcohol, soft drink, tea, tobacco, raw-fabric processing, cotton, woolen, linen, silk, knitting, apparel, headgear, footgear, tanning, leather, tan product, feather product, wood piece, board, woodwork, bamboo work, furniture, pulp, paper, stationary, athletic product, music, toy, game, crude oil, oil product, coking, fertilizer, organic chemical, cosmetics, pharmaceuticals, synthetic fabrics, fishery equipment, tires, power tire, crude rubber, rubber footgear, daily-used rubber product, crude plastic, plastic footgear, daily-used plastics, cement product, tiles and lime, glass, pottery, fireproof material, graphite, mineral product, iron, steel, light non-ferrous metal, rare metal and rare earth metal, cast iron pipe, container, construction metal, daily-used metal, furnace and motor, metal processing, bearing and valve, casting and forging, light-industry equipment, railway equipment, car, motorcycle, bicycle, ship building, airplane, electrical machinery, control and automation, daily-used electrical, lighting equipment, communications equipment, radar electronics and daily-used electronics.

3 Currently, as China is not part of the WTO, the market share of China's textile products in the USA was lost to Mexico that now has become the largest textile exporter to the USA (Yu et al., 2000).

References

Baldwin, R. E. (1985) 'The political economy of protection', *The Political Economy of US Import Policy*, Massachusetts, Cambridge: The MIT Press.

Cassing, J., McKeown, T. J. and J. Ochs (1986) 'Political economy of the tariff cycle'. *American Political Science Review*, 80(3): 843–62.

Caves, R. E. (1976) 'Economic models of political choice: Canada's tariff structure', *Canadian Journal of Economics*, 9(2): 278–300.

Chen, Baizhu and Yi Feng (2001) 'Openness and trade policy in China: an industrial analysis', *Chinese Economic Review*, forthcoming.

Feng, Yi (1997) 'China's economic reform: logic and dynamism'. *International Interactions*, 23: 315–33.

Feng, Yi and Hui Zhang (1999) 'Provincial distribution of direct foreign investment in China, 1992–96: a pooled time-series empirical study', in Baizhu Chen, Kim Dietrich and Yi Feng (eds) *Financial Market Reform in China: Progress, Problems and Prospects*, Boulder, CO: Westview.

Hillman, A. L. (1982) 'Declining industries and political-support protectionist motives'. *American Economic Review*, 72: 1180–87.

James, S. C. and D. Lake (1989) 'The second face of hegemony: Britain's repeal of the Corn Laws and the American Walker Tariff of 1846'. *International Organization*, 43(1): 1–30.

Kaempfer, W. and T. D. Willett (1989) 'Combining rent-seeking and public choice theory in the analysis of tariffs vs. quotas', *Public Choice*, 63: 79–86.

Magee, S. P., Brock, W. A. and L. Young (1989) 'Three simple tests of the Stolper-Samuelson theorem'. in *Black Hole Tariffs and Endogenous Policy Theory*, New York: Cambridge University Press, pp. 101–11.

McKeown, T. J. (1989) 'The politics of Corn Law repeal and theories of commercial policy', *British Journal of Political Science*, 19: 353–80.

Montinola, G., Qian Yingyi and B. R. Weingast (1995) 'Federalism, Chinese style: the political basis for economic success in China', *World Politics*, 48: 50–81.

Office Third National Industrial Census (1995) *The Data of the Third National Industrial Census of the People Republic of China in 1995 by Ownership Type*, Beijing: China Statistics Press.

Office Third National Industrial Census (1995) *The Data of the Third National Industrial Census of the People Republic of China in 1995 by Industry*, Beijing: China Statistics Press.

Pincus, J. J. (1975) 'Pressure groups and the pattern of tariffs', *Journal of Political Economy*, 83(4): 757–78.

Shirk, S. (1993) *The Political Logic of Economic Reform in China*, Berkeley, CA: University of California Press.

Tariff Department of Customs General Administration of the People's Republic of China (1996) *Practical Handbook on Import & Export Tax of the Customs of the People's Republic of China*, Beijing: International Culture Publishing Corporation.

Yang, Shenming (ed.) (1997) *Reforming China's Tariff System*, Beijing: China Social Science Publishers.

Yang, Shujing (1999) 'On China's joining the World Trade Organization', *China Press*, 5 June.

Yu, Yongding, Bingwen Zhen and Hong Song (2000) *The Research Report on China's Entry in WTO: The Analysis of China's Industries*, Beijing: Social Sciences Documentation Publishing House.

10

China's Choices: Scenarios for China in the Context of an Emerging Global Civilization

Howard V. Perlmutter

Introduction

'One of the great "ifs" and harsh ironies of history hangs on the fact that in January 1945, four and a half years before they achieved national power in China, Mao Tse-tung and Chou En-lai in an effort to establish a working relationship with the United States offered to come to Washington to talk in person with President Roosevelt. What became of the offer has been a mystery until, with the declassification of new material, we now know for the first time that the United States made no response to the overture. Twenty seven years, two wars, and *x* million lives later, after immeasurable harm wrought by mutual suspicion and phobia of two great powers not on speaking terms, an American President, reversing the unmade journey of 1945, has traveled to Peking to speak with the same two Chinese leaders. Might the interim have been otherwise?' B. Tuchman (1975).

'*Move to Span Gulf Between Taiwan and China*
Winston Wong, the son of one of Taiwan's greatest industrialists has agreed to join forces with Jian Mianheng, the son of the Chinese President Jiang Zemin, in a ground breaking $1.6 billion computer chip project that will span the political gulf between Taipei and Beijing.' *Financial Times*, 14 Sept 2000.

'*Asia's Informal Diplomacy: Track two, Discussions and Regionalism*
In a world of nation states it is natural to think of diplomacy as a formal and exclusive activity. Official speeches, white papers, and

> elaborate diplomatic etiquette further reinforced this impression. Government to government exchange, however, is not the only method by which diplomacy can be conducted. Nor for that matter is it a sufficient vehicle to help nations enhance their multilateral relations. In East Asia, Track two (T2) diplomacy otherwise known as private citizen diplomacy has acquired a peculiar and distinct form. Paralleling the formal dialogues held in the region, T2 has evolved into a plethora of multilateral exchanges designed to help governments deal with issues ranging from economic cooperation to peacekeeping and conflict prevention. These dialogues conducted in academically oriented conferences throughout the region are sustained by scholars and political analysts who work in think tanks... Governments in East Asia readily accept the research findings culled from T2 dialogues and there has been a neat, almost seamless working relationship between the public and the private (academic) sector on certain key issues'. Kim Beng Phar *Harvard International Review*, Spring 2001: 38.

The quotes above are relevant to the purpose of this essay. We examine China's choices as a function of the degree to which its leadership and citizenry come to prefer a set of international actions, policies, structures and interactive processes based on what we call the Global Symbiotic paradigm, a collaborative, global-partnership mindset. In my work with Eric Trist, we distinguished the Symbiotic paradigm from the Industrial and De-industrial paradigms (Perlmutter and Trist, 1981).

In its global version, the Symbiotic paradigm is based on the premise that to survive and to grow, it is necessary to establish collaborative structures and interactions which promote cross-cultural and cross-border relationships in different countries around the world. This paradigm is uniquely marked by a search for mutual gain, co-learning, reciprocal trust and respect, in short 'doing unto others as you would have others do to you'. The Global Symbiotic paradigm is further marked by global partnerships, with balances of autonomy and interdependence, in all societal domains, namely, political, economic, sociocultural, and in science, technology, medicine and ecology. An inclination to global engagement is consistent with this paradigm.

By way of contrast, the Global Industrial paradigm is based on a dominating, authoritarian, hegemonic, competitive mindset. It is further marked by a propensity to create ethnocentric, dominant–dependent and win–lose relationships worldwide. A concern with the global containment of what are seen as expansionist approaches of others is of central concern.

The third or Anti-industrial paradigm has many versions, including a mindset which is hostile to industrialization and globalization, and in one version, a strong preference for local traditions and environmental values. This can be manifested in an isolative, inward-oriented approach to international affairs, formerly associated with Libya and to a degree with North Korea and now still associated with Myanmar.

In any given time all three may coexist in a country. For example, the pragmatists may operate according to the Symbiotic paradigm, the conservatives or the military may prefer the Industrial paradigm and various protest groups may identify with the Anti-industrial world view.

In our current work, the idea of the Global Symbiotic paradigm led us to three additional concepts:

1 An emerging global civilization or the rapid growth of patterns of societal interdependence which are emerging.
2 Collaborative Social Architecture or interconnecting structures, organizations, ground rules and policies which are appearing and which promote mutually beneficial cooperation.
3 Deep Dialog Drivers or interactive processes between persons including delegates in the various societal domains, based on the presence of, to cite a few features, common direction, and mutual respect and trust.

We will ask how this paradigm fits with the futures of emerging global civilization and China's choices in the twenty-first century.

Three futures for the emerging global civilization

In a previous paper, we laid out a set of Rocky Road propositions (Perlmutter, 1991) in which we painted a picture of an emerging global civilization shaped by the macro forces of globalization and enabling communication technologies. Evidences of this global civilization are found in daily events from all regions of the world, and encompass economic, political, military, social, cultural, scientific, technological and ecological domains. Our interpretation is that the Symbiotic paradigm becomes a driving force, and is manifested in both globalization and technology trends. These forces are becoming stronger than the restraining forces of nationalism and protectionism.

One result today, is greater global openness, transparency of nations, and a greater density of linkages with persons and institutions in other countries. There is also a greater disposition to work for multilateral solutions, to recognize degrees of global interdependence and to find some shared values.

Another way to put it is: the configuration of global societal forces seem to be making a Symbiotic paradigm a more constructive mindset. On the other hand, there is clearly evidence of increasing ethnic and religious conflict where the Symbiotic paradigm does not prevail, from Bosnia to Belfast, from Israel to Indonesia, from Rwanda to Russia, and Chechnya and Algeria and other cases of civilizational clashes between Western values and Islamic fundamentalism. In various ways, they are based on the Industrial and De-industrial paradigms. Yet, Anti-industrial global isolation is really very difficult, as North Korea has found and Myanmar, Libya and Iraq are finding. And while global dominance is really not feasible even for populous China or for superpowers like the USA, in our times, it does not mean that it will be absent as an option in some contexts, for example, the military.

In other scenarios, as versions of capitalism become the dominant economic system, new bonds between countries are forged while existent ones are strengthened. These bonds of economic interdependence became most evident when tested during the Asian financial crisis and the default of Russian sovereign debt.

As the emergent global civilization outgrows its economic infancy, and when the era of super chips and broadband takes hold, we are likely to witness many global events which will require new global institutions including those which will be necessary with the growth of the Internet and a very rapidly emerging global cyber-civilization.

We shall focus on three of many possible global civilizational futures. These futures will be based on variations of three major macro trends and manifestations of the Symbiotic paradigm as evidenced in:

1 degrees of increasing global interconnectivity in all societal domains as evidenced in the proliferation of networks in all societal domains;
2 degrees of global civilizational accommodation as evidenced in the increased North, South, East and West networks of interdependencies in all societal domains – political, economic etc.; and
3 degrees of a paradigm shift for both nation states and firms, from isolated states who try to go it alone to more globally oriented, borderless, knowledge-based, horizontal, networked states in what is called the New World Economy.

The three kinds of global civilizational futures we chose, are then based on the speed, depth, and countertrends of variations of integration globally. Given the momentum of technological change, these futures are not seen as equiprobable over the long term. Nevertheless, we were able to develop some internally consistent scenarios for each future. See Table 10.1 for full details.

The low integration, the national fortress world or the fragmented isolationist world civilization

In this world, the forces against globalization prevail, and countries try to retreat into what Hammond (1998) has called the National Fortress World and we see the Anti-industrial paradigm in prominence. This world is marked by breakdowns in intercountry relations and a dramatic reduction in international trade and investment. A Fragmented Isolationist world is a nationalist world, where efforts to maintain boundaries are strong, and where the fear of foreign influence outweighs the benefits on global interdependence. The costs of this world are very great to countries who attempt to try it, as Libya, Myanmar and North Korea have found. They tried a low commitment to the Symbiotic paradigm. In some versions, there are ingredients of the Industrial and De-industrial paradigm. This scenario has a fundamental implausibility in the long term because it seems so impractical to cut off most communications. This applies especially in cyberspace and as the growth of enabling technologies grows, and the difficulty of resisting the trend towards global transparency increases.

The moderate integration or the pragmatic regionally oriented world civilization

In this world, the forces for globalization prevail, but countries at first aim for what Hammond (1998) has called the Regionally Oriented world. This is marked by a slower growth in interregional relations but over time, an increase in world trade and investment. This is a Pragmatic Reformist Oriented world civilization, one where the main orientation of countries is regional and reformist, where privatizing and globalization continue despite back lashes of the Seattle and Prague variety. The Symbiotic paradigm can prevail regionally with Western Europe as a model for facilitating mutually beneficial arrangements between nations in the region. But in this world the global digital divide between rich and poor countries is still very great. This world does not preclude some countries from adopting the Industrial paradigm and the accompanying desire for global superiority.

Table 10.1 Three global civilization integration scenarios

Low global integration: the fragmented isolationist world	**Moderate global integration: the pragmatic globally oriented world**	**High global integration: the virtual integration world**
Political		
• Political isolation and distrust • Re-emergence of the mulipolar international system • Intergovernmental institutions break down • Political standoffs with possible military confrontations • Self-interested nation-state mentality is very much alive	• Contingent political cooperation in maintaining world peace • Nation-states give way to regional alliances • More countries take steps toward democratization • Elections on local levels encouraged • Granting true religious freedom increases worldwide	• Politics no longer only conducted on a 'state to state' basis • A sense of a virtual global civilization, divided not by physical borders, but by cultural boundaries, on the rise • Political boundaries less important • The virtual nation state
Economic		
• Political uncertainty adversely affect worldwide financial markets • Information asymmetry continues or worsens • Speed of business decision-making and execution lags behind technological advances • Disintegrative economic policy-making • Consumer confidence decreases • Technology imports decrease while labour-intensive exports increases • Development of global brands and world-class enterprises unlikely	• More countries adopts Western like financial market regulations • Bourses succumb more to private enterprises' influence • Rise of private enterprises, replacing SOE's as the dominant economic entities • Countries shifts away from labour-intensive exports to technology and service exports	• Business at the speed of thought. Real-time business decision making • Financial markets subjected to common scrutiny • Adoption of world-wide standards in accounting and disclosure • Development of world class brands • Technology dominates economic output • A younger and more educated populace dominates the economic landscape • Global entrepreneurship flourishes in cyberspace
Social-cultural		
• Uneven development of social domains • Generational gap widens	• Acceptance and development of subcultures • Acceptance of ethnic practices	• A legal system free from political considerations established

Table 10.1 (continued)

Low global integration: the fragmented isolationist world	**Moderate global integration: the pragmatic globally oriented world**	**High global integration: the virtual integration world**
• Failing integration of all fifty-some culturally distinct ethnic groups • Population growth slows down with the continued implementation of population control policies • Human rights issues serve as political bargaining tools instead of legitimate social reform causes	• Human rights views will slowly conform to international standards in practice • Along with societal development comes unfamiliar social strains • Rise in private social institutions to deal with social problems	• Globalization of tastes in clothing, music, and food takes over • A rise in social institutions to deal with unprecedented social problems • Individuality replaces conformity • The education system gradually shifts from emphasizing conformity and inflexibility to emphasizing individuality and flexibility
Science Technology and Medicine		
• The potential of scientific and technological progress unrealized • Science and technology, instead of bringing cultures together, serve as major divides between the West and East • The lag between invention and diffusion of scientific discoveries does not shorten • Proprietary technological progress seen as a source of national pride • Sharing of technology remain a issue	• Technology cooperation among advanced and developing nations • Establishment of knowledge centres worldwide dealing with specific expertise • Upgrading of military technology, including nuclear power • Technology imports decrease as domestic technology sectors strengthens	• UN and International agreements to maintain stability in the region • World class research institutes established • Technological progress is shared to produce common good • Centrality of global cyberspace with information transfer costs = zero • Global cyber medicine is flourishing
Ecological		
• Resources for ecological initiatives diverted to the economy or military • International ecological efforts will be ineffective • Technologies that can improve the environment will be too slowly implemented	• International cooperation in preserving the environment • Development of ecological balance as well as economic balance	• Global shared efforts to improve the environment, tailoring to local and cultural considerations • People become more environmentally conscious as strains of economic development begin to surface

The high integration, globally interdependent virtual world civilization

In this world civilization, the Symbiotic paradigm is a global norm, and the forces for globalization prevail to a high degree. Countries no longer try to retreat but accept that they must play a major role not only regionally but in the world economy because, over time, there is no place to hide anywhere. This version of a world has been called a Global Market world (Hammond, 1998). It is marked by growth in symbiotic intercountry relations, a dramatic increase in international trade and investment, global Collaborative Social Architecture and a preference for Deep Dialog. A version of this world includes the enabling role electronic broadband technology might bring. In the longer term is a virtual world where both city and village bridge the digital divide. The result is a parallel and interpenetrating emerging global cyber-civilization. The third scenario is the most probable in a 20–50 year time perspective. It does not, however, preclude, countries making efforts to adapt the Global Industrial paradigm to cyberspace.

Three choices for China and the Global Symbiotic paradigm

The three paradigms are relevant to China's future choices. The Global Symbiotic paradigm applies to Chinese choices, reflected in various degrees in the economic area. It is consistent with the choices available to China in relation to Taiwan as a lesser province or Taiwan as a partner. For example, building economic partnerships with Taiwan in high technology, taking advantage of enabling technologies like the Internet for increasing global connectivity even at the village level can be consistent with a Global Industrial paradigm with different consequences.

The Global Symbiotic paradigm is expressed in China's choices which depend on dialogic relationships, so that differences can be bridged. We note here that the absence of dialog in the extraordinary missed opportunity of Mao not meeting Roosevelt was disastrous.

At this writing, the current conflict between China and the USA was being played out in the diplomatic activities after the collision between the US spy plane and a Chinese fighter plane. We shall discuss below how the Collaborative Social Architecture and Dialog process played a role in reaching a partial resolution of the conflict, specifically the return of the American crew. So while the conflict is not yet resolved, we can gain insights from the painful attempts at finding a way to bridge apparently cross-cultural differences such as a movement from the Chinese demands that the USA should apologize.

The absence of a clear and shared commitment to the Symbiotic paradigm and missing Dialogs of Mao and Roosevelt in the past, may have changed world history for 25 years. In the present, failure to reach a shared Symbiotic paradigm in the US surveillance plane incident threatened not only China–US trade, and consumer boycotts, but also a whole host of US–Chinese relationship including the most favoured nation status, location of the Olympics, and entry into the WTO. The consequences of missing and failed dialogs clearly can be very serious.

To identify China's choices for the future, we focused on a range from a high degree of global integration, meaning the prevalence of the Global Symbiotic paradigm, to a low degree of integration that refers to its relative absence. This led us to identify three choices for China based on the different degrees of correlation and integration of China into three emergent global civilization scenarios.

China's choices can match any one of these global scenarios or China can choose to pick one which will be robust in the long term regardless of short-term difficulties. Of these global civilizational directions, three future choices for China are based on different degrees of commitment to the Global Symbiotic paradigm: (1) China retreats from the world scene and chooses to limit outside relations, and picks an isolative, inward-looking future; (2) China expands regionally, forming its primary partnership to the Asian theatre; and (3) China expands globally with partnerships everywhere in the world.[1]

The latter two choices are somewhat arbitrarily based on China's accepting the primacy of the Symbiotic paradigm, a cooperative mindset with a regional or global international partnership approach. But Choice 3 is both global and virtual since, as a very long-term approach, the influence of enabling electronic technology will play a major role in achieving and maintaining global access to all countries.[2]

This means that two global futures for China will require, at different rates, different forms of Collaborative Social Architecture with other countries and engagement in more or less continuous Deep Dialog with persons in other countries in all civilizational domains, political, military, economic, socio-cultural in science, technology, medicine and ecology, from trade, arts and sports like the Olympics.

Our vision is that over a period of decades, the most robust future for China as for many other countries, including the USA, will be to evolve into a Virtual Global State, which is both home and host to local and Global cyber organizations of the future, and new forms of Collaborative Social Architecture. However unlikely this may seem today, where national identity is still primary, the process we describe is already under way, reaching deep into the urban populations of China, but including also the villages, with increasing connectivity which is available today through the Internet. But the challenge to state owned enterprises (SOEs), small entrepreneurial enterprises, and Chinese MNCs such as Haier are formidable. The range of these future challenges of the entire gamut of Chinese enterprises is well documented in Richter (2000).

Table 10.2 indicates China's choices. To review, the first choice for China is a Low Integration National Fortress China in which China in face of the disruptive internal forces of cultural conflict including religious, racial and economic disparities, chooses to retreat from the global economy. China gives up its efforts at reforms in the face of catastrophic unemployment from the conversion of SOEs, and backlash from the many constituencies who do not benefit from free markets. While we consider this choice highly improbable, it cannot be ignored in the face of the kind of turbulence which can be expected in the years ahead. This is a choice reflecting a low degree of commitment to the Symbiotic paradigm globally but rather to a Nationally-oriented Industrial or De-industrial paradigm. I consider this choice unlikely.

A second choice is a selectively open regionally oriented China, a Moderate Integration Pragmatic Reformist China. This is a version of the current situation in which more industrial and business sectors are privatized, but where the Internet does not yet play a major role because of the official fear of lack of control. The main risk of this choice is being cut off from the explosive impact of global technological changes, outside the region, changes which occur faster, broader and with deeper impacts. We consider this choice most likely to be preferred, in the short to middle term but basically infeasible in the long term. The Regional Symbiotic or Partnership paradigm would be confined to regional Asian activities. This reflects moderate degree of commitment to the Global Symbiotic paradigm and is really infeasible today and more so over time.

A third choice for China in the longer term we call a High Global Integration China, where China with its commitment to electronic technology becomes a virtual nation state. This would be transformational in that it involves a deep integration of China electronically in all the primary civilizational domains: political, military, legal, economic, socio-cultural, in science, technology and medicine, and ecology. The third scenario, with some cultural adjustments, has some long-term prospects because the emerging global cyber-civilization could bind Taiwan and China in seamless connections between the remotest villages

Table 10.2 China's choices in the emerging global civilization

Low integration: the fragmented national fortress China	**Selective integration: the pragmatic global integration China**	**High integration: the global virtually integrated China**
Political		
• China prefers political isolation and distrust • Reemergence of the bipolar international system with the US at one end and China at the other • Political standoffs with possible military confrontations • Taiwan's stifled through diplomatic isolation and force	• Contingent political cooperation in maintaining world peace • China becomes more active militarily, projecting its forces around South East-Asia in alliances • China takes steps toward democratization • Elections on local levels encouraged • China–Taiwan relationship improves as China becomes more democratic • Religious freedom but stifling any separatist attempts in Tibet and Xinjiang • China's military superiority in Asia serves to maintain stability in the region	• Politics no longer conducted on a 'state to state' basis • A sense of a global cyber-civilization, divided not by physical borders, but by cultural boundaries • Development of a multiparty political system in China • The CCP is no longer the dominant party • Taiwan and China unifies democratically and peacefully • Virtual China and Virtual Europe and US working together to unify the West and the East
Economic		
• Political uncertainty adversely affects worldwide financial markets • Information asymmetry in China continues or worsens	• China adopts Western like financial market regulations	• Business at the speed of thought. Real-time business decision making • Financial markets subjected to common scrutiny

• Speed of business decision-making and execution China lags behind technological advances • Disintegrative economic policy-making • Consumer confidence decreases • Technology imports decrease while labour-intensive exports increase • Development of Chinese global brands and world-class enterprises unlikely	• Bourses in Shanghai and Shenzhen become less susceptible to SOE influence, more to regional private enterprises influence • Rise of private enterprises, replacing SOEs as the dominant economic entities • West-China economic cooperation extends into policy making • With help from the West, China shifts away from labour-intensive exports to technology and service exports • Development of China's central plains	• Adopting of virtual worldwide standards in accounting and disclosure • Development of world class brands • Virtual technology dominate economic output • A younger and more educated populace dominates the virtual economic landscape • Entrepreneurship flourishes • Prominence of global cyber business
Social-cultural		
• Uneven development of social domains • Generational gap widens • Failing integration of all fifty-some culturally distinct ethnic groups • Population growth slows down with the continued implementation of population control policies • Human rights issues serve as political bargaining tools instead of legitimate social reforms causes	• Acceptance and development of sub-cultures that enrich China's social fabric • Acceptance of ethnic practices • Human rights views will slowly conform to international standards in practice • Along with societal development comes unfamiliar social strains • Rise in private social institutions to deal with social problems	• A virtual legal system free from political considerations established • Globalization of tastes in clothing, music, and food takes over especially in global cyberspace • A rise in social institutions to deal with unprecedented social problems • Virtual individuality replaces conformity • The education system shifts from emphasizing conformity and inflexibility to individuality and flexibility

Table 10.2 (continued)

Low integration: the fragmented national fortress China	**Selective integration: the pragmatic global integration China**	**High integration: the global virtually integrated China**
Science Technology and Medicine		
• The potential of scientific and technological progress unrealized • Science and technology, serve as major divides between the West and China and China and other nations • The lag between invention and diffusion of discoveries not short • Proprietary technological progress seen as a source of national pride	• Technology cooperation among advanced nations including China • Establishment of knowledge centres in China dealing with specific Asian expertise • Upgrading of military technology • Will eventually be able to project nuclear power throughout Asia • Technology imports decrease as regional technology sectors strengthen	• World class research institutes established • Technological progress is shared to produce common good • Global cyberspace has major roles in science and technology and medicine = centrality of global cyber civilization • Global technological progress in knowledge creation widely shared
Ecological		
• Resources for ecological initiatives diverted to the economy or military • International ecological efforts will be ineffective • Technologies that can improve the environment will be too slowly implemented	• International cooperation in preserving the environment • Development of inner China, improving ecological balance as well as economic balance	• Shared values. China part of global virtual efforts improve the environment, tailoring to local and cultural considerations

of China and Taiwan. It will require that Chinese and Taiwan political leadership develops a new global mindset (Dickie and Thornhill, 2001). In this scenario, China could choose to build in part a decentralized village-based economy, linked by wireless communication and efficient transport. As some observers have noted, this is a scenario where the world's most agricultural nation finds a way to bridge what is now a digital divide and 'leapfrog the industrial revolution straight to the information age' (Ogilvy and Schwartz, 2000). This choice reflects a high degree of commitment to the Global Symbiotic paradigm. This would be consistent with a trend for Asia seen by George and Usha Haley who see the Internet in the future taking a role in filling what they call 'an informational black hole' in Southeast Asia (see Haley, Tan and Haley, 1998).

The Global Symbiotic paradigm: Collaborative Social Architecture, Deep Dialog and China's choices

These three Chinese choices outlined above correspond to varying levels of commitment to building on the basis of the Global Symbiotic paradigm. The Global Symbiotic paradigm in turn leads to inventing different forms of Collaborative Social Architecture and requires what we call Deep Dialog processes with the world outside China in the political, economic, social, cultural, scientific, technological, medical and ecological societal domains.

The architectural innovations may be intergovernmental sponsored or non-governmentally sponsored, the latter a part of our evolving international civil society. In the high-integration scenarios, China is very active in various collaborative efforts on trade and finance, human rights, the environment, knowledge sharing, governing the Internet, working with members in the international civil society, and in environmental groups such as the World Wildlife Fund, the Sierra Club, and in seeking the Olympics in 2008. The DNA of the dialog process we call Deep Dialog are described in Table 10.3. To achieve progress the Deep Dialog Drivers must prevail over Deep Dialog Deficits.

The Collaborative Social Architecture – Deep Dialog framework provides us with a systematic approach to measure or to assess the quality of dialog between individuals, institutions and nations. This framework has offered particularly fruitful insights when applied to cross-cultural settings. Nearly all China's choices today involve different degrees of commitment to Deep Dialog. Conflicts can be explained by Dialog Deficits and the lack of Collaborative Social Architecture. For example,

Table 10.3 Deep Dialog Drivers, Deep Dialog Deficits, and the twenty-first century cybercorporation as collaborative social architecture

(a) Deep Dialog Drivers

1 Bridging – bridging time, language, cultural and geographical differences.
2 Bonding – dialog marked by distinctive relationship between persons based on mutual trust and respect.
3 Banding – dialog marked by collaborative team interactions and a willingness to band or join together.
4 Blending – opportunities taken to blend ideas, with frequent innovations forthcoming.
5 Bounding – focus on common directions and specific projects we could do together which contribute to shared objectives.
6 Binding – commitments to carry out joint projects.
7 Building – carrying out the commitment to implement projects.

(b) Deep Dialog Deficits

1 Fallow – no communications taking place.
2 Failed – persons find they cannot communicate.
3 Failing – persons find that current communications are getting worse.
4 Frozen – persons find that stalemates take place with polarized positions which are difficult to change.
5 Feeble – persons have minimal communication.

in the wake of the Asian financial crisis, worldwide economic and financial institutions have focused on promoting fairness, transparency and accountability, all of which are achievable through a web of dialog relationships involving intergovernmental and non-governmental institutions.

Furthermore, the Deep Dialog has profound implications for social architecture because Collaborative Social Architecture efforts are aimed at facilitating or improving dialog, cooperation, and understanding and vice versa. A Deep Dialog – Collaborative Social Architecture perspective allows users to dissect any event or encounter to identify the gaps or age, or deficits, not missing social architecture. The 7 Deep Dialog Drivers are Bridging, Bonding, Banding, Blending, Bounding, Binding, and Building. Together, they represent the essential processes through which Deep Dialog that occurs in China relates to other countries. The 5 types of Deep Dialog Deficits, Fallow, Failed, Failing, Frozen, and Feeble can also be evidence of mismatched and maladaptive or missing social architecture, in their societal vision and missions, governance, strategy, culture and organization design. Each deficit contributes to a specific type of deterioration in Deep Dialog.

After assessing the dialogic character of each scenario, we can envisage offering Collaborative Social Architecture – Deep Dialog solutions to areas of deficit and mismatch. The goals of this process would then be to move beyond identifying social architectural gaps and needs in each of the scenarios and to propose transformations in and establishments of unilateral, bilateral and multilateral institutions that will bring China further benefits and opportunities to contribute to the emerging global civilization.

China's desire to join the WTO is evidence of a desire to be connected to institutions based on a Global Symbiotic paradigm. This kind of Global Collaborative Social architecture is especially integral to the emergent global civilization as it deals with the designing of institutions that balance, interpret, and minimize the turbulence that is the defining characteristic of the emergent global economy today. For example, the Asian financial crisis was a negative manifestation of globalization in that local financial woes were magnified and transmitted to seemingly unrelated markets with astounding rapidity. It can be seen as a gap in the international financial infrastructure. New social architecture will be required to prevent or to limit another similar crisis, to deal with Third World debt.[3]

China's third choice and the twenty-first century global cyberorganization

The revolutionary conditions and consequences of the tidal wave of the spectacular and ubiquitous advances in telecommunications towards infinite bandwidth (Gilder, 2000) will lead to a major revolution in global networking. What happens when there is instantaneous global interconnectivity between all the villages of the world and between villages and urban centres? This transformational paradigm change will be mediated through persons and organizations which interact in productive partnerships for sharing knowledge worldwide (Von Krogh, 2000) based on a symbiotic paradigm[4] (see Table 10.4). We see the major evidence in the spread of diplomatic efforts in all societal domains between China and the outside world.

An open China would be host and home for firms who have instantaneous connections around the world and can engage in a definable set of deepening multilevel interpersonal and interinstitutional dialogic interactions with people and institutions in Asia (including Taiwan) and in all parts of the world, (including the United States).

The Deep Dialog competencies must be learned across cultures. There are many examples of Asian – Western Dialog, for example, of bridging, bonding, banding together, blending ideas, focusing on common

Table 10.4 Profile of the twenty-first century cybercorporation as Collaborative Social Architecture

Global societal vision – aspiration for global and local virtual leadership in value adding in specific societal (market) niches.
Global synarchic governance – less hierarchical leadership, less bureaucratic.
Global symbiotic strategy – a responsive global and local partnership strategy with stakeholders especially customers.
Global synergic culture – norms for Deep Dialog Drivers apply worldwide and virtually with knowledge sharing between persons inside and outside the organization.
Global spherical organization – the organization as a seamless, flexible, worldwide network, involving stakeholders such as customers, suppliers, governments and so on.

projects, binding the parties together and building new interface national, regional and global infrastructures which could benefit both China and its foreign partners. In Scenario III they could transform the new global economy of the millennium.

Two choices for China as a Virtual State

We see two choices for China as a Virtual State; China as a Virtual State based on the Industrial Paradigm and China as a Virtual State based on the Symbiotic paradigm. China will face these choices repeatedly in the years to come as it expands its reach globally, and regionally, not only with the United States but with the other countries of ASEAN. In Table 10.5, we compare what we believe to be the nature and consequences of the two choices as regards its role in Cyberspace. Paradigm I Virtual China, as the world's most populous nation, would seek to resolve differences based on a power-based Dominant–Dependent paradigm rather on the Symbiotic paradigm where one major manifestation will be for China to accept global ground rules and other forms of Collaborative Social Architecture reached through Dialog.[5]

Conclusions

We have painted some global futures of China based on an overarching proposition that over the next decades, information technology will support humankind's involvement in building our first global cyber-civilization. The rise of the Internet is an irreversible force, which while subject to controls in China and elsewhere, cannot impede in the long term, the building of global electronic networks for sharing ideas and interests everywhere in the world. If people in a country are motivated

Table 10.5 Two choices for China as a Virtual State

Dimensions of comparison	**Paradigm I (industrial)**	**Paradigm S (symbiotic)**
Orientation	Containment, confrontation, constricted collaboration	Engagement, cooperation, collaboration
Global dialogic character for global knowledge creation and sharing	Dialog Drivers decreasing, Dialog Deficits increasing for global knowledge creation and sharing	Dialog Drivers increasing, Dialog Deficits decreasing for global knowledge creation and sharing
Collaborative social architecture for global knowledge creation and sharing	In a limited number of societal domains, many missing structures for collaboration for global knowledge creation and sharing	Proliferation of many forms of global symbiotic social architecture in all societal domains for global knowledge creation and sharing
Role of military	Central	As just one important constituency
Regional relations (ASEAN)	Dominative, Hegemonic	Cooperative, collaboration
Relations in various societal domain: science, technology, medicine, ecology	Limited and under threat	Creative and productive, with participation in numerous worldwide networks
Roles in cyberspace in the emerging global cyber-civilization	Relatively marginal, because of the above	A central and proactive set of hubs and nodes in the emerging global cyber-civilization

by a Symbiotic mindset, they will gain the immense benefits of this civilization especially in global knowledge-creation and sharing.

In our view, it is not a matter then of whether a global cyber-civilization will be built, but on what kind of prevailing paradigm the global civilization will be built. To what degree will it be based on the Symbiotic Partnership paradigm, or the Industrial or Dominance–Dependence paradigm between nations or an anti foreign Industrial paradigm?

In the three choices for China, we ask which of China's choices are more likely to involve integration with the global economy where it is more likely that China will have a leading role and a better chance to improve the quality of life of most of its citizens. We believe Choice 3 is the long term direction. This means that if the Partnership paradigm prevails, not only will China's economy need to mesh with ideas of a sustainable global economy but also Chinese institutions and citizens will be involved in Collaborative Social Architecture and engaged in continuing dialogs on Western ideas and universal concepts of human rights, and other emerging and shared global values.

We also argue that participation in the emerging global cyber-civilization for China, and indeed any nation state, can be tracked by looking at the presence or absence of barriers to the dialogic process and the presence and absence of Collaborative Social Architecture in each of the civilizational domains, for example, political, economic, and so on. These processes are but the tip of the iceberg in terms of what changes will take place as the potential for instantaneous interconnectivity proliferates in the next decades. It is our view that those states that accept and prefer the prevalence of partnership norms and become part of a global knowledge creating and sharing process will see benefits for their own citizens in the cities and villages, and thus will see the benefits of becoming globally civilized.

Complexities and vicissitudes of Symbiotic paradigm: US–China surveillance plane incident

We have refered above to the intriguing idea that US–Chinese relations were severely compromised in 1945 through a mishap in communication between Mao and Franklin Roosevelt. No dialog was ever initiated and hence no Collaborative Social Architecture was built. This event was seen as one of the most costly Fallow Dialog Deficits in recent history.

In April 2001, we have an example of what could be construed as the possible erosion of the Symbiotic paradigm and the emergence of a shared Industrial paradigm between the USA and China based on confrontation and containment. A set of unpleasant experiences threatened to transform a relationship described as a 'strategic partnership' to one where confrontation and contention would be the norm. This would constitute a paradigm shift to the Industrial win–lose paradigm and the entire working relationship between the two countries. At the time of writing this, the latest encounter was considered unproductive and prospects were not very favourable.

It started on 1 April 2001 when a Chinese military jet plane collided with an American surveillance plane off the coast of Mainland China. The American plane crash landed in Hainan province with 24 crew members aboard. The Chinese pilot was killed. At the outset, the diplomatic activity was marked by strong public accusations (Dialog Deficits) between the USA and China. The USA asked for immediate return of the plane's crew and the Chinese demanded a sincere apology.

The communication process was largely defensive in the public and 'no doubt' private realm. Even though there were soon hints that some dialog was taking place with an effort to bridge differences, in a more collaborative manner, for a period of time it looked like no progress was possible. The one supportive Collaborative Social Architecture discovered to promote an opportunity for dialog was a Treaty signed by both countries in 1998 to promote military maritime safety.

But the Chinese military, who apparently were less enthusiastic about the Partnerships model, insisted on an apology and holding and questioning the American crew. The Chinese military unlike the Chinese ministers (or as well, some American constituencies) had in fact less opportunity or inclination for building relationships with its US counterparts, apparently showed disdain for their own 'pragmatists' and continued to demand an American apology. A stalemate or frozen Dialog Deficit prevailed when the USA refused to give one. Then some kind of creative dialog process seemed to have taken hold in the working group in search of a face-saving solution.

The joint committee worked on a draft letter which included an American expression of regret for the loss of life of the Chinese pilot who was trailing the American plane. Some version of the Symbiotic paradigm had prevailed during these intensive discussions so that an acceptable language could be found. For example, Mr Jiang, President of China noted that when people have a accident they say 'excuse me' (he used the English words). But this opened the possibility that there could be found an alternative in the Chinese expression *duibuqi* which is more informal and colloquial than the Chinese formal and legalistic expression *dao qian* which translates as 'apology' and implies the speaker has obligation to the offended party's loss of face. The former expression may have been more human and open the door to treating the matter as one of human relations as opposed to a legal confrontation and basis for many unpleasant consequences for both (*New York Times*, 2001).

The possibility that the Symbiotic paradigm was at serious risk became clearer after the American crew was released from China, and the USA showed evidence that the Chinese pilot, who had been just declared a Chinese martyr, was likely to be at fault; this position the Chinese found unacceptable. There was a serious conflict in accounts and facts about who caused the accident, such that instead of maintaining regrets to China, the USA saw their personnel put at risk by an over-zealous Chinese pilot who had been declared a martyr by China. Calls for punishment of China came from the US Congress. This included a long list such as (1) US sales of advanced arms (anti-missiles, submarines, etc.) to Taiwan; (2) opposing China's entry in the WTO; (3) vetoing China's quest for the Olympics; and (4) limiting favourable conditions for trading in the USA. There was US insistence that the plane be returned and the USA continue its surveillance missions.

Despite some major bonds of economic interdependence, there was the risk that the approach to increasing engagement with China in the Symbiotic mode, would be replaced by a containment orientation in the Industrial mode. The Symbiotic paradigm would be abandoned by both sides. There was a possibility that both the Conservatives and some Democrats would unite to express their desire to reprimand China for holding the American crew hostage for 11 days.

There was clearly a cross-cultural barrier that made the symbiotic solution difficult especially since the Chinese military was apparently taking a more prominent role. When an agreement was reached when the USA said it was 'very sorry' for the loss of life and for the emergency landing in Hainan, the crew was released.

This is intended to illustrate the cross-cultural and political vulnerability of the Symbiotic paradigm in United States–Chinese interstate relations and how a relatively minor event can at least temporarily threaten mutually beneficial economic interdependencies of China and in this case, the USA. For example, there were threats of boycott of Chinese products in the USA (Kahn, 2001).

I believe the recent US–Chinese spy plane conflict gives us a taste of what comes into play as, despite many opposing forces, hopefully the calmer mindsets of the symbiotic orientation will prevail and both US and China's choices come to contribute to the development of a more prosperous, equitable and humane global civilization.

Notes

1. There is another choice worth exploring: China deciding to choose the Industrial paradigm which means seeking to become an expanding, dominating, imperial, superpower. But we have chosen not to pursue this scenario in this essay because of the unlikelihood that any country including the USA can dominate all others in the Emerging Global civilization.
2. See Ogilvy and Schwartz (2000), 'Scenario One: China Web'. In this scenario, China builds a vast decentralized village based economy, linked by wireless communication and efficient transport. The world's most agricultural nation

finds a way to leapfrog the industrial revolution straight to the information age.

3 A World Bank – OECD memorandum proposed two new initiatives that will emphasize dialog and consensus building to improve the Collaborative Social Architecture of regional economic bodies and international organizations. They are aimed to improve corporate governance standards in emerging economies, which deserve part of the blame for the Asian financial crisis. The first is the Global Corporate Governance Forum, which will marshal the expertize that exists around the world in support of individual countries' efforts, both regulatory and voluntary. The second initiative will set up policy dialogue and development groups that will bring together representatives of governments in different regions of the world with OECD member country experts. Both measures aim to better equip emerging economies dealing with globalization. Institutions like these are steps in the right directions to thwart potential disaster.

4 The new forms of Collaborative Social Architecture which will be marked by what we call Deep Dialog can be based on positive or negative values. The proliferation of mafia connected activities, involved in drugs and sex trafficking of women an children will have to be matched by preventive, regulatory and prosecutorial institutions concerned with women's and children's rights.

5 It holds as well for the USA in its relations with the rest of the world. In our view, as a superpower, the USA is bound to be seen as a not-so-equal partner, one where the reality becomes one in which hegemonic, dominance-dependency will be the perception of other countries. This is a part of the complexity and vicissitudes of the Symbiotic paradigm in the uncertain times of the Emerging Global Civilization of the twenty-first century.

References

Dickie, M. and J. Thornhill (2001) 'Treading a quiet path to unification', *Financial Times*, 11 April.

Gilder, G. (2000) *Telecosm: How the Infinite Bandwidth will Revolutionize our World*, The Free Press.

Haley, G. T., Tan, C. T. and U. C. V. Haley (1998) *New Asian Emperors: The Overseas Chinese, their Strategies and Competitive Advantages*, Butterworth-Heinemann.

Hammond, A. (1998) *Which World? Scenarios for the 21st Century*, Island Press.

Kahn, J. (2001) 'Standoff over plane brings calls to boycott Chinese made goods', *New York Times*, 11 April.

New York Times (2001) 'Bush and Jiang exchange drafts of a letter stating US regrets', 7 April.

Ogilvy, J. and P. Schwartz (2000) *China's Futures: Scenarios for the World's Fastest growing Economy, Ecology and Society*, Jossey Bass.

Perlmutter, H. V. (1965) *Theory and Practice of Social Architecture*, Tavistock 1965.

Perlmutter, H. V. (1991) 'On the rocky road to the first global civilization', *Human Relations*, 44(9).

Perlmutter, H. V. and E. Trist (1986) 'Paradigms for societal transition', *Human Relations*, 39(1).

Richter, F.-J. (ed.) (2000) *The Dragon millennium: Chinese business in the coming world economy*, Quorum.

Tuchman, B. (1975) *Notes from China*, Council for Foreign Relations.

VonKrogh, G., Chijo, K., and I. Nonaka (2000) *Enabling Knowledge Creation*, Oxford University Press.

Part 4

Organizational Restructuring and Corporate Governance

11
Strategic Convergence or Divergence: Comparing Structural Reforms in Chinese Enterprises

Sek Hong Ng and Malcolm Warner

Introduction

This chapter attempts to explore the strategic implications of enterprise reform that have been undertaken at three major Chinese firms in the context of the recent wave of nation-wide policies aimed at promoting market socialism and China's projected entry into the WTO after the year 2000. These high-profile efforts have been directed at the national goal of building a market-oriented economy with Chinese characteristics (Child, 1994; Warner, 1995). The overall strategy, prescribed by the state, attempts to emulate the practice of the capitalist system known as marketization, which it hopes can still be accommodated within a doctrinal framework that still enshrines socialist principles (see *Fortune*, 1999). This hybrid blending of dialectical oppositions, between capitalist and socialist practices, is novel but has to date proved to be a workable piece of social experimentation at the wider level of the national economy. It is hence interesting to ascertain whether at the microlevel of the individual enterprise and workplace, such a fusion of the antithetical assumptions and practices of capitalism and socialism has been pursued with similar prudence and apparent success.

However, not all enterprises within China have been able to reconcile and integrate the two systems at an equal pace and with an equal harmony (see Chan, 1995). The factors and conditions shaping or constraining the performance of PRC enterprises are naturally diverse and pluralistic. However, it is likely that the different ways Chinese business and work units can cope with the paradoxical demands and implications of market socialism (or precisely, the capitalist or marketized system in a socialist context) may depend to a large extent upon the ownership and governance type to which an enterprise belongs (Naughton, 1995). This is to suggest, basically, that national enterprises are more liable to be captives of old-style socialist system production relations and hence less amenable to the requirements of a marketized system, as evident at the workplace level in the handling of employment and personnel establishment, or more precisely, de-establishment (see Warner, 1996). Conversely, where the enterprises are funded and managed by foreign capital or at least, with foreign participation, it is expected that capitalist arrangements excel better because of first, a less alien workforce and managerial psychology and second, a more market- (or capital-) friendly infrastructure of assumptions, practices and institutions. Between these two polar types, we find the newer forms of home-based Chinese enterprises (like the private collectivities) which are intermediate in terms of their propensity to deal with an innovative regime of market capitalism (Oi, 1999).

Much has changed since Mao's days; whilst in 1978, with the onset of Deng's reforms, over four-fifths of Chinese industrial output was produced by SOEs; by 1999, this proportion had been reduced to less than one-quarter. Indeed, such work-units (*danwei*) are now overshadowed by firms outside the state sector in not only output but also in the numbers they employ. Non-state sector workers now turn out well over half of the output of the whole economy (see *The Economist*, 19 June 1999: 104). Once a state-dominated economy, China now looks like becoming more and more like its neighbours, such as Japan and South Korea, with a core of giant firms and myriad numbers of small ones. In the context of the recent Asian crisis, this possibility has interesting implications but given the specificity of the Chinese context, it is likely that soft rather than hard convergence is on the cards (see Warner, 2000).

For purposes of the above exposition, this chapter shall hence present a spectrum of three case studies of classic PRC enterprises with each exemplifying the situation of a specific ownership type.[1] We prefer to use the term classic here, instead of the term stereotypical. The strategic issue, particularly in a so-called workers' state like the PRC, that we consider is basically the trade-off between factor efficiency and employment (for background, see Naughton, 1995; Nolan, 1998; Steinfeld, 1998); this is exemplified when we look at corporate governance since who actually runs the enterprise will determine who benefits, as will become clear as we look at each case in turn.

The dialectics of market socialism and its implications for enterprise management and corporate governance

Corporate governance in enterprises espouses the notion of industrial governance or in legal language, that of industrial jurisprudence as the legitimate prerogative and process of rule-making and of formulating decisions in key and strategic areas which affect the enterprise's agenda and its well-being. In the earlier decades of the 1970s and 1980s, the primary focus of governance issues in the West was seemingly coined in a pluralistic model and even encompassed collective bargaining and employee participation as alternative forms of practicing industrial democracy. Today, corporate governance appears to lessen the emphasis upon the bilateral relationship between the employer and the employed. Instead, the core institution for practising corporate governance has been consolidated to the governing entity of the board of directors, which is the shareholders' custodian in determining how ownership is to be constituted, evolved and replenished as well as how ownership and managerial control is to be exercised.

When China was still practising Marxian socialism in its orthodoxy, corporate governance hardly epitomized an issue which needed to be explicitly addressed as a policy choice. Governance at enterprises was ordained, first, by the doctrinal prescription that the workers were the masters (*zhuren*) in state enterprises under socialist ownership and second, as an extension of the state's authority structure under the imperatives of democratic centralism. Corporate governance at enterprises was literally non-problematic, inasmuch as the majority of such *danwei* was legally state-owned, thus hardly autonomous or self-governing (Lu and Perry, 1997). In spite of the ideological assumption about the community of interests and commonwealth in a socialist enterprise, division of purposes and power conflict still existed between the managers and the managed (see Kahn-Freund's 1972 classic treatment of the *raison d'etre* of labour law). Nevertheless, such a conflict of interest was ruled out ideologically and even suppressed politically, because a capitalist wage system was theoretically absent and irrelevant (see Ng and Warner, 1998).

However, the labour and capital divide has again emerged on the agenda of managing a workable system of governance for Chinese socialist enterprises when they were put on the long march of reform in order to become autonomous and commercially viable business-units. The creeping process of desocializing SOEs has emphasized, up to now, two focal areas of changes. One has been the structure and system of production relations, as the wage and employment reform policies have vested the SOEs with ample autonomy and yet also redefined their role as the employing units, namely, an employer as in a capitalist wage system. The other dimension has been the domain of ownership which has been, until recently, upheld and conserved doctrinally under the socialist principle of state-ownership. Private participation by individuals was still, for example, repudiated as ideologically alien during the early phase of the Four Modernizations in the mid- and late 1980s. This monolithic situation was, however, given a novel redefinition by the state when it began to engineer a process of furthering the SOEs' reforms, by the early and mid-1990s expressly aimed at, this time, the liberalization of ownership and governance control. As an extension of the logic of marketization, enterprises became eligible for their corporatization. Such a formula was at that time limited to a selected number of SOEs, however.

The above situation changed significantly by the year 2000 as a result of the recent introduction and the state's legitimation of the strategic notion of corporatization as an extension from the principle of marketization.[2] Such a new policy-initiative aims essentially at liberalizing ownership in order to widen the basis of capital formation and its sourcing. The entire notion is in this setting categorically distinct from that of privatization. The implications of this new policy of corporatization appear to be largely twofold. First, corporatizing in terms of legal status places a limit on the enterprise's and its owners' liability, as analogous to the equivalent arrangement of a limited company in capitalist (especially Anglo-American) economies. Second, the process of corporatization also enables a selected number of SOEs to be listed on the stock exchange. Third, it represents a major step for Chinese enterprises vis-à-vis globalization and projected entry into the WTO.

Restructuring the ownership and governance system of the SOEs involves, however, a basic dilemma in legitimating the role of these firms and demarcating the scope of their beneficiaries. During the pre-reform days, the picture was relatively unequivocal (see Warner, 1999a). It was basically, within the old doctrinal system, the state performing the agency role on behalf of the industrial proletariat, namely the working-class as the master of a socialist economy. However, the reform process of desocialization has now revived the importance of capital as a major factor. Although it is still the public (rather than private) ownership of capital per se which has the state's blessing, the restructuring exercise has announced, if only implicitly, that the key enterprises may work for capital's gain and not necessarily for the workers' interests. The classic divide between capital and labour, based on a we–they dichotomy, has again emerged or re-emerged (see Warner and Ng, 1999; Warner, 2000).

The emergence and re-emergence of a labour–capital distinction hence suggests an impasse which needs to be addressed either at present or eventually in future. The dilemma of having to deal with such a logic, normally associated with the capitalist wage system, especially at the SOE level, is probably best exemplified by the latest agenda of downsizing the workforce (see Warner, 1999b). The imperative of having to trim down drastically the size of personnel establishment of these SOEs in order to make them financially viable as autonomous and self-sufficient business units was and still is, alien to both the workers and even their managers brought up under the heritage of socialism since 1949. For them, job-ownership has always been held as a sacrosanct right, as a natural entitlement of the socialist worker under the norm of proletariat dictatorship and socialised public ownership (see Ng and Warner, 1998). In particular, downsizing has posed a far more problematic agenda in those vanguard SOEs where such a notion of proletarian ownership has been enshrined and upheld with stronger ideological faith. It is plausible to argue, in this connection, that unless the notion of ownership (of the enterprise and other forms of property) is clarified or redefined, the attitude of the workforce (especially among those affected) and even of the managers (particularly if they may be sacked) is likely to remain ambivalent about the legitimacy of retrenchment and removing workers from the employing units to which they belong. The emerging market is having a profound effect on both the employment, as well as the urban social security system. Additionally, market competition is leading all enterprises, state or non-state, 'to adopt a more flexible employment and wage system' (UNDP, 1999: 64–65). With up to one-third of the SOE workforce potentially redundant, 'the system of lifetime employment cannot last' (1999: 64).

Unemployment is, *pari passu*, growing by the day in China; the realistic total may be well over one in ten in many large cities; it may be over one in five in parts of the rust-belt in the Northeast (*dongbei*). A leading figure in the Chinese Academy of Social Sciences (CASS) recently described joblessness as the biggest challenge currently facing the Chinese economic system; professor Hu Angang, a CASS labour economist, cited figures to show that between 1993 and 1997, laid-off workers rose from 3 million to 15 million (with two in three from the SOEs). He estimated around 10–15 million more coming onto the dole by the start of the new millennium year. The highest reported jobless-ness cited is in Liaoning Province with over 22.4 per cent, followed by Hunan with 21.3 per cent; at city level, Chongqing at 18 per cent and Tianjin with 17 per cent, both had noteworthily high levels of unemployment (see Documentation, 1999).

The shifts now engendered and implied by the process of corporatization are therefore intriguing in this context. If the primary beneficiaries are no longer exclusively the workers or the industrial proletariat represented by the state, the subsequent changes in the constituency of the principal stake-holders to which the enterprise now owes its responsibility are obvious and even imperative. It is suspected, given the above exposition, that both private enterprises and SOEs inside China are likely to adopt a diversity of strategic approaches in restructuring the governance system of their business units and the authority structures underpinning it. They will in turn affect the relative ability of these enterprises to accept and to pursue what can still be viewed as drastic reform measures such as staff-cutbacks and de-establishing personnel.

The problems of bureaucratism and establishment above an efficiency threshold are probably most conspicuous in the publicly owned vanguard enterprises among the heavy-engineering industries, like steel plants. Paradoxically, it is also exactly these large SOEs which are also most apprehensive about and hence resistant to these structural reforms in governance, because of the uprooting and reversal of the doctrinal assumptions to which production relations have always been anchored (see Ng and Warner, 1998). It can also be argued that these standard-bearing socialist enterprises were in the past almost equivalent to an occupational community to which the industrial workers belonged and owed their existence and affiliation. Employment here had been permanent under the so-called iron rice-bowl (*tie fan wan*), workers had been assigned centrally by the state and in many cases, occupational inheritance from the parents to the children was also practiced. Such an exclusivity of the national enterprise as a community virtually endowed the socialist worker with a lifetime membership almost equivalent to a property-right, which was hardly alienable both in principle and in practice. If the downsizing agenda were sanctified as a prescription for uplifting the vitality of these national enterprises, the price to pay would be evidently the nullification of such a sacrosanct principle, one which has governed the *raison d'etre* of the SOEs since the liberation in 1949. The contradictions hence implied were formidable for the vanguard SOEs and up to now the state has hardly had a logical answer to this dilemma vis-à-vis the perils of disintegrating the socialist work-community, apart from the widely publicized re-employment programme (see UNDP, 1999: 71).

It is within such contradictions and structural ambivalence emanating from the state's quest for modernization and economic revitalization that this analysis proposes to examine a number of key cases of strategy-formulation and management of changes in corporate governance, as well as business and organizational structure, in three benchmark enterprises inside China. This trio of business organizations greatly differs in terms of ownership system, technology, marketing-strategy and employment policies. It is the intention here to argue that such differentials actually stem from the transient nature of the present reforms insofar as these variations may be expected to eventually narrow as the ownership-types converge.

Reforms at Shougang (Capital Steel) and its dilemmas

Shougang, the Capital Steel Corporation, provides almost a classic illustration of how enterprises and their managements have to cope with an impasse in restructuring their staffing and employment systems in the context of post-reform endeavours aimed at institutionalizing a marketized structure of ownership and governance, without however invoking the stigma of the capitalist system (Nolan, 1998; Steinfeld, 1998). This position appears to be problematic especially if perceived from the standpoints of first, rationalizing and streamlining the plant's staff and personnel establishment and second, safeguarding the jobs and wage security of the workforce (interviews exploring this were conducted on-site by the authors, November–December, 1998).

As the standard-bearer of the state's economic activities in a key strategic industry (heavy engineering) and vested with a mission to demonstrate the official commitment to reform, Shougang has always been innovative in the technical domain, as well as in exploring and developing its technological and business capabilities (see Nolan, 1998). It has a sizable research and development function, detached from the main parent as a subsidiary company and staffed by about over a hundred research personnel. It pledges an enterprise agenda of advancing the plant from the realm of manufacturing technology to that of tertiary-level process production. In pursuit of this goal, Shougang has been pursuing a strategy of diversification into associated industries of vertical and horizontal linkages with steel production. In part, these initiatives are emulative of Western experiences at revitalizing the iron and steel industries where these activities were also in the doldrums a decade ago in the 1980s.

With a history dating back over 75 years, Shougang,[3] employing over 60 000 employees in Beijing as well as many more elsewhere in China, around 230 000 by the end of 1998, is one of the largest Chinese SOEs (see Table 11.1). It has at present across the PRC (and overseas) 157 large and medium-sized plants, 52 domestic affiliates, 41 Sino-foreign joint ventures and 26 joint ventures or wholly funded enterprises. After 16 years of reforms, it has now become a multitrade, transregional, transnational firm involved in 18 industries involving iron and steel, mining machinery, electronics, construction, chemicals, light industry, building materials, ship building, shipping, tourism, garments, automobile, farming machines and finance. Its group turnover in 1998 was US$2975.9 million (over 24 billion RMB, as at the time of writing the official exchange rate was approximately 8.3 RMB to the US$), being number 402 in Asian ranking, compared with its Shanghai counterpart, Baoshan Steel with US$4636 million, ranked 259 (for further details of the Top Asian 500 firms, see *Asia Week*'s website, http://www.asiaweek.com).

However, Shougang has lived too long in the shadow of its socialist heritage for decades. Evidence appears to suggest that this vanguard national enterprise now faces a serious dilemma as how its business portfolio and production-system can be advanced and updated, without entailing any compromise of its basic ethical assumption that the workers' interests should not be sacrificed to the capitalistic profit-motive. In spite of a nationwide agenda, now almost imperative, for the SOEs to restructure and to rationalize their operations, there had long

Table 11.1 Development of Shougang since 1918

1918	Founded by Longyuan Mining Administration
1922	Initial pig iron plant completed
1945	Taken over by Guomindang; renamed Shijingshan
1949	Becomes Shoudu (Capital) Iron and Steel Corporation
1958	Decision to set up a fully-integrated iron and steel plant
1978	Renamed Shougang Iron and Steel
1979	Contract Responsibility System introduced
1983	Zhou Guanwu becomes Board Chairman and Party Sec., until 1995
1994	Becomes largest steel producer in the PRC
1998	Sales turnover now at almost 24 billion RMB
1999	Sales up by over 30 per cent over 1998 to 31.68 billion RMB
2000	Shougang to invest over 3.2 billion RMB in high-tech industry.

Sources: Nolan, 1998; Steinfeld, 1998.

been an evident amount of managerial reluctance to convert the veteran workforce with jobs-for-life to a hiring system of fixed-term labour contracts. Up to the mid-1990s, there was never a serious possibility of Shougang cutting costs by sacking workers due to government policy (see Nolan, 1998: 41). They had to look for growth to maintain employment rather than Western-style downsizing (1998: 41). Shougang had stated that they had a 'non-contract' contract (see also Interviews on-site, noted in Warner, 1995: 107–108) and only required newcomers to have a short-term labour contract. The latter course of action has been perceived with widespread apprehension, as laying the first step to retrenchment and discharge of the old-timers, who are seen as obsolete and redundant by the new technology and reorganized lines of the steel plant's businesses.[4]

The contradictions between a conservative (if not defensive) corporate philosophy and an innovative business strategy are clearly exemplified in the governance system of this giant steel firm. Its (formal) leadership has always been elitist and yet, for this reason, possibly conservative and lukewarm about fundamental and radical changes which could be rupturing to the status-quo conditions. Its governing board is hence still in effect dominated by government ministries. Probably, as a result of such an orthodoxy, the firm has prescribed a clear policy that anyone laid off from any exercise of downsizing needed to be reabsorbed by their reassignment to new postings. Redundancies at Shougang have hence been rigorously regulated by a personnel policy declaring no lay-offs, unless there were existing outlets for re-employing the surplus labour and where retraining was available. Unofficial sources have suggested that a modest slimming-down of the labour force was in vein. In 1999, over 2600 employees were laid-off in Beijing but three-quarters of these had been re-employed internally or externally, according to an inside source (interview by phone, February 2000).

It is hence almost naive and even wishful to assume that business strategy and decisions can be perceived in the same perspective as in a capitalistic system, where the governance structure of a vanguard type SOE like Shougang has essentially kept alive a pre-reform socialist model. What is recognizable in the Shougang experience are nominally liberal assumptions and attitudes of its management towards change and innovation. However, these stop short at the level of technical decision-making such as pertaining to the introduction of new product-lines and methods of production. However, outside the domain of technological and product innovation, the managerial decision-making system has been actually entrenched, inadmissive to basic change and at best making marginal concessions when asked to rescind the sacrosanct tradition of providing (and actually guaranteeing) a socialist commonwealth for all workers entitled as the masters (*zhuren*) of a socialist nation-state. In spite of an awareness about the limitations of the iron rice bowl mentality, which such a system has been known to perpetuate, it probably remains a fundamental belief held by ideologues that the capitalist prescription which calls for the demolition of the socialist system of state-backed security hardly applies either. The way by which the governing structure of Shougang was and is constituted, suggests that the influence of these ideologues is still decisive in shaping its establishment and personnel policies. It is perhaps premature, inasmuch as socialism is still nominally being upheld as the nation's *raison d'etre*, to expect a total conversion of this heavy-engineering plant into one shaped by market forces and commercial decisions. The Chinese steel industry estimates that the impact of entry into WTO will lead to short-term difficulties but will help competitiveness by forcing firms to reduce costs in the long-run (see *People's Daily*, 9 May 2000: 1; for further items on the topic, see http://www. peopledaily.com).

The experience of Beijing Founder

In contrast, an alternative experience at Founder seems to have suggested a possibility that a more commercialized or capitalist-like option of fashioning the business unit's corporate strategy may exist among SOEs which are hybrid in having assimilated and combined privatized initiatives and elements in their formation. Founder is basically a hive-off enterprise from Beijing University which is a leading national university belonging to the public sector (see Table 11.2). The company

Table 11.2 Development of Beijing Founder since 1987

1987	Founded by Professor Wang Xuan as Beida High-Tech
1989	Electronic publishing system approved for production
1993	Renamed as Beijing University Founder Group Corporation
1992	Sets up incorporated company in Hong Kong
1995	Adopts Group Structure, with subsidiaries and branch companies
1995	Initial public offer of Founder (HK) Limited shares
1995	Trial production of Founder PCs
1996	First among the state's top ten system integrators
1998	Eighth in ranking in Chinese electronics industry
1998	Sales turnover of 7.45 billion RMB
1999	Wang Xuan forced to resign
2000	Founder aims to be the largest Internet provider in PRC

describes itself as 'state-owned but privately managed' (interviews on-site, November–December 1998).

It has been described as follows:

> 'Beijing Founder Electronics (as a) Company Ltd. was set up . . . in 1987 by Beijing University with twelve employees. It was founded by Professor Wang Xuan, with the help of his host institution. It had a sales turnover in 1996 of around 4.6 billion yuan RMB, employing over 2000 employees. Its main products are in the field of electronic publishing technology, using the CC system . . . In 1995, it was floated on the Hong Kong Stock Exchange and is now a software corporation, as well as a hardware manufacturer. Over 80 per cent of China's 3500 major newspapers, magazines and book-publishing houses use its systems. In 1996, it paid a substantial 20 per cent remittance to Beijing University' (Warner, 1999a: 5).

By 1998, it had expanded its sales turnover to close to 7.45 billion RMB, (with profits of 151 million RMB in that year, with a 230 million RMB loss in 1999) and a sales target in the year 2005 of over 5 billion RMB. It was rated eighth in the Chinese electronics industry, with Legend Computers in first place selling 17.60 billion RMB in the comparable year.[5] Founder in 1998 had over 4000 workers, including its Hong Kong staff. By 1999, it had over 3500 employees, having laid-off around 700 of them (interview by phone, May 2000). Ninety per cent were said to be re-employed but turnover anyway was normally over 6 per cent.

This wholly owned subsidy of Beijing University is a remarkably successful hardware-cum-software house, yet able to enjoy autonomy as a privately managed business, particularly in electronic publishing-systems (see Lu, 2000). With the hybrid nature of its capital formation and governance structure, Founder has become an innovative organization which has been able to internationalize its business activities, with substantial freedom of opening overseas branches and entering into collaborative partnership with foreign MNCs to develop e-commerce and Internet-related activities. The latter activities have especially been instrumental for technological-transfer and 'know-how' assimilation by the plant. These policies have in turn helped Founder to sustain a proactive and innovative agenda of diversification, having extended both into new product-lines as well as overseas markets outside Mainland China itself.

An examination of the formative experience of Founder suggests a relatively Westernized style of management, in evolving and fashioning the governance and organizational structure of its hierarchy. Such a pattern is probably consistent with its flair as an innovative business organization, capable of technological inventions and entrepreneurial initiatives in managerial decision-making processes. The entrepreneurial spirit of Founder appears to have stemmed from its background as a subsidiary, branching out from a highly esteemed academic institution, Beijing University. This element apparently appears to have equipped the company with a cosmopolitan perspective and global horizon. For this reason, Founder has evolved a system of employment and personnel practices, albeit embryonic, which departs visibly from the established and bureaucratic pattern of the SOEs. The evolving arrangements at Founder appear to de-emphasize the centrality of the collective aspects of workplace labour- and production-relations. The role of trade union organization and associated activities of union–management negotiation yielding a collective contract are only given a nominal status within the administrative domain of the enterprise. As Founder is keen to stimulate and to encourage individualized incentives and initiatives, it has placed, instead, a heavier premium on assessing its staff's individual performance and implementing performance-based pay. The practice is apparently emulative of the human resource management model as popularized among enterprises in Western market-based economies (see Pange, 1999), where the latter are concerned with an enhanced agenda to streamline business performance by stressing human performance, assessed individually rather than collectively.[6]

However, the appearance of modernity in the personnel practices of this software house needs to be qualified. This necessity comes about because of an existence of a dual system in the personnel hierarchy and staff establishment of Founder, due to a hybrid blending of the old and the new systems. As a branch of Beijing University, Founder has to be maintained as a public enterprise at its nucleus. For this reason, it has retained its core staff, mostly personnel on secondment from Beijing University, on a permanent employment basis for their lifetime work. Other kinds of personnel, who were selected and hired by Founder directly, were placed instead on fixed-term labour contracts. The core permanent staff, who belonged to the personnel establishment of Beijing University, were hence exempted from the Labour Law (1994) requirement to sign a labour contract with Founder. As public-sector employees, they continued to enjoy an array of privileges and protection which used to cover most permanently-hired workers at the SOEs before the present reforms.

In spite of the above limits on Founder in marketizing the personnel system of its entire hiring structure, the corporate scheme it has adopted following the principle of corporatization has enabled it to pursue a business strategy and associated activities which suggest a commercialized portfolio. Up to now, except for basic and fundamental issues like Human Resource Development, personnel policy and so on, decision-making at Founder appears to be free from the bureaucratic grip of the pre-reform socialist forms of democratic centralism. Instead, as to be discussed in greater detail later, Founder has appeared to have enjoyed ample elasticity and freedom in commercial decisions, resembling closely its Western counterparts in responding to the imperatives of the market place.

Beijing Jeep: a joint venture model

Compared to Shougang and Founder, a third variant of new enterprise formation being evolved at a popularized pace is a joint-venture business amalgamated from the shared ownership of a foreign and Chinese partner. The benchmark case of the pioneering and now established Sino-foreign partnerships of this nature, also located in the capital, is Beijing Jeep Corporation (BJC) (see Aiello, 1991; Hoon-Halbauer, 1996; Goodall and Warner, 1997; Mann, 1997). This automobile car assembly plant owes its foreign participation to a leading US automobile manufacturer, initially American Motors, later Chrysler, now DaimlerChrysler. It was allegedly the first manufacturing joint venture in China, set up in early 1984. The Chinese government has designated it many times as the Best Chinese Foreign Investment Enterprise but recently it has fallen from favour.[7] It has aimed to produce and promote a hybrid and adapted model of its heavy-duty land vehicles, the Cherokee Jeeps, through allied engineering and production with its host-nation partner in China.

Beijing Jeep's sales turnover in 1998 was 4.13 billion RMB, with profits of 20.69 million RMB (Shanghai Volkswagen sales were 23.31 billion RMB, with 4.01 billion RMB profit). By 1999, sales in the Beijing firm were 2.00 billion RMB, with losses of 84.86 million RMB. The BJC was the fifteenth largest Foreign Invested Enterprise (FIE) in China, (Shanghai VW is first in the list) and was a US$300 million joint venture, owned 42 per cent from the Chrysler side and 58 per cent by Beijing Automotive Corporation. Beijing Jeep now has an annual capacity of around 100 000 Jeep Cherokees and lower-end Beijing Jeeps. Although the first automotive joint venture in China, Beijing Jeep falls short of the minimum yearly production capacity (150 000) the central government requires before a company can introduce a new vehicle model (see *China Business Review*, January 1998: 2). Given the overcapacity in the Chinese sedan car-market, the central government has reportedly asked it to continue to concentrate on production of sports, utility and light vehicles. About a third of its production in 1999 were Cherokee Jeeps.

As a hallmark of the new generation of modern Sino-foreign joint venture enterprises sponsored by the reformist state, Beijing Jeep has adhered closely to the official regulations and legal standards which have been proclaimed to regulate the business activities and labour–management relations at the workplace level. This automobile plant has, for example, distinguished itself for having negotiated a bench-marking collective labour contract with the grassroots workplace union at the plant, as early as 1984 (see Gong, 1994; Warner and Ng, 1999). Having had a collective contract for 15 years, invented by this company, it has erected a representation-system instituting a regular labour–management dialogue, which purportedly combines both consultation and collective bargaining in a non-adversarial pattern as prescribed by the letter and spirit of the 1994 Labour Law (see Warner, 1995). The representation system discusses wages and conditions with the All China Federation of Trade Unions (ACFTU) union branch, within the terms of the contract. Once a year, there is a formal meeting on industrial relations and HRM matters with Chrysler, alternating between the USA and the PRC. There is a joint management–labour committee that meets twice a year in Beijing on strategic industrial relations (IR) matters and reports back to both sides. Such workplace arrangements are seen to be consistent with the blueprint as envisaged by the state on a nationwide basis as a new hybrid formula to nurture and to regulate a new employment relations system, compatible with and supportive of the new economic order of market socialism, which the state-ordained reform initiatives have brought to the Chinese workplace (interviews on-site, November–December 1998). Wi Jianxing, President of the ACFTU, noted that equal consultation and collective contracts were vital to enable the deepening of reforms in enterprises, on a visit to Beijing Jeep in December 1999 (*People's Daily*, 8 December 1999: 1).

As a foreign-funded enterprise, Beijing Jeep has also enjoyed nominal autonomy of self-discretion in hiring, personnel selection and recruitment, as well as other aspects of HRM pertaining to incentive and performance pay.[8] However, these corporation-specific decisions about employment, labour and wage need to be reconciled with the regulatory activities of the Ministry of Labour and its local labour bureaus, in the context of macroregulation of the provincial and nationwide labour market. The personnel establishment at Beijing Jeep has also been affected by the ongoing wave of staff cuts and downsizing. It had reduced its establishment by 600 workers in 1998, followed by over 450 subsequently in early 1999 – in all over 1000 – to meet the US partner's requirements to increase productivity per employee and reduce labour costs. Around 26 million RMB was saved in 1998. The pace of attrition at reducing the workforce size has been in the ratio of just under one in three over the last two years or so taking into account normal labour turnover additionally, due to a substantial slump in sales (interviews on-site, November–December 1998; interviews by phone, 1999). Whilst it is possible that the vagaries of the market for the Cherokee vehicles Beijing Jeep produces have been responsible for the sizeable rate of redundancy, it is nonetheless surprising that even such a flagship joint venture has been so heavily downsized. A new low-cost sports utility vehicle (SUV) was introduced in September 2000 to compete better in the home market and to prepare for the coming challenges (see http://www.chinaonline.com/industry/automotive/newsarchive/secure/2000/html).

The corporate strategy of Beijing Jeep is, understandably, a compromised mix of the objectives of a foreign multinational partner seeking to extend a market foothold inside Mainland China on one hand and of the intention of its Chinese partner to tap Chrysler's technological know-how and its managerial and financial resources on the other. This compromise may have contributed to and enhanced a managerial consciousness for prudence in partnership negotiation and actions of this nature. However, Beijing Jeep may also have been subjected to a substantial amount of ambivalence, internal conflicts and rigidities, precisely because of its hybrid nature. The BJC–Chrysler alliance, nonetheless, is set to be extended when the 20-year contract ends in 2004; BJC has announced that it will spend 1.96 billion RMB during the coming five years to enable it to compete better when China enters the WTO, according to internal sources (see http://www.chinavista.com/business/news/archive/june06-01.html).

It is suspected that at Beijing Jeep, in spite of the apparently commercial decision-making in a business alliance between the Sino-foreign partners, state intervention and policy preferences were still important and even key factors affecting the corporation's behaviour in strategic areas, like personnel. As a standard-bearing enterprise in the foreign-funded sector, business strategy at Beijing Jeep may be probably closest to that of its counterparts in Western capitalist societies. The

Table 11.3 Development of Beijing Jeep since 1983

1983	Agreement signed between Beijing Auto and American Motors
1984	Initial operation of joint venture for 4-wheel-drive vehicles
1984	Pioneering Collective Labour Contract with ACFTU
1987	Chrysler Corporation takes over American Motors
1989	Tiananmen Square events and political uncertainty
1994	More restrictive auto-industry policy in PRC
1997	Total PRC auto production capacity approaches 1 million units
1997	Severe slow-down in overall PRC auto sales
1998	Cherokee Jeeps attain only 2 per cent of PRC market
1998	BJC's sales turnover exceed 4.13 billion RMB
1999	Sales of Beijing Jeeps fall by over 30 per cent
2000	Launch of low-cost SUV model to prepare for entry into WTO

development of Beijing Jeep since 1983 is shown in Table 11.3. Yet such a nominal aptitude for fully commercial activities still needs to be reconciled with the state's macro policies of regulating its post-reform economy and embryonic labour markets. The pursuance of these state-policy initiatives always entails a possibility of official intervention by public and government agencies like the Ministry of Labour and its bureaus, hence placing an effective limit constrains the scope of strategic and autonomous decision-making by Beijing Jeep as a business unit.

Discussion: strategic and structural convergence

A spectrum of corporate forms may be identifiable in our analysis; we shall now explore the implications of this phenomenon. We have listed above three case studies to exemplify the situations and constraints respectively of a 'national' enterprise (i.e., an SOE), a privately managed subsidiary of a public sector organization (a state-funded public university) and a highly esteemed Sino–US partnership as a standard-bearing joint venture between Chinese and foreign capital. After having sketched-out a profile of each of these enterprises, we proceed next to review these three corporate types in terms of their relative strengths and weaknesses in the industrial and socioeconomic domain of post-reform China, especially in the context of anticipated WTO entry after the year 2000.

Shougang can be labelled as one of the key elite establishments among the SOEs, as it has always enjoyed an eminent position as a model steel plant among its ranks within the country (see Nolan, 1998). Such a standard-bearing role has, however, unwittingly bred handicaps and problems which are endemic to the socialist system which is still upheld by many as the orthodox *raison d'etre* of the nation. Behind the logic of the state's blueprint of the economic and enterprise reforms is an assumption that legal and institutional innovations must be reconciled with economic, strategic and technological changes. Such a policy orientation we may argue also becomes – it follows – a built-in feature of the strategy adopted at almost every large SOE in the pursuance of enterprise reforms. When the basic fabric of a socialist and state-backed constitution of these prominent nationally known industrial enterprises was called into question because of their shift towards financial autonomy, the state attempted to reconcile with the paradoxical implications of the commercialization (or, literally, the desocialization) of these formerly vanguard socialist enterprises, by adopting an emulative formula, perhaps analogous to the limited-company system in Western economies. This process has been labelled as the corporatization of the SOEs. However, at Shougang, a dilemma is apparently encountered by its management inasmuch as the present wave of reforms poses a serious ideological problem for the enterprise management as to where the highly ambivalent boundary is between what is permissible as the basket of the marketized type of reform packages for an SOE and what has to be upheld as the sustained political institutions of a socialist workplace-based community. Shougang was also very late in adopting the individual labour contract model and has dragged its feet in implementing a collective one. Shougang Group's General Manager, Lou Bingsheng, still looks for growth and diversification to maintain jobs but sees the need for stronger strategic restructuring to meet the challenges of internationalization, such as going into hi-tech developments, real estate and services, better quality steel products and overseas expansion (Lou, 1998: 6–7). With the prospect of WTO entry looming, the group is looking at investment in high-tech and Internet-related activities (see *People's Daily*, 5 September 2000: 1). Diversification looks like being its strategic response to the challenges involved.

Such a dilemma was, however, earlier masked by the pace of reform but later became exposed when the hallmark of socialist collectivism, which used to guarantee to the proletarian Chinese workers a membership-right in their enterprises, was thrown into peril because of the nationwide agenda of downsizing these establishments in order to convert them into *bona fide* business units which were financially self-sufficient. It is likely that the potential challenges to the socialist nature of the workplace could be perceived by the doctrinal ideologues to be so fundamental that the entire agenda of de-establishing and desocializing the flagship steel firm might provoke widespread resistance, both at the grassroots and managerial levels. The trauma could be so pervasive that uncertainty and inertia could prevail at Shougang in the wake of an explicit and substantial downsizing policy.

Prima facia, it appears that Founder, on the other hand, was able to enjoy ample enterprise autonomy as a privately managed business entity hived-off from an academic institution.[9] However, it is not specific to the Chinese situation but rather a commonplace worldwide pattern that universities and public-funded research institutes have served as a springboard inspiring and sponsoring the satellite formation of high-technology business enterprises. The history of Founder, in this sense, as an electronics firm evolving from a pilot-case of academic entrepreneurship into a global business conglomerate, has been a substantial achievement. The group has now established an extensive business network in many parts of the world. In the PRC, the group has a total of 37 branch offices with more than 300 distributors throughout major provinces and cities. Apart from Founder Limited in Hong Kong (see http://www.founder.com.hk), with its financial travails in 1999, the group has subsidiaries in Canada, Japan and Malaysia, and distributors in Japan, South Korea, Macau and Taiwan. This gigantic sales network has opened up local and overseas markets to the group's products. It has, for example, a major JV agreement with Digital, signed in June 1998, on systems integration. Further diversification vis-à-vis WTO entry after the year 2000 looks most likely.

In spite of Founder's commercial auspices and innovative propensity – its motto is 'Create Science and Culture' – it appears to have been eclipsed by its background as a spin-off from a public institution, Beijing University and their mutual linkages. Such an element of ambivalence is shown, for example, in the personnel and employment aspects of Founder's management, although it has purported to assume a market-oriented approach, as disguised by the Westernized label of HRM. At Founder, it is possible to identify such instruments as performance appraisal, job evaluation and performance pay which are suggestive of the human resource functions normally found in western MNCs (interviews on-site at Founder, November–December 1998; interviews by phone, 1999; 2000). However, a more detailed enquiry at this new model enterprise hints strongly that many of its organizational traits are still reminiscent of the pre-reform enterprises. Free market personnel sourcing and entry were, for example, still limited by way of open and competitive recruitment, inasmuch as centralized assignment by the state or parent establishment (Beijing University) were still the norm, with the probable exception of the non-core personnel. For this reason, staff stability has been high and labour turnover correspondingly moderate (Warner, 1999a: 13).

In this context, institutional continuity from the hallmark arrangements and provisions for workplace control and labour welfare has persisted into the corporate infrastructure of Founder, as it was previously characteristic of the official '*danwei*' (see Francis, 1996). Important vestiges of such a tradition inherited from the pre-reform SOE model include, *inter alia,* the availability of medical insurance for all staff and families, housing and social insurance for the core staff members and permanent workers, as well as a high level of unionization and a worker congress (see Cook and Maurer-Fazio, 1999; Warner, 1999a: 12–13, 10).

However, perhaps the most salient symptom of the strategic ambivalence emanating from these conflicting orientations of Founder in steering a new style and commercially sensitive business strategy and reconciling with the politico-ideological dictates to remain as a socialist workplace is best epitomized by its less-than-positive attitude to instituting a collective contract, to be jointly negotiated with the workplace labour union. Such a lukewarm attitude evidently fell short of the enthusiasm with which the high-tech firm has endorsed implementation of individual labour contracts.

As envisaged by the architects of the enabling Labour Law of 1994, the institutionalization of the collective labour contract was intended as the new bulkwark for enshrining a new set of workplace devices supposedly commensurate with the marketization and desocialization of employment relations. However, while the individual labour contract was widely accepted at enterprises by management as conducive to their personnel autonomy and efficient human resource utilization, many, at both the private and national level, harbour general suspicion and even apprehension about the functional role of the collective contract. The reason is twofold. The first is a managerial fear about the possibility of an erosion into the enterprise autonomy, as the collective contract implies substantial scope for both union and labour bureau intervention into its employment affairs. The second reason is a widespread scepticism about the possible drift of such a practice to evolve and lapse into the adversarial activity of a form of collective bargaining, Western style and characteristic of the capitalist marketized economies (see Warner and Ng, 1999).

In a hybrid enterprise like Founder, managerial attitudes have been hence equally equivocal and problematic about the orientation of the corporation's future (see *Beijing Review*, 15 November 1999: 21ff). The key question appears to be whether the growth path of Founder as a high-tech electronics firm, sufficiently competitive on both the local and overseas (and even global) markets, and the anxiety of its managing cadres to adhere to the socialist fabric of a workplace commonwealth, can be reconciled, in spite of the inherent contradictions apparent. The trade-offs in order to maintain a prudent balance in the current state of impasse could prove to be costly.

Concluding remarks

To sum up, it can be seen that there is a wide spectrum of strategy, ownership, structure and performance (amongst other factors) in the classic Chinese enterprises we have selected as case studies (see Table 11.4). It is apparent that each of these cases has made a trade-off between

Table 11.4 The spectrum of classic PRC enterprise case studies

Company	Shougang	Beijing Jeep	Founder
Size (employees)	>80 000*	>7000	>4000**
Date of founding	Pre-1949	1984	1992
Product(s)	Iron and steel	Automotive	Electronics
Technology	Process	Mass	Mixed
Strategy	Early reform	Mid-reform	Late-reform
Ownership	Old SOE	JV	New hybrid SOE
Structure	Highly diversified	Less diversified	Relatively diversified
Governance	Corporatized	Subsidiary of MNC	Corporatized
Management	Strong Chinese idiosyncratic management model	Mix of Chinese, Western management	New style Chinese management
Labour–Management relations	Classic *danwei* model: slow to implement individual and collective contract	Classic (early) individual and collective contract	Individual labour contract but reluctant vis-à-vis collective contract
HRM	Personnel administration	Mix of Chinese and Western HR practices	Hybrid
Downsizing	Limited reductions	Substantial cuts	Recent lay-offs

* Includes Beijing-based employees only; ** Includes Mainland plus Hong Kong-based employees only.

the contradictory demands of the market model on one hand, and the ideological and political imperatives of operating in the PRC, on the other. In terms of forging a new form of corporate governance to cope with the dilemmas the above issues pose, the strategic response elicited has been corporatization but this has taken different paths. As the post-reform adjustments persist, the differentials between the three types may narrow. Beijing Founder looks like a promising model for the PRC to adopt in the state-sector; however, corporatization and privatization are hard to segregate. Founder too has not been without its setbacks.

Since in all the three cases the companies have had to adapt to market pressures, pushing towards convergence *grosso modo*, it is clear that whilst there have been strategic, structural and other shifts that have been made by each, the older classic work-unit (*danwei*) namely Shougang, has been most resistant to change; the early classic JV, Beijing Jeep, has belatedly had to conform to external pressures from its parent; the late classic high-tech SOE, Founder, has been able to absorb most of its environmental pressures. Corporatization or not, the issue of overmanning has to be faced but the response has not been uniform.[10] Coming to terms with downsizing has been a common feature of firms, large and small, in face of the recent Asian economic and financial crisis (see Godement, 1999). The PRC has been somewhat insulated from the above crisis in terms of its direct effects but nonetheless its impact has been felt, vis-à-vis, for example, Chinese exports to the Asia Pacific region which have fallen; indeed there has been pressure on the RMB to devalue.

In the HRM field, there is clear evidence of strategic divergence. It is clear that the label 'with Chinese characteristics' applies more aptly to the one relatively downsizing-resistant case, Shougang, than to the now workforce-slimming Beijing Jeep, with Founder possibly better able to cope due to a faster-expanding market for its high-tech products. Even so, as we have seen, the last of these firms has not been without its ups and downs commercially and structurally. It is clear that corporatization as such does not necessarily lead to comparable organizational and people-management responses. We may thus conclude that whilst there are pressures towards strategic convergence in Chinese enterprises, there have also been countervailing pressures to maintain a relatively clear degree of differentiation.

Finally, looking at the wider implications, China may need to confront directly the ideological impasse that has resulted from retaining socialism by moving closer to the market, in order to steer the economy onto a more stable path of reform vis-à-vis the processes of globalization now unleashed by its steps to make itself more interdependent with the world trading community. If it does this (like the new policy explicitly recognizing the role of privately owned enterprises), it may come closer to soft convergence (see Warner, 2000) with its Asian counterparts, especially vis-à-vis anticipated entry into the WTO. Moving from so-called corporatization as a policy for the SOEs, to more open forms of privatization at the microeconomic level may be a necessary step, as may RMB-convertibility.

The afore-mentioned impasse may perhaps be more definitively resolved at the macroeconomic level by moving closer to even more openly recognizing market forces ideologically or by further abandonment of existing notions of market socialism as previously defined by Deng. Clearly, much depends on the PRC enjoying a rapid rate of economic growth, say at least 10 per cent per annum, for this may help politically sell the proposed changes in policy; otherwise, slow growth, say as low as 6 per cent over the year, may further increase the jobless total, and this may heighten social tensions, promote nationalistic tendencies and make it difficult for ideological shifts to take place so that there can be a fuller incorporation of the WTO logic and all it entails.

There is a strong argument for China's leaders to continue to move pragmatically, indeed step by step, as they have done since 1978 when the Open Door was first promoted as the way to implement the Four Modernizations. The full WTO programme, involving ultimately not only manufactured goods but also services, may be too much for the Chinese economy to digest in the short-term. Even if we take what has been agreed in terms of deregulating and liberalizing product markets, it may take a transitional period of at least five years to implement all the detailed clauses, sector by sector. The impact on labour markets may be too much to cope with, if the anticipated lay-offs take place without corresponding absorption of displaced workers in other non-state sectors, such as the TVE and private firms that have burgeoned in recent years. Moving too precipitously may lead to political and social reaction that may erode support for the deepening of the reform agenda within the country; China's leaders are walking a tightrope here and they know it.

Acknowledgements

We are grateful to the British Council and the University of Hong Kong Business School for their support in this project. We should also like to thank the Beijing Administrative College for its assistance in carrying out the field investigation.

Notes

1 The field work for this study was carried out in Beijing in late 1998 and involved visiting enterprises, government ministries and trade unions in the capital; the material was updated by interviews by phone and internet searches in 1999 and 2000.
2 The full text of the new government policy is to be found in the *Beijing Review*, 12 October 1999.
3 Shougang was founded originally in 1918 by the Longyuan Mining Administration (see Nolan, 1998, for a short historical account; see also Table 11.1 above).
4 An Examinations Committee had been in place for some time; it could promote, demote or dismiss workers, often on the 'say so' of 'their boss alone' (Warner, 1995: 108).
5 For the ranking of Chinese enterprises, see http://www.cei.gov.cn/eent/htm
6 The HR director stressed the human resource management philosphy of the company (interviews on-site, November–December 1998).
7 In recent (late 1999) articles on MNCs in the automotive industry in the PRC in the official *Beijing Review*, there has been no mention at all of Beijing Jeep.
8 It has reduced its median wage from 2100 RMB in 1997 to 1500 RMB per month in 1998, due to the decline in sales (interviews on-site, November–December 1998).
9 It is sometimes the case that privately-owned firms euphemistically call themselves as collectives. The term private may be used to refer to non-state sector firms generally, including collective, privately-owned, foreign-owned and joint venture firms. In the Chinese electronics industry, Legend, Stone and Founder, for instance, may be dubbed non-governmental enterprises (*minying keyi qiye*). Stone is still legally a collectively owned enterprise (*jiti suoyouzhi*); Legend and Founder are categorized as in state-owned whole-people ownership (*quanmin shuoyouzhi qiye*) (see Lu, 1997: 20). Privately-owned (*siyou* or *siying qiye*) refers to those enterprises specifically held in strictly private ownership. Some high-tech firms in China might be categorized as *minban* (collective established through private initiative and autonomous in their management); others may include *guanmin* firms (established via the initiative of a university – see Francis, 1996; 84, n 21). An example of the latter category would be Founder (see Warner, 1999a).
10 Whilst productivity at Shougang in the early 1990s was one-tenth of that of its competitors in advanced economies, labour costs were about a quarter of those of equivalent steel firms elsewhere (see Nolan, 1998: 46–47). Thus, cheap labour, it was said, mitigated the international productivity differential.

References

Aiello, P. (1991) 'Building a joint venture in China: the case of Chrysler and Beijing Jeep Corporation', *Journal of General Management*, 17(1): 47–64.

Chan, A. (1995) 'The emerging patterns of industrial relations in China and the rise of the two new labour movements', *China Information: A Quarterly Journal*, 9(4): 36–59.

Child, J. (1994) *Management in China During the Era of Reform*, Cambridge: C.U.P.

Cook, S. and M. Maurer-Fazio (1999) 'Introduction', in Special issue, 'The workers' state meets the market: labour in transition', *Journal of Development Studies*, 35(3): 1–15.

Documentation section (1999) *China Quarterly*, No. 160, December, p. 1106.

Francis, C. B. (1996) 'Reproduction of Danwei institutional features in the context of China's market economy: the case of Haidian District high-technology sector', *The China Quarterly*, 147: 839–59.

Fortune (1999) 'Special report: inside the new China', *Fortune*, No. 19, 11 October, pp. 66–127.

Godement, F. (1999) *The Downsizing of Asia*, London: Routledge.

Goodall, K. and M. Warner (1997) 'Human resources in Sino-foreign joint ventures: selected Case studies in Shanghai and Beijing', *International Journal of Human Resource Management*, 8(5): 569–94.

Gong, Y. (1994) 'Collective contract', *Chinese Trade Unions* (ACFTU), 9–11 August.

Hoon-Halbauer, Sing-Keow (1996) *Management of Sino-Foreign Joint Ventures*, Lund: Lund University Press.

Kahn-Freund, O. (1972) *Labour and the Law*, London: Stevens and Sons.

Lou, Bingsheng (1998) 'Reform Shougang Group Corp. for the needs of the twenty-first century', Paper to Conference on the *Reform of State-Owned Enterprises: the UK and Chinese Experience*, CASS, Beijing PRC, 7–8 October, 7pp.

Lu, Q. (2000) *China's Leap into the Information Age: Innovation and Organization in the Computer Industry*, Oxford: OUP.

Lu, Xiaobo and E. J. Perry (1997) *Danwei: The Changing Chinese Workplace in Historical and Comparative Perspective*, Armonk, New York and London: M.E. Sharpe.

Mann, J. (1997) *Beijing Jeep: A Case Study of Western Business in China*, Boulder, Colorado and London: Westview.

Naughton, B. (1995) *Growing Out of the Plan: Chinese Economic Reform 1978–1993*, *Cambridge*: Cambridge University Press.

Nolan, P. (1998) *Indigenous Large Firms in China's Economic Reforms: The Case of Shougang Iron and Steel Corporation*, Research notes and studies, No. 12, London: School of Oriental and African Studies.

Ng, Sek Hong and M. Warner (1998) *China's Trade Unions and Management*, London: Macmillan and New York: St Martin's Press.

Oi, J. C. (1999) 'Two decades of rural reform in China: an overview and assessment', *The China Quarterly*, No. 159, September, pp. 616–28.

Pange, L. (1999) '"Human resistance or human remains?" – how HR management in China must change', *China Staff, Incorporating Hong Kong Staff: The Human Resources Journal for China and Hong Kong*, 8 (July/August): 8–11.

Steinfeld, E. S. (1998) *Forging Reform in China: The Fate of State-Owned Industry*, Cambridge: C.U.P.

UNDP (1999) *The China Human Development Report*, Beijing: United Nations Development Programme.

Warner, M. (1995) *The Management of Human Resources in Chinese Industry*, London: Macmillan and New York: St Martin's Press.

Warner, M. (1996) 'Chinese enterprise reform, human resources and the 1994 labour law', *International Journal of Human Resource Management*, 7(7): 779–96.
Warner, M. (1999a) 'Human resources and management in China's "high-tech" revolution – a study of selected hardware, software and related firms in the PRC', *International Journal of Human Resource Management*, 10(1): 1–20.
Warner, M. (ed.) (1999b) *China's Managerial Revolution*, London: Frank Cass.
Warner, M. (2000) 'Introduction: Asia pacific HRM model revisited', in Special issue on *International Journal of Human Resource Management*, 11(2).
Warner, M. and Sek Hong Ng (1999) 'Collective contracts in Chinese enterprises: a new brand of collective bargaining under "market socialism"', *British Journal of Industrial Relations*, 37(2): 295–314.

12
Crisis and Reform in Corporate Governance in Asia

Thomas Clarke

Introduction

Collapsing currencies, equity and property markets in East Asia in 1997–98 exposed underlying vulnerabilities in corporate governance structures and values. Financial liberalization and large current account deficits financed by short-term foreign loans, left these economies open to large international movements of capital. However, an international confidence crisis was fuelled by a growing realization of the structural weaknesses of economies often governed by crony capitalism, opaque accounting and auditing systems, and too close relations between business and the state.

Unprecedented growth over three decades brought overconfidence with savings not always applied to productive investments, currency appreciations, mismanaged firms and misaligned strategies. 'Speculative bubbles involve the mass delusion that asset prices will rise relentlessly' (Lingle, 1997: 88). In many senses the Tiger economies are victims of their success, with burgeoning prosperity encouraging excessive borrowing and the wasteful use of resources, inadequate supervision of the financial sector and lack of transparency in business. Complacency during the time of seemingly endless economic growth was replaced by inability to act decisively at a time of crisis.

The recovery process will require attention to regulatory systems and compliance, together with reforms of corporate governance and disclosure standards. As Rohwer (1996: 18) presciently argued, 'The biggest flaw in the success stories of modern Asia – including Japan – has been their failure to develop the transparent and objective public institutions needed to run the more sophisticated societies and economies that their fabulous economic growth is producing.' The critical element in restructuring, refinancing and acquiring of distressed companies is that of the reliability and accuracy of financial statements. However, to assume what is necessary is directly an adoption of Anglo-Saxon inspired international governance and regulatory systems underestimates the distinctive cultural foundations of governance systems.

More critically, the original assumption of Alan Greenspan of the US Federal Reserve and others, that the Asian financial crisis could be confined, neglected the global integration of financial markets accelerated by computer and communication technologies and deregulation. As the contagion spread to other emerging economies most spectacularly in the case of Russia and Brazil, it was not only the weaknesses in corporate governance systems that were exposed, but the overwhelming volatility and irresponsibility of the operation of international financial markets (Cohen, 1997; IMF, 1998; Soros, 1998).

Miracle economies?

'From 1965 to 1990 the 23 economies of East Asia grew faster than all other regions of the world. Most of this achievement is attributable to seemingly miraculous growth in just eight economies.' (World Bank, 1993: 1) The World Bank research report, The East Asian Miracle, characterized the High Performing Asian Economies (HPAEs) led by Japan, into the four Tiger economies of Hong Kong, Republic of Korea, Singapore and Taiwan, joined later by the Newly Industrializing Economies (NIEs) of Indonesia, Malaysia, and Thailand. What caused East Asia's success? The World Bank (1993: 5) offered the following explanation:

'In large measure the HPAEs achieved high growth by getting the basics right. Private domestic investment and rapidly growing human capital were the principal engines of growth. High levels of domestic financial savings sustained the HPAE's high investment levels. Agriculture, while declining in relative importance, experienced a rapid growth and productivity improvements. Population growth rates declined more rapidly in the HPAEs than in other parts of the developing world. And some of these economies also got a head start because they had a better educated labour force and a more effective system of public administration. In this case there is little that is "miraculous" about the HPAEs' superior record of growth; it is largely due to superior accumulation of physical and human capital.'

This sustained economic growth ranked with the economic miracles of post-war Germany and the period of fastest growth in the 1960s of the Japanese economy. The IMF in its annual reports endorsed this path to rapid economic expansion, and other commentators added their approval (Gereffi and Wyman, 1992; Overholt, 1993; Kim, 1995). Of course as the World Bank argued in its 1996 report, from plan to market, high investment alone does not guarantee fast growth. It is the composition and quality of investment, as well as human capital and technological know-how that is critical.

A further difficulty the World Bank and the IMF did have with these economies was the extent of policy intervention by the state (in fact the 1993 World Bank research on the East Asian economies was funded by the government of Japan). Policy intervention took many forms (World Bank, 1993: 6):

(a) targeting and subsidizing credit to selected industries;
(b) protecting domestic import substitutes;
(c) subsidizing declining industries;
(d) establishing and financially supporting government banks;
(e) making public investments in applied research;
(f) establishing firm and industry-specific export targets;
(g) developing export marketing institutions; and
(h) sharing information widely between public and private sectors.

In addressing the question of whether such selective interventions were good for growth, the World Bank offered two possible explanations. A neoclassical view stressed the importance of getting the macroeconomic basics right, grudgingly accepted that interventions did not significantly inhibit growth, but suggested that if in some instances in Northeast Asia (Japan, Korea, Taiwan and China) government interventions resulted in higher and more equal growth, the prerequisites for success were clear performance criteria, and prudent control of costs. Secondly, a revisionist school argued that East Asian governments led the market in critical ways. In contrast to the neoclassical view which acknowledged relatively few cases of market failure, revisionists contended that markets consistently fail to guide investment to industries that might generate the highest growth for the overall economy. In East Asia, it is argued, governments remedied this by deliberately getting the prices wrong – altering the incentive structure – to boost industries that would not otherwise have thrived (Amsden, 1989; World Bank, 1993: 6–9).

A question the World Bank did not address in their 1993 report was, whatever its causes, whether this rapid rate of growth was sustainable in the East Asian economies. Alwyn Young (1994) and Paul Krugman (1994) have both dismissed East Asia's economic growth as the inevitable result of a dramatic rise in the quantity of inputs in the economic system at an early stage of industrialization. Gains from input-driven growth cannot continue indefinitely unless there are accompanying increases in efficiency. Growth in East Asia can be attributed to a great mobilization of resources, combined with a self-sacrificing level of personal savings. Lingle (1997: 79) contends: 'Dynamic, and thus sustainable economic growth relies upon gains in total productivity. Increased labour participation rates, employment expansion, as well as increased investments in education, health, and physical capital are blunt, one-shot methods for generating economic growth. The perpetuation of high growth rates demands that qualitative improvements must coincide with quantitative increases in outputs.'

The World Bank 1996 report (p. 41) supported this view, insisting that as savings and investment rates reach a high plateau, then productivity gains become increasingly important in years to come. With shrinking scope for achieving efficiency through further shifts in resources, achieving gains increasingly will depend on broadening enterprise and financial sector reforms that boost efficiency at the firm and industry level.

Damaging to the effort to achieve qualitative economic improvements is an apparent lack of innovativeness and creativity in the East Asian economies. 'East Asian economies have been following rather than leading the rest of the developed world, by relying upon ready access to Western technology and open markets. As the age of mass industrialization passes, the competitive advantage of many East Asian economies will be challenged. Without producing their own domestic entrepreneurial talent and self-generated technological advance, these countries will continue to lag the developed economies in what could prove a perpetually dependent relationship' (Lingle, 1997: 85).

For example, Asian countries have specialized in the production of semi-conductors, and South Korea is a world leader in the production of memory chips, with silicon wafer production concentrated in Taiwan and Singapore. Malaysia has had great success in developing assembly plants servicing major computer hardware corporations such as Motorola, Intel and Texas. But what is the future in this business? 'Prices are plummeting as the glut hits the market, but there is no sign of a slackening of the pace. Malaysia and Singapore are building a large number of new silicon wafer plants, while major companies in Taiwan, such as Formosa Plastic, are eager to get into the industry – the island nation is building 12 silicon wafer factories at an estimated average cost of US$1 billion each' (Gough, 1998: 107).

These production strategies could not have helped, but deeper social and structural flaws in the East Asian economies were soon to be revealed. As Lingle (1997: 83) contends, 'The more inclusive and transparent nature of political relationships necessitated by a modern economy poses a challenge of equal magnitude to the ability of East Asian economies to remain on a high growth path.'

East Asian financial crisis

It is difficult to overestimate the extent of the speculative euphoria which seized the East Asian economies in the early 1990s. As Philip Pillai (1998: 2), a Singaporean lawyer, described it, 'The elements of a conventional bubble were everywhere to be seen wherein seemingly inexhaustible capital pursued seemingly inexhaustible projects, which were premised on a never ending growth curve and a fear amongst lenders of being left out of the Asian miracle. As in all bubbles, it burst in the wake of events which do not appear to justify the magnitude of the crash.' Manifold evidence of excessive speculative activity included greatly inflated stock prices, land prices, housing prices, and the highest hotel room costs in the world. In turn this provoked a massive building boom throughout East Asia in office and apartment blocks, luxury hotels and shopping centres.

The financial crisis when it came was brought on by an over-reliance on credit, both domestic credit and foreign borrowing. Phil Parton of the ANZ bank, Shanghai, suggests three inter-related immediate causes of the crisis: a build-up of short-term external debt; concern over East Asian domestic banks; and mounting national current account deficits. East Asian economies accumulated debt in the 1990s, to the extent that debt-to-GDP ratios had risen across the board. Much of the build-up of debt was by domestic banks, raising cash for domestic funding purposes. Businesses also borrowed directly from foreign banks, with managed exchange rates playing a crucial role in minimizing borrowers' perceptions of currency risk. The fixed exchange rate bands supported markets characterized by high domestic interest rates and low US dollar short-term interest rates, which induced domestic borrowers to seek US dollar funding, often on a short-term basis for long-term needs. Concurrently, foreign banks, particularly European and Japanese banks looking for increased market share, were aggressive in Asian lending. Short-term debt soared in East Asia, for example, Indonesia's short-term debt increased from US$17.1 billion at the end of 1994, to US$34.2 billion by December 1996.

The currency crisis immediately impacted upon domestic banks. In emerging economies, capital markets are often underdeveloped, and because of the lack of an alternative, banks become the most important channel for access to foreign capital. In Asian countries therefore, bank credit as a percentage of GDP is higher than in Western economies. Unfortunately, at this point, the international creditworthiness of Asian banks was called into question because of their exposure to highly geared corporate borrowers (South Korea and Indonesia) to the property sector (Thailand, Malaysia, Indonesia and the Philippines) and to out-of-money share investors (Malaysia). Asian banks were critically undermined by the collapse in asset prices, the property oversupply, and the distress in the business sector generally. As a result Asian banks were downgraded by rating agencies, and consequently foreign banks reduced their exposure to Asian banks by refusing to roll over maturing loans and suspending unutilized lines of credit (Parton, 1998: 2).

However, from the moment that the Thai government announced a managed float of the baht, confirming warnings indicated by the bankruptcy of Hanbo Steel Korea at the beginning of the year, and the collapse of Finance One, Thailand's largest finance company, in May 1997, the financial systems in rest of East Asia trembled. Interventions by successive governments, and repeated attempts by the IMF could not prevent a contagion of currency depreciation, accompanied by collapsing stock markets, tumbling asset prices, and increasing corporate failures and financial insolvencies. A self-reinforcing process intensified as domestic credit dried up and foreign investors fled, with a loss of total stock market capitalization in dollar terms ranging from 42 per cent (Hong Kong) to 88 per cent (Indonesia) in the period 30 June 1997 to 3 July 1998 (Table 12.1). This was no ordinary financial crisis, and the scale of the disaster for the countries concerned was similar to the great Wall Street crash in which there was an 86 per cent loss in market capitalization between 1929 and 1933 (Soros, 1998: 145).

The weaknesses of Asian modes of governance

The question remains how could all this have happened in economies that were formerly celebrated for their robustness and efficiency? In a modern economy, companies are disciplined by a combination of internal and external controls. Internally, the company directors' duty is to ensure adequate financial controls are exercised, and this is reinforced by independent audit of the annual accounts. Externally, there is a legal framework of corporate law, policed by regulatory authorities.

Table 12.1 Dimensions of the East Asian crisis 1997–98*

	Currencies (%)	Stock index (%)	Market fall in dollar (%)
Indonesia	–83.2	–35.0	–96bn (–88%)
Thailand	–40.2	–48.0	–40bn (–66%)
Malaysia	–39.4	–56.0	–217bn (76%)
Philippines	–36.1	–33.8	–43bn (–58%)
South Korea	–34.1	–58.7	–111bn (–71%)
Singapore	–16.5	–43.5	–91bn (–53%)
Hong Kong	Nil	–43.2	–223 (–42%)

* Fall in currency exchange rate for US$ between 30 June 1997 and 3 July 1998. Percentage decline in stock-market index between 30 June 1997 and 3 July 1998. Fall in stock market capitalization in US$ billions, between 30 June 1997 and 3 July 1998.
Sources: Bank of International Settlements; IMF; World Bank; *Asia Week*, 17 July 1998; Jones Lang Wootton; Dataquest.

Finally there is the capital market which exercises a commercial discipline upon companies. Though this institutional structure was broadly in place in the East Asian economies, the problem is that it did not work properly. Surveying the institutional structures of Korea, Malaysia and Thailand, Prowse (1998) concludes: 'Market and regulatory institutions that play an important role in ensuring market disciplines are relatively undeveloped in the East Asian economies. In a less-evolved regulatory, legal and institutional environment, information asymmetries are more severe, contracting costs are higher because standard practices have not developed, enforcement of contracts is more problematic because of weak courts, market participants and regulators are less experienced, and the economy itself is likely to be undergoing more rapid change than in developed countries. In addition to having a weak judicial system, developing countries are unlikely to have administrative agencies that can handle issues that benefit from detailed rule making and non-legal administrative enforcement such as accounting standards, financial disclosures and stock market listing rules.'

Firstly, East Asian economies are typified by a considerable concentration of ownership, most public companies having either a majority shareholder, or small group of dominant shareholders, or the company is part of a corporate network which in turn has majority shareholders. 'The most frequent organizational form in East Asia is the diversified conglomerate, closely held, controlled and managed by a family' (Prowse, 1998). Companies with widely dispersed ownership are quite rare. In this context the rights of minority shareholders are difficult to protect, and though often strict laws and penalties exist against insider trading, and there are provisions on related-party transactions, substantial transactions, and on takeovers, there are questions about how rigorously and frequently these are enforced.

On the boards of companies, there is often no clearly defined role for non-executive directors, and lack of knowledge of the obligations and functions of company officers is widespread. Decision-making bodies are often not effective in carrying out their formal roles, sometimes they are unable to exercise their rights, and boards are co-opted by the dominant shareholders. Disclosure and transparency tend to be kept to a bare minimum, with the result that it is much more difficult for the legal and regulatory authorities to take action if they were inclined to do so. Similarly, there is an underdevelopment of institutional investors and fund managers, which diminishes the likelihood of informed monitoring by powerful external agencies.

In the West, banks and other financial institutions play an important role in ensuring companies operate along sound governance principles and have incentives to follow prudent policies. In East Asia, government intervention in the banking sector to rescue depositors when banks have got into trouble has provided an incentive for relaxing risk controls. Such guarantees reduce risk associated with commercial operations and eliminate the incentives for prudent management. In this financial environment, the economy can become vulnerable to overinvestment, with the resulting boom and bust cycles of the property and share markets.

In East Asia, corporate finance is more typically dominated by banks, for example in Malaysia, the country with one of the more developed corporate securities markets in the region, banks in 1997 provided over 85 per cent of the funds raised in the private sector, compared to under 15 per cent from the capital markets. The tendency of East Asian governments to bail out many insolvent businesses diminishes the disciplining effect of debt by reducing the fear of bankruptcy, and encourages firms to increase leverage. Corporate leverage increased significantly in recent years, which Krugman (1998) argues is based on the incentives, rising asset prices and a belief that the government is operating a too-big-to-fail policy gives firms to borrow as much as they can invest in fixed assets.

Running like a thread through many of the flaws of the governance systems of East Asia is an inclination towards secrecy, obedience and incestuousness which is deeply damaging to the effort to promote a dynamic open economy. The official proponents of Asian values have often abused the values they claim to uphold. The deeply held commitment to hard work, sense of thriftiness, and concern for the family, belief in education, desire for consensus and respect for authority are the bedrock of the value system that has served Asia in the early decades of its industrialization. However, these values have often been translated into nepotism, cronyism and corruption by dynastic rules and paternalistic industrialists. Such a system of patronage crowds out a spirit of initiative and independent entrepreneurship. As Lingle (1997: 19) argues, 'Many Asian economies are uniquely distinguished by an institutional bias against individualism. Asian cultures that inculcate conformity at the expense of initiative restrain the enterprising spirit that underpins the innovative process necessary for sustained economic growth.'

Signs of economic recovery in some of the East Asian economies, as the painful processes of restructuring and recapitalization proceeds, cannot disguise the severe dislocation and substantial output cost of this crisis, with the sacrifice of several years of economic growth (Table 12.2). Throughout the slowdown, exports in key sectors have continued, but this should not be deflected from the urgent programme of institutional reform, which is inescapable if sustained recovery is to be achieved.

At this point, the position of China is important. China's determination to maintain economic stability during the East Asian financial crisis, and refusal to devalue, was a steadying force in the region for which the international agencies were deeply grateful. To prevent a damaging recession, the Chinese government launched a public spending package of US$12 billion, with a similar amount provided by the state banks, investing in infrastructural projects and postponing the privatization of small state enterprises. However, this may add to problems of overcapacity,

Table 12.2 Economic growth in the East Asian economies 1997–2000

	1997	1998	1999	2000
China	8.8	7.6	7.7	7.2
Indonesia	4.7	–15.5	–3.0	3.0
Thailand	–0.4	–7.0	2.0	4.5
Malaysia	7.8	–4.7	–0.5	3.5
Philippines	5.1	–0.5	2.0	4.5
Chinese Taipei	6.8	4.5	4.0	5.5
Singapore	7.5	0.0	0.5	3.2
Hong Kong, China	5.2	–4.5	1.5	5.5

Source: OECD, *Economic Outlook*, December 1998.

excess inventories and non-performing loans, and could direct resources away from other sectors of the economy. Though China has contained both political and economic tensions, they are still there. As the Organizations of Economic Cooperation and Development (OECD) concludes, 'While China has weathered the regional crisis quite well, the financial crisis of other Asian countries which shared similar structural problems with China have raised concerns that its current strains could develop into something considerably worse' (1998: 23).

Reform of East Asian corporate goverenance

Given the systemic nature of the problems of corporate governance in East Asia, only a fundamental programme of reform on institutions and practices, conducted in an energetic and committed manner over a considerable period of time is likely to produce results. There is much evidence of a profound inclination towards reform in the countries concerned, but should this dissipate as the East Asian economies move towards recovery, there is an array of external agencies with an interest in ensuring the process of reform is followed. The IMF, World Bank, and Asian Development Bank all have launched significant initiatives to encourage and to facilitate the reform process. International investors are unlikely to be sympathetic towards countries and companies that are not significantly improving their corporate governance standards.

Progress towards reform will follow different paths in the different countries concerned, but some general principles may be outlined. The important objectives for the development of more robust modes of governance include:

- clarifying and strengthening internal control structures within firms;
- strengthening external monitoring and control through improvements in the legal framework, enhanced by regulatory agencies and greater disclosure of information;
- developing training and information programmes to improve the understanding of corporate governance procedures and issues.

To clarify and to make more effective internal control structures, reform of the Companies Acts in the countries concerned may well be required. In addition, developing a code of best practice in corporate governance is now essential. With the widespread failure of any system of voluntary standards of corporate governance in East Asia, a more prescriptive approach appears to be necessary. Though companies can participate in the drafting of the code, it is probably necessary to ensure that a powerful regulatory body in the form of a Securities Commission ensures compliance. Important elements of any code would be provision for:

- a clear and legally enforceable structure of decision-making bodies and individuals within the firm to ensure that the internal mechanisms of corporate governance are in place including roles for remuneration committees and non-executive directors;
- clearly defined rights and responsibilities of each constituent body, and clearly defined procedures for exercising these rights;
- monitoring and reporting requirements to ensure the transparency of the management's actions and the company's performance.

To enhance the enforcement of corporate governance standards, a disclosure-based regulatory regime is necessary. This will require firms to disclose all material information at the time of new listings and thereafter on a periodic and continual basis. In countries with developed capital markets, firms rely on market practice and due-diligence obligations to ensure the disclosure of all material information. In East Asia, the capital markets are less well developed and regulators will need to play a more active role in defining and enforcing specific accounting, financial reporting and disclosure standards. Enforcing the code of best practice can be reinforced by inducing companies at the entry points to market listing, credit rating, and government contracts to demonstrate their compliance with best governance practice.

Other procedures to encourage good practice include instituting the legal requirement for interested parties to abstain from voting on connected party transactions; and ensuring the prior approval of shareholders to both substantial and interested party transactions. Improving the quality of legal enforcement against insider trading, and the rigour of take over codes will help. Improving accounting, auditing, financial reporting and disclosure standards, enforcing due diligence and fiduciary obligations of both financial intermediaries and company officers and directors will allow minority shareholders to protect themselves against abuse by majority shareholders. Similarly, more timely and continuous disclosure will contribute to more accurate assessment of credit and market risk.

Finally, enhancing and developing the knowledge and capacity of shareholders, company officials and other stakeholders in their rights and responsibilities can form a vital part of institution building that will help the implementation and enforcement of corporate governance standards. This will allow self-enforcement by a more active role in governance, or through legal actions to force compliance in cases of violations.

In conclusion, corporate governance reform in East Asia requires action on three fronts: strengthening the mechanisms in firms for more accountable and transparent operations; providing more effective control and regulation of firms by external agencies; and education and training to develop understanding of sound corporate governance practices. Together these reforms will permit investors to make more intelligent and critical judgements on which companies to entrust with their money. However as important as reform of corporate governance may be in the national context, there is a worrying sense that such reforms could be vitiated by the destabilizing impact of future incursions of the international capital market.

Economic recovery and progress towards corporate governance reform 1998–2000

As export-led economic growth has returned to the East Asian region, with improving GDP growth rates each quarter, the revival of consumption, and indications of some recovery in investment has occured. The critical question is whether this recovery and growth has occurred on firmer economic and institutional foundations than the rapid speculative growth that precipitated the Asian crisis. Will Asia develop a more stable model of industrial development, or will another spurt or reckless growth lead inevitably to another cycle of crisis and forced restructuring?

In their survey of recovery in the region, Segal and Goodman (2000) highlight the disproportionate role of Japan which alone accounts for two-thirds of all Asian GDP. The recent economic failures of Japan originally sparked the crisis in Asia, and the failure of Japan to remedy in any convincing way its enveloping economic malaise, has sustained the economic weaknesses of East Asia. Powerful Japanese economic growth from the 1960s increased the interdependence of the region, and when the Japanese speculative bubble economy burst in 1990, it was just a matter of time before this impacted upon neighbouring economies. Segal and Goodman conclude that in terms of global stability and regional economic success, undoubtedly the most important factor will be the return to health of the Japanese economy (2000: 5).

In addressing the elements of recovery in the region, Segal and Goodman stress three interrelated themes: political reform, economic reform, and the role of international institutions. Though fiercely contested in the Asia Pacific, they insist 'the weight of evidence indicates that achieving sustainable economic reforms requires deeper political and social change ... Financial transparency requires a political system which allows, indeed orchestrates, fierce questioning of officials in public debate. It also requires the rule of law, in which civil servants and citizens are subject to impartial justice, not the rule of man, as well as a system structurally committed to pluralism. While China's behaviour shows that lack of political reform and openness can provide some short-term protection, in the longer terms, sustaining economic growth in post-industrial economies requires change' (2000: 5).

With regard to economic reform, in the essential search to restore sources of domestic and international investment, guided the of corporate governance codes developed by the OECD, World Bank and Asian Development Bank, all of the East Asian economies have been persuaded to look at their standards of corporate governance, and Singapore, Malaysia and Korea have made the greatest efforts to improve corporate governance. Malaysia's National Economic Recovery Plan gives high priority to improving transparency and regulatory environments and urges the Kuala Lumpur Stock Exchange and Securities Commission to enforce regulations vigorously and consistently. In 1999, Malaysia tightened its company listing rules requiring the issue of quarterly financial statements and preventing individuals sitting on too many company boards (EAAUa, 1999: 63).

The results in Malaysia, as indeed in all the East Asian economies, are mixed. A Dresdner Kleinwort Benson report lists ten major Malaysian companies with good corporate governance records, including fair treatment of minority investors (1999).

However, audit and company restructuring reports also point to insider dealings and maneuvering at the expense of minority shareholders. For example, Arthur Anderson's 30 June 1998 audited accounts of the Malaysian company Ekran were qualified because of large sums paid to parties related to one of its directors without the relevant approval from the Securities Commission, and possibly in breach of the companies law.

Continuing the effort to reform, in February 1999, Malaysia produced a corporate governance report with a 70-point programme to improve transparency and board accountability to shareholders and to protect minority shareholders. Malaysia intends to use this study to lead corporate governance reform discussions in APEC. The recommendations in the report fall into three categories:

1 developing a Malaysian Code of Corporate Governance;
2 reforming laws, regulations and rules to strengthen the regulatory framework for publicly listed companies; and
3 providing training and education to expand the pool of qualified directors and managers.

The best practice code recommends independent or outside directors constitute at least one-third of corporate boards, directors' attendance and remuneration details be released and each board establishes committees of non-executive directors and names a lead non-executive director. Other proposed changes include anti-cronyism rules restricting controlling shareholders from voting when they have a conflict of interest and requiring companies to offer mailed proxy votes. The report argues for greater policing of breaches of minority investor rights. These proposed changes were to be fully implemented by December 2000, and though the code of practice is voluntary, under proposed new stock exchange listing rules, companies would have to disclose compliance with the code or reasons for non-compliance (EAAUa, 1999: 64).

Singapore which weathered the crisis better than any other East Asian country, and which takes pride in the stability of its banking and corporate sector, has sought to strengthen further its banking system by improved corporate governance. Since 1996, Singapore has been working to develop and to refine corporate governance rules and principles for listed companies. The Monetary Authority of Singapore will require all banks to appoint nominating committees to handle appointments and reappointments to the board and key management positions. Members of nominating committees must be chosen from the board and approved by the Monetary Authority. The listing rules require companies to establish audit committees and their annual reports must state whether and how companies have complied with the best practice guide. This focuses more on the substance of governance rather than the form.

Korea has passed legislation to improve minority shareholder rights, increase independent membership of boards and introduce international accountancy standards. Korean conglomerates must now release consolidated company accounts for the activities of all subsidiaries (EAAUb, 1999). However, as the East Asia Analytical Unit of the Australian Department of Foreign Affairs and Trade concludes, 'Improving corporate governance requires a significant shift in corporate culture and ethics; this cannot be achieved just by passing legislation. Strict enforcement and some highly publicised convictions can assist this process' (EAAUa, 1999: 65).

The case of Thailand, where the Asian crisis erupted, is instructive of the determination to reform, the residual problems, and the likely results. Prasarn Trairatvorakul, the Secretary General of the Securities and Exchange Commission of Thailand, has indicated the lingering problems among the signs of economic recovery which threaten the sustainability of economic growth. Thailand still has the problem of non-performing loans which were in mid-2000 around 37 per cent of the total banking systems' outstanding loans. An additional complication was the problem of corporate debt restructuring which still awaits cure. The Thai government has promoted the establishment of a private Asset Management Corporation (AMC) to buy the problem loans out of financial institutions, and established a task force, the Corporate Debt Restructuring Advisory Committee, to promote market-based corporate debt restructuring. Policy initiatives to eliminate impediments and broaden the incentive framework for debt restructuring are aimed at achieving a dramatic reduction in non-performing loans.

However, the devastated Thai securities market may prove more difficult to revive. 'Since the outbreak of Thailand's financial crisis in the last quarter of 1997, no new public company has been able to list in the Stock Exchange of Thailand and raise funds from the public. The old listed companies could only raise 5.3 per cent of their total new funds by public offerings of securities in 1999' (Trairatvorakul, 2000: 3). Investors had lost confidence in the Thai stock market, there were perceived to be fewer and fewer good products, and the market itself was becoming too small to invest funds. The Thai Securities and Exchange Commission (SEC) at this point, like the SEC's in other emerging markets, departed from its traditional brief to keep the stock market fair, transparent and efficient and to attempt to restore the market. 'How can we have a fair, transparent and efficient market if the market does not even exist . . . when there is no demand and no supply, there is no market?' (Trairatvorakul, 2000: 5).

The SEC in Thailand launched a campaign to bring back investors focusing on three strategies:

1 inducing a good supply of securities;
2 creating a good market system;
3 empowering and protecting investors.

To induce a better supply of securities, the SEC proposed to accommodate a broader spectrum of companies by making the listing requirements more flexible on minimum registered capital, track record and profitability, while keeping in place the tightening rules on good corporate governance. Secondly, it encouraged state enterprises under the government's privatization programme to list on the stock exchange. Thirdly, it facilitated Thai small- and medium-sized enterprises to list, with better access to venture capital funds and credit guarantees. Finally, it developed the bond market as an alternative investment vehicle with the establishment of a debt management office to coordinate debt management to ensure the consistent issuance of government bonds creating an interest-rate benchmark for the market.

To create a better market system, two policy measures were implemented firstly enhancing good corporate governance practices by improving the accountability of boards, and requiring all listed companies to establish an audit committee. A code of best practice in corporate governance was developed and improvements in the Thai accounting standards to conform with international accounting standards introduced. Secondly, the SEC sought to enhance the integrity of the clearing and settlement system by instituting proper mechanisms for internal control, risk management and customer protection.

The final SEC strategy to empower and protect investors comprised four policy measures:

1 Improving the legal infrastructure by offering protection for shareholder rights, amending the Public Company Act to strengthen the responsibilities of corporate officers, to make legal proceedings by shareholders less cumbersome, and tightening auditing requirements;
2 reducing the transaction costs of the market by liberalizing brokerage fees, and utilizing Internet technology;
3 promoting investor education, beginning in secondary schools; and
4 promoting institutional investors including mutual funds and provident funds, to provide more professional investment services.

This would all be very reassuring if taken at face value, but Jamie Allen the Secretary of the Asian Corporate Governance Association dispels any unfounded optimism: 'While I believe that a global set of corporate governance principles is emerging, and are applicable to Asia, if you simply transplant them to Asia without modification, they will, in most cases wither in barren soil . . . More than 90 per cent of companies do not want to hear the corporate governance message. Inertia and stubborness are powerful forces. Most companies, whether family owned or not, do not like having change imposed on them. Changing entrenched practices and mindsets is hard and it carries a cost. But it also carries significant benefits for those who bother' (*Governance*, September 2000). It appears that while Asian countries may have adopted aspects of the OECD code of corporate governance, this has certainly influenced the thinking of company regulators, and that while company and securities laws offer rights to shareholders, equitable treatment, disclosure and transparency, the point is whether the spirit of these laws is being followed, and if not what sanctions have been applied. 'The answer in most cases is, respectively "No" and "Very Few". But this is because the market has not demanded more from companies. In the end, investors get the corporate governance they demand' (*Governance*, September 2000). Comfortingly, Allen suggests that there was a similar reluctance to commit to the spirit rather than the letter of corporate governance reforms in Western companies when these were first introduced; however if spectacular corporate failures occur from time to time in most Western countries, the problem is they are more endemic in East Asia.

In contemplating the chances for a sustained recovery in Asia, it is important to examine the progress of China, the other superpower in the region. China stabilized the Asian crisis at some cost to itself, but as a consequence the reform process appears to have become stalled. A startling report from the Shanghai Stock Exchange (SSE), following a three year corporate governance survey of managers at more than 1000 companies, presents grim reading. The SSE insists that over 99 per cent of key business decisions including board appointments and pay, have to be ratified by Communist Party officials within the company. More than two-thirds of listed companies remain under the direct supervision of government ministries or other agencies. 'Due to government interference dramatic fluctuations in corporate performance, frequent asset restructurings, window dressing of financial statements, stock market manipulation and insider trading, there is no significant correlation between the market value of a company and its intrinsic value.' The report goes on to suggest that boards of directors are no more than rubber stamps for the executive management and controlling shareholders, that independent directors make up just 0.3 per cent of the 3000 directors covered in the survey, and that 'Directors pursue their own interests instead of maximizing shareholder value, and they cannot fulfill their fiduciary duty' (*Governance*, November 2000). When it is realized these observations concern the supposedly reformed sector of Chinese industry, and that the reform of SOEs has slowed considerably, and reforming and recapitalizing the banks is also proceeding slowly, then the possibility of the crisis in the Chinese economy and society deepening becomes very real.

An unreformed China, combined with political instability in Indonesia and Malaysia, suggests that at least the political element of recovery in the region is fragile, and economic success hardly assured (Segal and Goodman, 2000: 7). But whilst the implications of this instability are threatening for the Asian countries themselves and for the economic well-being of their people, to suggest this is potentially a cause of instability in global markets is somewhat wide of the mark. Global financial markets are currently more than capable of compounding their own instability.

The instability of international financial markets

Regulating a global financial system in which hedge funds can leverage themselves geometrically and with little supervision, and in which money flows are instantaneous and electronic is, as US Treasury Secretary Rubin put it, 'exceedingly complicated'. Mr Rubin noted that 'over the last 30 years global capital flows have increased exponentially', and he emphasized the market's herd mentality, insisting that just as capital once flowed into emerging market economies without due regard for proper risk analysis, 'it is now flowing out in a non-discriminatory, overly negative reaction' (*International Herald Tribune*, 3–4 October 1998).

The IMF (1998: 23) puts the responsibility on national governments of emerging economies to discourage speculation through more extensive disclosure: 'The solution is to provide better information to the markets on government policies and the conditions of domestic financial institutions in order to encourage investors to trade on fundamentals rather than to run with the herd. This means releasing full information about current government policies and about contingencies that might affect future government policies, as well as using interest rates and other financial variables under the government's control to clearly signal policy priorities. It means not presenting hedge funds and other private investors, whose combined resources constitute a market vastly larger than the assets of central banks and governments, with an incentive to take large positions against a currency by offering them the irresistible combination of inconsistent policies and unsustainable currency pegs.'

Roger C. Altman, the investment banker who served in the US Treasury for both the Carter and Clinton administration has argued: 'The worldwide elimination of barriers to trade and capital . . . have created the global financial market place, which informed observers hailed for bringing private capital to the developing world, encouraging growth and democracy' (*New York Times Magazine*, 1 March 1998). However, Jagdash Bhagwati has questioned the wisdom of the free movement of trade and the free movement of the vast capital flows which greatly exceed anything happening in the non-financial economy. Bhagwati records how in 1996 the total capital inflows to Indonesia, Malaysia, South Korea, Thailand and the Philippines were US$93 billion, up from US$41 billion in 1994. In 1997 this suddenly changed to an outflow of US$12 billion. 'Hence it has become apparent that crises attendant on capital mobility cannot be ignored' (Bhagwati, 1998: 8). Charles Kindleberger of MIT has noted that capital flows, unlike trade in most commodities, are characterized by panics and manias.

Efforts to restore the confidence of those responsible for capital flight, typically involve dramatic increases in domestic interest rates for the countries concerned, and 'across Asia this has decimated firms with large amounts of debt' (Bhagwati, 1998: 9). The case for free trade has been 'hijacked by the proponents of capital mobility ... to bamboozle us into celebrating the new world of trillions of dollars moving about in a borderless world, creating gigantic economic gains, rewarding virtue and punishing profligacy ... But interests have also played a central role. Wall Street's financial firms have obvious self-interest in a world of free capital mobility since it only enlarges the arena in which to make money' (Bhagwati, 1998: 11).

The logic which benefits Wall Street is not necessarily a logic which will benefit emerging economies, argues Xiang Bing who emphasizes the 'Fundamental vulnerability of an emerging economy with financial liberalization: both the country's stock market and the currency market, characterized by thin trading, are too insignificant in scale to withstand rational trading activities of large international capital' (*Hong Kong Economic Journal*, 15 February 1998). Exactly how the East Asian economies felt they were being overwhelmed by a tsunami wave of capital movement is illustrated in Figure 12.1, which compares the total market capitalization in July 1998 of the New York Stock Exchange at US$10 465 billon with the stock market capitalization of Jakarta, Bangkok, Manila, Seoul and Kuala Lumpur, which together mustered US$178 billion. The fluttering of a few eyebrows in Wall Street really can cause financial havoc in emerging economies on the other side of the world in a system with this kind of imbalance.

A further irony is that a major beneficiary of the capital flight out of East Asia was the USA, as the world's largest capital market and the

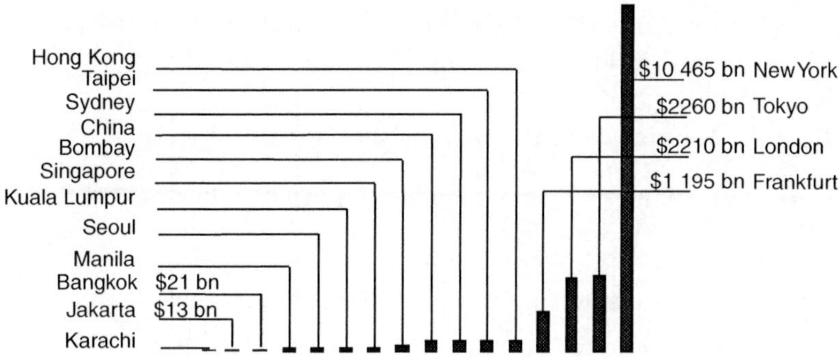

Figure 12.1 Market value: total capitalization, 6 July 1998
Source: Salomon Smith Barney, *Asiaweek research*.

holder of the leading currency. It was not a coincidence that as the markets drained in East Asia, Wall Street enjoyed a revival of its prolonged bull market (Hale, 1998: 11). There was a sharp divergence in the fortunes of Asian stock markets and the rest of the world, as the stock exchanges of East Asia lost more than half their capital, with the emerging markets of Latin America following behind, the markets of Western Europe and North America continued to increase in value. The sense that world growth could continue despite the Asian collapse was encouraged by many authorities including the IMF.

There was an air of unreality about all this as the US stock market became increasingly unhinged from economic fundamentals despite Alan Greenspan's occasional warnings against irrational exuberance. Some commentators were happy to throw caution to the wind: 'The Dow Jones Industrial Average is more than four times as high as it was six years ago. The New York and NASDAQ stock exchanges have added over $4 trillion in value in the last four years alone – the largest single accumulation of wealth in the history of the United States' (Zuckerman, 1998: 18). A scenario similar to the Japanese speculative bubble seemed to be developing as a growing proportion of US households were persuaded to part with their savings – and go into debt – to plunge into stocks through mutual funds, despite only modest productivity growth in the US economy and slow GDP growth, creating for a time at least a self-fulfilling prophecy of substantial growth in the US market, even, the end of history (Henwood, 1998; Krugman, 1998; Martin Wolf, *Financial Times*, December 1998). However as J. K. Galbraith recently commented, 'In the United States we now have more mutual funds than there is intelligence, perhaps integrity, to handle them. They are a bridge between the innocent and eventual loss' (address to Harvard University Club, London 17 June 1998).

The architecture of the new world economic order

An effective default on Russia's payments on foreign loans at the end of August 1998, and continuing worries for the financial stability of Thailand, Malaysia, Indonesia, South Korea, Brazil and Venezuela, provoked the fear that emerging markets might be shut out of international financial markets for some time, with severe reverberations upon the rest of the global financial system. (*Financial Times*, 2 September 1998). The G-7 finance ministers responded by promising coordinated action to promote growth and to lower interest rates, and measures to alleviate the effects of the crisis on the poorest countries with augmented financial assistance. Concern was expressed about the general withdrawal of funds from emerging markets without respect for the diversity of their prospects, and significant progress being made in countries carrying out macroeconomic policies and structural reforms.

Later in the Autumn of 1998, building on a series of three reports by the G-22 group of economies on crisis prevention and management, a series of financial reform proposals by the G-7 were heralded as promising a new architecture of the world economic order. The finance ministers and central bankers of the leading industrial countries agreed to a plan for a new safety net of the IMF to bail out troubled countries, with greater coordination and regulation of cross-border capital flows. Support was expressed for a code of conduct for all open economies, requiring rules for disclosure of financial information with an agreed approach on corporate governance. The policies are designed to increase the transparency of the international financial system; to enhance stability, particularly through more effective regulation; and to improve ways to respond to crises, through orderly arrangements and better insolvency regimes. However, as Martin Wolf argues, among the matters not fully considered in the policy statement was the critical question of exchange rate regimes, and whether in emerging economies these should be regulatory, prudential or market based. This determines whether countries adopt fixed or floating exchange rates, and the extent of intervention and regulation of the financial system and capital movements, which is quite fundamental (*Financial Times*, 4 November 1998).

In terms of practical proposals for preventing similar crises occurring on a periodic basis, two sets of measures received increasing support, the introduction of capital controls, and bolstering the IMF as an international lender of last resort. To lessen the surges of short-term hot money, Joseph Stiglitz argued that it was time to consider 'some form of taxes, regulations, or restraints on international capital flows' (*Business Week*, 12 October 1998). The IMF acknowledges that prudential controls on inward capital flows could be a useful tool before a crisis hits, but are not a substitute for financial reform, and are of little use in preventing investor flight. In support of prudential controls, Jagdish Bhagwati has insisted, 'I am against full-scale capital-account convertibility for nearly all developing countries. It is premature, given their political and economic fragility, to allow total freedom to take any amount of capital out of or into these countries. I also believe there should be close monitoring and review of short-term borrowings, keeping them in line with fundamentals, reserves, ability to borrow in need' (*Far Eastern Economic Review*, 15 October 1998).

Enhancing the capacity of the IMF to act as an international lender of last resort encountered the objection that this might simply increase the moral hazard of countries and speculators taking risks knowing they will be bailed out if things go badly wrong. (However, the severity of the impact of IMF rescue policies upon the economies of countries experiencing difficulties is unlikely to influence them to subject themselves willingly to similar IMF interventions in future.) Perversely, when IMF rescues have occurred, the people who have benefited first are the short-term foreign lenders who helped to cause the problem. The IMF's response to this dilemma is to propose that private lenders should be forced into participating in IMF rescue operations. This would provide an incentive to investors to pay closer attention to the quality of their investments.

Emerson has highlighted the inconsistency between free-market ideology and the available remedies when disaster occurs: 'The IMF's members are not corporations but states. But the crisis has been driven not by public debts but private ones, incurred by Asian banks and firms' (1998: 49). Hale outlines the different roles of the IMF during market stress: to offer macroeconomic policy advice that national politicians can sell to their voters as their own; to act as a global lender of last resort in a liquidity crunch, similar to the role played by national central banks during domestic crises; to promote economic reforms that might otherwise be unacceptable' (1998: 7). However the impact of IMF policies in the Asian crisis has not proved exactly benign: 'To date the IMF-led rescue plans for these nations do not appear to have worked. Unemployment and interest rates have soared, the value of their currencies has plummeted, and prosperity has turned into dislocation and riots. The flow of private funds into these countries has screeched to a halt' (*Business Week*, 12 October 1998).

In their review of the impact of IMF programmes in Indonesia, Thailand and Korea, executive directors of the IMF admitted that they had over-reacted. In attempting to break the vicious circle of capital outflows and currency depreciation, while dealing with its immediate financial and social fallout, the IMF had imposed a monetary tightening that helped to propel these economies into a much deeper recession than envisaged. Capital continued to exit even after the programmes were implemented, and a greater fiscal stimulus could have been delivered more promptly as the extent of the slowdown became apparent (IMF, 1999).

In holding up Clinton's commitment to supplement IMF funds by US$18 billion to help to deal with the crisis (bringing the IMF's total capital to US$280 billion), Republican congressmen claimed the IMF was simply encouraging recklessness in the management of countries' finances. Perhaps nearer to the truth is Hale's assertion that the IMF has served as a proxy agency for US foreign policy since the Cold War: 'Great economic crisis do not occur in political vacuums. In the 1930s depression led to global war and cost millions of lives. In Indonesia today, the streets of Jakarta have already seen bloodshed and attacks on ethnic Chinese . . . The IMF interventions should be classified as financial peacekeeping, not just economic assistance' (1998: 13).

If not the IMF, then some form of international lender of last resort is clearly essential to maintain political as well as financial stability in the world, otherwise this would mean the rich industrial countries 'standing idly by while currencies plummet, countries run out of foreign exchange, trade and investment comes to a halt, and crises in one region spread to others' (Hass and Litan, 1998: 3). Emerson has drawn attention to the importance of the search for 'alternatives to unregulated markets and the vulnerability and instability that comes with them' (1998: 47). The G-7, IMF and World Bank, together with the national treasuries and central banks of most of the countries of the world for the last two years, have been struggling with this dilemma, which could be described as the governance of markets. As Jack Boorman, the director of the IMF's Policy Development and Review Department concluded: 'The crisis quickly turned into a vicious circle. Capital outflows pushed the value of currencies downwards, creating risks of insolvency for companies that were indebted in foreign currencies and adding momentum to capital outflows. In a global financial market linked by almost instantaneous communications, money moves with a speed that leaves policy makers little room for hesitation' *(International Herald Tribune*, 20 January 1999).

The hope of those engaged in developing a new architecture of international financial governance is that in the future, crises such as that in East Asia in 1997–98 may be prevented, and that if they do occur, they can be managed more effectively. The OECD offers a more sanguine view: 'No amount of strengthening of the international architecture can be expected to prevent difficulties from emerging in countries that do not address their domestic problems. And no institutional framework or regulatory environment is likely to insulate the world from excesses by financial markets unless the major participants are obliged to face more of the negative consequences of their own decisions with greater frequency than has often been the case at present' (1998: 32).

Conclusions

The Asian financial crisis proved a severe shock to the confidence of the region previously celebrated as miracle economies. It revealed that a quarter of a century of rapid economic growth was based on rather ramshackle foundations of corporate governance. In the promising effort to rebuild the East Asian economies, it is clear that lessons have been learnt concerning the importance of disclosure, transparency and accountability, and international codes of corporate governance conduct have been willingly adopted at least by national regulators. However, the worry is that these reforms do not run deep enough in terms of company practice and director behaviour, and will be quickly forgotten if the present restructuring gives way to another economic boom. However, the Asian crisis was a symptom, not a cause, of a much more profound instability in the operation of international financial markets. Unregulated international financial markets have demonstrated the power to bring prosperous countries to their knees, and to lead the world perilously close to complete financial collapse.

References

Amsden, A. H. (1989) *Asia's Next Giant: South Korea and Late Industrialisation*, New York: Oxford University Press.

Bhagwati, J. (1998) 'The capital myth', *Foreign Affairs*, 77(3): 7–12.

Cohen, B. (1997) *The Edge of Chaos: Financial Booms, Bubbles, and Chaos*, London: Wiley.

Department of Foreign Affairs and Trade (1999) *Asia's Financial Markets – Capitalising on Reform*, Commonwealth of Australia.

De Trenck, C., Cartledge, S., Daswani, A., Katz, C. and D. Sakmar (1998) *Red Chips – And the Globalisation of China's Enterprises*, Hong Kong: Asia 2000 Ltd.
Dresdner K. B. (1999) *Malaysian Corporate Governance: Better Than You Thought*, Malaysian Research Team, Singapore.
East Asia Analytical Unit (EAAUa) (1999) *Asia's Financial Markets: Capitalising on Reform*, Commonwealth of Australia, Department of Foreign Affairs and Trade, Canberra.
East Asia Analytical Unit (EAAUb) (1999) *Korea Rebuilds: From Crisis to Opportunity*, Commonwealth of Australia, Department of Foreign Affairs and Trade, Canberra.
Emerson, D. (1998) 'Americanizing Asia?' *Foreign Affairs*, 77(3): 46–56.
Gereffi, G. and D. Wyman (eds) (1992) *Manufacturing Miracles: Paths of Industrialisation in Latin America and East Asia*, Princeton: Princeton University Press.
Goodman, D. S. and G. Segal (1997) *China Rising – Nationalism and Interdependence*, London: Routledge.
Gough, L. (1998) *Asia Meltdown – The End of the Miracle?* Oxford: Capstone.
Hale, D. (1998) 'The IMF, now more than ever: the case for financial peacekeeping', *Foreign Affairs*, 77(6): 7–13.
Hass, R. and R. Litan (1998) 'Globalisation and its discontents', *Foreign Affairs*, 77(3): 2–6.
Henwood, D. (1998) *Wall Street*, London: Verso.
IMF (1998) 'Hedge funds and financial market dynamics', Occasional Paper 166, International Monetary Fund, Washington.
IMF (1999) 'IMF supported programmes in Indonesia, Thailand, and Korea: a preliminary assessment', International Monetary Fund, Washington.
Kim, Y. C. (ed.) (1995) *The South-East Asian Economic Miracle*, New Brunswick, N.J.: Transaction Publishers.
Krugman, P. (1994) 'The myth of Asia's miracle', *Foreign Affairs*, 73(6): 62–78.
Krugman, P. (1998) 'America the Boastful', *Foreign Affairs*, 77(3): 32–45.
Krugman, P. (1996) *Pop Internationalism*, London: IMF Press.
Lingle, C. (1997) *The Rise and Decline of the Asian Century*, Hong Kong: Asia 2000 Ltd.
Overholt, W. (1993) *China: The Next Economic Superpower*, London: Weidenfeld & Nicholson.
Parton, P. (1998) 'Causes of the Asian Financial Crisis', *ANZ Bank Economic Review*, Shanghai: ANZ Bank.
Pillai, P. (1998) 'Corporate governance and transparency revitalising Asian tiger economies', ROC International Conference on Corporate Governance: Responsibilities, Risks and Reform, 7–8 July 1998, Kualar Lumpur, Malaysia.
Prowse, S. (1998) 'Corporate governance in East Asia: a framework for analysis, managing capital flows: national and international dimensions', Conference on 15–16 June 1998, Bangkok, Thailand.
Rohwer, J. (1996) *Asia Rising*, London: Nicholas Brealey.
Segal G. and D. S. G. Goodman (2000) *Towards Recovery in Pacific Asia*, London: Routledge.
Soros, G. (1998) *The Crisis of Global Capitalism*, London: Little Brown and Company.
Trairatvorakul, P. (2000) 'Challenges of restoring investor confidence following a financial crisis', 25th Annual Conference IOSCO, Sydney.
Young, A. (1994) 'Lesson's from the East Asian NIE's: a contrarian view', *European Economic Review*, 38: 964–73.

World Bank (1993) *The East Asian Miracle – Economic Growth and Public Policy*, Oxford: Oxford University Press.
World Bank (1996) *From Plan to Market, World Development Report 1996*, Oxford: Oxford University Press.
World Bank (1997) *The State in a Changing World, World Development Report 1997*, Oxford: Oxford University Press.
Zuckerman, M. (1998) 'A second American century', *Foreign Affairs*, 77(3): 18–31.

13

Corporate Governance and Restructuring in Korea: Before and After the Crisis*

Keun Lee

Introduction

While the Korean economy had boasted a strong recovery with almost 10 per cent real growth in 1999, the situation in 2000 and now does not seem that bright. Now, the perception increasingly is that post-crisis restructuring, once regarded as successful, is not really satisfactory – only half the required job has been done. This chapter will look at the post-crisis changes in corporate governance and business structure in Korean firms. To evaluate post-crisis corporate restructuring in Korea, the chapter starts with examining the root of the corporate system in Korea.

As a matter of fact, successive bankruptcies of the *chaebol* in 1997 had damaged the credit-worthiness of the Korean firms and economy, and served as one of the triggering factors for the crisis. Both Koreans and foreigners thought that the *chaebol* would never go bankrupt, always backed by the Korean government and its concern with the socio-economic impact of any failure within the big *chaebol*. But the myth proved to be false, which stopped the roll-over of Korean-held debts in international banks. At the bottom of this crisis lies the *chaebol*'s mismanagement of risks, namely the simple pursuit of heavily indebted growth. Questions such as what drove them to pursue such aggressive growth and why the banks and other stakeholders were not able to check such *chaebol* behaviour, will be attempted to be answered here as the chapter examines corporate governance and finance in the Korean firms.

The focus is on the *chaebol*, the family-controlled business groups that have been the backbone of the Korean economy. La Porta et al. (1998)

and Bebchuk et al. (1999) find that firms of controlling minority structures (CMS), such as the Korean *chaebol*, are widespread around the world. Not only in Korea but also in many other countries, CMS firms have recently come under close political and market scrutiny, especially after the 1997 crisis in Asia. In the CMS firm, a shareholder exercises control while retaining only a small fraction of the equity claims on a company's cash flows. Such a radical separation of control and cash flow rights can occur in three principal ways – through dual-class share structure, stock pyramids, and cross-ownership ties. These three methods are exactly what is used by the Korean *chaebol*. The CMS structure resembles controlled structure insofar as it insulates the controller from the market for corporate control, but it resembles dispersed ownership insofar as it places corporate control in the hands of an insider who holds a small fraction of equity (Bebchuk et al., 1999).[1] Thus, the CMS threatens to combine the incentive problems associated with both controlling structures and dispersed ownership in a single-ownership structure, as well noted by Bebchuk et al. (1999). However, this important distinction of the *chaebol* as a CMS is missed in most of the literature, including the more recent, post-crisis conference on *chaebol*, for instance Hyun (1999) and Nam et al. (1999).

Granovetter (1995) defines business groups as those collections of firms bound together in some formal and/or informal ways, characterized by an intermediate level of binding, namely neither bound merely by short-term strategic alliances nor legally consolidated into a single entity. The Korean *chaebol* fit into this definition, and are also consistent with Strachan's (1976) definition as there are strong personal and operational ties among the member or affiliate firms in a *chaebol*.[2] As noted in the literature, specific forms that business groups take in each country vary depending upon not only economic but also political and legal conditions of the countries. In the case of Korea, a protected domestic market, state-controlled banking sector, active industrial policy by the government, and so on, are the important influencing factors for the development of the *chaebol*. Although the chapter will naturally touch upon these issues, the focus will be on the impact of these factors on corporate governance and growth of the *chaebol*. In this chapter, the term *chaebol* is used to indicate the whole business group as a unit consisting of the member or affiliate companies. The terms, member firm, group-affiliate firm, or *chaebol* firm (company), are interchangeably used to refer to an individual firm belonging to a business group, namely a *chaebol*. Actually, these affiliate firms are legal persons, often listed in the stock markets and interlocked by circular share-holdings, but a business group or *chaebol* is not a legal person in itself.

In the next section, the growth of the *chaebol* are discussed in terms of their source of growth potentials, the reasons for their diversification and circular shareholding. The ensuing section discusses corporate governance problems in Korean. The next section maintains that the relative strength of the *chaebol* system depends a lot on the external environment, and that the sudden deterioration of the environmental condition increased the costs and reduced the benefits of the *chaebol* system. Thus, this section examines the change in the external environment focusing on the change in the role of the government and the 1990 wave of liberalization and globalization. Next, the chapter provides an overview of post-crisis changes in financial systems, corporate governance, and capital and business structures in Korean firms. Finally, the chapter concludes with policy implications and remarks.

How the *chaebol* grew in Korea

Rapid growth with diversification is one of the most salient features of the Korean *chaebol*. According to Penrose (1995), diversification is a way of utilizing available resources in a more profitable way for the firm. This means that for diversification to happen two conditions need to be satisfied. The first is that an opportunity for profitable expansion of the firm exists; and the second is that the firm has extra resources to invest in a new business. Depending upon the situation, either of the two conditions may be binding. For example, when there is ample opportunity for profitable expansion, a more binding constraint is the firm's (internal) resources. This seemed to be the case for the Korean *chaebol*.

During the high-growth period of the 1960s and 1970s, the protected domestic markets and the preferential loans from the state-controlled banks opened up numerous profitable business opportunities (namely rents) for the Korean *chaebol*.[3] For example, during the heavy and chemical-industry promotion drives by the government in the 1970s, the government directed banks and non-banking financial institutions to supply more than 50 per cent of total domestic credit as heavily subsidized loans (Cho and Kim, 1995; Nam et al., 1999). Given this, the *chaebol* had to stretch their resources to the maximum to take full advantage of the growth opportunity, and, at the same time, recruit more financial and managerial resources from the outside. The tendency to use this strategy resulted in very aggressive expansion often times without the backup of internal resources and the concentration of economic resources in the economy into ten of the *chaebol*. Undeniably, it also laid the basis for a sudden break-down sometime in the future when such careless pursuit of growth was no longer profitable. For example, it is now well-known that the Daewoo group, at this point itself bankrupt and thus dissolved, once even considered acquiring Samsung Automobiles in 1998 right after the financial crisis.

Stories about the growth of several *chaebol*, including the diversification story of LG Group, formerly Lucky-Gold Star, are well known, and introduced in textbooks such as Milgrom and Roberts (1992). One of the important implications of such stories about rapid growth with diversification is that with imports restricted and demand guaranteed, the only constraint for a *chaebol*'s growth was finding financial resources to invest into production facilities. Thus, real managerial skills were not as important as personal connections with government bureaucrats to bargain out preferential loans from the state-controlled banks. In this sense, the state granted two kinds of rents to *chaebol*, the rents of extra profits associated with market protection and entry control and the rents of preferential loans.

For those *chaebol* that were allowed the rents for growth, the two major concerns were to keep the controlling shares in the firms and to finance the growth at the same time. However, as the history of capitalism indicates, these two objectives are not easily reconciled, and thus history saw the natural separation of ownership and management, and the emergence of managerial capitalism (Berle and Means, 1932). However, the Korean *chaebol* found a way to achieve both of the objectives through circular shareholdings. By forming a complex web of circular shareholdings, the founding owner-manager was able to control the whole enterprise group even with a very small share owned by his family. Whenever the *chaebol* started a new business, they did so by establishing a new member firm in the *chaebol* group. Capital for the new firms was financed in very little part by the owner family's funds and came mostly from the other member firms and the banks. Relatively few firms were raised openly in the stock markets until the 1990s.[4] In other words, establishing a new firm was a much easier and cheaper way to finance the new start-up than forming a new division inside the old firms using its funds alone.

Table 13.1 shows the share composition in the *chaebol* firms. On average, the owner and relatives own only about 10 per cent of the *chaebol* group's stock in the top 30 business groups. More than 30 per cent of the stocks are owned by the other member firms in the same *chaebol* group. However, these stocks are mutual exchanges among themselves.

Table 13.1 Ownership structure in *chaebols* (as of 1 April 1996)

Chaebols	**No. of member firms**	**No. of business sectors**	**percentage of shares owned by**		**Insiders' shares (A + B)**	**Adjusted shares A/(1 – B)**	**Equity to asset ratio**	**Degree of openness (percentage)**	
			Owners and relatives (A)	**Member firms and self-owned (B)**				**By capital stock**	**By no. of firms**
Hyundai	46	38	15.39	46.02	61.4	28.51	20.99	44.31	34.78
Sumsung	55	30	2.97	46.04	49.01	5.5	32.7	55.22	25.45
LG	48	29	5.97	33.91	39.88	9.03	24.2	60.21	22.92
Daewoo	25	27	6.35	35.35	41.69	9.82	22.91	86.19	36
SunKyong	32	24	16.1	32.54	48.64	23.87	23.27	56.86	15.63
Average									
1st–5th	41.2	29.6	8.2	39.65	47.85	13.58	25.14	62.34	26.69
5th–10th	24.4	24.6	9.53	21.63	31.16	12.16	20.94	64.14	30.32
11th–20th	19	16.8	9.81	29.83	49.64	13.98	17.21	54.95	23.15
21st–30th	15.1	12.4	10.17	32.69	42.86	15.1	16.47	66.17	23.17
1st–30th	22.3	18.8	10.32	33.82	44.14	15.59	22.34	62.08	25.56

Note: Equity to asset ratio refers to non-financial institutions only. Degree of openness measures the proportion of the member firms that are listed in stock markets either by the number of them or in terms of values of the capital.
Source: Korea Fair Trade Commission.

For example, firm A in a *chaebol* group owns a share of firm B worth 100 million won, firm B owns a share of firm C worth 100 million won, and finally firm C owns a share of firm A worth 100 million won. This 100 million won does not represent a real asset and it is a paper asset existing only in the accounting system. However, this paper asset contributes to keeping the controlling share of the member firms in the owner families. In other words, as Table 13.1 shows, the insiders' share ratios (the sum of the shares owned by the owner-relatives and the member firms) are as high as 44 per cent in the 30 largest *chaebol* in Korea. In this way, the owner-families were able to keep their control over a large number of the member firms with only a less than proportional amount of real financial capital. However, the adjusted insider share ratio amounts to only 15.6 per cent, if we exclude the circular holdings of paper assets.

Table 13.2 shows how the Korean *chaebol* financed the acquisition and growth of their assets. In 1986, about 32 per cent of the newly increased assets were internally financed. This ratio of internal financing continued to decrease to only 12 per cent in 1996. As a consequence, the share of the owner and relatives decreased from 16 per cent in 1987 to 10.3 per cent in 1996.

If there were rents in terms of domestic market protection and preferential loans, it would be natural for the *chaebol* to take advantage of these rents in pursuing growth. However, existence of rents does not sufficently explain the expansionary tendency of the *chaebol*, especially given the substantial degree of market liberalization and reduction of subsidized loans since the 1980s. As a matter of fact, the *chaebol* are perceived to acquire, or to enter, a business which is often not justifiable in terms of rates of return on investment. Theoretical models presented

Table 13.2 Asset growth and financing in the Korean firms (in billion won)

	1986	1987	1988	1989	1991	1992	1993	1994	1995	1996
Values of asset increases (A)	8 422	15 934	13 827	22 152	37 626	21 063	33 293	55 234	48 050	48 877
Cash flow (B)	2 656	3 234	4 043	3 664	4 798	3 974	5 309	9 152	14 121	5 631
Rate of internal financing	0.32	0.20	0.29	0.17	0.13	0.19	0.16	0.17	0.29	0.12

Notes: Values of asset increase is defined as asset value of the present year minus asset value of the previous year; cash flow is the sum of the net income, depreciation allowance and other exempted taxes.
Sources: Bank of Korea, Performance Analysis of the Firms in Korea (in Korea), various years.

in Bebchuk et al. (1999) give us a persuasive clue to this question. The models explain why inefficient projects are chosen and unprofitable expansion is pursued by a CMS firm such as the Korean *chaebol*. Another model in Bebchuk et al. (1999) shows that given any distribution of opportunities to expand and to contract, the likelihood that a CMS firm will make an inefficient decision – and thus incur the expected agency cost – grows larger as the controller's equity stake becomes smaller. In this model, too, the deciding factor is the magnitude of private benefits accruing to the controller when he keeps or acquires the asset, and private benefits tend to come from self-dealing or appropriation opportunities.

In the Korean context, typical private benefits also took the form of arbitrary and preferential borrowing from the firms and many kinds of outright cash payments to the controlling shareholders. These models suggest that the unique agency-cost structure of the CMS firm pushes the *chaebol* to pursue more growth than otherwise. For example, the largest *chaebol*, Samsung, had to enter the automobiles business because it was strongly backed by the command or desire of the owner-chairmen although many within the group were sceptical about the viability or the rate of return of the new automobile business. This foray turned out to be a wrong decision and Samsung sold its automobile business to Renault in 2000.

Problems of corporate governance in the *chaebol*

In American firms, the main issue in corporate governance is how to monitor hired management under dispersed share ownership, and the job is mainly done by markets (Jenson and Meckling, 1976; Fama, 1980). In Japanese firms, the main banks play an important role as the final monitor over management (Aoki, 1987; 1990). The Korean firms do not fit either of the two cases mentioned earlier. As discussed in the previous section, the owner and relatives own only 10 per cent of the shares but control 100 per cent of the firms. This means that the governance problem in Korean firms is the bulk of power disproportionately divided in favour of the managers with 10 per cent of the shares vs. the rest of the shareholders with 90 per cent of the shares. In a sense, the title 'owner' (which is often used in Korea) of the *chaebol* is not an appropriate one as they hold only 10 per cent of the shares. At the same time, the owner families are also different from professional management in the diffusely owned firm as they actually control the firm with their own stocks combined with circular shareholding, and more importantly, they have long-time horizons. In this light the structure of the Korean *chaebol* can be considered as a variant of the CMS as analysed in Bebchuk et al. (1999). There are two major problems in the Korean-style CMS. The first is the ignorance of the rights of minority shareholders; the second is the ignorance of the rights of debt-holders. These two problems are discussed below.

The governance structure in the Korean *chaebol* gives extraordinary protection to the controlling incumbent management, while the rights of minority shareholders are minimal. It is well known that the price gap between common stocks and preferred stocks, which is a measure of management premium, is very large in Korean firms; in an international comparison, the price of common stocks is often twice as high as that of preferred stocks in Korea. Another measure of shareholder rights should be the amount of dividends. Dividend rates relative to profits are also very low in the Korean *chaebol*, only 14–20 per cent, compared to about 40 per cent in the USA and Japan. One of the reasons for such a low dividend ratio is that the owner-managers want to avoid the heavy income taxes imposed on their dividend incomes. Instead, they want to be compensated in the form of arbitrary and preferential borrowings from the firms and many kinds of arbitrary cash payments to the owner-shareholders. In practice, the distinction between the official money of the firm and private money of the owner is often blurred in Korea, as has been revealed in the cases of several bankrupt *chaebol* in 1997.

Also, the return to dividends measured by the ratio of dividends to the price per share (about 1.5 per cent) is very low compared to interest rates (9 to 10 per cent) in Korea. In the USA, the ratio of dividends to shares reaches up to one half of the interest rates. This situation in Korea tends to make stock investment less attractive to bank savings, which explains the decreasing stock capitalization ratio and decreasing stock investor population in the 1990s. The stock investor population decreased from 2.4 million in 1990 to 1.46 million in 1996.

Furthermore, institutional investors in Korea, including pension funds, investment and trust funds, forfeited their voting rights as shareholders, as a result of the overprotection of the incumbent manager-owners. Even for individual shareholders, their rights as shareholders are almost nil in terms of the right to call for shareholders' meetings, to attain access to the accounting books of the firms, to raise lawsuits against the management, and so on.[5]

Since the voices of minority shareholders are very weak, the management with the controlling shares is not subject to constructive checks from the minority shareholders. While it has the benefit of promoting managerial initiatives, it carries the intrinsic costs of managerial dictatorship. Thus, the costs of such one-man dominated management is substantial in that strategic decision-making can go wrong due to the misjudgment of the owner. It is reported that in many cases of Korean *chaebol* bankruptcies, one of the most important causes for the decline of the firms had to do with wrong strategic decisions made by the owner, especially by second generation owner-managers who inherited the companies from their fathers.

Table 13.3 shows the list of the recently bankrupted companies and whether the *chaebol* had a succession from a founder to his descendants before the bankruptcy. It is shown that out of 24 cases, 14 cases had a succession several years before the bankruptcy. The typical behaviour and motivation of the second generation owner-management is observed to include a very aggressive mindset and a desire to prove that he is as good as his father, and that he can achieve something new and different. Such a mentality leads to careless expansion into new business areas, which often puts the whole group into jeopardy.

Weak protection of shareholders' rights leads to weak investment motivation, which tends to translate into higher capital costs (OECD, 1998); however, that was not the case with the Korean *chaebol*. Money borrowed from the banks was very cheap in many respects, and thus they did not feel much need to bother to issue shares to attract new money.

In comparison to American firms, firms in Korea, Japan and Germany tend to rely more on borrowing from banks. In Japan, banks not only lend to firms but also own shares, and the relationship between banks and firms is characterized by the main-bank system, where the main bank of each firm plays the role of its monitor.[6] In German firms, banks are able to participate actively, based not only on their own share holdings but also on the delegated voting rights they have, to act as monitor and adviser to the firms (Berglof, 1989; Cox, 1986). The Korean *chaebol* firms fit none of these representations.

What was the role of Korean banks? Their role during the high-growth period was to provide the so-called money for growth whenever the firms needed it and when the government asked or commanded the banks to lend to the firms. The banks were nationalized right after former President Park Jeong Hee took power by military force in the early 1960s, and were under *de facto* control by the government, specifically the MOF, even after nominal privatization since the 1980s. Thus, the effective lending criteria of the banks were the signals or orders from

Table 13.3 The cases of bankruptcies and the successions in the Korean conglomerates[a]

Name of the firm	Forms of bankruptcy	Date bankrupt	Succession	Succession year
Woo-seong	CA[b]	19 January 96	Yes	1990
Dong-A	SL[c]	10 January 97	Yes	1977
Han-Bo	CA	28 January 97	Yes	1996
Jinro	SL/CA	20 March 97	Yes	1984
Sammi	CA	20 March 97	Yes	1980
Hanshin	CA	31 May 97	Yes	1983
Kia Auto	CA	18 July 97	No	N.A.
Dae-Nong	SL/CA	11 September 97	Yes	1989
Ssang-Bang-Ul	SL/CA	20 October 97	Yes	1997
Newcore	SL	04 November 97	No	N.A.
Su-San	SL/CA	18 November 97	No	N.A.
Tae-Il	SL/CA	18 November 97	No	
Sin-Ho	SL	28 November 97	No	N.A.
Halla	SL/CA	08 December 97	No	N.A.
Hanhwa	SL	16 December 97	Yes	1981
Jin-Do	SL	16 December 97	Yes	1981
Ssangyong	SL	10 January 98	Yes	1975
Hanil	SL	15 January 98	Yes	1981
Nasan	SL/CA	15 January 98	No	N.A.
Kukdong	CA	20 January 98	Yes	1991
Kohap	SL	30 January 98	No	N.A.
Chung-Gu	SL/CA	23 April 98	No	N.A.
Geo-pyung	Default	20 May 98	No	N.A.
Hai-Tai	SL	03 November 98	Yes	1981

[a] All firms belong to the top 60 largest conglomerates in terms of the asset values as of the end of 1996, assessed by the Bank Supervision Authority of Korea.
[b] 'Court Administration'. Those firms, which are assessed to be hopeless even with cooperative syndicated loans, were directly subject to court administration.
[c] 'Cooperative Syndicated Loans', which is to give emergency loans for the *de facto* bankrupt firms in the form of syndicated loans by the involved banks. In some cases, the initial SL led to the CA later. In other words, the cases are often mixed.

the government. That was the only way for bankers to keep their positions. The banks were also very cooperative with the MOF because many high-level positions tend to be filled by the former staffs of the MOF. Consequently, the basic behavioural pattern of the banks was passive and incentives did not exist for them to keep watch of how money was spent in the firms. The primary lending criteria, as applied by the government, was the promotion of specific export-oriented industries while the profitability of the project itself was only a secondary matter. For the banks, there was no incentive to monitor the *chaebol* since they had all their loans backed by collateral and/or cross-guarantees by the member firms. As a result, the banks did not have to examine the creditworthiness of the borrowing firms. Furthermore, the Korean capital markets were always in sellers' market conditions and closed from the threat of foreign competition. So banks' levels of efficiency were quite low.

The weak monitoring by the banks can also be partly explained by regulations on the banks' equity participation in non-financial firms. Under the 10 per cent, or more recently 15 per cent, ceiling on their equity share, the banks' main motivation to hold shares in non-financial firms was not management control or influence, but capital gains (Nam et al., 1999).[7] Furthermore, the banks' role as a shareholder was severely limited due to regulations mandating shadow voting, an obligation to vote with the management side. Despite the fact that the banks did not enjoy any rights as debt holders or equity holders and had no say over management, they took most of the financial burden when firms went into bad situations. The financial distress of firms often led to debt reduction, roll-over, or even more lending from the banks, leading to a typically soft-budget constraint (Kornai, 1980) or moral-hazard situation similar to those experienced by firms in socialist planned economies. As a matter of fact, the Korean government was heavily involved in massive bailouts on numerous occasions, including the emergency debt freeze in 1972, restructuring of major heavy and chemical industries in the early 1980s, and industrial rationalization measures in overseas construction and shipping industries during the mid-1980s (Nam et al., 1999). The tradition continues as shown by the recent restructuring of Daewoo Group and Hyundai Construction in 2000. Government bailouts exacerbated the already weak market discipline, and excessive corporate leverage based on implicit risk-sharing by the government created the so-called too-big-to-fail hypothesis, which worked as an important exit barrier (Nam et al., 1999).

The existing moral hazard situation under soft-budget constraints led to excessive risk taking by the owner-management. As Milgrom and Roberts (1992) observe, excessive risk was expected as the costs of any failure were shared or transferred to the lenders, whereas benefits of any success were monopolized by the incumbent management. This situation followed the debt-growth spiral, in which more and more debts were incurred to finance more growth (see Table 13.2). However, it was clear that the *chaebol* did not practice any risk management or worry about their loans since they did not believe that the banks would ask them to pay back the loans suddenly and assumed that the banks were always ready to roll-over the debts. As a matter of fact, *chaebol* firms borrowed money with cross-guarantees among the member firms, so that default by one firm could lead to a chain-reaction effect to other firms in the same group since their total cross-guarantees greatly exceeded their pay-back capabilities.

The unchanged *chaebol* under a changed environment: the seeds for breakdown

The year 1997 saw the collapse of one *chaebol* after another in Korea and finally of the economy itself, which led to Korea having to beg the IMF for an emergency loan. What went wrong with the *chaebol* in Korea? The answer to this question dates back to the origin of the growth of the *chaebol*. As discussed earlier, the environment nurturing the growth of the *chaebol* was an economy which abounded with artificial rents and protection. The fundamental change in the nature of the external economic environment lies at the bottom of the crisis of the *chaebol* and the economy itself.

We should note the two important changes in the external environment. First, the government gradually stopped the explicit promotion of, or giving favour to, specific industries and the firms. This does not mean that the government stopped intervention in the private sector, but that many kinds of once legal promotional policies of the government disappeared. These policies included the so-called policy loans which were given to the designated firms in the target industries at interest rates much lower than market rates, special export credits given at lower interest rates, and arbitrary tax exemptions to target industries. It was actually during the 1980s that the government declared it was switching from policies of selective intervention to those of functional intervention. The change meant that the government intended to recover normal market-mechanism functions from past distortions. Also, to be recognized as an elite economist of the economic ministries in Korea, and especially to be welcomed by the *chaebol*-led business community, one had to wear the brand of being a man of market principles. Although uncertainty remained regarding the degree to which the economists really understood the concept of market principles, they all seemed to agree that they could no longer give outright favours to specific industries or certain firms only.

In general, the changes in the government's attitude and its actions toward the private sector contributed to the lowering of the rents

Table 13.4 Trends of effective protection rate and customs tax rate for manufacturing good imports in Korea
(a) Trends of effective protection rate, 1963–90 (in per cent)

	1963	1970	1975	1978	1980	1983	1985	1988	1990
Primary industry	37.3	27.7	31.5	78.7	73.3	86.3	89.6	113.6	160.0
Manufacturing industry	243.9	15.3	–3.8	9.5	18.6	15.0	8.3	–0.2	4.0
Light industry	266.8	8.7	–15.1	–5.7	10.7	8.7	–2.5	–13.5	–5.8
Heavy and chemical industry	158.7	25.5	6.8	37.4	44.2	26.2	15.2	9.9	12.9

Note: (1) It is estimated by the Corden approach using the sales revenue data. 1963 figures are calculated by Lee Jai Min. The figures for 1970, 1975 and 1978 are from Kim, Kwang-Suk and Hong Sung-duk (1982, p. 48). The figures after 1980 are calculated using the data from Hong Sung-duk (1992, pp. 27, 29) and the input-output tables by Lee Jai Min. (2) Light industry include food processing, tobacco processing, textile industry, garments and other fiber products, leather, woods products, paper-making and paper products, printing and publishing, rubber products, plastic products, non-mental mineral. Heavy and chemical industry include chemical, petroleum and coal mining and dressing, primary metals mining and dressing, metals dressing and several machinery.
Source: Lee Jai Min (1995).

(b) Trends of customs tax rate for manufacturing good imports, 1983–94 (in per cent)

	1983	1984	1985	1986	1987	1988	1989	1990	1991	1992	1993	1994
Customs taxes rate	22.6	20.6	20.3	18.7	18.2	16.9	11.2	9.7	9.7	8.4	7.1	6.2

Source: Ministry of Finance, reported in Kim (1996).

enjoyed by the *chaebol*. However, many bureaucrats started to claim a part of the private firms' rents or profits for illicit private gains, abusing their power and discretionary authority in giving business licenses and permissions, inspections, tax impositions and collections and so on. They are the ones who opposed the general drive from the top leadership for deregulation, fearing that their share of the illegal pie would disappear. Roughly speaking, the government gave up promotional industrial policies but bureaucrats continued to interfere with the private sector for private gains.

Second, we should note the rising wave of globalization and the WTO spirit of free trade in the 1990s. In the 1990s, the Korean economy saw the fulfillment of most of its liberalization programmes, including both trade and capital markets. Such liberalization measures caught further

Table 13.5 Profit (net income) to equity ratio by size of the firms (in per cent)

Year	Large	Medium	Small
1980	–8.8	–4.4	–3.7
1981	–0.2	0.8	2.3
1982	–4.5	2.5	4.5
1983	7.4	11.5	13.9
1984	7.4	9.9	10.4
1985	4.0	8.4	6.4
1986	16.3	12.1	13.9
1987	18.6	14.6	15.4
1988	16.0	14.6	15.5
1989	11.7	14.1	13.0
1990	1.7	7.0	8.1
1991	0.4	7.0	7.4
1992	–2.0	1.2	1.4
1993	2.8	3.5	2.9
1994	4.6	5.9	5.0
1995	–1.3	0.4	2.3
1996	–4.5	–1.6	0.3
Average by period			
1980–84	0.3	4.1	5.5
1985–89	13.3	12.8	12.8
1990–96	0.2	3.3	3.9
1980–96	4.1	6.3	7.0
Standard deviations			
1980s	9.2	6.6	6.5
1990s	3.1	3.4	3.0
1980–96	7.9	6.0	5.9

Source: Yoon (1998).

momentum following Korea's entry into the OECD. Table 13.4 shows the downward trend of effective protection rates over the 1963–90 period. Toward the end of the 1980s, the effective protection rates for manufacturing goods were reduced to less than 10 per cent or even fell to negative levels. Table 13.6(b) shows that custom rates for the imported goods decreased from more than 20 per cent in the early 1980s to about 5 per cent in the mid-1990s.

With the domestic market opened and liberalized, the Korean firms including *chaebol* have faced increasing competition from foreign firms. In the world markets, on one hand, Korean comparative advantages as a low-wage country have disappeared with the rise of ASEAN and Chinese exporters; and, on the other hand, Korean products cannot afford to

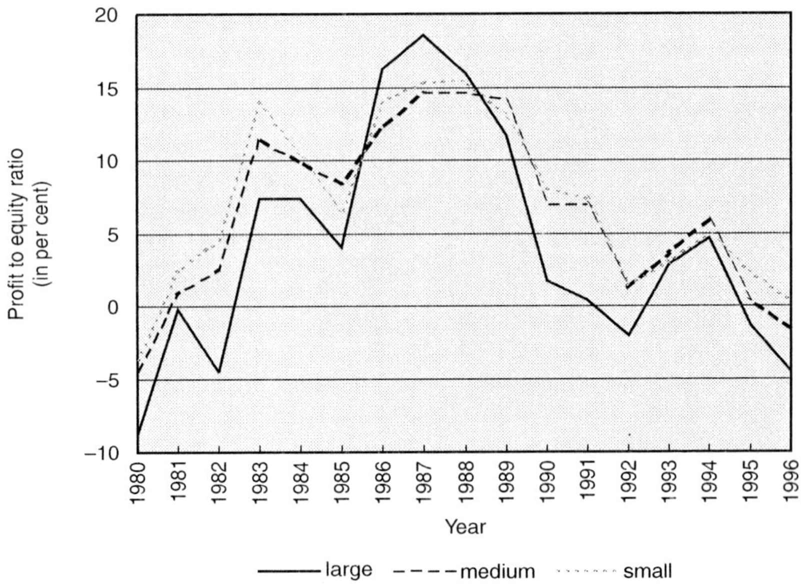

Figure 13.1 Profit (net income) to equity ratio by size of the firms (in per cent)
Source: Table 13.5.

compete with the products from an advanced country, like Japan, in terms of quality and product differentiation. In general, this trend of globalization and liberalization has contributed to the lowering of rents and the decrease of profit rates enjoyed by the Korean *chaebol*.

Table 13.5 and Figure 13.1 show the long-term trends of profit rates or Rates of Equity (ROE), where ROE equals net income to stock holders' equity, over the 1980–96 period. The profit rates in Table 13.5 are adjusted measures, which are different from the profit rates measured in terms of book values; they are estimated using the market values of the firms' assets.[8] In general, Table 13.5 shows a decreasing trend over the concerned period. For the large-sized firms, which include most of the *chaebol* firms, the profit rates changed from 0.3 per cent during the 1980–84 period, and 13.3 per cent during the 1985–89 period, to 0.2 per cent during the 1990–96 period. It is important to note that the profit rates for the large-sized firms, mostly *chaebol* firms, tend to be consistently lower than the small- or medium-sized firms since the mid-1980s when the trend of profitability passed the peak.

Rising wage costs are an additional factor which contributed to the eroding profitability of Korean firms. As McKinsey (1998) observed, the

Table 13.6 Changing profitability of the *chaebol* (in per cent)

	1994	1995	1996
(a) *Profitability of the 30 largest chaebol in Korea*			
Operation profit/equity	6.23	1.11	0.87
Normal profit/equity	0.31	0.42	0.09
Operation profit/sales revenue	0.22	0.23	0.17
Normal profit/sales revenue	0.07	0.09	0.02
Operation profit/total asset	0.22	0.25	0.18
Normal profit/total asset	0.07	0.09	0.02
(b) *Profitability of the 10 largest chaebol in Korea*			
Operation profit/equity	15.37	28.95	24.66
Normal profit/equity	8.46	10.38	0.75
Operation profit/sales revenue	6.22	6.23	4.7
Normal profit/sales revenue	1.9	2.29	0.21
Operation profit/total asset	6.34	6.74	5.02
Normal profit/total asset	2.16	2.65	0.4

Source: Calculations based on the data from Choi, Seungno (1995; 1996; 1997), The Large Corporate Groups in Korea (in Korean).

Return On Investment (ROI) was lower than interest rates. It should be taken into consideration that although Korean firms faced relatively high capital costs (interest rates), their ROI's were lower than those of other countries. It is in this sense that McKinsey (1998) calls what is happening in the Korean industry, value destruction rather than value creation.

Table 13.6 measures the short-term change of profit rates for the 30 and 10 largest *chaebol* during the 1994–96 period. It is shown that over this period, all the measures of profitability declined by a substantial margin for the 30 largest business groups although the base year of 1994 was a special year at the peak of a small-business cycle. The trend is more clear-cut for profitability measured using ordinary income rather than operating income. The difference between these two is financial expenses including interests paid. Ordinary income to stockholders' equity rates declined from 8.46 per cent in 1994 to a mere 0.75 per cent in 1996 for the ten largest *chaebol*.

What do these changes mean for the balance sheet of costs and benefits of the *chaebol*-type firms? It is clear that the benefits side has lost. With lower benefits, balancing the costs and benefits of the *chaebol* have become difficult, and now the costs side has started to loom large. In other words, the costs of overdiversification are suddenly felt much more strongly than before. As mentioned before, diversification was a somewhat rational response of the *chaebol* to the environment. But, now that the environment has changed, and there has been an increase in competition, it is not easy to make money in many industries. Unfortunately, the *chaebol* did not command enough flexibility to meet the new challenges, or were too big to change quickly. The source of the inflexibility has to do with both the seemingly M-form like overdiversified organization with few exit possibilities and the unchanged mind of the top management.

The quality of the top management might have actually worsened as the founder-managers were succeeded by their sons, who did not have verified managerial talents. The challenge to the inherited management was in general more demanding as the size of the firms had grown bigger and entry into the global business environment was more complicated as well. In other words, the burden on top management had become much heavier and the need for decentralization was evident. Decentralization was necessary as the member firms in the Korean *chaebol* enjoyed much less autonomy than the division in the M-form and because the necessary separation of strategic and operational decision-making processes was not made. In addition, the benefits from the strong implementation power of the owner-managed firm had become less important as the government stopped explicit industrial policy.

The above discussion indicates that both external environment and internal conditions in the 1990s were quite different from those in the 1970s and the 1980s. If the tendency of declining profitability was real, then we have to ask why the *chaebol* did not stop their relentless pursuit of simple expansion. For example, even in the 1990s the average number of affiliate firms of the top five *chaebol* continued to increase, and, more importantly, their debt/equity ratio increased to the 500 per cent level (for the top 30 *chaebol*) just before the crisis in 1997 (Hyun, 1999). This was a very rapid increase since the debt/equity ratio was around 400 per cent in 1996, and around 330 per cent during the 1991–92 period (Nam et al., 1999). Intrinsic rigidity or inflexibility running against any changes should not be a sufficient answer. As discussed earlier, with the help of theoretical models presented in Bebchuk et al. (1999), the agency-cost structures implied by the CMS led to a situation where inefficient projects were chosen and unprofitable expansion was pursued. In other words, given the private benefits associated with expansion, the controlling minority shareholders tended to acquire or to enter businesses not justifiable in terms of their rates of return.

Post-crisis reform of corporate governance and finance

Two major economic policies on the agenda after the crisis were reform of corporate governance and financial systems. The strategy of the Korean government in this regard was to reform the financial system first so that the banks and other financial organizations may be in a good position to deal with their corporate clients, namely giving them pressure for change (Hyun, 1999). Improvement of corporate governance systems in general have proceeded as a part of overall corporate restructuring, which began with the Five Principles of Corporate Restructuring agreed to between the government and business leaders in January 1998. The government has revised and introduced various laws or provisions to push the private sector in the direction of improving their corporate governance, capital structure, and redirection of business focus with less diversification and concentration on core competence areas. In this section, three aspects of the reforms will be discussed in the sequence of financial reforms, corporate governance and corporate restructuring to change capital and business structures.

Financial reform

Restructuring of the financial system took off in June 1998 as the financial supervisory authorities ordered the five commercial banks, out of a total of 20 or so in Korea, to be closed. The other seven banks are to continue their operation conditionally and were given some time for improvement of capital structure. Thus, out of these seven, the big two, Citizens Commercial Bank and Hanil Bank, merged to become Hanvit Bank, and three others (Choheung, Kangwon and Chungbuk) merged too. Relatively good performing banks were also subject to merger drives, for instance, the merger of Hana and Boram banks, and merger of Kukmin and the Long-Term Credit Bank. The Foreign Exchange bank succeeded in improving its capital structure by introducing foreign capital from Germany, and the Kukmin bank also sold the largest bloc of stocks to the Goldman Sachs. Co. The Cheil Bank, one of the top banks, has recently become controlled by foreign management with the take-over of controlling shares by New Bridge Capital (an American investment group).

In sum, within the period of just one year, a total of 11 banks were closed or merged, closing more than 1000 branches, and downsizing by 40 000 employees. Thus, financial restructuring is now regarded as one of the most successful aspect of post-crisis economic reform in Korea. With the exit of non-viable financial institutions and the injection of fiscal resources, many Korean banks were reported to obtain clean-bank status with BIS ratios of 10–13 per cent, although the problem is not completely solved. Since then, the government has taken responsibility for enforcing more strict regulatory and prudential standards in banks. Most importantly, most banks are now subject to better internal monitoring of management as they have adopted a board system with a majority of non-executive directors; now, most commercial banks in Korea appoint seven to nine non-executive directors and two to three executive directors.

In a sense, the corporate governance systems of banks can be said to have improved much better or faster than those in non-bank corporations which have only one independent director on their boards. However, as you can tell from the recent situation in the Korean banking sector, the problem is not over yet and the government is still pouring more money to clean up the banks.

Corporate governance

Corporate governance systems can be discussed in terms of fairness, transparency and accountability (OECD, 1998). For better transparency, a number of measures have been implemented. First, the business groups or *chaebol* are required to produce their Combined Financial Statements (CFS), beginning in fiscal year of 1999, which should help to disclose the details of complicated intragroup transactions. According to a recently released document by the Korea Security Commission, 22 business groups comprising 1152 firms have been ordered to report CFS's. For example, the Daewoo Group is supposed to combine the largest number (248 firms) of the firms in their CFS, while Hyundai has 139 firms and Samsung has 171 firms. The firms to be included in the CFS are determined by whether it is under the *de facto* control by the same shareholders or not, which should be regarded as more comprehensive and strict, compared to past practices involving linked financial statements.[9] The CFS's offset within-group transactions, such as lending or borrowing of capital, shareholding, sales or purchasing to report only the purely external transactions so that one can clearly see the real picture of the groups' business performance and conditions. In addition, Korea's Generally Accepted Accounting Practices (GAAP) was revised to be more in line with international accounting standards. Also, the top 30 *chaebol* and all listed companies were required in February 1998 to introduce independent audit committees with minority shareholder and creditor representatives.

To increase fairness and accountability in corporate governance, a series of reforms have been introduced. First, formerly forfeited voting rights of institutional investors were fully recognized in September 1998. Also, the threshold for filing stockholder derivative suits was lowered from 1 per cent to 0.01 per cent of total shares (see Table 13.7). In addition, to make the controlling shareholders accountable for their management, the related laws were revised in December 1998 to regard a controlling shareholder as a *de facto* director. This should be an important improvement since in the old system, although the controlling shareholders were actively involved in management and made all the important decisions, they did not take any responsibility for their actions since they did not hold either the official title of the CEO or the directors on the board. Maybe most importantly, all listed companies are required by law to appoint at least one outside director. It is reported that by October 1998 all 752 listed companies had appointed 764 outsider directors (Hyun, 1999).

Table 13.7 Comparison of Shareholder Rights in Korea and the USA

Korea	**USA**
Access to the shareholder registery and the records of the board meetings	
Allowed without limitations	Allowed with some limitations
Derivative litigations	
0.01% share required (listed co.) 5% share required (unlisted co.)	One share required
To demand disappointment of directors	
0.5% share required (listed co.) 5% share required (nonlisted co.)	10% share required
Multiple voting rights (in electing directors)	
Recognized in law but companies have rights not to introduce	Guaranteed in 6 states in the rest, simple voting schemes or optional choice of the companies
Rights to have their shares purchased by the controlling shareholders or management (when they do not like some management decisions or policies)	
Allowed in both listed and unlisted co.	Mostly not allowed, including Delarware state; also allowed only to common stocks
Proportion or number of non-executive or independent directors	
Need to have more than one (most have just one)	Need to have some (most have a majority of non-executive or independent directors)

Source: Jung-Ho Kim, Comparison of shareholder rights in Korea and the USA (Seoul: Korean Economic Research Institute, 1999); OECD, Corporate Governance, Paris: 1998.

With all the revisions and additions in the related laws, some people argue that the rights of shareholders are now even comparable to US standards (Kim, 1999). For example, the US system requires more than 10 per cent of stock ownership to demand the resignation of executive directors, whereas it is only 0.5 per cent in case of the listed companies. Furthermore, any shareholder is given free access to the register of shareholders and the records of board meetings. However, there is always a gap between laws and actual practices. For example, the US and Korean system is similar in requiring a certain number of independent directors. But, in the USA most listed companies allow a majority of independent directors on their boards (OECD, 1998), whereas in Korea generally there is only one independent director on a listed company's board. Furthermore, in Korea, the directors are not really independent since they are chosen from among friends of the CEO's. At present, in most cases, these independent directors are known not to play any active role in corporate governance, with a few exceptions such as the SK company, a core company of the SK group. Another example of differences in law and practice involves the introduction in the Corporation Law of multiple voting rights, which are to offer an effective way for non-controlling shareholders to appoint directors representing their sides.[10] But, out of 516 listed companies which held their shareholders' general meetings in early 1999, the majority (75 per cent) of them introduced a clause to exclude the implementation of the multiple voting rights scheme as the companies have been given rights to do so by the same law.

But, in general, we can say that rights of general shareholders are now much better recognized and exercised in Korea than before. We are now seeing and hearing many cases, unlike before, where minority shareholders raise objections to, or challenge in a court of law, the doings of the top management or controlling shareholders, for instance, in Mando Machinery Co., Cheil Banks, Samsung Electronics and so on. Actually, increasing the rights of minority shareholders has become a part of a social movement, involving an organization called Solidarity for Participation. Meanwhile, management is now saying that their independence is increasingly threatened by activists promoting shareholders' rights. Such sentiments from management is understandable too, given the lack of sufficient business-judgment safe harbours as in the American system (OECD, 1998). An increasing number of Korean companies are now buying their directors' insurance for their legal liabilities in preparation for increasing law suits. In sum, the important matter should be how to balance the interests of management and shareholders, and, furthermore, how to align these two interests. The OCED (1998) suggests that performance-based compensation is a useful tool for this purpose, with stock options as one of the best. However, in Korea, stock options are just being introduced although they are spreading very rapidly. Out of 516 companies that held their general meetings in early 1999, about 11.6 per cent of them introduced stock options for top management.

Increasing recognition of the rights of non-controlling shareholders has also to do with the rise of foreign shareholders. Not only serving as an additional source of capital, foreign portfolio investment is also perceived as being able to improve the corporate governance of Korean firms where the foreign investors are encouraged to play active roles on the boards or as shareholders or take-over bidders. Foreign investment related laws were revised in May and October 1998, and now allow all forms of mergers and acquisitions. Actually, there have been many incidences of foreign investors acquiring major or minor shares of Korean companies. As a matter of fact, in several of the best Korean companies, foreign shares are reported to be higher than 51 per cent, such as in Samsung Electronics, Samsung Fire Insurance, Bank of Housing and Medisson. Also, a survey by the Korea Stock Exchange (reported in *Maeil Business News*, 16 March 1999) indicates that listed companies with higher foreign shares tend to perform better in terms of profits and debt reductions. The survey's results compare the 40 companies with highest ratio of shares held by foreigners with the other 700 listed companies to find that in the former group, the average debt to equity ratio is 169 per cent as of March 1999, decreased from the previous year's 259 per cent; whereas in the latter group, the ratio is still as high as 357 per cent. The former group also showed a profit increase of 132.5 per cent in 1998; whereas the latter group experienced a threefold increase of their loss in 1998.

Changes in capital and business structures

To pressure the heavily indebted companies to improve their capital structure, the 64 largest companies were forced to sign financial pacts, with their respective creditor banks, stating their commitment to reduce their debt to equity ratios to below 200 per cent. New cross guarantees were prohibited from April 1998 onwards, and all the existing cross guarantees are now practically eliminated. The top five *chaebol* have kept their promises to slash their debt-to-equity ratios below 200 by the end of 1999 and to improve their financial structures by means of asset sales, recapitalization, and foreign capital inducement.

To improve their capital structures, the firms are to rely more on equity markets, and for this purpose, the binding requirement for public offerings was eliminated in February 1998 so that firms may go freely to the equity market for financing. At the same time, the notable ceiling in the amount of aggregate total capital investment within each group was removed for the top 30 *chaebol*.

Many *chaebol* are working successfully on changing their capital and business structures. Although the big *chaebol* complained bitterly, the largest five have now met their target of lowering their debt-to-equity ratios to below 200 per cent. This should be taken as very important since in the past, the typical strategy by *chaebol* in response to any government reform initiative against the *chaebol* tended to be a time-earning strategy that delayed the implementation of any specific measure as much as possible. The top five *chaebol* have already eliminated substantially the cross-debt guarantees within each group. Table 13.8 confirms the general reduction of debt-to-equity ratios in both the largest fifth and sixth to thirtieth *chaebol*. However, although debt-to-equity ratios were reduced, the absolute amount of gross debts has increased in the case of the top five *chaebol*. Specifically, there is some criticism that the top five *chaebol* are simply enlarging their equity rather than reducing their debts to meet the target of 200 per cent debt-to-equity ratios (S. Kim, 1999). Thus, one estimation reported in Table 13.8 is that if we exclude those capital increases and asset revaluations, the average debt-to-equity ratio is as high as 547 per cent, compared to its book value of 335 per cent. As a matter of fact, due to increasing capital investment, the ratio held by insiders has increased to 53.5 per cent in the case of the top five (see Table 13.8).

Such a phenomenon led to public awareness of the increasing concentration of economic power in the top five vis-à-vis other *chaebol* and the rest of the economy. The share of the top five in the total assets of the top 30 *chaebol* had increased to 65.8 per cent by the end of 1998, compared to 62.7 per cent by the end of 1997. The big five have succeeded in raising more equity capital owing to their increasing dominance of financial markets. Their dominance has increased as they acquired several financial companies during the wave of financial restructuring and as people go to these bigger and seemingly more reliable financial companies run by the top five *chaebol*, rather than to less prestigious financial companies. For example, the share of the top five *chaebol* in secondary financial institutions (including security, insurance, investment and trust, and credit cards) is reported to have increased to 34.7 per cent, a more than 10 per cent increase from 22.5 per cent two years before. Security companies belonging to the top five *chaebol* are reported to have raised more than 100 billion won (accumulated total) in selling

Table 13.8 Changing capital structure and performance since the crisis

	Top 5 *chaebols*	6th–30th *chaebols*	Top 30 *chaebols*
Debt/equity ratio			
1998 end	335.00%	497.70%	
1997 end	472.90%	616.80%	
Gross Debts (trillion won)			
1998 end	234.54	132.39	
1997 end	221.37	136.43	
Share of insiders in shareholding			
1998 end	53.50%	43.50%	44.14%
1995 end	47.85%	31.2% (6th–10th) 49.6% (11th–20th) 42.9% (21st–30th)	
Profits or losses (trillion won)			
1998			– 19.5
1997			– 3.2
Net profit/sales (%)			
1998	– 3.30%	– 7.90%	– 4.50%
1997	0.00%	– 2.00%	– 0.80%
Share of top 5 in the top 30 total			
1998 end	1997 end		
In asset	65.50%	62.70%	

Debt equity ratios: Actual Book values and if without capital increase or asset revaluation (1998 end)

	Book values (%)	Without capital increase or revaluation (%)
Top 5 average	335	547
Hyundai	483	1374
Daewoo	355	720
LG	314	405
Samsung	252	285
SK	240	439

Source: Korean Fair Trade Commission (released April 1999).

various security notes, including mutual funds, which is more than 40 per cent of the total funds raised in the same way in the markets.

Given the group-based structure of many Korean *chaebol*, the overall capital structure of the *chaebol* can be improved substantially when they are able to sell out or close non-viable member firms or business divisions. Actually, there are relatively high-exit barriers in the Korean economy associated with rigid, lengthy, and inconsistent regulations and laws regarding the exit of firms. Thus, several bankruptcy related laws were amended in February 1998. The amendment simplified legal processes for corporate rehabilitation and bankruptcy filing, and gave more roles or voice to creditor banks in the resolution process. Following the 7 December agreement of business swap, the top five *chaebol* signed financial pacts with their respective creditor banks to dramatically reduce the number of their subsidiaries from 272 at the end of 1998 to 136 by the end of 2000. Also, in May 1998, the creditor banks established formal review committees to assess the viability of 313 client firms showing signs of financial weakness. Upon completion of their evaluation, creditor banks declared 55 firms as non-viable, of which 20 were affiliated with the top five *chaebol*, and 31 with the top 64. Creditor banks prohibited new credit and cross-subsidy bailouts to these firms, which would facilitate exit of these 55 non-viable firms. To facilitate corporate restructuring, a government-initiated corporate restructuring fund, amounting to 1.6 trillion won, was launched in October 1998.

Business swap, which is often called 'big deal' in Korea, was envisaged as a way to deal with relatively big firms or businesses which are not easily handled by pure market transactions. The focus has been the business swaps between the top five *chaebol* to streamline over investment in such key industries as semiconductors, petrochemicals, aerospace, rolling stock, power-plant equipment and vessel engines. In December 1998, the top five *chaebol* reached a general agreement on swaps, and have already closed several deals or are still working out the details to close the deals. However, as of now, except the selling of LG's semiconductor business to Hyundai, many big deal plans, including the exchange of Daewoo's consumer electronics and Samsung's automobiles, have gone astray. As a matter of fact, Daewoo itself became subsequently bankrupt, and Samsung automobile was sold to Renault.

Policy implications and concluding remarks

Based on the discussions so far and on recent events in Korea, the following observations are in order. First, the *chaebol* style corporate model seems to have a limited life expectancy. While it served well as the engine of growth in the pro-growth environment in the past, its fitness and strength has gradually weakened as the external environment has changed to a more open, competitive and complex one from a closed, protective and simple one. While Hyundai and Daewoo survived the 1997 crisis, they are now undergoing some trouble (Hyundai Construction) or even bankruptcy (Daewoo) as their restructuring was not sufficiently thorough. More transparent and accountable management still provides an urgent agenda for restoration of market confidence and investment attraction, and focus on the core competence areas seem to be a critical matter for firms' survival in global competition.

Second, markets do not seem to consider corporate restructuring in Korea as fully satisfactory. After a strong recovery in 1999 with the stock market index rising above 1000, currently, as of winter 2000, the index plummeted back to 500 levels although it is substantially higher than the peak-of-the-crisis level of around 200 something. Given the low price-earning (PE) ratios, some investors are saying that Korean stocks are undervalued. However, others observe that the low PE ratios reflect international recognition that while Korean corporate reform has achieved some surface-level improvements, it has not changed deep-seated realities, especially in terms of transparency and accountability.

Third, as reforming old business groups is not an easy job, the Korean economy also needs to rely on new corporate models which are more suitable to the new economy. Actually, the strong recovery of the Korean economy after the crisis is not so much attributed to the revival of the *chaebol* as to the strong emergence of new groups of firms, usually small- and medium-sized hi-tech or information technology-based firms. The momentum for the growth of these firms was the establishment of the KOSDAQ stock market, like NASDAQ in the USA, by the Korean government. Only a few years after its establishment, KOSDAQ has emerged as the mother of hundreds of small- and medium-sized venture companies and start-ups. Many ambitious youth are joining KOSDAQ firms from universities and many talents are leaving the *chaebol* to join these new-style firms. Having financed their investment from stocks rather than from bank borrowings like the *chaebol*, these new and flexible firms boast very high equity-to-asset ratios and very low debt ratios but are growing rapidly. Venture capitalists are the typical major shareholders for these firms. In many cases, these firms' market values are becoming as large as those of key *chaebol* affiliates: for example, Saerom Technology Co. with less than 70 employees, is valued higher in the stock market than Hyundai Contruction Co., one of the pillar companies of the Hyundai Group. Their behavioural patterns and characteristics should be a new important subject of investigation (see Lee and Kim, 2000 for further analysis of this new style of Korean firms).

Notes

* This chapter draws upon the author's on-going project on corporate governance in the Korean Firms. The author would like to thank Usha Haley for useful comments and Xiyou He, Sung Su Kim and Minho Yoon for research assistance.

1 Controlled structure means that a large blockholder owns a majority or large plurality of a company's shares.
2 This is how Strachan (1976) distinguishes the typical American conglomerate from business groups. In the case of the former, component companies are acquired and divested mainly on financial grounds, and there are few operational or personal ties among the member firms, which are inherently unstable (Granovetter, 1995).
3 For the estimation of the amount of the rents, see Cho (1996). To see the nature and degree of oligopolistic market structure in Korea, see Chung (1993). The effective protection rates are presented later in Table 13.9.
4 Of course, this also had to do with the primitive nature of the Korean stock market itself.
5 Actually there are various devices in place to protect minority shareholders but they are all nominal and never utilized in practice (Nam et al., 1999).
6 For a recent assessment of the main-bank system, see Weinstein and Yafeh (1998).
7 Regarding individuals or *chaebol*'s ownership of shares of the banks, there was initially an 8 per cent ceiling in 1982 when the banks are privatized. Later, the restriction was further strengthened, and the ceiling was lowered to 4 per cent in 1994 as financial liberalization made progress.
8 The estimation is done in Yoon (1998); the adjusted rates tend to be lower than the original rates during the 1990s, and higher during the 1980s. This difference occurs because during the 1990s, the price of land and other assets declined substantially.
9 Linked financial statement only link firms where group affiliates hold more than 30 per cent of the stock.
10 When there are *n* number of openings for board-member positions, each share is assigned not one vote but *n* votes. Thus, by concentrating their votes on one target candidate director, even minority shareholders could elect the director who can represent their interests.

References

Aoki, M. (1987) 'The Japanese firms in Transition', in Yamamura, Kozo and Yasukichi Yasuda (ed.) *The Political Economy of Japan*, Stanford: Stanford University Press.

Aoki, M. (1990) 'Toward an economic model of the Japanese firm', *Journal of Economic Literature*, 28 March: 1–27.

Bebchuk, L., Kraakman, R. and G. Triantis (1999) 'Stock pyramids, cross-ownership, and dual class equity: the creation and agency costs of separating control from cash flow rights', Discussion paper no. 249, Harvard Law School, Olin Center for Law, Economics and Business.

Berglof, E. (1989) 'Capital structure as a mechanism of control – a comparison of financial systems', in M. Aoki, B. Gustafsson and O. E. Williamson (eds) *The Firm as a Nexus of Treaties*, London: Sage Publications, pp. 237–62.

Berle, A. A. Jr. and G. C. Means (1932) *The Modern Corporation and Private Property*, New York: MacMillan.

Cho, Yoon Je (1996) 'Government intervention, rent distribution, and economic development in Korea', in M. Aoki, H. Kim and M. Okuno-Fujiwara (eds) *The Role of the Government in the East Asian Economic Development*, Oxford: Oxford University Press.

Cho, Yoon Je and Joon-Kyung Kim (1995) 'Credit policies and industrialization of Korea', World Bank discussion paper no. 286.

Chung Kap-young (1993) *Structural Understanding on Korean Industrial Organization*(in Korean), Seoul: Bakyong Press, p. 55.

Cox, A. (1986) 'Ch. 1. State, finance and industry in comparative perspective', in A. Cox (ed.) *State, Finance and Industry*. Brighton: Wheatsheaf Books.

Fama, E. F. (1980) 'Agency problems and the theory of the firm', *Journal of Political Economy*, 88: 288–307.

Granovetter, M. (1995) 'Coase revisited: business groups in the modern economy', *Industrial and Corporate Change*, 4(1): 93–130.

Hong, Sung-duk (1992) 'Structural changes in the nominal and effective protection rates', *Policy Research Material*, 92–01, KDI.

Hyun, Oh-Seok (1999) 'Korean's corporate governance system: applying new remedies', Paper presented at the Conference on *Corporate Governance in Asia: A Comparative Perspective* jointly hosted by the OECD, KDI and the World Bank.

Jenson, M. C. and W. H. Meckling (1976) 'Theory of the firm: management behavior, agency costs, and ownership structure', *Journal of Financial Economics*, 3: 305–60.

Kim, Jung-Ho (1999) *Comparison of Shareholder Rights in Korea and the USA* (in Korean), Seoul: Korean Economic Research Institute.

Kim, Kwang-Suk and Sung Duk Hong (1982) *Long Term Trends of the Nominal and Effective Protection Rates in Korea* (in Korean), Research monograph 82–02, Seoul: KDI.

Kim, Nam-Doo (1996) *Analysis of the Costs of the Trade Protection* (in Korean) Seoul: KIEP.

Kim, Sejin (1999) 'Policy issues in non-financial institutions in Korea (in Korean)', Paper presented at the annual convention of the Korean association for financial economics.

Kornai, Janos (1980) *Economic of Shortage*, Amsterdam: North Holland.

La Porta, R., Lopes-de-Silanies F. and A. Schleifer (1998) 'Corporate ownership around the world', NBER working paper 6625.

Lee, Jai Min (1995) 'Dynamic comparative advantages and industrial policy in Korean industries', San-Up-Yon-Gu (industry study in Korean), 1: 3–24.

Lee, Keun and Sungsoo Kim (2000) 'Characteristics and economic efficiency of the venture firms in Korea: comparison with *Chaebols* and other traditional firms', *Seoul Journal of Economics*.

McKinsey and Company, Inc. (1998) *Reinventing Korea*. Seoul: Maeil Business Newspaper.

Milgrom, P. and J. Roberts (1992) *Economics, Organization and Management*, New York: Prentice Hall.

Nam, I. C., Kang, Y. and J. K. Kim (1999) 'Comparative corporate governance trends in Asia', Paper presented at the Conference on *Corporate Governance in Asia: A Comparative Perspective* jointly hosted by the OECD, KDI and the World Bank.

OECD (1998) *Corporate Governance*, Paris: OECD.

Penrose, E. (1959, new edition 1995) *The Theory of the Growth of the Firm*, Oxford: Oxford University Press.

Strachan, H. (1976) *Family and Other Business Groups in Economic Development: The Case of Nicaragua*. New York: Praeger.

Weinstein, D. and Yishay Yafeh (1998) 'On the cost of a bank centered financial system: evidence from the changing main bank relations in Japan', *Journal of Finance*, 53.

Yoon, Jong In (1998) *A Study on the Return on Stockholders' Equity in Korea* (in Korean), PhD Thesis, Economics, Seoul National University.

14 Revolutionizing Japanese Corporate Governance

Caroline Benton and Yoshiya Teramoto

The co-evolution of corporate governance and business models

A corporation's governance model is deeply entwined with its business model. In a business where cost and efficiency are of paramount importance, a corporate governance model that tightly coordinates, controls and audits operations is necessary, whereas in a business where knowledge and new value are core, a governance model that accentuates networking among business partners and customers is key. Accordingly, as evident in the revolution in Japanese business and management practices occurring in the last decade, both models are mutually influential and co-evolve with changes in a corporation's internal and external environments (see Figure 14.1).

Since the burst of the Japanese economic bubble in the early 1990s, a series of socioeconomic changes – such as the growing number of high-profile corporate corruption scandals, wide-ranging deregulation, influx of foreign businesses and capital, changing *keiretsu* relations, emergence of young IT companies, and shifts in investor make-up and goals – have occurred. These have had profound and far-reaching consequences and are acutely affecting the way corporations operate, manage and govern their businesses.

This chapter will attempt, first, to give a synopsis of these major issues and changes in the Japanese market; second, to present how these changes have affected the style of Japanese corporate governance using Sony as an example; and third, to present strategies for corporate governance in the twenty-first century.

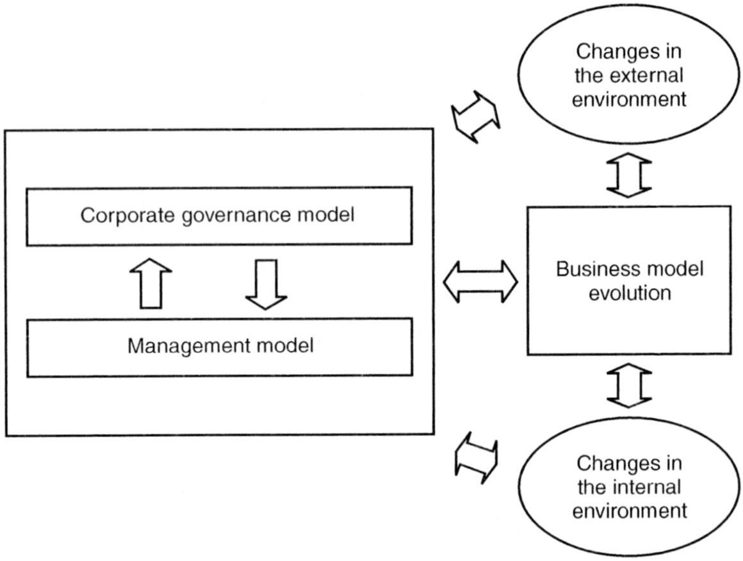

Figure 14.1 The co-evolution of corporate governance and business models

Japanese corporate governance at risk

Japan is still in the midst of a decade-long recession from which the earliest signs of recovery are just being felt. The burst of the economic bubble has caused significant shifts in the attitudes and practices of every market sector. Corporations and industries are struggling to stay above water; those that have succeeded have done so by reformulating their business models to meet the needs of the emerging environment. The conventional Japanese business philosophy aimed at perfecting how to bring a product or service to the market, this has proven to be no longer effective with the growing sophistication of consumers in this age of the global economy and the Internet. Corporations must now focus their efforts on developing unique value for their customers, shareholders and employees. All this has had a huge effect on Japanese corporate governance.

Japanese investors (institutional and individual) are demanding greater returns on their investments and have become less likely to maintain their once stable, long-term stock holdings.[1] This is pressuring corporations to improve their severely weakened financial positions by redeeming unconverted corporate bonds that were issued during the late 1980s and by selling off unnecessary investments. The volatile state of the stock market has also led to a growth in the number of institutional investors (especially foreign investors), while driving off most substantial corporate purchasers.[2]

Moreover, investors and consumers alike are calling for fair play, full disclosure and transparency by both businesses and government bureaucracies. Subsequent to the burst of the bubble, the breadth and depth of corporate and governmental corruption and incompetence has become more conspicuous than ever before, as it has become more difficult to hide evidence of mismanagement and dubious activities with increased public scrutiny. Also, the Japanese media – which have been less likely to confront industry and government than their Western counterparts – have become more aggressive in investigating improper activities with declining public trust in corporations and government as the economy continues to stagger. Just a few examples of recent scandals are listed below:

- The *jusen*, mortgage-lending industry, collapsed in the early 1990s as a result of burgeoning bad loans due to the lenders' sloppy, and in many cases illegal, loan approval processes during the bubble period, causing taxpayers trillions of yen.
- Major banks' common practice of wining and dining MOF officials to solidify ties and to obtain information on the ministry's auditing schedules came to light. Naotaka Saeki, chairman of the Federation of Bankers Associations of Japan, was forced to apologize to the public in a news conference in January 1998 (*Japan Times*, http://www.japantimes.co.jp/news/news1-98/news1-13.html).
- Domestic banks' attempts to hide the full amount of their bad loans and sour investments have dwindled away public faith in the financial industry's competence and ethics. Japanese institutions were forced to adopt US-style disclosure rules for bad loans in 1998 as a result of intense criticism from the public. Under the new rules, the banks will have to disclose non-performing loans if borrowers fail to make interest payment for three months (*Japan Times*, http://www.japantimes.co.jp/news/news1-98/news1-13.html).
- Nomura Securities and most of the major brokerage firms were issued administrative sanctions in 1991 (including suspension of operation/trading) by the government after revelations of loss-compensation for investments made by VIP customers, which severely angered average customers who did not benefit from this preferential treatment (*Japan Times*, http://www.japantimes.co.jp/news/news7-97/news7-15.html).

- Two high-ranking inspectors of the MOF were arrested in a bribery scandal in early 1998. The fallout included the thitherto unconceivable raiding of the once proud and untouchable MOF by the Tokyo District Public Prosecutors' Office (*Japan Times*, http://www.japantimes.co.jp/news/news1-98/news1-26.html).
- Major corporations, such as Mitsubishi Corporation, Nomura Securities and the now-defunct Yamaichi Securities, were shamed in a series of highly public *sokaiya* scandals over the last five years that further diminished public confidence. *Sokaiyas* are rouge dealers (many are associated with organized crime) who are paid by corporations to squash any deliberations or questioning during shareholders' meetings. In many cases *sokaiyas* are actively sought out by major corporations to ensure that their meetings lasted only several minutes, while others blackmail corporations with threats to disrupt the meetings with allegations of corruption.
- Recently, numerous scandals involving various prefectural police departments have been widely publicized in the media. These include stories of internal investigators fraternizing (wining and dining) with the target of their inquest and of police officials concealing the crimes of fellow officers.
- In June 2000, Snow Brand Milk Products' low-fat milk caused widespread food poisoning (reportedly, over 10 000 people were taken ill after consuming the product) due to contamination as a result of alleged unsanitary production processes. Typical for Japanese corporations, which are not used to the vehement public and media outcry that followed, the company's top management blotched the handling of the scandal and was accused of arrogance, corporate negligence and cover-up in the media, further eroding public confidence in the company. (*Japan Times*, http://www.japantimes.co.jp/cgi-bin/getarticle.pl5?fl20000720pb.htm).
- After announcing a recall of over 6.5 million tires in the USA on 9 August 2000, Bridgestone and its US affiliate, Bridgestone/Firestone, faced allegations of having delayed the recall (delayed the timing), which may have led to further accidents. Chairman of the American subsidiary, Masatoshi Ono, was forced to testify before the US House of Representatives in September. (*Japan Times*, http://www.japantimes.co.jp/cgi-bin/getarticle.pl5?nb20000831a5.htm).
- In September 2000, The Transport Ministry formally lodged criminal accusations against Mitsubishi Motors for allegedly concealing approximately 1700 user complaints last year. This was the first time that the ministry filed criminal accusations against an automobile

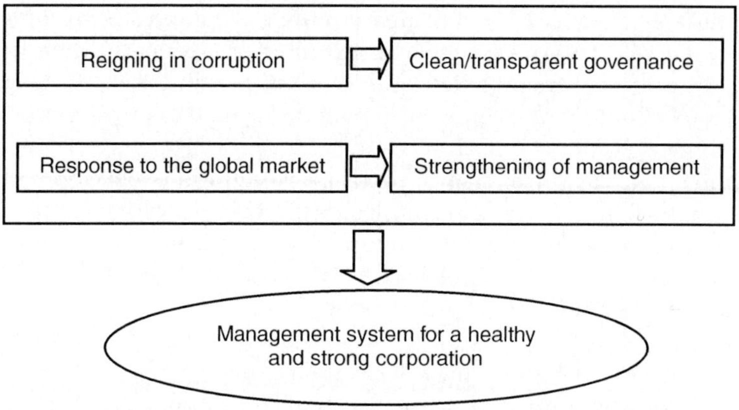

Figure 14.2 Emerging issues in corporate governance

> manufacturer for suspicion of violating the law over recalls. The president of the company announced his intention to step down to take responsibility on the same day. (*Japan Times*, http://www.japantimes.co.jp/cgi-bin/getarticle.pl5?nn20000909a2.htm).

The above examples are merely a short list of the countless number of improper activities by businesses, government and elected officials that have surfaced since the economy's downward spiral. For a culture that traditionally held deep reverence and respect for authority, the revelations have caused a great deal of shock and embarrassment.[3] Corporations (and government) are being impelled by increasing public scrutiny and regulatory changes (especially in accounting standards) to review not only their business models to regain profitability and financial/fiscal responsibility, but also their corporate governance models to ensure fairer and more transparent play (see Figure 14.2).

Changing governmental policy on corporate governance

In addition to growing public outcry over corporate corruption, three major impetuses have moved the government to implement wide-ranging regulatory changes of accounting practices and commercial code that acutely affect Japanese corporate governance. These are (1) requests from the business world for regulatory changes that will allow for greater freedom and options with regard to corporate governance and business practices; (2) pressure from the international environment (especially the USA) to bring Japanese rules of business in line with global standards; and (3) desire of the government itself to change its basic stance from relying on corporate regulations to monitoring corporations.

In the past, the government's model for handling and developing the economy and industry has been to guide actively selected industries, to implement measures to avoid unnecessary competition and to promote exports. The major factors of this model, as reported by Porter et al. (2000) are as follows:

1 activist, central government with a stable bureaucracy;
2 targeting of priority industries to enhance economic growth;
3 aggressive promotion of exports;
4 extensive guidance, approval requirements and regulations;
5 selective protection of the home market;
6 restrictions on foreign direct investment;
7 lax anti-trust enforcement;
8 government-led industry restructuring;
9 official sanctioning of cartels;
10 highly regulated financial markets and limited corporate governance;
11 government-sponsored cooperative R&D projects; and
12 sound macroeconomic policies.

However, this government model is obsolete and no longer valid in the current global environment. It has stunted competition, which has adversely affected Japanese corporate competitiveness, strategic capabilities and innovation. Porter et al. (2000) also found that this model is more accurate for the Japanese government's policy toward industries that have failed than to those that have succeeded. It is hoped that the recent deregulatory measures will bring about a freer market environment, leading to greater competitiveness, innovation and strategic capabilities of Japanese corporations, and that the ensuing move toward global standards in accountability and disclosure will be a catalyst for enhanced performance. These changes, which are discussed below, have in effect changed the set of game rules by which corporations can operate, and have directly and indirectly influenced corporate governance in Japan.

Easing of requirements for shareholders' suits against directors

In 1993, the government revised the commercial code to make it easier for shareholders to bring suits against directors. Shareholders with a

3 per cent or more share in a company are now able to view a company's books (prior to the revision, only those with 10 per cent share could do so). The court fee for the suits was also reduced across the board to 8200 yen regardless of the size of the suit. As a result, the number of suits rose dramatically from 31 on-going shareholder suits throughout all regional courts on 31 December 1992, to 74 at the end of 1993 and 174 at the end of 1996 (complied by the Japanese Supreme Court).

New accounting practices for disclosure

The government implemented changes to accounting standards and practices in March 2000, in order to promote the disclosure of consolidated financials and cash flows. In the past, corporations were required to consolidate subsidiaries in which they had over 50 per cent ownership, and could choose to consolidate a subsidiary in which it had between 20 per cent and 50 per cent ownership. With the new standards, any subsidiary over which a corporation has substantial controlling power must be consolidated regardless of ownership ratio.

The government also introduced the following changes to accounting practices: market valuation for securities held for trading purposes (i.e., securities should be assessed according to market price at the end of business year) starting from fiscal year ending March 2000; market valuation of long-term stocks, including mutually held stocks, starting from fiscal year ending March 2001; disclosure of insufficient accumulation of funds to cover pension obligations. Continued deliberations on implementing consolidated taxation for corporate groups have also been scheduled (MOF, http://www.mof.go.jp/english/tax/tax2000.htm).

For shareholders, the most significant consequence of these proposed reforms in accounting standards is greater disclosure and transparency. Corporations will find it more difficult to hide or to transfer losses to their subsidiaries and will have to take greater responsibility not only for parent-companies' performance, but also for that of subsidiaries. In other words, corporations will have to manage the value of their group as a whole.

Deregulation of holding companies

Pure holding companies without an operational base were prohibited under the anti-trust law in order to avoid the accumulation of power and wealth in the pre-war industrial groups (*zaibatsu*) and other large conglomerates. The government relaxed this restriction and gave the go ahead to the formation of holding companies in 1999. Corporations are now able to concentrate in control and monitoring functions at a holding company, while leaving the responsibility of day-to-day operations to their subsidiaries, accelerating decision-making at all levels.

Introduction of stock exchange scheme

Last year, the National Diet approved a corporate stock exchange scheme that will permit corporations to exchange their stocks for those of subsidiaries. Effective from 10 November 1999, this scheme makes it possible for a corporation to privatize a publicly-listed subsidiary through the exchange of stock, based on a ratio that is deemed appropriate for the performance/financial situations of both companies (Tokyo Stock Exchange, http://www.tse.or.jp/news/release/article/199911/991110_a. html).

Facilitation of division spin-offs

In May 2000, the Diet enacted revisions to the commercial code that will facilitate corporate spin-offs. A law to protect workers and detailing the succession of labour contracts at the time of a spin-off was also concurrently approved. The revised code targets two types of spin-offs – the spinning off of a division to form a new company and the transfer of a division to an existing company. It is hoped that these changes will help corporations to regroup and to rebuild their global competitiveness (*Japan Times*, http://www.japantimes.co.jp/cgi-bin/getarticle.pl5?nb-20000525b1.htm).

Fundamental reformation of commercial code

For the first time in roughly 50 years, the government is considering a fundamental reformation of the commercial code, which is aimed at modernizing regulations for promotion of international competitiveness, managerial flexibility and increased decision-making speed. The proposed reformation focuses on shareholders' meetings and boards of directors (*Nihon Keizai Shimbun*, 7 September 2000).

With regard to shareholders' meetings, the following issues will be deliberated: decreasing the quorum regulation (with the increase in foreign shareholders, it has become difficult for corporations to meet the current quorum requirements at general shareholders' meetings); pushing forward the deadline for which shareholders can introduce issues on the agenda from six weeks to eight weeks prior to the meeting; and allowing meetings to be conducted via circulation of documents for small- to mid-sized corporations that are not publicly traded.

The issues regarding boards of directors that will be discussed are (1) releasing directors who are without fault from having to take responsibility for damages caused by illegal trading, dividend distribution and so on, in order to facilitate the recruitment of external directors; (2) making financial auditors take responsibility for overlooking improper accounting practices; and (3) allowing small corporations that are not publicly traded to have only one director rather than the current requirement of three.

Expanding the target of stock options will also be considered. Currently, managers of subsidiaries are not able to receive stock options from the parent company. This has made it difficult for managers to take advantage of stock options after a spin-off or regrouping of divisions with the introduction of a holding company and so on.

Industry is also requesting the following changes: (1) limiting the issues that need to be approved by shareholders; (2) strengthening of regulations regarding corporate officers; (3) allowing for certain company documents to be saved on digital media rather than on paper; and (4) letting shareholders' meetings be conducted over the Internet.

Managing corporate value through governance – a case study of Sony

Japanese corporate governance has traditionally emphasized the goals and needs of internal management and committees at the expense of shareholders and other external stakeholders. The main entities responsible for corporate governance (Figure 14.3) have been the board of directors and top management committees that are comprised mainly of in-house personnel. Important external entities have tended to be limited to regulatory authorities and organizations such as main banks and suppliers with which corporations have crucial operational relationships. In contrast, in the USA, autonomous entities outside the corporation such as external directors, public accountants and institutional investors play a major role in corporate governance (Figure 14.4). This involvement of autonomous external entities ensures not only an influx of diverse knowledge that can be tapped into, but also greater objectivity as there is less vested interest in maintaining status-quo relationships and business practices. This difference in governance style, however, is diminishing as a result of the aforementioned regulatory and environmental changes that are catalyzing reforms.

Sony's issues and their solutions

Sony's President and CEO, Nobuyuki Idei, stated that for corporations the rules of economics have changed, requiring a fundamental review

	US corporations	Japanese corporations
Internal	Top management Board of directors (comprised mainly of external directors) Various committees (comprised mainly of external directors)	Top management Committee of senior managing directors (comprised of all internal directors) Audit committee (mainly internal HR) In-house labour union
External	Public accountants Institutional investors Labour unions (intercompany, industry/ job-specific)	Main banks Regulating authorities Business partners

Figure 14.3 Entities responsible for corporate governance

	Board members		Corporate officers
	Total	External directors	
GM	16	14	54
GE	14	10	26
Merck	13	12	27
IBM	11	9	24
AT&T	10	8	24
Du Pont	13	9	22
Citicorp	14	10	109
P&G	17	13	36
Wal-Mart	13	9	42
Exxon	10	7	20

Figure 14.4 Samples of directors of major US corporations
Source: 1997 Sokai Ininjo Sanko Shorul and Corporate Yellow Book, Spring 1997.

of traditional business practices (with regards to both management and operations). He is most concerned about five issues: (1) the tremendous growth and impact of the digital economy; (2) the importance of market capitalization in an era where relatively new and small knowledge-based corporations, such as America On-line,[4] achieve spectacular market capitalization; (3) increasing returns on scale with the emergence of knowledge-based businesses; (4) being a rule breaker to succeed in the changing market; and (5) managing value creation to satisfy not only customers and employees but also shareholders (N. Idei, *Shukan Toyo Keizai*, 7 August 1999).

For Sony, the solution to these issues has been to implement a radical redesign not only of the business models of its Strategic Business Units (SBUs), but also of its corporate governance model. Through these measures it hopes to create greater value for all stakeholders by vitalizing its business divisions through greater operational autonomy and by centralizing policy-strategy and restructuring its board of directors to speed up top-level decision-making. It was the first domestic company to introduce in-house companies[5] (1994) and to restructure its corporate board by reducing membership and introducing a system of corporate executive officers (1997).

In March 1999, Sony announced plans to 'realign and strengthen its group architecture', that entailed the following three measures: (1) privatizing three group companies that were listed on the Tokyo Stock Exchange, going against the typical Japanese business mindset that equates success with the public trading of subsidiaries; (2) strengthening of the company's core electronic business through a further regrouping of in-house companies; and (3) enhancing group management capabilities to speed up decision-making (Teramoto and Benton, 2001).

In a second phase of reform and realignment, Sony announced subsequent steps in fiscal year 2000 to focus further group strength and to separate corporate governance and policy formation from operational management and control. These included: (1) accelerating corporate reform by strengthening headquarters' management team; (2) positioning group headquarters, termed (eHQ), so that it focuses on developing overall strategy and coordinating the group's entire business, while considering a possible transformation to a holding company; (3) establishing an eManagement Committee (eMC) that is an executive body of eHQ to manage total group businesses and to set strategy for net business; and (4) forming eSony Development Group within eHQ to assist the eMC and realize business decisions (Sony, http://www.world.sony.com/News/Press/200003/00–13E/).

Accelerating corporate reform

In the most recent series of reforms, Sony announced in March 2001 a further evolution of its corporate governance with a new group structure that is designed for the 'next stage of integrated and decentralized management' (Sony, http://www.sony.co.jp/en/SonyInfo/News/Press/200103/01–017/E/). The structure is intended to allow for both synergy (integration) and autonomy (decentralization) of management, while enabling headquarters to fortify its corporate governance capabilities. The three major components of the new structure that intimately deal with corporate governance are the establishment of a new group headquarters that acts as a hub for overall group strategy and draws together key businesses, the formation of a management platform to provide staff support functions globally, and the creation of a separate business headquarters for its main and most complex business area, electronics.

Concretely, Sony's group headquarters was reorganized as a global hub that concentrates on creating overall management strategy and a unified global vision, while promoting synergy among and autonomy of key business units (see Figure 14.5). For decision-making speed, the global hub is managed by the company's three top executives – its Chief Executive Officer (CEO), Chief Operating Officer (COO) and Chief Financial Officer (CFO), who will cooperate to raise total corporate value by bringing together strategically the resources and activities of five business areas – electronics, financial services, Internet/communication services, games and entertainment. The consolidation of Sony's vital resources including brand value, electronics hardware expertise and entertainment business know-how and venture business development is advocated, while effective corporate governance of the group as a whole through strategic planning is carried out.

The management platform is a horizontal organization that comprises vital support functions including accounting, finance, information systems, human resources, legal and intellectual copyright services and public relations for the corporate group. By consolidating these functions, Sony is able to make optimal use of common resources and

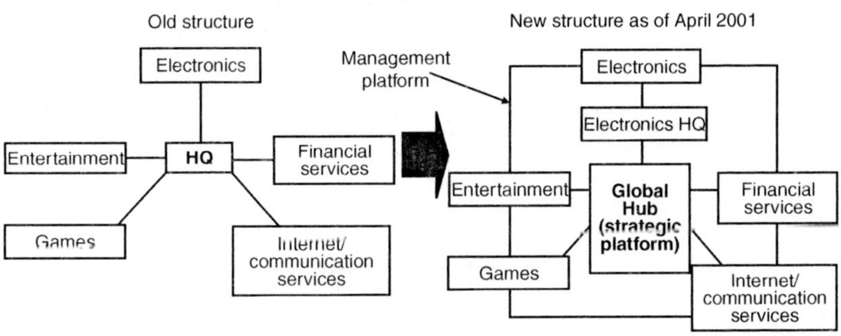

Figure 14.5 Sony's group governance and management structure
Note: Adapted from Sony's home page, (http://www.sony.co.jp/en/SonyInfo/News/Press/200103/01–017E/).

to integrate IT and work processes to increase management speed. To oversee this platform, Sony has instituted a new position, Chief Administration Officer who will guide this organization.

The Electronics Headquarters seeks to bring together the group's electronics and network-compatible products to prepare for the next generation of advanced information and communications technology. Games, electronic hardware and Internet/communications companies are placed under the management of the new headquarters for the development of integrated products that can lead and make use of the broadband technology of the future. Three technology centres and a sales platform will support these companies for greater time and operational efficiency.

In addition, in this new corporate governance and executive management structure, the role of chairman of the board (currently the position is held by Norio Ohga) is to represent shareholders' interests, which have been and are still habitually given a lesser degree of priority and importance than those of internal management and executive committees in Japanese companies. Board of directors' meetings are also being held throughout the world (and have taken place in Beijing, Silicon Valley and Berlin already) so that regional issues can be focused on amidst diverse environment and market contexts. Likewise, Sony's board of directors recently held a joint meeting with their counterparts from the American computer manufacturer Hewlett-Packard, for even further expansion of business perspective and knowledge exchange (see Figure 14.6).

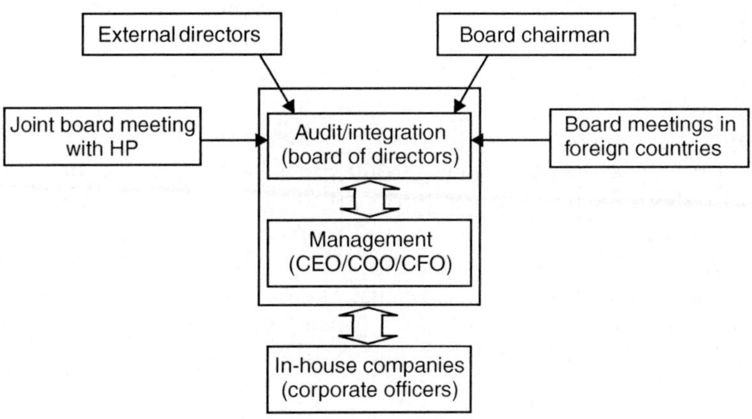

Figure 14.6 Reform in Sony's global corporate governance

Redefining Japanese corporate governance for the twenty-first century

In the digital era of the twenty-first century, Japanese corporations must re-examine their corporate governance model and bring it in line with global conventions, while the government must continue with deregulatory measures that support healthy implementation of these efforts. The new model must not only respond to surging public dissatisfaction and distrust, but must also support an effective knowledge system to create innovation and heighten competitiveness. By increasing transparency and promoting an open society, corporations can better tap into internal and external knowledge by exposing themselves to the scrutiny of diverse stakeholders. This de-emphasizing of current status-quo policies, strategies and vested interests with influx of external knowledge will heighten strategic capabilities that are so lacking in most domestic corporations. The knowledge obtained can be used to create even more complex and newer knowledge. In this manner, corporations' governance and business models co-evolve to feed a knowledge-creating spiral.

For the government, Porter et al. (2000) propose the following agenda for changes in macroeconomic policy: (1) trust in Japan's ability to compete without regulatory protection; (2) recognize that open trade will make Japanese companies more competitive; (3) build a world-class university system; (4) modernize archaic, inefficient domestic sectors such as retail and wholesale; (5) create a true system of corporate accountability; (6) create a new model of innovation and entrepreneurship; and (7) encourage decentralization, regional specialization and cluster development.

The important rules of corporate governance that should be considered by Japanese society as a whole are separation of policy formation and operational management, greater corporate accountability, accounting practices, disclosure stipulations, anti-trust and commercial codes, labour regulations, safety nets for workers faced with restructuring and downsizing, and environmental protection laws. In an era of a borderless economy, these rules must be compatible with the more transparent global standards. For example, accounting practices should quantify the true value of corporations by requiring market price for investments and assets and consolidated performance measures, and full disclosure should be mandated.

In contrast, the style of corporate governance is not codifiable and cannot be imported from other foreign cultures. Style must reflect the

Structural issues	Procedural issues
• Reduce board members • Institute corporate officers • Recruit external directors • Enforce auditing committee, external auditors • Establish individual board committees • Establish holding companies	• Emphasize stock value (ROE, ROA, EVA) • Link shareholder value with stock options • Enforcement of IR activities, including full disclosure • Stage meaningful shareholders' meetings • Realign group architecture • Move toward consolidated financials

Figure 14.7 Revolution in structural and procedural issues of corporate governance

strategies, traditions, culture and social values of the internal and external environments, as no corporation is disconnected from its surroundings. This will allow corporations to formulate a governance model that is transparent and globally explainable, while simultaneously being relevant and understandable to the Japanese market place.

Many factors that affect the style of corporate governance have been the chief strengths of Japanese businesses. These should not be abandoned but should be made to fit in with the emerging competitive environment, and include but are not limited to long-term viewpoints of management, long-term employment in exchange for loyalty, focus on operational and energy efficiency, the usually cooperative relationships between industry and government, and group-oriented work ethics, and must be contemplated when implementing the new governance and business models.

For individual corporations, a strong model for the future will encompass a redefinition of head-office functions, a separation of policy-making and operational control to promote strategy-making capabilities and accountability, and the enforcement of external directors to ensure responsibility toward shareholders. This will entail a consideration of both structural and procedural issues of corporate governance (Figure 14.7).

Structural issues deal with the entities that are involved, including a downsizing of the corporate board for faster decision-making, implementing a system of corporate officers to separate the responsibilities of policy (board directors) and operational management (corporate officers), increasing the number of external directors to bring in new knowledge and objectivity, strengthening the power of auditing committees (in particular external auditors), and establishing board committees that tackle individual issues. For some corporate groups, the formation of a holding company to support the separation of governance and policy-making from operational management can also be a viable structural solution.

Procedural issues are those that deal with the method of carrying out corporate governance. For example, managing corporate value based on Returns On Equity (ROE), Returns On Assets (ROA) and Economic Value Added (EVA), solidifying investor relations with full disclosure, linking stock options with value created for shareholders, and staging meaningful general shareholders' meetings are important factors for better (more transparent, efficient and effective) corporate governance. The ROE/ROA/EVA valuation clearly quantifies corporate value to shareholders and other stakeholders, and is a move away from the traditional Japanese practice of emphasizing growth in market share at the expense of profit. Full disclosure gives stakeholders access to information necessary for judgement, while linking performance with stock options makes management more accountable for their decisions and actions. Organizing meaningful general shareholders' meetings allows the owners of the company to question and to monitor top management. For corporate groups, restructuring of the businesses and a move toward emphasizing consolidated performance can fortify group governance.

Both the structural and procedural reforms discussed above will support the development of a more effective knowledge system that creates unique value by opening up the companies to internal and external environmental knowledge. This in turn will feed the dynamic spiral of corporate governance and business model co-evolution. In this manner,

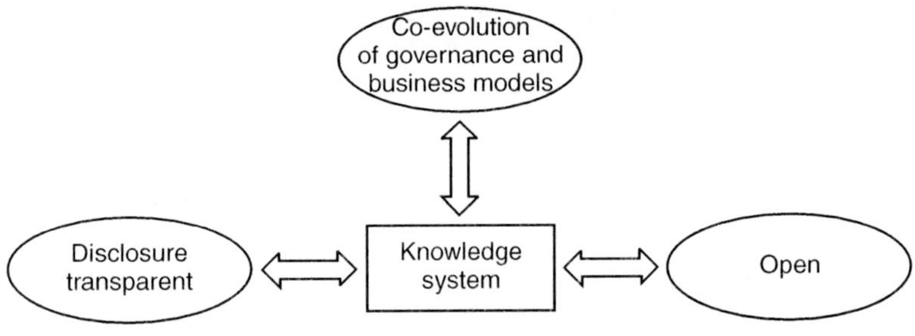

Figure 14.8 Effective knowledge system for the twenty-first century

Japanese corporations can adapt to the ever-changing environment of the digital twenty-first century (see Figure 14.8).

Notes

1 In 1997, US corporations averaged an ROA of over 15 per cent compared to an average of roughly 4 per cent for Japanese corporations (Daiwa Securities Analyst Guide, Compustat).
2 In the first quarter of 1999, foreign investors accounted for over 40 per cent of trading on the Tokyo Stock Exchange.
3 As history scholar Samuel Huntington has stated, in traditional Japanese culture Caesar is God, meaning that government and other high-ranking entities have authority over both spiritual and temporal matters (Huntington, 1996). In other words, Japanese authorities tended to be revered and thought of as being above moral and temporal wrongdoings.
4 With less than one-tenth of Sony's sales, America On-line's market capitalization in 2000 was more than double that of the company's.
5 A system of in-house companies is different from a system of business divisions in that companies are each allocated capital and have much greater responsibility for performance and investments. The merits of in-house companies are faster decision-making, vitalization of organization, and clarification of operational responsibility (*Shukan Toyo Keizai*, 3 April 1999).

References

Huntington, S. (1996) *The Clash of Civilization*, New York: Simon & Schuster.

Idei, Nobuyuki (1999) 'Watashi Ga Kagaeru Itsutsu No Koto Wo Kataro' (loose translation: 'The five issues I am considered about'), *Shukan Toyo Keizai*, 7 August.

Japan Times, http://www.japantimes.co.jp/news/news7-97/news7-15.html

Japan Times, http://www.japantimes.co.jp/news/news1-98/news1-13.html

Japan Times, http://www.japantimes.co.jp/news/news1-98/news1-26.html

Japan Times, http://www.japantimes.co.jp/cgi-bin/getarticle.pl5?fl20000720pb.htm

Japan Times, http://www.japantimes.co.jp/cgi-bin/getarticle.pl5?nb20000831a5.htm

Japan Times, http://www.japantimes.co.jp/cgi-bin/getarticle.pl5?nn20000909a2.htm

Japan Times, http://www.japantimes.co.jp/cgi-bin/getarticle.pl5?nb20000525b1.htm

Ministry of Finance, http://www.mof.go.jp/english/tax/tax2000.htm

Nikkei Business (1999) 'Idei Nobuyuki Shacho Ga Kataru Sony No Daitan Kiko Kaikaku' ('Interview with President Idei on Sony's Bold Realignment'), 22 March.

Nihon Keizai Shimbun (2000) 'Shoho Bappon Kaisei He, Kidouteki Keiei He Kankyou Seibi' (loose translation: 'Fundamental revision of commercial code, adjusting environment for flexible management'), 7 September.

Porter, M., Takeuchi, H. and M. Sakakibara (2000) *Can Japan Compete*, MacMillan Press, London.

Shukan Diamond (1999) 'Kigyo Kachi No Sozo Wo Mezasu Sony Soshiki Kaikaku No Yomikata' (loose translation: 'How to read Sony's organizational realignment aimed at creating corporate value'), 27 March.

Shukan Toyo Keizai (1999) 'Kyoso Rule Ga Kawaru' (loose translation: 'Rules of competition is changing'), 3 April.
Sony, http://www.world.sony.com/News/Press/200003/00-13E/
Sony, http://www.sony.co.jp/en/SonyInfo/News/Press/200103/01-017/E/
Teramoto, Y. and C. Benton (2001) 'Networking knowledge for value creation', *Intangibles in Competition and Cooperation*, Palgrave, New York.
Tokyo Stock Exchange, http://www.tse.or.jp/news/release/article/199911/991110_a.html

Part 5
Post-crisis Business Environments

15

Here There be Dragons: Opportunities and Risks for Foreign Multinational Corporations in China

Usha C. V. Haley

Introduction

In 2000, Morgan Stanley's economist Andy Xie noted changes in the profile of China's foreign investor: 'We have a switch in FDI from overseas Chinese to multinational companies, which tend to have bigger projects, longer timetables and more well-thought-out strategies' (Areddy, 2001). For multinational corporations (hereafter referred to as 'multinationals'), the assessment of China's huge potential markets against the risks of assaults on their competitive advantages and core competencies needs reassessment.

Haley (2001) identified the characteristics of multinationals including investment in their intangible assets such as research and development, advertising, reputation and managerial skills which give them competitive advantages over local firms' knowledge of local markets and conditions. However, multinationals also require strategies that protect their sustained, long-term investments in these intangible assets; secure returns on their investments; and, obviate freeloader problems. Euphoria over market potential and inappropriate risk appraisal comes with a price tag for multinationals. 'In current cases like the Carlsberg venture, foreigners are realizing that they cannot be successful in their current situation, and they have to pay a "learning fee" of several million dollars to exit', said Jürgen Kracht, managing director of Fiducia, a European investment consultant that has researched profitability in China (Holland, 2000).

Old maps for seafarers sometimes carried the phrase 'Here there be dragons' to warn of potential dangers in uncharted territories that could overturn exploring ships and kill the crews. As in the days of yore, the Chinese market poses enormous potential and horrendous obstacles; effective strategizing by multinationals will need to consider both safe harbours and dragons in a reasoned light. The first section of this chapter analyses historical trends of FDI into China. The ensuing section estimates various risks associated with doing business in China including market potential, copyright violations, political manoeuvrings and corruption. The final section offers some suggestions for effective strategies by multinationals operating in China in the new millennium.

Reading the charts

Analysts said China's probable entry into the WTO in 2001 or soon after, and recovery in parts of the regional economy, have helped to buoy multinationals' enthusiasm in the Chinese market and to maintain its status as the largest recipient of FDI among developing countries. China is second only to the USA in FDI inflows; however, the trends show a distinct leveling off in these flows. The multinationals that now serve as the primary vehicles of FDI into China appear to have reservations about their investments and expected returns after China's WTO entry, despite the prospects of even greater market potential in this already high potential market. In this section, we first look at FDI flows into China and then at the characteristics and expectations of the multinationals operating there.

Foreign direct investment trends

China reported a marginal 0.93 per cent increase in actual FDI to US$40.77 billion in 2000, reversing an 11 per cent plunge in 1999 (Hu, 2001). Statistics released by China's Ministry of Foreign Trade and Economic Cooperation (MOFTEC) also showed a nominal 50.84 per cent surge in contracted FDI, which indicates future intentions, to US$62.65 billion. Beijing approved 22 532 new multinationals in 2000, bringing the total to 364 345 by the end of the year.

China's manufacturing sector attracted US$16.52 billion in FDI in the first nine months of 2000, according to the latest figures from China's National Bureau of Statistics (NBS). According to the NBS, agreed FDI for 11 185 manufacturing projects in the nine-month period totalled US$26.63 billion. Real estate received the next highest amount of FDI, attracting US$3.23 billion. Up to US$1.56 billion of FDI went into the production and supply of power, gas and water, while another US$1.49 billion was pumped into the social-service sector, according to the NBS. About 30 per cent of FDI went into the IT sector in China in 2000 (*Xinhua News Agency*, 2001).

Actual FDI in China peaked at US$45.46 billion in 1998, but slumped to US$40.31 billion in 1999, largely due to the Asian financial crisis and sluggish domestic demand. Early in 2000, capital injections from Taiwan increased rapidly, although inflows from Southeast Asian economies continued to fall. All analysts agreed that the WTO factor helped to revitalize enthusiasm in investing in China, and to some, it also helped to explain the huge disparity between the growth rates in actual and contracted FDI. For example, Huang Yiping, a senior economist at Salomon Smith Barney Hong Kong said, 'Without that final [accession] document... my reading is that some investors may not rush at the moment because they don't know what might happen' (Hu, 2001).

The statistics also show that by historical standards, FDI did not rush into China in 2000 at the same rate as it had for several years prior, suggesting that WTO membership serves as less of a magnet for capital than many analysts and policy makers have expected. One US attorney, whose clients included some of the largest foreign multinationals in China, said he could muster only limited enthusiasm for FDI in the near term and noted that signing the WTO agreement would not necessarily trigger a rush into China (Areddy, 2001). His law firm's activities in 2000 had not helped foreign multinationals fashion Greenfield investment projects in China, but instead, to restructure existing arrangements. For example, many multinationals in joint ventures had moved to buy out local partners, usually penurious state-owned companies. The brunt of his law firm's WTO work, he said, had been reviewing the legal status of multinationals already in China. Some multinationals had expressed concern that China's WTO membership would adversely affect them because of the Chinese government's murky approvals regarding initial investment, which could cause the government to change course, either by ordering closure or partial sale of their operating facilities. The attorney concluded that none of this activity by multinationals amounted to increasing investment and 'It's anybody's guess, once China gets in (to the WTO), how it will work' (Areddy, 2001).

Despite the stagnating statistics, China has witnessed a rise in FDI commitments or contracted investment as opposed to actual investment. But again, a Beijing lawyer said he took a dim view of letters of intent: 'They don't mean anything', he said. 'The word "commit" is really false', he continued, noting that his experience showed much contracted FDI would never materialize into actual FDI flows. Even if investment actually does come about, 'it could take two years to negotiate the deal and another year before the money goes in', he said (Areddy, 2001).

Yet, commitments to invest in China do appear to carry more weight than in prior years. Actual investment amounted to 75 per cent of commitments made in 2000, after having risen annually from as little as 41 per cent in the mid-1990s, according to the US–China Business Council, a lobbying group. The extent to which China lived up to its pledges in the WTO would determine how fast the committed FDI actually moved into China, according to Friedrich Wu, an economist at the Development Bank of Singapore. Potential FDI approximates US$55–60 billion by 2003 and US$65–70 billion by the end of 2005, he estimated (Areddy, 2001). Wu added that China had a great incentive to encourage FDI, based on his estimate that every dollar in FDI (US$1.0) boosts the country's GDP by US$1.15. Further, he noted that FDI inflows could help offset the outflows expected as imports increase under the WTO regime (Areddy, 2001).

Multinational corporations' characteristics and expectations

Multinationals that now dominate as vehicles for FDI in China have very different risk profiles and characteristics from the overseas Chinese companies that have traditionally served as China's major investors (Haley et al., 1998). Among the multinationals, telecommunications and automobile companies dominated the list of the major multinationals in China, in terms of sales, according to the WWW site of the official Chinese newspaper, *International Business Daily*. Shanghai Volkswagen Automotive Co., a 50–50 joint venture between Volkswagen AG and Shanghai Automotive Industry Corp., topped the list with 26.7 billion yuan (about US$3.2 billion) in sales from November 1999 to October 2000 (dela Cruz, 2001). Shanghai Volkswagen has held the number one spot for nine consecutive years, the newspaper said. The multinationals did not disclose their net income figures.

Can foreign multinationals make profits in China? The Chinese market presents formidable obstacles for multinationals to make returns on their investment, and one new report suggested that WTO membership could exacerbate problems for multinationals. 'Although we have no doubts that the value of FDI will remain strong for many more years, a much bigger uncertainty is the extent to which such investors will be able to show a respectable profit… (and) WTO membership is only going to make the environment more competitive', according to the Political & Economic Risk Consultancy Ltd., a Hong Kong advisory firm. Another cautionary note for multinationals considering FDI is that while business people in Hong Kong said they looked forward to China's membership in the WTO, and expected positive results, around 62 per cent of Hong Kong Chamber of Commerce member companies reported in December 2000 that the WTO would not prompt them to switch any operations to the Chinese mainland (Areddy, 2001).

Over the past decade, the Chinese market has attracted many multinationals, each believing vast potential profits lay just around the corner. But those years also generated horror stories about broken contracts, counterfeiting, corruption and bureaucratic red tape, especially following the gold rush of 1994–97, when multinationals fell over themselves to get in early on China's growth cycle. As multinationals nursed their bruises, profits in China often seemed elusive. Peugeot's Guangzhou joint venture epitomizes one of the most conspicuous commercial failures in the first 20 years of China's reform and opening. Established in 1985, Peugeot's joint venture had the Chinese central government's approval to manufacture 30 000 passenger cars a year. In 1993, factory production peaked at 16 400 cars. In 1997, in its final year of operations, only 1700 cars rolled off the assembly line (*South China Morning Post*, 2000b).

According to Wang Zhile, a professor at the Chinese Academy of International Trade and Economic Cooperation, about one-third of the 354 000 multinationals in China currently turn a profit (Holland, 2000). Yet, a 1999 survey by the American Chamber of Commerce in China showed that, while 58 per cent of its member multinationals had lower profit margins there than in other global operations, 88 per cent had plans to expand. Does this mean that investors do not want to concede that their euphoria over China could be wrong thereby continuing to throw good money after bad? Some prominent failures, such as a recent rout in the brewing industry, involving Carlsberg, Bass and Asimco, and the pull-out by Britain's National Power, have just raised such concerns. The next section outlines some of the dragons in China's unchartered markets.

Deciphering travelers' tales

As the most populous country in the world, China presents awesome potential markets for multinationals: indeed, automobiles and telecommunications may present two of the largest potential markets in the world, and as indicated earlier, multinationals from these industries have attained high sales. Yet, despite high sales, profits have eluded the bulk of the multinationals operating in China, including those in automobiles and telecommunications. The lure of enormous markets and profits comes entangled with various problems including inability to ascertain the market's true size, infant distribution channels, copyright violations that strike at the core of the multinationals' competitive advantages, high regulatory risks and corrupt business environments.

Market potential and size

The American Chamber of Commerce's survey in 1999 showed that 87 per cent of its member multinationals came for the Chinese market's size and potential (Holland, 2000). Two industries with enormous market potential and sales, though not profits, include automobiles and telecommunications.

Foreign automobile manufacturers invested heavily in China's auto industry over the past 15 years, yet most have struggled, selling expensive sedans and family wagons that few Chinese can afford. Consequently, most foreign automobile manufacturers in China operate at just a fraction of capacity, selling primarily to companies and government agencies. To combat this, General Motors Corp. (GM) plans to start producing a compact family car in China in 2001, a move the US multinational hopes will finally give it access to this country's potentially huge pool of individual buyers. General Motors Corp. hopes the new car, priced at about US$12 000, will bring it within buying range of China's burgeoning middle-class (Leggett, 2000). Ford Motor Co. is currently finalizing a deal with Chongqing Changan Auto Co. to make a compact car also expected to go for about US$12 000. Similarly, in the northern city of Tianjin, Japan's Toyota Motor Corp. and Tianjin Automotive (Industrial) Group Co. also hope to roll out their own compact car in 2001. Meanwhile, Volkswagen AG and Shanghai Automotive, allied since 1984, plan to launch a model based on the original People's Car that Volkswagen made in Germany.

With China's WTO membership rapidly approaching, the Chinese central government is taking steps to boost the automobile industry, among them making it easier for buyers to finance car purchases with bank loans. Critics, however, have contended that even priced at around US$12 000, the new economy cars may not garner enough buyers. With average income among Chinese still under US$1000 a year, many individuals are saving to buy homes and to pay for rising education and medical costs. Most Chinese still view cars as luxury items. Additionally, deeply ingrained protectionist policies set by local governments in China, such as exorbitant sales and license taxes, could force the price of the compact cars even higher, driving down demand.

Despite their high sales, foreign automobile manufacturers' aggressive expansion in China may prove an erroneous strategy in view of the country's relatively small but highly protected market. Graeme Maxton, the global economist of The Economist Group, said he had reservations that China would really open up its market to foreign multinationals after its WTO entry, and because of cultural barriers, would gradually become controlled by local competitors (Sito, 2000). Foreign automobile manufacturers currently account for the majority of the country's car sales. Yet, the mainland's biggest foreign automobile manufacturer, Volkswagen of Germany, with joint venture factories in Shanghai and Jilin, produced only 230 836 vehicles in 1999. Similarly, despite the launch of its family car, GM expects only half of its production capacity of 100 000 will be used in 2001.

Although the Chinese central government has agreed to cut import tariffs of 80–100 per cent on cars to 25 per cent within six years of its entry into the WTO, Graeme Maxton of The Economist Group said foreign multinationals' analysis of the growth potential of the automobile market may prove inaccurate (Sito, 2000). Some foreign multinationals believe that if only 10 per cent of China's 1.3 billion people became their customers that would provide a big market. But China's passenger car market, excluding trucks, appears relatively small when compared with other countries. The market, with car sales of 675 000 in 2000, was smaller than the sum of the Netherlands' and Belgium's markets – Europe's two small car markets. By 2010, Graeme Maxton predicted, car sales in China would increase about three fold, to 2 million units, yet, 'the market would still be smaller than France's (Sito, 2000).

The experiences of Cerestar, a subsidiary of the Paris-based Eridania Beghin-Say agro-industrial group, and one of the largest foreign multinationals in China with a US$200 million investment, show some of the difficulties of estimating market size in China. After its initial joint-venture partner ran out of money, Cerestar lined up a new partner, Jilin-based grain trader Jiliang Group. The plant plans to open in the second half of 2001 to produce high-grade starch, as well as the corn sweeteners dextrose, glucose syrup and dried glucose, and a bulking agent, maltodextrin, all aimed primarily at the Chinese market.

Tintin Delphin, who arrived in 1999 as vice-president of the joint venture's commercial department, discovered that demand for the product did not synchronize with expectations: the Chinese used native starch differently from Westerners (Lawrence, 2000a,b). In the West, starch serves as a thickener in food and pharmaceuticals, while in China, 40 per cent of starch produces the flavour enhancer monosodium glutamate. Consequently, in China the price of starch assumes more importance than its quality. Cerestar's financial projections, based on the joint venture's charging a premium for its starch because of its high quality, had to be revised downwards. 'It is still a huge market', Delphin said, 'but it is not quite the niche that we thought' (Lawrence, 2000b). Delphin also learned that the dextrose market in China differed from that in the West, as Chinese manufacturers use dextrose in pharmaceuticals but rarely in food. Exploring the market for dried glucose, Delphin found it 'very limited, because they don't know how to use it'.

To estimate market size, Cerestar initially relied on its joint-venture partner's estimates as the Jiliang Group had two of the largest plants in China for starch products. Yet, the Jiliang Group's estimates proved grossly erroneous and misinformed. Also, publicly available market information that Delphin could obtain was generally at least two years out of date. Delphin eventually obtained the market information she needed through exhaustive hands-on research, begun late in the joint venture's life. Delphin and her staff compiled a list of thousands of possible starch users, then began cold calling, eliminating trading firms, distributors and representative offices, none of whom use starchy products directly. The information gathering evolved into an extremely frustrating experience: 'Telephones have been disconnected. Many are reluctant to talk to strangers. Others are bankrupt. Or they've moved' and fewer than 10 per cent emerged as genuine, potential customers (Lawrence, 2000b).

Cerestar also had to think creatively about how to adapt transportation of products for its customers. The joint venture's liquid sweeteners, such as glucose, a product used in beverages, posed the biggest problem. A highly viscous substance, glucose thickens as the temperature drops. In Europe and the USA, Cerestar ships glucose in giant steam-jacketed tanks that maintain the temperature, so the glucose stays sufficiently liquid till its destination. But food-grade large tanks proved difficult to obtain in China, even without steam jackets. Cerestar pondered importing the tanks from Europe, but the roads leading south from the plant, two-and-a-half-hours' drive north of Changchun in Northeast China, could not accommodate 20-tonne shipments of liquid glucose in heavy tanks carried on even heavier trucks. One short-term solution the joint venture is currently considering involves transporting the glucose in small drums to Southern China, where most of the plant's customers may reside. 'Once it arrives in Shanghai in winter, it will be very thick, but they can warm it up', Delphin said. She noted, though, that this would constitute an expensive option and reduce any profits even further (Lawrence, 2000b).

Also, while many multinationals' market research shows large potential for the Chinese market, the research often fails to account for competitors also entering the market, resulting in excess capacity, fierce price-cutting and a realization that China's immense market faces strong regional protectionism. Besides the French car maker Peugeot, referred to earlier, those high-profile investors that lost money because of an inability to compete include US white-goods maker Whirlpool, a DaimlerChrysler truck venture and Australian brewer Foster's. Stiff competition originates from other foreign multinationals as well as some local companies. In sectors such as white goods and brewing, a handful of local companies such as Qingdao Brewery, air-conditioner maker Kelon and refrigerator maker Haier developed into efficient businesses as they learned from their foreign rivals and turned being local into a strength. Zhang Ruimin, President of the Haier Group said: 'For foreign companies, China remains that last big frontier; but we are already well known here, and we know the market too. So as long as we learn from multinationals and keep up our quality standards, we can have certain advantages.' He pointed especially to local companies' better access to distribution networks and connections within China's rambling bureaucracy (Holland, 2000). In fact, the Chinese government's favourite maxim as far as its domestic companies go is to 'study, cooperate, compete', against foreign enterprises in China in order to build economic strength. Beijing fiercely promotes hi-tech transfers and overseas training programmes offered by foreign multinationals, in order to get its domestic companies up to speed.

Copyright and intellectual-property violations

For overall risk, Peter Humphrey, chief representative in China for Kroll Associates (Asia) Ltd., the global business-risk-consulting firm, put China on a par with Asian neighbours Indonesia, India, Thailand and South Korea. For intellectual-property violations, however, Humphrey placed China in a league of its own. Humphrey called the country 'a major world center of counterfeiting' (Lawrence, 2000c). According to Humphrey, perpetrators of copyright violations include unscrupulous business people, abetted by present or former employees of the multinationals being ripped off; and the organized-crime gangs from Hong Kong, Macau and Taiwan who now run extensive counterfeiting syndicates in China (Lawrence, 2000c).

Even a casual observer should notice that China is awash in bogus goods. In recent weeks, media reports have uncovered shadow markets for almost anything with a trademark or a margin, from soaps to cigarettes and motor parts to rice, including prescription drugs and blood products. Some mainland-based Western pharmaceutical manufacturers put the counterfeit rate for some branded drugs at 10 per cent or more (*South China Morning Post*, 2000a). The Chinese government estimates the value of fake goods produced domestically at about 130 billion yuan annually (about US$15.7 billion), resulting in direct losses of 25 billion yuan (about US$3.01 billion) in taxation revenue. However, according to the China Anti-Counterfeiting Coalition, a lobby group of 49 multinationals, including Nike, Bayer, Gillette, Philip Morris, Kodak and Heineken, counterfeiters cost the Chinese government much more – upwards of hundreds of billions of yuan in lost taxes each year. The counterfeiters employ increasingly sophisticated techniques to manufacture, to package and to market their goods, causing great apprehension among foreign multinationals. For example, some counterfeit soap merchants have separated their manufacturing and packaging operations to limit their liabilities when governmental authorities close illicit factories. Similarly, pharmaceutical counterfeiters are establishing risk funds to cover legal expenses and lost revenues accruing from members' arrests.

As more and more multinationals suffer losses, decisions about whether to make further investments in China may be put on hold or dropped altogether. Proctor & Gamble's (P&G's) running battle against copyright violations capture some of the travails of operating in China. Since P&G set up its first joint venture in China in 1988, the consumer-products multinational has invested US$300 million in the country. Like many other model multinationals in China, it has lost money hand over fist to counterfeiters. Conservatively, 15–20 per cent of all P&G-labeled products on the shelves are fakes. That adds up to potential losses in sales of US$150 million annually. In addition, P&G spends US$2–3 million a year on raids and other anti-counterfeiting action and conducted 450 raids in the first eight months of 2000 alone (Saywell, 2000). In November 2000, P&G was forced to cancel contracts with two of its biggest suppliers, Dalian Dafu Plastic and Colour Printing Co. and Zhongshan Dafu Plastic Packaging, after it discovered counterfeit shampoos and detergents were using Dafu-manufactured packaging (*South China Morning Post*, 2000a).

For all the time and energy it spends chasing counterfeiters, however, P&G has had surprisingly few successes. Under current regulations, victims of counterfeiting can press criminal charges only if administrative officers have caught and fined a counterfeiter thrice. The low fines typically encourage counterfeiters to resume business within a day of getting caught. On the rare occasions when counterfeiting cases get court dates, government officials, law-enforcement agencies and even local courts often protect counterfeiters. In some cases, local government departments control wholesale markets that trade in counterfeit goods. P&G has won just two criminal cases that have gone to court and the counterfeiters received paltry jail terms of between two and three years apiece.

So far the counterfeiting problem has not stopped P&G from investing, but it could become a deciding factor in the future. 'If the problem continues to escalate, I can guarantee it will become the determining factor on whether we invest or not', said William Dobson, P&G's Guangzhou-based Vice-president of external relations. 'We might decide to put a plant in another place where we would have more control over the whole supply chain: raw materials, production and packaging' (Saywell, 2000). The counterfeiting problem has also influenced P&G's ability to raise the prices of its products, ranging from shampoos and soaps to Pampers-brand diapers. Counterfeiters can undercut on price, sometimes by as much as 50–90 per cent. 'It's a factor in pricing', admitted Dobson. 'Any time you increase the margin of the price differential between you and a counterfeiter, you're giving them an opportunity to make more money' (Saywell, 2000).

Foreign multinationals such as P&G face not only loss of their revenues in China through counterfeiting, but also loss of their export markets and their reputations. P&G has found China-made copies of its goods in markets as far afield as Thailand, the Philippines and India. Similarly, bogus mainland-exported Yamaha motorcycles have been spotted in US showrooms. Companies affiliated in some way with state-owned corporations export many of the products. Moreover, when counterfeiters sell inferior or unsafe products, they undermine loyalty to the brand and harm its owner's reputation with consumers. For the last three years, 60–70 per cent of all the consumers' comments that P&G has received have been related to counterfeit goods – from requests that the company certify whether a purchased item is genuine to claims for compensation (Saywell, 2000). Similarly, a US congressional committee in 2000 put the blame for the damaging effects of gentamicin, an antibiotic linked to deafness and kidney damage, on contaminated bulk gentamicin imported from the Long March Pharmaceutical Co. in Sichuan province.

In the automobile industry, lack of severe punishment and local government protection of some bogus parts-makers has resulted in resounding losses for multinationals, including top-selling Shanghai Volkswagen. Shanghai Volkswagen, maker of the popular Santana model in China, reported it spends 1.4 billion yuan (about US$170 million) to repair parts annually for the Santanas (Han, 2000; *Xinhua News Agency*, 2000). However, Volkswagen sells only a third of the replacement parts for the 1.5 million Santanas driven in China and makers of bogus, unauthorized parts claim the other two-thirds. A fake Santana headlight sells for 90 per cent less than a legitimate one, also hindering Volkswagen from recouping resounding losses by raising prices (Han, 2000). The Chinese government has demolished 770 factories producing illegal goods and confiscated 90 million yuan (about US$10.9 million) worth of Santana parts over the past two years, but these efforts have touched just the tip of the iceberg. Similarly, copycats have taken at least 20 per cent of Bosch Trading's (Shanghai) potential 40-million yuan (about US$4.83 million) market. Bosch, a German company, has found a fake version for almost every one of its components on the Chinese market (Han, 2000).

In the automobile industry, as with other consumer goods, crackdown efforts by the central government have proven futile because local governments protect counterfeiters as a way to keep jobs and tax revenues in their jurisdictions. The enormous profits and windfall tax income have allowed counterfeiters to become pillar industries in provinces such as Zhejiang and Jiangsu. Ineffective criminal prosecution and light penalties have also curbed efforts to stem counterfeiting (Han, 2000). Foreign multinationals fear that China's impending entry into the WTO may open global markets to smaller mainland exporters, thereby allowing the flood of fakes to breach local borders and pour into world markets; as a corollary, in early 2001, MOFTEC announced the Chinese government was preparing to loosen its restrictions on private companies seeking foreign trade licenses.

Political and regulatory risks

Political risk, or governmental and country stability, constitutes a major factor in the strategic decision-making of multinationals operating in foreign countries. Peter Humphrey, chief representative in China for Kroll Associates (Asia) Ltd., argued that worse scenarios on political risk exist for several parts of Asia over China including Indonesia, Indochina, the Philippines and parts of India. But even in China, Humphrey pointed out that acts of terrorism and sabotage have risen involving

Muslim separatists in the far northwest. He also noted the possibility that Tibetan separatism could 'take an ugly form' as a younger generation of Tibetans, unhappy with Dalai Lama's eschewing of violent tactics, comes to the fore (Lawrence, 2000c). Humphrey expressed worry that because China has been relatively peaceful for 20 years, many multinationals have become complacent about its stability. The Tiananmen demonstrations and crackdown of 1989 and the violent popular reaction to NATO's bombing of China's embassy in Yugoslavia last year should have been wake-up calls, he said, for multinationals. The anti-NATO protests, which resulted in the burning-down of the US consul-general's residence in Chengdu, plus assaults on foreigners and stone-throwing attacks on some foreign multinationals, were a reminder that 'nowadays things can happen quickly in China. It no longer needs months to build up. It can happen in 24 hours' (Lawrence, 2000c).

A startling new report, 'China Investigation Report 2000–01: Studies of Contradictions within the People Under New Conditions', by the Communist Party's inner sanctum (Eckholm, 2001) also describes a spreading pattern of collective protests and group incidents arising from economic, ethnic and religious conflicts in China. The report identifies relations between the party officials and masses as 'tense, with conflicts on the rise' (Eckholm, 2001). The report also describes mounting public anger over inequality, corruption and public aloofness. Painting a bleak picture of seething discontent, the report warns that the coming years of rapid change, driven by China's entry into the WTO, will likely lead to even greater social and political conflicts: 'Our country's entry into the WTO may bring growing dangers and pressures and it can be predicted that in the ensuing period the number of group incidents may jump, severely harming social stability and even disturbing the smooth implementation of reform and opening up' (Eckholm, 2001). Political risks in China certainly appear to be increasing.

Simultaneously, regulatory risk, or uncertainty about which factions and interest groups will make what governmental policies tomorrow, remains the big downside of the world's most tempting market. China's fast-growing telecommunications market captures some of the regulatory risks facing multinationals. China's telecommunications market has seen amazing growth: A decade ago, China's phone system had one fixed line for every 100 people, and no mobile phones; today, China has five times as many fixed lines as India, and 25 times as many mobile subscribers. In 2000, 70 million Chinese subscribed to mobile phone services and by 2005, the number of subscribers could reach 240 million, making China the largest mobile-phone market in the world (*Economist*, 2000a). The importance of China's telecommunications market extends far beyond its own borders. The Chinese are already making their influence felt abroad, in such matters as the battle among technology standards for next-generation mobile phones. Within the International Telecommunication Union, a standard-setting body of the United Nations, China chairs a key committee and simply by anointing one standard or another in its vast home market, China might sway the global contest between European and US standards. However, every move China made to liberalize its telecommunications industry occurred, at least initially, against the wishes of Wu Jichuan, China's telecommunications minister, officially minister of information industry, and widely considered the most powerful man in the world's potentially biggest telecommunications market (*Economist*, 2000a).

Wu Jichuan used to run China Telecom, the country's fixed-line telephone monopoly, as an arm of his ministry. When other ministries tried to create some competition in 1994 by forming a rival, China Unicom, Wu deprived Unicom of a fixed-line license. Wu's worst ire has however always been reserved for foreign multinationals. In 1997, Wu told the US commerce secretary that China would not open its telecommunications market for at least 20 years. To a foreign journalist, he once intimated that he was not keen on foreign multinationals participating in China's Internet sector – ever (*Economist*, 2000a). Zhu Rongji, Prime Minister of China, has opposed Wu from implementing some of his protectionist ambitions. Indeed, Beijing's telecommunications policy appears as the product of a power tussle among Wu, Zhu and Li Peng, China's second-in-command after Jiang Zemin, and another strong protectionist who opposes FDI and economic liberalization.

Regulatory risks of operating in China have affected Qualcomm, a US company that champions the Code Division Multiple Access (CDMA) standard for mobile phones. The multinational lobbied long and hard for China Unicom to use its technology alongside the European Global System for Mobile Communications (GSM) standard favoured by China Telecom. Wu frustrated these efforts whenever he could (*Economist*, 2000a). Irwin Jacobs, Chairman of Qualcomm, first thought he had broken the GSM stranglehold in February 2000, when Qualcomm won a deal with China under which state-run China Unicom would build a CDMA network with 10 million users by the end of 2000. That deal crumbled in June when China Unicom said it would wait for the next generation of CDMA, a decision that would keep Qualcomm out of the China market for yet another year. Qualcomm's shares plunged on the news. China Unicom reversed course again in October after Jacobs made a trip to Beijing and met with Zhu Rongji and other leading Chinese officials. Jacobs quickly said the deal would probably cause the company to revise worldwide sales projections upwards in 2001 and 2002; he also was quoted as saying he was 'cautiously optimistic' for the fiscal year ending September 2001, in part because of the Chinese market's potential. Recent Chinese statements show that some Chinese authorities, lead by Wu Jichuan, remain determined to ensure that domestic companies reap the lion's share of any profits from the fast-growing telecommunications industry and Qualcomm's emphasis now clearly veers on the 'cautious'. Jacobs has acknowledged disappointment with China Unicom's flip-flops and delays, which he has attributed mainly to Chinese politics. 'I think it became complicated because a number of manufacturers within China were all competing to be among those selected to be licensed and were asking for the people they knew in government to perhaps help them, and that slowed things down', said Jacobs (Biers and Wilhelm, 2000).

Multinationals in telecommunications such as Qualcomm have experienced that no matter how promising China's market looks, politicians such as Wu mould and shape this market. Power shifts fast in Beijing, and Wu might not always have Zhu Rongji to reverse his decisions. Ascertaining which group holds power does not constitute an easy task in China. Indeed, China emerged as the laggard in a new PriceWaterhouseCoopers' survey measuring the transparency of 35 countries, which the authors said directly correlated to borrowing costs (Reuters, 2001). PriceWaterhouseCoopers through its opacity index argued that lack of clear, accurate, formal and widely accepted business practices increased the cost of capital and posed a major obstacle to FDI. China came out as having the most opaque system in the world, with a score of 87, followed by Russia.

Culture of corruption

According to the latest corruption perceptions index published by Transparency International (TI), a Berlin-based non-governmental organization that fights corruption worldwide, China ranks as the eighth most-corrupt country in the world (with Nigeria winning the dubious distinction of most corrupt). Launched in 1995, the TI index ranks countries based on how much corruption is perceived to exist among politicians and public officials. These rankings derive from 16 surveys of businessmen, the general public and country analysts from eight independent institutions (*Economist,* 2000b).

Backman (1999) argued that corruption formed the primary cause for the disintegration of favourable business environments in Asia and the Asian financial crisis. China's culture of kickbacks and corruption poses a huge problem for foreign multinationals operating here too. Suppliers routinely pay kickbacks to buyers for foreign multinationals, and then pass the cost of the kickbacks along to the multinationals in the form of higher prices for inputs, eroding the multinationals' margins (Lawrence, 2000c).

Stories of corruption filter in from official Chinese sources. A Chinese governmental audit of embezzlement in the first half of 1999, which the central government published in August 2000, showed that some 20 billion yuan (about US$2.42 billion) had been diverted from the state into personal bank accounts. Another 1 billion yuan (about US$121 million) had been bilked from the pension funds of the state railways, post and telecommunications. Additionally, about 6 billion yuan (about US$724 million) of pension funds from the state coal bureau had been misused (*Economist*, 2000c). The Communist Party's official mouthpiece, the *People's Daily*, said that 120 billion yuan (about US$14.5 billion) of state funds were misused (on a wider definition) in the first half of 1999 – equivalent to one-fifth of the central government's tax revenues.

Some incisive research shows that most Chinese market-oriented reforms to the state sector have failed and appear to feed into the root of the culture of corruption (Steinfeld, 1998). The reforms started in the 1980s with the introduction of the contract-responsibility system that allowed enterprises to sell their goods for profit in the open market once they had fulfilled their quotas under the plan. The contract-responsibility system served as the cue for quantities of state goods to leave the factory by the back door, with the proceeds kept by the managers. For much of the 1990s, the central government praised modern, scientific management and managers of SOEs were given more autonomy to generate profits. The managers were not, however, penalized for racking up losses, which remained the state's responsibility. Unscrupulous managers could milk their companies' assets through shell companies and subsidiaries (*Economist*, 2000c). New milking opportunities presented themselves with the Communist Party's endorsement in 1997 of a shareholding system to turn small- and medium-sized state firms into companies with mixed public and (sometimes majority) private ownership. Small state firms were soon being privatized at a frantic pace. Managers would often bully workers into buying shares, forming nominal collectives to disguise what was going on. When the central government tried to slow down the process, outside observers said China's leaders were backtracking on reform. More likely they realized, horror-struck, how easily the state's assets were being pilfered (Steinfeld, 1998). The dominant and staggering SOE system continues to contribute to corruption in China. The next section explores how multinationals may chart an effective course in China.

Setting an expeditious course

What can multinationals do to engender profitable operations in China? No easy answers exist, nor despite China's impending WTO entry do the dragons look like they will disappear any time soon. Clearly profits will not come plentifully and easily for foreign multinationals in China. In earlier forays into China, especially in the 1980s and early 1990s, many foreign multinationals relied on joint ventures with local partners to decipher the local terrain. The local partners ideally would provide knowledge of local conditions and business environments, thereby complementing the multinationals' core competencies in their intangible assets. However, as Cerestar and P&G did, most foreign multinationals experienced setbacks and unhappiness with joint-venture partners in China ranging from cultural misunderstandings to copyright violations; in effect, the costs of maintaining these local partnerships proved more costly for most multinationals than their benefits. Consequently, in the last 5 years, joint ventures with local partners no longer serve as the premier mode of entry for foreign multinationals into China, and most have decided to make a go of it alone as sole captains of their ships. Under these circumstances, effective understandings of the business environments and the dragons that lurk in them become pressing imperatives for multinationals.

At a minimum, foreign multinationals have to undertake extensive, hands-on market research, which does not rely on archival data and includes customers' tastes, buying habits and competitor's operations to estimate true market potential and viable profit targets. Archival data are often dated as soon as they are published because of the double-digit annual sales growth in so many of China's industrial markets; additionally, governmental statistics provide notoriously misleading information. As Cerestar did, many successful multinationals have created their own estimates based on approaching potential customers; as Cerestar found, most multinationals have found this process for generating market data costly, time consuming and a serious deflator of previous market estimates.

On copyrights and trademark protection, simple steps, which some multinationals overlook, include registering the multinational's trademarks in China, and making sure that patents have been approved, and not just applied for, before bringing any technology to China. Multinationals should also do due-diligence on their partners, and to write into contracts the clients' rights to do spot checks on licensees. For example, 'you may have licensed someone to make a million razor blades', said Peter Humphrey, chief representative in China for Kroll Associates (Asia) Ltd. 'They may be making 2 million' (Lawrence, 2000c). Where counterfeiting appears serious, Humphrey has instructed multinationals to investigate and to get local law authorities to conduct raids. 'The authorities however do not take much interest in fraud in privately owned companies', Humphrey lamented, so multinationals have to watch out for themselves, by implementing a strong system of internal checks and balances, and carefully screening new hires (Lawrence, 2000c).

Multinationals facing overcapacity and losses may attempt to restructure and to downsize; yet, workplace violence has also increasingly become an issue in China, often sparked by efforts to downsize and to restructure multinationals. When one of Kroll's clients decided to liquidate voluntarily a formerly state-owned bottling plant it had acquired, workers badly beat up the four accountants sent to do a pre-liquidation audit, detained them for a day, and then threatened to attack the premises of the accounting firm (Lawrence, 2000c). Kroll had to put some of the accountants and their families in safe houses. The workers withdrew their threats two weeks into the stand-off, after being given the impression that the investor had fired the accounting firm. The accounting firm should have conducted a security-threat assessment before sending their people to perform the audit.

On longer-term strategic issues, unfortunately no easy answers exist and multinationals have to chart their independent courses, taking into account the warnings to beware of dragons in the largest potential market in the world. China presents a high-risk, high-potential market and will probably remain one after its WTO entry. When potential copyright violations and trademark infringements could threaten the multinationals' export markets and core competencies, the business circumstances and opportunities spawning them should be avoided, no matter what the temptation of the lucrative Chinese market. On the other hand, when the technology is aging or when technology cycles are shorter, the multinational should seriously consider investing in China to get a foothold in this immense market and to maintain the same portfolio of options as other competitors. After all, here there be dragons, but also rainbows and pots of gold. Journey cautiously wise traveller.

References

Areddy, J. T. (2001) 'China watch: despite WTO, China FDI prospects mixed', *Dow Jones Newswires*, 7 January.

Backman, M. (1999) *Asian Eclipse*, John Wiley.

Biers, D. and K. Wilhelm (2000) 'Telecoms – a cautious courtship', *Far Eastern Economic Review*, 7 December.

dela Cruz, R. (2001) 'Telecom, auto cos top list of China FIEs in terms of sales', *Dow Jones Newswires*, 11 January.

Eckholm, E. (2001) 'Chinese warn of civil unrest across country', *International Herald Tribune*, 2–3 June.

Economist (2000a) 'The minister of arbitrary power', 9 December.

Economist (2000b) 'Corruption', 16 September.

Economist (2000c) 'The honeycomb of corruption', 6 April.

Haley, U. C. V. (2000) *Strategic Management in the Asia Pacific: Harnessing Regional and Organizational Change for Competitive Advantage*, Butterworth-Heinemann.

Haley, U. C. V. (2001) *Multinational Corporations in Political Environments: Ethics, Values and Strategies*, World Scientific Publishing.

Haley, G. T., Tan, C. T. and U. C. V. Haley (1998) *New Asian Emperors: The Overseas Chinese, their Strategies and Competitive Advantages*, Butterworth-Heinemann.

Han, J. (2000) 'Slack enforcement foils battle against fake parts', *South China Morning Post*, 24 November.

Holland, L. (2000) 'A brave new world?', *Far Eastern Economic Review*, 5 October.

Hu, B. (2001) 'Direct inflows show slight gain', *South China Morning Post*, 18 January.

Lawrence, S. V. (2000a) 'From villain to hero', *Far Eastern Economic Review*, 5 October.

Lawrence, S. V. (2000b) 'Formula for disaster', *Far Eastern Economic Review*, 5 October.

Lawrence, S. V. (2000c) 'For better or worse', *Far Eastern Economic Review*, 5 October.

Leggett, K. (2000) 'GM plans to make a compact car for China's market', *Wall Street Journal*, 1 September.

Reuters (2001) 'Switzerland: Davos-China, Russia laggards in transparency survey', 25 January.

Saywell, T. (2000) 'Fakes cost real cash', *Far Eastern Economic Review*, 5 October.

Sito, P. (2000) 'Foreign firms seen overrating market sector expected to be dominated by local makers in future', *South China Morning Post*, 14 November.

South China Morning Post (2000a) 'Crackdown on fakes failing to stem trade', 23 December.

South China Morning Post (2000b) 'Honda gets into gear', 30 May.

Steinfeld, E. (1998) *Forging Reform in China: The Fate of State-owned Industry*, Cambridge University Press.

Xinhua News Agency (2000) 'Non-starter: the proliferation of fake car parts', 24 November.

Xinhua News Agency (2001) 'China Statistics Bureau data on foreign investment in manufacturing sector', 24 January.

16
Impact of the Asian Crisis on Capitalism in Post-crisis Asian Business Environments

Fred Robins

Introduction

The Asian crisis of 1997 has already had powerful national, regional and global consequences. At the present time, three years later, regional recovery is well underway although the possibility of an aftershock cannot be entirely ruled out. Yet the crisis caused more disruption in the East Asian region than any other economic event of the past 50 years.

A cursory familiarity with the consequences makes clear that the full impact of the crisis embraces financial, economic, political, social and institutional elements. It is, therefore, appropriate to explore the impact of these events on the business and political economy of states within the region. In particular, it is interesting to explore the impact of the crisis on those aspects of the government–business relationship which reflect the Asian model of economic development. This model may also be referred to, as here, by the term Asian capitalism. Those consequences which have been observed and documented, so far, are probably just the beginning of a fairly long adjustment process. In any event, current controversy over globalization of the international trade and investment environment make it interesting to speculate on where these early changes are leading. Such is the purpose of this chapter.

Labels

There is already an extensive literature suggesting that business practice in East Asia may differ in important respects from business practice in the other parts of the world, notably the West. In the academic literature of business schools, this includes the very extensive volume of published research into the characteristics of East Asian business, and even more so, into government–business relationships in the region (Whitley, 1992; MacIntyre, 1994; Sheridan, 1998; Richter, 2000). At a more popular level, it emerges in the frequency with which we see the epithets: Japan Inc., Taiwan Inc., Malaysia Inc., Singapore Inc. and so on (Jayasankaran, 1999; Kunii and Takahashi, 1999; Lloyd-Owen, 1999; Haley, 2000). It also emerges in the recurrent trade related, diplomatic argument between the USA and Japan over, for example, foreign access to Japan's flat glass market (Shimizu, 1999).

Different labels are variously attached to those characteristics which are seen as differentiating East Asian from Western business. These include the Asian way of doing business, the Asian model of capitalism, and Asian values. Although not always done, it is probably best to apply each of these three labels to just one particular level of analysis, thus:

- *The Asian way* – is probably best reserved for the business conduct of firms – the microeconomic level of analysis.
- *The Asian model* – is usually and probably best reserved for analysis of the industrialization process as a whole or economic development theory – the macroeconomic level of analysis.
- *Asian values* – is perhaps appropriate for general political and social analysis – but probably best reserved for philosophical analysis and the history of ideas; the most difficult label to apply rigorously (Sen, 1997).

This chapter, which focuses on business and government–business relations, uses only the first two of these labels.

Direct consequences for business

It is self-evident that a sudden drop in domestic currency values, equally sudden rise in interest charges, major credit squeeze and economic slowdown, has a dramatic impact on most businesses. Indeed, the 1997 crisis in East Asia was so severe that it bankrupted many of the region's banks and financial institutions as well as more conventional businesses. Malaysia's Finance Minister, Daim Zainuddin, said in April 1999 that 'Malaysia lost about five years of development as a result of the financial crisis – and to catch up is a gigantic task'. More dramatically, Ronnie Chan, Chairman of Hang Lung Development Group of Hong Kong and 18 other companies spread across the world, told students at

Fairfield University School of Business: 'the Asian economic crisis set back Asian companies 10–20 years in one month' (DeFusco, 1999). While such remarks can now be seen as exaggeration, it need be no surprise that many of the businesses which have survived have changed as a direct consequence of these events. In the words of James Shapiro, Head of Asian operations for the New York Stock Exchange: 'Changes in attitudes among Asian firms in the past 12 months have been revolutionary' (Brancato, 1999).

Examples of consequent changes in business thinking, business practice and corporate structures can be documented from across the region. The priority of business in the immediate aftermath of the crisis was to access new capital and to reduce debt in the face of greatly increased debt-servicing charges and reduced availability of working capital, at a time of falling sales and decline in revenues.

The crisis began in Thailand, so it is reasonable to look first for examples there. It happens that the country's largest business group, Charoen Pokphand (CP), came very close to default and had to restructure. Its problems were made worse by demands for early repayment by Korean banks in Hong Kong (Vatikiotis, 1998). The consequence for the group was a major sale of subsidiary businesses, majority and minority stakes, the closure of some subsidiaries and the consolidation of 11 of its core Thai agri-businesses, including six previously unlisted companies. Given the regional scope of the group's operations, many of these asset sales were outside Thailand and some, like sale of its Shanghai brewery interests, were to existing joint-venture partners. As a result, what before the crisis was a sprawling, loosely coordinated conglomerate, has been substantially slimmed down and, though still diversified, it has become much more focused on its core activities and in its attention to profitability. Before the crisis, some group companies carried debt up to ten times their equity. Since the crisis, group companies have been ordered to cut debt levels to no more than two-thirds their equity. This represents a substantial change of corporate culture. In addition, the group's holding company, which before the crisis had guaranteed loans to group companies in China and Indonesia, is now kept debt free. Speaking to journalists (Biers and Vatikiotis, 1999), Group Chairman, Dhanin Chearavanont, commented on the lessons of the crisis as follows: 'We expanded too fast. This is the lesson. In our core businesses we had done very well. It was not too fast or too slow. What expanded too fast were those non-core businesses'.

Another of Thailand's diversified, industrial conglomerates is the Siam Cement Group. This company operated in a relatively stable environment before the crisis, was widely perceived as well managed and utilized strategic planning tools (Chang, 1999). However, the impact of the crisis on Siam Cement was not dissimilar from its impact on CP. The burden of $4.3 billion of debt required the sale of assets and significant corporate restructuring. Consequently, the group sold off or reduced its stake in dozens of non-core operations enabling it to focus on just three of its strongest businesses: cement, petrochemicals and paper, which together accounted for about 60 per cent of revenue. Since the crisis, company policy has become very clear indeed. It is to specialize in activities yielding strong profits, returns on investment and long-term competitiveness. Group President, Chumpol NaLamlieng, is quoted as saying (Mertens, 1999): 'We are not restructuring debt. It's a business restructuring, in line with a changed environment which we feel is not temporary. Boom times may be years away and, if they return, the rules of the game will be changed.' Such a statement explicitly recognizes that post-crisis business conditions are different and that, therefore, companies need to adapt and to change.

The example of just two companies from one-crisis economy does not by itself prove very much. Yet, there is anecdotal evidence to suggest that such business responses are in fact widespread; not just in Thailand but across the region. The modest assertion here is simply that some such corporate changes are occurring and that they are occurring as a direct response to the pressures brought on by the crisis. By implication, they would not otherwise have occurred as quickly or so widely, or, perhaps at all.

The initial shock of the crisis brought about some financial and corporate restructuring to Thailand, plus the direct policy involvement of the IMF. Progress was patchy and gradual but there were important advances in bankruptcy legislation, the sale and restructuring of non-viable banks and in putting the public spotlight on political corruption. There was also some slow but effective corporate restructuring. By the latter months of 2000, with a new general election looming, this gradual and still incomplete reform process appeared to be coming to a premature halt. Indeed, at the time of writing it is impossible to say what moves, if any, the next Thai government may make. Despite improving economic fundamentals, including booming exports, share prices on the Bangkok Stock Exchange fell 40 per cent, the baht fell 15 per cent against the dollar, and capital flight accelerated over the first three quarters of 2000 (Cheeseman, 2000b); so, a sure hand remains necessary.

Differences between countries, except in the case of South Korea, tend to reflect differences in the severity of the crisis rather than differences in the character of response. In Indonesia, for example, according to the rating agency, Fitch, non-performing loans in December 1998 amounted to a very high proportion of 57 per cent. Exacerbated by domestic political factors, the crisis there was so severe that the Indonesian Bank Reconstructing Agency (IBRA) was at one stage sitting on $14.3 billion in industrial assets consisting of equity stakes in 215 companies. One Jakarta-based consultant was quoted as saying this amounted to the largest nationalization of private enterprise since the communist take-over of China (*Economist*, 1999). The figure suggests the Indonesian government had effective control over industrial assets equivalent to about 25 per cent of GDP. Although reform in Indonesia has been very limited, in large part due to the priority need for political reform, these assets will sooner or later pass into the hands of different business owners; another direct consequence of the crisis. In the case of Astra International, Indonesia's largest car maker, this has already occurred. After two years of drama and uncertainty, IBRA's 40 per cent stake in Astra was sold in March 2000 to a consortium led by Singaporean car distributor, Cycle & Carriage, for US$506 million (Murphy and Dolven, 2000).

Like Thailand, Indonesia responded to the crisis by bringing financial and corporate sector behaviour under a degree of institutional scrutiny which did not exist prior to the crisis. In the Indonesian case, even more than in Thailand, these changes have taken place slowly. Moreover, their impact has been very considerably weakened by the government's preoccupation with non-economic matters – including Timor, a range of other internal armed revolts and moves by disaffected but powerful interests to promote instability. To this external observer, at least, Indonesia also appears to be characterized by greater institutional resistance to change than does Thailand.

South Korea differs from all the Southeast-Asian economies in being bigger and more technologically advanced. It also differs, as is well-known, in that the domination of the economy by hitherto state-favoured conglomerates (*chaebol*) is even greater than elsewhere. The biggest of these, again more than elsewhere, have shown they can be stubbornly reluctant to accept the need for any change at all; a stance exemplified by the now defunct Daewoo Group under Founder and Chairman, Kim Woo Chong (Burton, 1999a; Clifford, 1999). This remains so, despite the fact that the debt-to-equity ratio of the top five *chaebol* at the end of 1997, according to Korea's Fair Trade Commission, averaged a massive 473 per cent and despite heavy government demands that they achieve a maximum ratio of 200 per cent by the end of 1999. The top four surviving *chaebol* did appear to reduce their debt-to-equity ratios to this level in line with government policy, but the reality did not match the appearance. The ratio reduction was in large part achieved by increasing capital rather than reducing debt (Kwak, 2000).

Daewoo was Korea's second largest conglomerate and many judged it too big to be allowed to fail, its assets being greater than the GDP of the Philippines (Burton, 1999b). Yet, without massive asset sales it could not service its $50 billion debt and the group's founder and owner long resisted the necessary restructuring. The consequence was a kind of slow corporate poker involving Daewoo Chairman Kim, domestic and foreign creditors, and the Korean government. In 1998, the company claimed it would sell multibillion dollar shipbuilding and electronics businesses but they remained unsold at the high prices asked; at the same time the company resolutely resisted sale of two highly profitable financial institutions. By August 1999, the restructuring of Daewoo had become something of a litmus test of the government's resolve to tackle the nation's excessive corporate debt problem. Perhaps for this reason, government and creditors finally agreed to break up the group, take immediate control of profitable Daewoo Securities, and sell off all of Daewoo's other businesses, including the group's car manufacturing operation. Daewoo Motor holds about 25 per cent of the Korean car market (Moon et al., 2000a). By the start of 2000, insolvent Daewoo Motor was up for auction with both Ford and General Motors closely interested. However, the company's US$5.8 billion assets were dwarfed by acknowledged debt of US$16.5 billion. Potential buyers were nonetheless having to probe for further hidden debt even though a final sale had been scheduled by the government for the middle of 2000. By September 2000, both the preferred bidders had pulled out of any deal on terms immediately attractive to the creditor banks and the likelihood of a clean sale, without dismemberment of the company, was receding (Yoo, 2000).

Smaller and less powerful *chaebol* have generally responded to the crisis more like firms elsewhere in the region. Daesang, for example, the country's twenty-seventh largest *chaebol*, agreed in March 1998 to sell off one of its major divisions to the German giant BASF. Hanwha, the eighth largest, which was on the very edge of bankruptcy as a result of the crisis, immediately sold off whole or partial stakes in nine affiliates in December 1997 and in the course of 1998 made more drastic asset sales thereby reducing its debt ratio from 1200 per cent at the end of 1997 to 255 per cent in mid-1999 (Lee, 1999).

Doosan is one of the oldest and the thirteenth largest *chaebol*. Best known for its Oriental Brewery (OB) beer, the company was actually in trouble before the crisis began and had already been put under the control of a younger, US business-school educated, family member in 1996. At that time, Doosan was wildly overdiversified and overleveraged, with a debt to equity ratio of 600 per cent. By the time of the crisis, Doosan had consolidated its subsidiaries from 29 to 23 and sold off its share of joint-venture operations with Nestle, 3M, Kodak and Coca-Cola, to its joint-venture partners. Staff were cut and company cars sold off; this cost cutting substantially boosted cash flow. Company President Park Yong Maan has said: 'Without restructuring, we would've been gone'. Then when the crash came, Doosan consolidated further by merging its 17 remaining subsidiaries into five focused firms (Larkin, 1999). In 1998, negotiations were opened with overseas firms potentially interested in securing a stake in some of Doosan's local operations. This was in order to attract foreign investment. However, the company aggressively courted those foreign partners which could offer desired managerial expertize. The twin objectives were to reduce further the now 300 per cent debt ratio and to raise overall competitiveness (Lee and Biers, 1998) which is all very different from the typical pre-crisis *chaebol* perspective of market share, growth and expansion regardless of cost. By the end of 1998, the company had entered a 50–50 joint venture with Belgium-based Interbrew and the joint-venture then went on to take over Jinro Cass Brewing in December 1999, thereby securing a total beer market share for the company of over 50 per cent (Nho, 2000).

In summary, it may be said that in South Korea, restructuring in both financial and corporate sectors has been pursued more vigorously and has gone further than in either Thailand or Indonesia. In particular, the government has displayed greater zeal and consistency. Yet even in Korea, in neither the financial nor the corporate sector, is either debt reduction or other restructuring yet complete.

Although Japan is definitely not one of the 1997 crisis economies, Japan is, as we shall note later, the archetype and model for all the high-performing East Asian economies. It is therefore interesting to note that the changes occurring in Japanese business practices at this time are the most profound for two generations. Of course, this is in response to Japan's own problems but the consequent changes in Japanese management practice are not altogether dissimilar. Toshiba and Fujitsu, like their followers in the crisis-stricken economies, have begun to sell non-core businesses, form joint ventures with foreign firms to help expand markets, and to study ways of improving their corporate structure. For the first time, they are now setting goals for return on equity (Keenan and Landers, 1999). Moreover on 1 April 2000, a new bankruptcy regime, modelled on Western-style bankruptcy protection, took effect in Japan, as did new accounting standards which require companies to consolidate subsidiaries for the first time. Subsidiaries were, up to this time used for hiding losses, a practice which was widespread. These changes significantly enhanced transparency. Other uniquely Japanese managerial practices such as lifetime employment are also eroding.

Legal and institutional consequences

The following paragraphs offer an indication of the legal and institutional consequences of the crisis – first, on the financial sector, then on the corporate sector and, last, on the issue of crony government–business relationships.

The immediate post-crisis priority, throughout the region, was to rescue bankrupt banks and to rehabilitate broken financial systems. So moves towards bank reconstruction and recapitalization, the recreation of functioning banking systems, and the introduction of new, more transparent and seriously administered financial supervision, have all been very important outcomes of the crisis. These moves have involved the establishment of emergency financial institutions, the passage of new legislation and changes in established patterns of bank behaviour.

Consequences for the corporate sector have been just as far-reaching. As in the financial sector, bankruptcy and insolvency posed the most urgent problem. As a result, accounting practices and corporate governance in general, including shareholders' rights and some established local business practices, have all come under critical scrutiny. Consequently, there has been new business-sector legislation and, it is widely hoped, some permanent changes in business practice.

At the same time, changes have also occurred within firms as a result of crisis-induced adjustments in established government–business relationships. Two different kinds of government–business relationship have been directly affected by the crisis. One is the overall style of governance with respect to business; the other is industrial development policy. It is helpful to keep the two apart. The distinction makes it easier to assess the effect of cronyism, collusion and corruption, which tends to be all-pervasive, independently of the more focused commercial impact of industry policy, which in some circumstances may affect only specific sectors of an economy. Since the 1997 crisis has directly impacted on both cronyism and industry policy, many companies are having to adjust their responses with regard to both. We look only at cronyism in this section and industry policy later.

First, one of the more obvious consequences of the crisis has been the widespread establishment of emergency institutions to deal with bank failure. Thailand now has its Financial Sector Reconstructing Agency (FSA), Indonesia has its Indonesian Bank Reconstruction Agency (IBRA), South Korea has its Financial Supervisory Commission (FSC) and even Japan has its Financial Supervisory Agency (FSA). Malaysia has actually established a duo of similar government agencies (Shari, 1999a). The task of all of them is to provide guidance and support for the rehabilitation of failed financial infrastructures and to create safeguards against the continuation of past weaknesses. Prior to the crisis, few regional governments or central banks had useful information about the volume of short-term, foreign currency debt held by banks under their nominal supervision and even less did they know the levels of foreign currency debt held by their corporate sectors. The need to improve on this state of affairs is now recognized everywhere. The crisis made clear that central banks need full and timely information to be able to exercise effective authority in difficult times. In short, they need to be able to assess the solvency and exposure of institutions under their regulatory jurisdiction. The new agencies are changing things in this direction and, in some measure, promoting the establishment of more effective financial supervision.

Another widespread consequence, important for both financial institutions and the corporate sector, is the establishment of modern bankruptcy legislation and judicial process. For example, Thailand opened its first central bankruptcy court in June 1999 (Crampton, 1999). Thailand's introduction of modern, Western style bankruptcy legislation proved a most delicate and time-consuming institutional adjustment. It required amendment of older bankruptcy and foreclosure laws which, although a necessary step forward, did not begin to overcome a very great reluctance to push prominent bankrupts into the public spotlight of court proceedings. The same problem existed in Indonesia where the pre-crisis bankruptcy law dated from 1905 was written in Dutch. As a result of the crisis, and as required under the terms of an IMF memorandum, this colonial legislation was superseded in 1998. The outcome was the establishment of a special Commercial Court with formal rules and written procedures. Further, a Dutch lawyer was made available to give expert advice and the appointed judges received special training before taking up their new positions. As in Thailand, this development represents a major legislative advance but outside observers do not judge the early performance of the court a success. So far, efforts by the government and foreign creditors to take bad debtors to bankruptcy court have been in vain. This is why the IMF is encouraging Indonesia to reform its corrupt legal system, including the purging of corrupt bankruptcy court judges (Praginanto, 2000a): 'The [bankruptcy] court doesn't work' (John Dodworth, Chief Representative, IMF, Jakarta).

In a formal sense, there has been some improvement in the institutions of financial supervision in all the crisis-affected economies. Yet, it remains very hard indeed to gauge how much practical difference this will make. Only time will tell. The collective failure of the world's leading nations to agree upon an improved, up-to-date and comprehensive international financial architecture means that there are no easily applied standards by which to make a judgement. The tests will come when difficult conditions return.

More fundamentally, the 1997 crisis demonstrated a widespread need right across the region not just for robust financial institutions, but for modern commercial law backed by the capacity to apply it and promotion of the rule of law in general. Crisis highlighted the urgent need to modernize these elements of the commercial environment. For example, under pre-crisis Indonesian accounting standards, illegal levies were categorized as unanticipated costs and were deductible expenses; a category not recognized by international standards. The need to improve on this situation is now formally recognized regionwide, probably most strongly in South Korea. There, in keeping with an undertaking made to the World Bank in September 1998, the government has tried to make a start on improving the quality of corporate governance. It has reduced the minimum requirements for equity shareholders to exercise a voice at shareholder meetings, required corporations to appoint standing auditors and introduced an innovative system of appointing outside directors to corporate boards. Indeed, in his 1999 Liberation Day speech, President Kim Dae-jung re-emphasized his determination to bring about reforms in *chaebol* governance to deal with the uncontested managerial rights of *chaebol* heads (*chongsu*), overdiversification, and illegal insider trading (Kwak, 1999). A year later, however, a dramatic leadership and succession saga in Hyundai, the country's largest *chaebol*, highlighted the magnitude and difficulty of this task. Moreover, cross-holdings within the 30 largest *chaebol* were said to be worth US$32 billion in June 1999, double the 1997 figure (Moon, 2000b), reflecting self-serving adjustments by the *chaebol* owners designed to retain their control. Indeed, according to Lee Nam-kee, the Head of the Fair Trade Commission, '*Chaebol* are now more clever in funneling funds to each other. It's unbelievable' (Burton, 2000). Similarly, a survey showed that no less than 80 per cent of outside directors at the *chaebol* were handpicked by the groups' owners (Larkin, 2000). Nonetheless the crisis in South Korea, assisted by political change, has brought matters of corporate governance in that country under greater critical scrutiny than ever before. As one Professor of Law has written (Jeong, 1999): 'What Korea needs now is not perfunctory reform of corporate governance but rather a new business philosophy...' A top policy-maker, Chung Duck-koo, Minister of Commerce, Industry and Energy, has spoken in similar terms to the local American Chamber of Commerce (Nho, 1999): 'In the past, companies reaped high profits at times when there was a business upturn but the losses they incurred when business was poor were compensated for by bailouts from creditor banks or with taxpayers' money. The latter practice will no longer be tolerated.'

Things have indeed changed. Prior to the crisis, Korea tightly controlled FDI in order to exclude foreign control. Since the crisis, FDI has been permitted and mergers and acquisitions involving local firms formally encouraged. Restrictions on the foreign ownership of land have been removed, as have those on the establishment of foreign banks and financial institutions. Further, new legislation requires all Korean companies to adopt international accounting standards and the *chaebol* must steadily reduce intragroup debt guarantees among their many affiliates.

Overall, given the severity of Korea's worst economic crisis in modern times and taking political and economic policy responses to this crisis together, Korea's recovery has to be regarded positively. More than in the countries of Southeast Asia, Korea's crisis was home grown and required a domestic cure. Firmly backed by Washington and supported by the IMF, the incoming administration of Kim Dae-jung proved up to this challenge and quickly stabilized the situation. Of course, not all is yet cured and the country's economic health is not yet robust. In particular, corporate restructuring by the larger *chaebol* and debt reduction by smaller *chaebol* are being delayed by vested interests. The professionalism of the financial sector also requires upgrading to equip it for international standard credit analysis and lending practices (Beck, 2000). Nonetheless, Korea now ranks seventh in the world in spending per capita on R&D and is in the top ten in patent registration. It also has the most liberalized telecom sector in Asia. Samsung is one of the world's largest producers of chips and IT now makes up 8 per cent of the national economy; a more dynamic, smaller-scale, digital economy is rising alongside the old (Bremmer and Moon, 2000).

There are even a few hints of change in Indonesia. In June 1999, the Director General of the Indonesian Ministry of Forestry and Plantations publicly spoke out against 'corruption, collusion or nepotism' (Praginanto, 1999b). No Indonesian Minister could possibly have made such a statement and kept his job three years ago. Moreover this was done while commenting on his ministry's decision to revoke eight forestry concessions; seven of which were controlled by Soeharto's children or his long time golf buddy Bob Hasan. Such open reference to insider and crony deals is probably a necessary first step in moving away from such practices. Somewhat similarly, an influential former Director of the Jakarta Stock Exchange, Felia Salim, is quoted as saying (Vatikiotis, 1999): 'What we need is to improve the credibility of our own institutions, not bring in IMF auditors.'

However, institution-building takes time. In the aftermath of crisis, innovations such as modern bankruptcy courts can be brought into existence quite quickly but only time can give these new institutions the respect and moral authority required to change customary business habits. As illustrated above, there are signs that changes have begun to occur. On the other hand, it is scarcely realistic to expect dramatic changes in business habits to come about quickly. This becomes self-evident when we look more carefully at the KKK question, that is, cronyism, collusion and corruption.

There are two reasons for looking into this matter. First, it is widely seen to be a significant feature of the East Asian business scene and one which significantly adds to the costs of doing business in the region. Second, the crisis has exposed some of the inherent negatives of cronyism and may yet result in its diminution. Most larger businesses are now having to adjust to a situation in which some pre-crisis habits of both government and business are being openly questioned and government and business are coming under some pressure to change, within and beyond the crisis economies themselves. This is especially so with respect to the three crisis economies which came under IMF supervision: Thailand, Indonesia and South Korea.

There are many examples of crony-style government–business relationships in East Asia. Indonesia under ex-President Soeharto offers many of the best known examples. The impact of the crisis has been to accelerate political change in Indonesia and to weaken the residual business influence of former President Soeharto, his family and friends. However, the region also includes examples of unhealthily intimate government–business relationships which are themselves direct consequences of the crisis. So the overall picture is mixed. Some post-crisis cosy deals include recent purchases by Petronas, Malaysia's state-owned, cash-rich, oil and gas monopoly. In 1998, Petronas bailed out Malaysia International Shipping through a $1.5 billion increase in its equity stake, at the same time spending a further $220 million to buy 11 tankers from an associated company, Konsortium Perkapalan, controlled by Mirzan Mahatir, a son of the Prime Minister. Other Petronas purchases, unrelated to its core businesses, include the 1998 purchase of $272 million of unsecured, low-interest bonds issued by a public housing developer. Another may be the purchase of the remaining state interest in Proton, the national car company. Rumour is that Petronas is being called upon to pay US$263 million for a 27 per cent stake (Balfour, 2000). If this eventuates, Petronas executives are said to want to resell Proton as soon as it becomes politically permissible to do so (Shari, 1999b). It is important to add, however, that Petronas, is state-owned.

Classic crony relationships involve private-sector companies or individuals rather than SOEs. Cronyism is usually said to exist when the former enjoy specially favoured treatment by government and government-controlled interests. Patronage of this kind is visible in post-crisis Indonesia. For example, in June 1998, less than a month after Soeharto's resignation, the former Head of Pertamina, the state-owned oil and gas monopoly, announced that 159 contracts which had been awarded to well-connected companies contained clauses detrimental to his company; there had been no competitive bidding so Pertamina had been forced to settle for costly deals (Praginanto, 1999a). Some of these contracts have since been revoked.

Evidence of Indonesian ambivalence about abandoning crony relationships may be gained from the short history of Indonesia's Bank Restructuring Agency (IBRA), which was created under IMF tutelage in January 1998. Bank Bali was one of many bankrupt banks to pass under IBRA control. In July 1999, Standard Chartered Bank performed due diligence on Bank Bali with a view to purchasing a 20 per cent stake. In the process, they identified $80 million which had mysteriously gone missing. It emerged that this money went to a company owned by a senior official of the then President Habibie's ruling Golkar party. When these facts became public knowledge IBRA reluctantly admitted they knew of the payment which they chose to call a debt collection fee. However, if so, this was a 60 per cent fee for collection of debt already guaranteed by the Indonesian government itself! This curious affair is not an isolated example. There are plenty of other suggestions of cosy relationships in high places, including IBRA. One is evidence that Bank

Indonesia bent its own rules to save seven banks which should have been closed down in March 1999 under the bank restructuring programme. One of the beneficiaries was Bank Nusa Nasional (BNN), owned by the Bakrie family, probably the country's leading *pribumi* industrialists, one of whose members was as the time sitting on President Habibie's board of economic advisers and who was also a close associate of the then economics minister. According to the rules, banks with a capital adequacy of less than –25 per cent were to be closed; BNN had a capital adequacy of –210 per cent yet was allowed to survive (Dodd, 1999a,b,c). According to the press (Murphy, 1999a), a report prepared for Bank Indonesia by McKinsey's showed that in February the government had determined that 45 banks, including BNN, were too sick to save. The then President Habibie intervened at the last minute and only 38 were liquidated; seven others, including BNN, were nationalized instead. The official explanation was that closing them would disrupt the payments system but IBRA officials are said to admit it was due to the owners' ferocious lobbying.

Evidence of business as usual, pre-crisis style, is not limited to the banking sector. Recently, the Indonesian government together with a group of leading foreign banks halted bankruptcy proceedings against Semen Cibinong, the listed cement company of the Tirtamas Group. In restructuring negotiations the company had claimed to possess $234 million in cash. Then at a meeting with creditors at which this cash was to be used as collateral for a new loan, the Group Chairman declared it was no longer there. The company did not explain this about-face (Thoenes, 1999). The Chairman of the Tirtamas Group is the brother of a son-in-law of former President Soeharto.

The impact of the crisis on cronyism across the region is hard to assess. As the above instances illustrate, not all the documented evidence points in the same direction; nor is the balance the same across countries. Yet, it can safely be said that the crisis has made a difference. This is manifest in a formal sense in the small-print of the Letters of Intent and various Memoranda of Economic Policies to the IMF from the governments of those countries it is directly assisting, for example:

- Thailand Letter of Intent and Memorandum on Economic Policies — 14 Aug 1997
- Korean IMF Stand-By arrangement — 5 Dec 1997
- Indonesian Memorandum of Economic and Financial Policies — 15 Jan 1998

These formal documents contain plural references to the desirability of improving transparency, corporate disclosure and the need to apply uniform and transparent criteria across institutions.

Within the countries themselves, the best evidence of post-crisis changes may well be public debate about the need for change, transparency, openness and fairness. These features are all noticeably absent from economies in which cronyism, nepotism and corruption are prominent. In this view, public statements calling for greater transparency in business affairs strongly suggest the direction of change is towards openness. What follows is an indicative selection of relevant statements from the three countries receiving IMF support.

At the time the crisis broke, Thailand had a council of experts working on a new draft constitution. One of these was the Dean of Chulalongkorn University. He has written as follows (Eng, 1997): 'Political reform would benefit businessmen who are prepared to compete in a fair manner instead of by connections with politicians. The draft constitution contains numerous mechanisms, ... These mechanisms would arm businessmen to combat nepotism and corruption.'

Illustrative of the character of public debate in the years since, is a headline in the *Bangkok Post* of 3 May 1999 which read: 'Bucking the system of patronage: trying to stay free from both political influence and the need to pay homage to those in higher office has its price.'

A slightly sharper change, made possible by more dramatic political developments, has occurred in Indonesia. Shortly before the crisis, the front cover of *Business Week* (16 June 1997) posed the question whether an economy built on 'cronyism, monopolies and one-man rule' could survive. That was at the time when Indonesia's famous corrupt customs service, under a Director General married to one of then President Soeharto's relatives, was getting its job back after 12 years during which customs operations were contracted out to the Swiss firm SGS (Shari, 1997). The aftermath of the 1997 crisis has helped answer that front-cover question. Within two years, the personal fortune of the 'one man' was being publicly probed, his younger son Tommy had been indicted on 43 counts of fraud, and a large number of his family's hitherto privileged businesses were publicly listed among the country's 200 top debtors. We could also read in the country's largest circulation English-language business magazine that, 'Hostility toward the conglomerates is heightened by the fact that despite their sound skill, many of their businesses are built on collusion and nepotism with former President Soeharto, who, in return, gave them business protection in the form of monopoly and exclusive rights' (Hakim, 1999).

By implication, such arrangements are no longer considered acceptable. Indeed, the government has proposed anti-monoploy and unfair business practice legislation. If such legislations were to be introduced and enforced, it would represent the most striking move away from the pre-crisis past.

Similar changes in attitude towards cronyism and corruption have come to South Korea. There, as in Indonesia, political developments reinforced these changes but whereas in Indonesia the economic crisis came first and precipitated political change; in Korea, a scheduled Presidential election and normal constitutional change just happened to coincide with the crisis. The importance of this coincidence of timing is hard to overstate. The outcome is a reform-minded President who is free of political debt to the existing financial and corporate power structure. This has created a political climate in which criticism and, more importantly action, against cronyism, non-transparency and corruption is more acceptable than at any time in the recent past.

It is scarcely necessary to demonstrate the endemic nature of commercial corruption and government–business collusion in pre-crisis Korea. It suffices to state that according to TI, in 2000, Korea was ranked forty-third among 85 countries in its league table; on a par with Zimbabwe. This figure represents a level of corruption far greater than most of its competitors in the region, including Japan (25th) and Taiwan (29th). Indeed, in 1993 the Daewoo Economic Research Institute estimated that: 'By 1992 nearly one-third of corporate profits were being doled out as bribes and other payments to unaccountable bureaucrats and politicians.'

What has now changed is that the Korean government publicly aspires to a major reduction in corruption and, encouraged by a small $345 grant from the World Bank, is actively seeking to develop ways of achieving this. Indeed, the government has set the target of rising to twentieth place on TI's ranking by the year 2003. The World Bank's role has been to fund the establishment of the government's anti-corruption scheme. However, it is the crisis which has directly forced serious attention on the corruption issue by requiring government and business, alike, to focus on making Korea attractive to foreign investors.

The outcome has been a package of anti-corruption measures. The Minister in the Premier's Office responsible for administrative coordination, Chung Hai-joo, who launched the package, spoke as follows: 'In the past, the government's anti-corruption steps were focused on unearthing irregularities by officials and punishing them. However, the new schemes are designed to create an infrastructure to eradicate the root causes of corruption and pave the way for citizens to take part in the efforts as monitors.'

According to official figures, the number of civil servants charged with corruption quadrupled between 1991 and 1998. In 1999, more than 7000 government employees were disciplined for bribery, including one low-echelon official who proved to be a multimillionaire (Shin, 1999). In addition, there were 12 elected representatives facing corruption charges and no less than 13 per cent of 248 elected local administration heads had been convicted in Court of abuse of power, or, were awaiting verdicts on such charges. Moreover, in the elections of 2000, the National Election Committee posted the names of candidates with criminal records on its website. According to the Committee, nearly 15 per cent of the 1170 candidates had served jail sentences for serious crimes (Veale, 2000).

The post-crisis Korean reform package views corruption as a combination of government–business collusion, excessive indulgence in entertainment, non-transparent corporate accounting, unrealistic administrative red tape and low pay for government employees. In other words, the problem lies in the political system rather than with moral lapses by individuals. So the package is aimed at structural and systematic elimination of corruption through a solid legal foundation, administrative reform, and equal punishment for bribe-givers and bribe-takers (Kim, 1999). One of the problems of implementation may be a possible clash between the anti-corruption drive and long-standing tradition. According to Chung Young-kug, a researcher at the Academy of Korean Studies: 'It would be quite difficult to tell a bribe from an expression of simple gratitude, which is quite common in Korea's tradition and culture.'

However, an even more serious problem may be public indifference. A 1999 Gallup poll indicated that 72.4 per cent of respondents were highly cynical of the government on the issue. It follows from the foregoing that in addition to formal legal and institutional consequences of the crisis, there is also some identifiable movement on cronyism, collusion and corruption in all three countries examined. Moreover the clear direction of this movement is against corruption, in favour of more open, transparent and law-based behaviour. The magnitude of this change, however, will take time to be discernible.

Consequences for the developmental state

Post-crisis soul searching in the affected economies has not been limited to reassessment of cronyism. In fact, it has embraced most aspects of economic life, including core attitudes towards the role of government in industrialization and even extending to the organizational underpinnings of the Asian model of development, the philosophical underpinning of the Japan-inspired developmental state. Although events since 1997 have influenced both elite and popular opinion, the focus here is on elite opinion, that is, the opinions of those currently in a position to initiate and mould political and economic change.

In the words of Sihasak Phuangketkeow (1998), Director of the Policy and Planning Division of Thailand's Ministry of Foreign Affairs: 'The crisis has been a wake up call. It has generated public support for, and awareness of, the need for both political and economic reforms, which had been lacking before. It has made us realize that in a global economy and in a globalized world, the way we have conducted the affairs of business and government left much to be expected. Moreover, the crisis has given us the opportunity to take a long hard look at the concept of economic development ... I am pleased to note that nowadays the words "good governance, transparency and accountability" lie at the heart of our economic and political reform efforts.'

A few early consequences of this kind of attitudinal change can be identified. One is an increase in the activities and effectiveness of the Bank of Thailand. In July 1999, a government-appointed panel reporting on the collapse of the Thai currency two years earlier, described Bank decision-makers as 'completely useless' (Reuters). Then, two years later, Assistant Governor Kiatisak Meecharoen said the Bank was examining how a devaluation of the Chinese yuan would affect the other economies in the region and was drawing up an emergency plan to protect the baht in such an event. This contingency planning indicates greatly enhanced organizational effectiveness. However, Thailand's bureaucracy has long been regarded as dysfunctional and as the Bangkok Head of US law firm Baker & McKenzie, Kitipong Urapeepatanapong, has said (Engardio, 1998): 'Changing the laws doesn't mean attitudes will change overnight'.

The claim being made here, though, is that attitudes are indeed changing, or, at least beginning to change. Moreover this change is in quite basic attitudes such as that towards what in the West is termed corruption. The author is encouraged in this view by statements such as the following by Bank of Asia Chairman, Chavalit Thanachanan: '... Thailand was now having to search for honest, hard-working and capable people to replace the corrupt civil servants and politicians who had contributed so much to the country's downturn.'

Moreover the influence of such opinion is strengthened by the fact that pessimists, who hold contrary views, recognize the dire consequences of their judgement. One such is Amaret Sila-On, Chairman of Thailand's Financial Sector Reconstructing Authority (Suzuoki, 1999). Speaking in Hong Kong on 26 May 1999 he said: 'If the rule of law still remains weaker than the rule of men, Thai banks will return to their old ways despite restructuring efforts. Banks may be recapitalized and there may be new management, but the social norms may still be the same. In that case, another crisis will be inevitable.'

The message of such a statement from someone with such a critically important responsibility is that there are now members of the establishment pushing for basic changes in social, bureaucratic and business behaviour. This is new. It is, moreover, a direct consequence of the crisis and it is regionwide.

Indonesian Minister for Economy and Finance, Ginandjar Kartasasmita, made equally relevant observations. His advice to the bureaucrats of his country, who had no prior experience of a change of regime, was to switch to a neutral mentality and to abandon their obsessive loyalty to the ruling Golkar party. When asked what should be done, the Minister replied: 'More transparency, accountability and better governance' (Murphy, 1999b). Of course, there are cynical voices in Indonesia too. Former ministers Elim Salim and Mohamad Samli have echoed Sila-On's comments saying: 'You can make beautiful rules but old habits die hard'. This is pertinent to corruption. The obvious fact in Indonesia, as in some other parts of the region, is that many bureaucrats are dependent upon unofficial payments to survive. Moreover, the culture of corruption is embedded in the civil service through patronage networks and personal loyalties, making it unlikely that real change will come quickly (McBeth, 1999). Small wonder, then, that the World Bank has warned that Indonesia needs a 'vigilant, skilled and effective bank supervision system' (Murphy, 1999a), and that the IMF has asked the President to commit the government to a full and open investigation of the Bank Bali scandal (Dodd, 1999b). Perhaps a realistic assessment, given Indonesia's relatively low living standards and low pay, is that the country will prove a regional laggard in raising standards of public propriety and accountability.

For the immediate future, little can be said about economic prospects except to note that the country directly benefits from the currently high international oil price. Beyond that, it is necessary to make explicit reference to the high level of political risk involved in any commercial assessment involving Indonesia and to pinpoint the urgent need, right across the archipelago, to reduce the level of social tension and unrest. For the moment, issues of personal security and institutional predictability have to be factored into any significant international contract. New business growth requires, in the shortest feasible time, establishment of the rule of law, to make risk manageable, and establishment of predictable, trustworthy institutions, to fill the void which currently exists. When this might happen is impossible to predict.

South Korea is totally different. Reform in Korea is not being driven by outside pressures so much as 'a deep desire among the grass roots for greater openness and for the adoption of global standards' (Larsson, 1999). Furthermore, this desire is shared at the top. The President, Kim Dae-jung, has publicly called on the *chaebol* to scrap their inefficient centralized and paternalistic management style and to pursue business specialization. This view parallels that of outside observers who comment on the desirability of change: 'Korea needs a new model of corporate behaviour. Corporate thinking has to change, the ways banks interact with corporations has to change, the way the government interacts with the banks has to change' (John Dodsworth, then IMF representative in Seoul).

Although not always put so simply, the same message can be heard from many Koreans. For example, Lee Ki-ho, chief economic advisor to President Kim, says '*chaebol* control of the financial sector must be checked and so-called "circular cross-unit equity investments" banned' (Chon, 1999). At the present time, the top five *chaebol* own 39 non-bank financial institutions. Further, the government's Financial Industry Development Committee has argued for tougher regulations on *chaebol*-affiliated investment trust companies and insurance firms to prevent them from using customers' money to assist their affiliated firms (Sim, 1999).

The foregoing is but a detail of the contemporary debate in East Asia about corruption and the future economic role of government. It is brief and offers no more than insight. It cannot be either representative or balanced; it is not even intended to be so. Its purpose is merely to demonstrate that such a debate is taking place and that its participants include individuals in powerful official positions and other influential members of the elite.

This questioning of the status quo ante, which is directly attributable to the crisis, has had a ripple effect. Rising doubts about particular factors, such as inadequate prudential supervision of banks and non-consolidation of corporate accounts, has resulted in wider questions being raised. As indicated above, the whole panoply of East Asian government–business relationships is now under critical scrutiny in East and West alike (Lee, 1998; Lohr, 1998). Indeed, the very concept of the developmental state, long criticised in the West, is now coming under review in the East, not least in Japan, as never before (Bhaskaran, 1998; Fujita, 1999).

One core dimension of the developmental state has been industry policy. With the partial exceptions of The Philippines and Hong Kong, the governments of all the crisis economies, like Japan before them, have had active industry policies to accelerate and to direct their industrialization and development. South Korea is the classic Tiger economy. There, more than elsewhere, we can point with confidence to a government which has played a decisive role as initiator, promoter and master of the industrialization process (Amsden, 1989). The Southeast-Asian countries have employed far less comprehensive and less prescriptive industry policy practices and, unlike Korea, have actively courted FDI. In all cases, however, it is the judgement of this author that it is primarily the mechanism of industry policy, rather than primacy of the development role of government as such, which is being criticized. Acceptance of a major role for government in the industrialization and growth process, outside South Korea at least, remains largely undiminished. So, while industry policy is currently being reassessed at both a practical level and in principle, the outcome of this reassessment is likely in the end to be a totally pragmatic response to changed circumstances. The policy priority of industrialization and growth will essentially remain, but there will be increased recognition that the means to this end will probably have to change. It is therefore most likely that new industry policy mechanisms, compatible with WTO norms and the new international trading environment, will be devised and adopted.

So where does this leave the Asian model of development? Already in September 1997, just two months after the crisis broke in Thailand and even before South Korea finally succumbed in December of that year, the leading editorial article of *Business Week* (1 September 1997: 60) displayed the heading: 'Asia needs a new economic model'. It concluded that: 'It is time for Japan and Asia to shift their economic model.' Again, at the end of the year, in a much less superficial editorial, *The Economist* (20 December 1997: 15) asked the question: 'Has the "Asian model" gone wrong?' The conclusion this time was: 'The economies in difficulty do not share anything that can be sensibly described as an "Asian model", still less an ideology'. So we should first perhaps acknowledge that this so-called model has never been very exactly defined (Fujita, 1999). Nevertheless, the widespread acceptance of its existence must also be acknowledged. Interestingly, former President Lee Teng-hui of Taiwan, an economy which today enjoys a higher per capita income than anywhere else in East Asia except for Japan and the cities of Singapore and Hong Kong, told a journalist (Eguchi, 1999) that: 'One of the key reasons for Taiwan's development was that it had a superb teacher in Japan'.

The President of Japan International Cooperation Agency, Kimio Fujita (1999), has taken a more aggressive stand on the issue and in doing so raised a critical question seldom asked outside the region: 'The principles of the Japanese economic model have been successful in many countries in East Asia . . . , and no one in Asia is blaming these principles for the current economic difficulties they are facing . . . Have there been any successful cases of the American model transplanted to the developing world?'

A short chapter is not the best place to pursue this rather philosophical debate, which is more fully explored elsewhere (Wade, 1998); the debate nonetheless informs the brief comments which follow. Japan is the source, inspiration and model of the broad approach to industrialization adopted by East Asian societies during recent decades. Yet, Japan itself no longer displays such great confidence in its own model. Kan Naota, one of the country's more popular politicians, recently said: 'Japan is at a dead end . . .'. More relevantly to business, Miyoshi Toshio, Chairman of Matsushita, somewhat similarly said (McCormack, 1999): 'The old ways that delivered Japan to the status of economic superpower are failing us; they are even working against us'. This judgement is shared by another of Japan's most internationally minded business leaders, Yotaro Kobayashi, Chairman of Fuji Xerox, who has said (Lloyd-Owen, 1999): 'I think Professor Yasuo Takeuchi got it right in his book "The End of Japan" in which he described Japanese capitalism as not really capitalism in its pure form.'

In practical terms, it is easy to see that a Japan in which lifetime employment and promotion by seniority are being cut back, cross-shareholdings wound down and anti-competitive laws and regulations weakened, is coming a little bit closer to the pattern of corporate governance familiar in the West. There is plenty of evidence. Japanese companies are closing their subsidiaries at a record rate. *The Nikkei Weekly* editorial of 11 January 1999 stated: 'The traditional pillars of Japan's economic strength are now doing the most harm to the economy . . .'. A researcher at Japan's National Institute for Research Advancement (Cornell, 1999) has said: 'Japan's policy-making system seems to have reached the limits of usefulness.' Such sentiments are indicative of vigorous, open and highly critical debate. This intellectual turmoil and reduced self-confidence is being carefully noted throughout the region.

Even Malaysia's Prime Minister, Dr Mahathir, a long-term disciple of the Japanese development model, has written (Mahathir, 1999) 'It seems that Japan wants to do away with government/private sector cooperation which has been dubbed "Japan Incorporated" by the West and to replace it quite suddenly with the "so-called" Western concept of separation between government and the private sector.' The debate within Japan will most certainly influence the reassessment of the 'Asian model' currently taking place across the region.

So, what are the other countries of the region actually doing? Given that energies remain concentrated on getting over the shock and hangover of the 1997–98 crisis and the re-establishment of growth and prosperity, the most common answer is to accept the need for deep reforms of both financial supervision and corporate governance and to work hard at improvement despite difficulties of implementation. Leaving financial institutions on one side, this requires the corporate sector to face elements of liberalization and deregulation at home plus liberalization of FDI from abroad. For those countries still influenced by the IMF and World Bank, at least, it also involves a new and genuine concern about the business impact of cronyism, collusion and corruption. These concerns, alone, even if not yet translated into political or legal action, represent a very substantial modernization. They may also indicate one direction of future change.

In Japan itself, the worst elements of the Asian model now lie exposed. Hitherto hidden mountains of debt and corruption have slowly emerged into view and, in response, changes have even more slowly been introduced by government and business. Korea is somewhat similar but the government there is more proactive. Thailand and Indonesia are different in character, with less state emphasis on productivity and greater acceptance of private patronage, but comparable problems are being handled from a broadly similar perspective albeit in a rather less decisive way. Some of the remaining economies differ significantly in their responses. Malaysia seems to be reforming its financial sector with some vigour while maintaining existing crony corporate networks intact (Shari, 1999a). The Philippines under President Estrada is taking a step backwards with the business community there increasingly worried about renewed growth in influence-peddling (Tiglao, 1999). Singapore and Hong Kong may for the moment be going in opposite directions. Singapore's government is delicately relaxing some of its controls on business, hoping thereby to sharpen the international competitiveness of its domestic enterprises. For example, a planned deregulation of the telecom sector was brought forward by two years early in 2000, to start on 1 April that year, rather than two years later. At about the same time, the Monetary Authority of Singapore lifted the 49 per cent limit on foreign ownership of local insurers, thereby allowing free entry of direct insurers and brokers into the market for the first time (Richardson, 2000). Meanwhile, Hong Kong is formulating new industry policy and intervening in the economy more than in the past in order to foster high-tech enterprise; even to the extent of awarding one $1.7 billion contract for a cyberport to a favoured son without going through a proper tender process. Indeed, the contractors for another major contract, to establish a Hong Kong Disneyland, are also said to have been selected without full competition (Chong, 2000; Dwyer, 2000).

So, overall, there are clear signs that there may eventually be broadly based institutional reform and policy adjustment across the region; even if not quite everywhere and even if differences between countries remain. Interestingly, Singapore's Prime Minister told the Asia Society in Sydney (Hiscock, 1999), that differing willingness between countries to make changes may later result in a two speed Asia. In most regional economies, however, there is now likely to be a steady unbundling of pre-crisis government–bureaucracy–banking–business relationships in order to increase efficiency and to achieve increased transparency, beginning with Western-style prudential and accounting standards, through WTO-compatible economic development and industry policies, to a much less pervasive and much less costly level of corruption. Of course, such substantial changes are as much political and social as they are narrowly economic and commercial, so they cannot possibly come about quickly. They can nonetheless begin. In some years, time, with hindsight, it should cause no surprise if Asia's 1997 crisis proves to have been a catalyst for change and a formative influence on the development of Asian capitalism.

Culture's consequence . . . ?

At the formal and institutional level, both the practical and the intellectual consequences of the crisis have been commented upon already. Before drawing conclusions, however, it is advisable to take a reality check by explicitly acknowledging the human, cultural dimension. This is attempted only in a summary, illustrative way.

As we have seen, the financial and corporate consequences across the region are broadly comparable and, overall, the region's responses to grossly excessive debt represent an observable step towards Western-style accounting, procedural transparency, and towards making profitability, the business priority. To this generalization, however, must be added the practical constraint of deeply entrenched social custom. The power of such factors can be illustrated by the family feud involving control of Hyundai Motor (Oh, 1999). The story begins in 1998 when the 84-year-old founder, Chung Ju-yung, undertook a groupwide reorganization. As a result, the founder's eldest son emerged as heir apparent. However, the founder's respected younger brother, who had himself largely created the company's position as a car maker, had his own plans and he derailed the reorganization. What is revealing is how this key *chaebol* power struggle was then resolved. The founder and elder brother simply called in his younger sibling, told him his plot had been foiled and that he was to give up. He did! He followed up with a press conference at which he cried and renounced all management control. As a result, Hyundai followed classic patrimonial, hereditary and lineal succession from father to son. As the episode illustrates, while some convergence between Eastern and Western business practice may be occurring in response to the crisis, differences of style reflecting deep-seated cultural tradition, nonetheless remain.

Intriguingly, the Hyundai family saga moved beyond these events and took a decidedly more modern turn. Although family rivalry continued, maintaining instability at the top of the Hyundai businesses, it was government and a group of creditors which really brought about change. By 2000, there were open calls for the 85-year-old patriarch to relinquish all his managerial rights in the group. Many believed that his removal would show the world that Korea's corporate governance had reached the level of Western countries (Oh, 2000). When the old man did finally retire, on 31 May 2000, he also announced the effective retirement of the two rival sons with him, leaving the Hyundai Group apparently able to hire outside professional managers, including foreigners, for the first time.

Another consequence of crisis sometimes regarded as cultural in character, is subtle change in political attitudes towards the Asian model of development. Established regional attitudes on this issue have certainly been challenged by the crisis and its consequences. This has come about, in part, because the model offered few obvious answers to immediate post-crisis needs, and partly because the model is now under strong challenge in its country of origin. While it is the political and institutional dimensions of Asian capitalism which attract most interest in the West, it is particular mechanisms of industry policy which are most under scrutiny within the region. Policy mechanisms like government-directed policy loans in Korea and tariff protection of national projects in Malaysia and Indonesia, are clearly falling out of general favour. At the same time, the objective of the model, which is to help governments achieve rapid economic growth, remains as central as ever to East Asian politicians and bureaucrats. So do its cohesive social underpinnings in those societies characterized by intimate government–business relationships. For example, many societies in the region cultivate gift giving of a style hard for Westerners to distinguish from graft. In these societies, winning contracts may often require gifts and dealing with officialdom and may often require unofficial payments to ensure that goods or documents do not go astray. Where such occurrences are merely goodwill gestures, rising living standards and changes in traditional attitudes may eventually cause such customs to fade away. Where such occurrences are necessary to maintain recipients' standard of living, they are most unlikely to fade away. So differences between East and West and also within the East Asian region will remain.

Conclusions

The clearest conclusion, to date, is that some convergence in financial supervision and corporate governance, and some diminution in the distinctiveness of Asian capitalism, is occurring. These changes are direct consequences of the Asian crisis. They are partial, gradual and long-term in nature. They are, however, likely to endure. Yet, they are also likely to remain powerfully constrained, in some of the countries of the region, by customary social and business convention.

A second conclusion is that the character of the business environment, across the region, has been permanently changed by the crisis and its aftermath. The confident complacency within and about the region which was characteristic before the crisis, especially on the part of the global financial sector, is history. Today, within and beyond the region alike, there is for the first time an acceptance of informed analysis and an expectation of demanding scrutiny. Countries, industries and individual firms are all under the microscope; not least by overseas investors who react negatively to opaque, unconsolidated accounts and non-transparent transactions. Put simply, the facile generalization and benign acceptance of pre-crisis years have been replaced by serious-minded analysis and a new attention to detail.

Of course overall, the business environment in the economies of East Asia is largely determined by rates of economic growth, the buoyancy of domestic demand and the international competitiveness and global appeal of national output. However, the crisis has emphasized the need for prudential supervision, modern institutional processes and the rule of law. This has brought individual country differences to the fore. These differences are now seen to be critically important. In consequence, the contemporary commercial appeal of each country is essentially driven by the combined effect of two factors. One is the country's attractiveness to domestic and foreign investors which, in turn, reflects the competence and depth of that country's post-crisis reform and reconstruction; the other is the price and availability of capital and other business inputs, which, itself, is also a reflection of the competence and depth of post-crisis reform and reconstruction. So throughout the region, irrespective of how deeply a particular economy was affected, today's business environment is very much a function of the local response to the events of 1997–98. This is as true of Singapore, which was less affected, as of Malaysia, which was more affected. From a global perspective, moreover, it is important to recognize that for investors and businesses from elsewhere in the world, all of East Asia appears much riskier than before. The pre-crisis trust and confidence, or, hubris, has been broken by events and will not easily return.

In terms of economic fundamentals, Indonesia obviously excepted, most crisis economies today are in many respects as soundly based as they have ever been. In addition, more is known about these economies and their commercial enterprises than ever before. However, perceptions of risk have irreversibly changed, as have standards of what is acceptable. To attract FDI, for example, more is expected of a host country's legal system, its supervision of financial institutions, and the accounting probity of potential partner firms, than was the case in 1997. It is an altogether different world now. This change is best understood with reference to detail in specific countries.

In Thailand, for example, corruption among bureaucrats remains rife, with many officials still demanding unofficial payments. In 2000, one survey by a Thai business chamber found that 75 per cent of its members still paid bribes to government officials to speed up export procedures and investment applications. (Cheeseman, 2000a). A senior bureaucrat may still pay 20 million baht for his job but expect to recover this outlay many times over (Alford, 2000).

Indonesia, as we have already noted, is hobbled by political tension. The country's instability means, for example, that its privatization programme, which was scheduled to raise up to a US$1 billion in 2000, is in trouble due to the country's poor reputation among investors.

Indonesian Finance Minister, Prijadi Praptosuhardjo, has publicly admitted that 'plans to privatize seven state-owned companies by the end of the year would be hard' (Dodd, 2000). In September 2000, former Minister of Investment and State Enterprises, Laksamana Sukardi, went further saying: 'If I were an investor, I would not do business in Indonesia' (Praginanto, 2000b).

In South Korea, the government declared Daewoo Group insolvent in July 1999. Yet at the time of writing, September 2000, not one of twelve key Daewoo companies has been closed down or sold to a foreign bidder. None of the 12 has put in place the financial structure which would enable it to re-emerge as a competitive company. With combined debt of at least US$80 billion, some $26 billion more than their assets, sale of the group is not helped by its reputation for murky accounting (Moon, 2000c).

None of the above issues represents anything new. The issues have characterized the East Asian business environment through 30 years of unprecedented growth. They are old issues, not new ones. But the 1997–98 crisis has given rise to a discontinuity in attitudes and perceptions. While none of the above issues would have had any discernible impact on business decisions pre-crisis, today, post-crisis, they might. Each item of this kind is nowadays given thought, often perceived negatively, and is therefore potentially damaging to the economy. For investors and businesses from elsewhere in the world, East Asia simply does not look the same.

Yet at the same time, for those in a position to assess risk and for those with sufficient resources to sustain risk, the fundamentals are positive and speak for themselves. The rebound from crisis has been rapid and vigorous. Domestic businesses can derive optimism from strong recovery in local employment and domestic household expenditure. Although public expenditure in some countries is at non-sustainable levels, abrupt changes are not necessary. So, a lot of local businesses will continue to be able to ride the continuing recovery. Although restructuring remains incomplete in all the most affected economies and although further progress will encounter problems, the broad picture for the region's business is positive. Cyclical factors aside, for so long as the region's export industries can continue to expand into the global market place, this is likely to remain the case.

For overseas firms, there are further grounds for optimism, like before the crisis, the region offers above-average economic growth, high savings rates, high investment rates, responsible budgets and lots of commercial dynamism. In addition, since the crisis, balance of payments weaknesses have been overcome and foreign reserves replenished. Exports have boomed and FDI has begun to recover. So, while competition may be greater for some than before the crisis, in many countries of the region, most other risks are less.

There is, however, one important caveat. We do need to note that the potentially destabilizing influence of unregulated investment funds remains unchanged since 1997. So renewed financial sector-led instability cannot be excluded.

In summary, commercial prospects in East Asia are again generally bright. New factors for business to consider are an enhanced need for local knowledge and a greater need for close and continuous monitoring. Compared with the pre-crisis past, differences between countries are more important, industry structures in the modern sectors are more fluid and competitive, and risk of global financial market instability seems to be with us to stay.

References

Alford, P. (2000) 'Thai time-servers buy plum jobs', *The Australian*, 21 September, Sydney.

Amsden, A. (1989) *Asia's Next Giant: South Korea and Late Industrialisation*, Oxford: Oxford University Press.

Balfour, F. (2000) 'Cronyism: Malaysia still hasn't learned its lesson', *Business Week*, 28 August, p. 19.

Beck, P. (2000) 'Building a New Economy', *The Korea Times*, 24 February, Seoul.

Bhaskaran, M. (1998) 'R&R – Singapore Style', *Far Eastern Economic Review*, 17 December, p. 50.

Biers, D. and M. Vatikiotis (1999) 'Back to school', *Far Eastern Economic Review*, 8 April, pp. 10–14.

Brancato, C. K. (1999) 'Building on sand', *Asian Business*, August, p. 9.

Bremmer, B. and I. Moon (2000) 'Korea's digital quest', *Business Week*, 25 September, pp. 20–5.

Burton, J. (1999a) 'Union backs Daewoo break-up', *Financial Times*, 10 August.

Burton J. (1999b) 'Creditors to dismantle Daewoo', *Financial Times*, 17 August.

Burton, J. (2000) 'Probe into South Korea illegal trading', *Financial Times*, 21 September.

Business Week (1997) 'Asia needs a new economic model', Editorial, 1 September, p. 60.

Chang, Yu Sang (1999) 'Facing crisis with solid planning', *Asia 21*, July, pp. 28–9.

Cheeseman, B. (2000a) 'Foreign investors lose patience with Thais', *The Australian Financial Review*, 4 September.

Cheeseman, B. (2000b) 'Thai bank in defence mode', *The Australian Financial Review*, 25 September, p. 5

Chon Shi-yong (1999) 'President summons *chaebol* leaders to meeting to urge corporate reform', *The Korea Herald*, 19 August.

Chong, F. (2000) 'HK clean but China looms as a polluter', *The Australian*, 2 February, p. 28.
Clifford, M. (1999) 'Daewoo boss is playing a dangerous game', *Business Week*, 16 August, p. 18.
Cornell, A. (1999) 'Policy adviser slates bureaucrats on slow reforms', *The Australian Financial Review*, 10 June, p. 13.
Crampton, T. (1999) 'Thailand 2 years later', *International Herald Tribune*, 26–7 June.
DeFusco, D. (1999) 'Hong Kong businessman says US mishandling Asian economic crisis'. See www.fairfield.edu/whatsnew/press/chan.html
Dodd, T. (1999a) 'Bank Bali's missing $120m generates bribery rumours', *The Australian Financial Review*, 11 August, p. 12.
Dodd, T. (1999b) 'Indonesia hit again by high-level corruption', *The Australian Financial Review*, 13 August, p. 34.
Dodd, T. (1999c) 'IMF demands inquiry into Bank Bali scandal', *The Australian Financial Review*, 18 August, p. 12.
Dodd, T. (2000) 'Instability undercuts Jakarta sell-off plans', *The Australian Financial Review*, 6 September, Sydney, p. 8.
Dwyer, M. (2000) 'HK cyber star is speaking Beijing's language', *The Australian Financial Review*, 22 February, p. 13.
Economist, The (1997) 'Asia and the abyss', Editorial, 20 December, p. 15.
Economist (1999) 'Commanding depths', 24 June, pp. 65–6.
Eguchi, Katsuhiko (1999) 'The road to democracy', *Asia 21*, August.
Eng, P. (1997) 'Redressing thailand's culture of corruption', *Asia Inc.*, July, p. 88.
Engardio, P. (1998) 'Cleaning up Thailand's mess: the long struggle ahead', *Business Week*, 12 October, pp. 51–2.
Fujita, Kimio (1999) 'Intellectual masochism and ethical silence', *Asia 21*, May.
Hakim, A. (1999) 'The end of big business?', *Indonesian Business*, January, pp. 42–3.
Haley, U. C. V. (2000) *Strategic Management in the Asia Pacific: Harnessing Regional and Organizational Change for Competitive Advantage*, Oxford: Butterworth-Heinemann.
Hiscock, G. (1999) 'Make or break for East Asia', *The Weekend Australian*, 17–18 April, p. 54.
Jayasankaran, S. (1999) 'Saving Malaysia Inc.', *Far Eastern Economic Review*, 12 August, pp. 10–13.
Jeong, Byung-seok (1999) 'Corporate governance must be renovated', *The Chosun Ilbo*, 7 April, reproduced in *Korea Focus*, 7(3) (May – June): 134–6, Korea Foundation, Seoul.
Keenan, F. and P. Landers (1999) 'Staggering giants', *Far Eastern Economic Review*, 1 April, pp. 10–14.
Kim, Ji-ho (1999) 'Government launches anticorruption crusade', *The Korea Herald*, 18 August.
Kunii, Irene and Takahashi, Tomoko (1999) 'At last new blood at Japan Inc.', *Business Week*, 8 March, pp. 16–17.
Kwak, Young-sup (1999) '*Chaebol* reform, protection of middle class to top gov't economic agenda', *The Korea Herald*, 15 August.
Kwak, Young-sup (2000) 'Banks set to continue monitoring of *chaebol* debt reduction efforts', *The Korea Herald*, 23 May.
Larkin, J. (1999) 'The bitter pill', *Asian Business*, August, p. 14.

Larkin, J. (2000) 'Lessons Unlearned', *The Far Eastern Economic Review*, 21 September, pp. 64–6.
Larsson, T. (1999) 'Globalization is putting down roots in South Korea', *Asia 21*, July, pp. 14–15.
Lee, C. (1999) 'Saving the body', *Far Eastern Economic Review*, 20 May, p. 42.
Lee, M. (1998) 'Testing Asian values', *New York Times online*, 18 January.
Lee, C. and D. Biers (1998) 'Remaking Korea Inc.', *Far Eastern Economic Review*, 30 April, pp. 10–13.
Lloyd-Owen, J. (1999) 'The end of Japan Inc.?', *Asia 21*, March, pp. 7–9.
Lohr, S. (1998) 'Asian Values may change in wake of economic crisis', *New York Times online*.
MacIntyre, A. (ed.) (1994) *Business and Government in Industrialising Asia*, St Leonards, NSW: Allen & Unwin.
Mahathir, M. Dr. (1999) 'Japanese economic recover tied to Asian prosperity', *The New Straits Times*, 6 July, p. 10.
McBeth, J. (1999) 'Old habits die hard', *Far Eastern Economic Review*, 19 August, p. 22.
McCormack, G. (1999) 'Japan – a question of leadership at home and in the region', *The Asia-Australia Papers*, April, No. 1, pp. 29–35, The Asia-Australia Institute, The University of New South Wales, Sydney.
Mertens, B. (1999) 'Putting back the pieces', *Asian Business*, April, pp. 22–9.
Moon, I., Armstrong, L., Thornton, E. and K. Kerwin (2000a) 'Kicking tires in Seoul', *Business Week*, 24 January, pp. 14–15.
Moon, I. (2000b) 'The next frontier in remaking the *chaebol*', *Business Week*, 17 April, p. 24.
Moon, I. (2000c) 'The crawl of reform', *Business Week*, 4 September, pp. 18–19.
Murphy, D. (1999a) 'New dogs, old tricks', *Far Eastern Economic Review*, 19 August, p. 12.
Murphy, D. (1999b) 'Baptism of fire', *Far Eastern Economic Review*, 19 August, pp. 8–10.
Murphy, D. and B. Dolven (2000) 'Wheeler-dealers', *Far Eastern Economic Review*, 6 April, p. 64.
Nho, Joon-hun (1999) 'Owners, investors to be held accountable for mismanagement', *Internet Korea Times*, 12 August.
Nho, Joon-hun (2000) 'Interbrew's strategy of going local spells success with OB', *Internet Korea Times*, 17 April.
Oh, Young-jin (1999) 'Hyundai family feud shows essence of Asian values', *Internet Korea Times*, 3 August.
Oh, Young-jin (2000) 'Chung Ju-yung vs Western values', *Internet Korea Times*, 30 May.
Phuangketkeow, Sihasak (1999) 'The finance and currency crisis in East Asia: where did business and governments go wrong', *The Asia-Australia Papers*, April, No. 1, pp. 65–9, The Asia-Australia Institute, The University of New South Wales, Sydney.
Praginanto (1999a) 'Indonesia moves to break Pertamina's grip on oil industry', *The Nikkei Weekly*, 5 April, p. 20.
Praginanto (1999b) 'Cleanup planned for corrupt Indonesian timber industry', *The Nikkei Weekly*, 26 July, p. 20.
Praginanto (2000a) 'Indonesia's desperate budget bid', *The Nikkei Weekly*, 18 September, p. 3.

Praginanto (2000b) 'Wahid's foundations under fire', *The Nikkei Weekly*, 25 September, p. 24.
Richardson, M. (2000) 'Singapore opens door to foreign insurers, utilities', *The Australian*, 22 March, p. 29.
Richter, F.-J. (2000) *The East Asian Development Model*, London: Macmillan.
Sen, A. (1997) 'Human rights and Asian values', *The New Republic*, 14 July.
Shari, M. (1997) 'An Indonesian nightmare may soon recur', *Business Week*, 31 March, p. 20.
Shari, M. (1999a) 'Take a good close look at this cleanup', *Business Week*, 5 July, p. 24.
Shari, M. (1999b) 'Turning a cash cow into a beast of burden', *Business Week*, 16 August, p. 20.
Sheridan, Kyoko (1998) *Emerging Economic Systems in Asia*, St Leonards, NSW: Allen & Unwin.
Shimizu, Yasumasa (1999) 'Flat-glass dialogue heats up as US makers cry foul', *The Nikkei Weekly*, 21 June.
Shin, Yong-bae (1999) 'War on corruption to tackle fundamental problems', *The Korea Herald*, 18 August.
Sim, Sung-tae (1999) 'Gov't to ban *chaebol* from using group names for financial subsidiaries', *The Korea Herald*, 19 August.
Suzuoki, Takabumi (1999) 'Economic crisis produces different results across Asia', *The Nikkei Weekly*, 12 July.
Tiglao, Rigoberto (1999) 'Estrada and Co.', *Far Eastern Economic Review*, 12 August, pp. 38–40.
Thoenes, S. (1999) 'Vanishing cash halts debt rescue', *Financial Times*, 12 August.
Vatikiotis, M. (1998) 'Trouble at the mill', *Far Eastern Economic Review*, 28 May, Hong Kong, pp. 60–62.
Vatikiotis, M. (1999) 'Pride and prejudice', *Far Eastern Economic Review*, 5 August, pp. 20–1.
Veale, J. (2000) 'South Korean candidates fret as the net closes in', *The Australian Financial Review*, 10 April, p. 16.
Wade, R. (1998) 'The Asian crisis and capital triumphalism', *Overseas Development Council Commentary*, 19 March. See http://www.odc.org/commentary/rwspeech.html
Whitley, R. (1992) *Business Systems in East Asia*, London: Sage Publications.
Yoo, Cheung-mo (2000) 'Daewoo Motor sale hurt by ebb of GM interest; General Motors says it will not submit a binding offer in the new bidding', *The Korea Herald*, 23 September.

17

Political Risk After the Asian Financial Crisis: A Proposal to Consider the Significance of Uneven Political and Economic Transformation

Michael A. Santoro and Chang-Su Kim

Introduction

The dramatic growth of international capital flows was one of the most remarkable and far-reaching economic phenomena of the late twentieth century. In less than a decade, net capital flows to emerging countries quadrupled – from $50 billion in 1987 to over $200 billion in 1996. The financial crises which swept through Latin America and Asia in the last decade of the century led, however, to reversals of these capital flows – portfolio and banking flows in particular – away from developing countries in these regions. Net capital flows to emerging countries dropped to $148 billion in 1997 and further to $66 billion in 1998, but they are projected to rebound in 2000 (IMF, 1999) (see Tables 17.1 and 17.2). In the longer term, capital flows to developing countries are likely to increase. As the twenty-first century begins, Third World nations will continue to seek foreign investment for their development needs, and financial institutions in rich nations will continue to look for opportunities to diversify their portfolios.

As a result of the harsh commercial and social impacts engendered by the Asian financial crisis, government officials and policy makers from institutions such as the Financial Services Authority of Britain, the Swiss Federal Banking Commission, the US Federal Reserve Bank, the IMF, the World Bank, as well as scholars and pundits have sought to understand the causes and lessons of the crisis. Numerous proposals have been

Table 17.1 Net capital flows[1] to emerging market economies[2] (in US$ billions)

	1991	1992	1993	1994	1995	1996	1997	1998	1999	2000
Net private capital flows	118.1	120.6	176.3	143.4	192.9	213.8	148.8	66.2	68.3	118.5
Net direct investment	31.5	35.3	57.9	84.7	93.0	113.5	142.6	132.4	118.5	128.4
Net portfolio investment	24.7	55.6	98.7	104.9	38.3	74.0	66.7	27.1	21.6	40.2
Other net investment	36.0	29.7	19.6	–46.3	61.7	26.4	–60.5	–93.3	–71.8	–50.1

[1] Net capital flows comprise net direct investment, net portfolio investment, and other long- and short-term net investment flows, including official and private borrowing.
[2] Emerging markets include developing countries, countries in transition, Korea, Singapore, Taiwan and Israel. No data for Hong Kong SAR are available.
Source: *World Economic Outlook*, 'From Crisis to Recovery in the Emerging Market Economies', October, 1999.

Table 17.2 Net capital flows to crisis-hit Asian countries[1] (in US$ billions)

	1991	1992	1993	1994	1995	1996	1997	1998	1999[2]	2000
Net private capital flows	24.8	29.0	31.8	36.1	60.6	62.9	–22.1	–29.6	–18.1	–8.2
Net direct investment	6.2	7.3	7.6	8.8	7.5	8.4	10.3	9.7	9.4	8.4
Net portfolio investment	3.2	6.4	17.2	9.9	17.4	20.3	12.9	–7.3	4.5	5.6
Other net investment	15.4	15.3	7.0	17.4	35.7	34.2	–45.3	–32.0	–32.0	–22.2

[1] Crisis-hit Asian countries include Indonesia, Korea, Malaysia, the Philippines and Thailand.
[2] The value of 1999 and 2000 is projected.
Source: *World Economic Outlook*, 'From Crisis to Recovery in the Emerging Market Economies', October, 1999.

made to prevent future crises in Asia and elsewhere. Among the issues being studied are the need for improved transparency in the lending operations of banks in developing countries; the need for improved financial supervision and regulation in both the borrowing and lending countries; the role of moral hazard and corruption in overaccumulation and misallocation of foreign capital; the possible role of controls on the flow of short-term and long-term capital in and out of developing countries; and the contribution of various exchange-rate regimes to financial stability. One of the least understood lessons of the Asian financial crisis, however, has been the light that it shone on the inevitable connection between political and economic development.

The end of the twentieth century witnessed a series of financial crises all over the world – in Latin American countries (principally Mexico, Brazil and Argentina) through the 1980s and 1990s, Japan in the early 1990s, Russia since 1992 and the East Asian countries (most notably Thailand, Indonesia, South Korea and Malaysia) in 1997. While it seems plausible to suggest that the distinctive political cultures of East Asia shaped the depth and character of the financial crises in those countries (Gehani, 1999), the varieties of political experiences accompanying similar crises elsewhere provide a sobering caveat to the effort to characterize that influence.

The sequencing of political and economic reform seems one promising factor for determining the sustainability of economic development. Confounding this notion, however, is the fact that countries in the various regions suffering economic crises experienced political and economic transformations in various sequences and intensity. No sequence of political and economic development would appear to immunize a country against financial crises. For example, the bromide one often heard in the Asian context was that for sustainable development to occur, economic reform needed to precede political reform. However, the evidence from Asia suggests that this sequencing did not insulate countries from economic, or indeed political crisis.

We believe that a more promising variable would focus on the correlation between economic and political development. According to this theoretical perspective, in assessing political risk we should seek to ascertain whether political and economic liberalization are proceeding at a roughly equal pace. It is, we believe, unrealistic to expect that political liberalization will be enduring without economic development. Conversely, it is also unrealistic to expect that economic liberalization will be sustainable without political liberalization. The lesson of the Asian financial crisis is that building political depth through a stronger governing institution is critical for the sustainability of economic development. Indeed when one examines the evidence from Southeast Asian and other developing countries, the gap between economic and political development appears to be a better predictor of financial crises than traditional country-risk measurements (see Santoro and Kim, 2001).

Redefining political risk in Asian context

A focus on the correspondence between political and economic development can help to restore credibility in using political risk as a factor in East Asian investment portfolios. One of the most important questions emerging from a post-mortem of the Asian financial crisis was why the crisis was not predicted by the market – why, that is, foreign capital continued to flow in as usual for a long time until just before the crisis commenced (Rahman, 1998). Until the crisis started in mid-1997, the Euromoney Country Risk Assessment ratings of the East Asian countries hardest hit by the crisis changed curiously little (*Euromoney*, March 1997). There were, in other words, not nearly enough warning signals for those countries. Credit rating agencies such as *Standard & Poor's* (March 1997) and *Institutional Investor* (March 1997) also did not provide any indication of the crisis in their ratings of the sovereign debt of the East Asian countries. This failure to presage the crisis in any way calls into question the methodology and accuracy of currently prevailing forms of country-risk assessment. In particular, we believe, the failure to predict the crisis was due to an inadequate mechanism for factoring political-risk variables into country-risk analysis.

Political risk is concerned with the impact of events which are political – in the sense that they arise from power or authority relationships in the society as a whole – and which affect the firm's operations (Kobrin, 1979). When it comes to international investment decisions, however, evidence suggests that political factors are not a major determinant of capital investment (Schneider and Frey, 1985). When measures of political risk were included in studies in parallel with economic factors, economic factors were found to be more statistically significant (UNCTC, 1992). Various explanations for this result have been posited. First, the relevant political factors, as perceived by companies, may be harder to model effectively than the economic factors. Second, it may be that firms themselves may fully recognize the need to allow for political risk, but may find it difficult to do so adequately in terms of fine tuning a capital portfolio that takes into account such political-risk factors (UNCTC, 1992). Whatever the motivation for failing to incorporate political risks in portfolio allocations, it seems clear in the case of Asia that private firms inadequately conceived and assessed political risk. A better screen for political risk – incorporating our suggested emphasis on the correspondence between political and economic development – would have created a heightened awareness for the onset of the financial crisis and thereby ameliorated both its private and public negative impacts.

In recent years, numerous studies have made a positive association between economic and political developments (e.g., Scott and Lodge, 1985; Barro, 1997). These studies all suggest that there is a connection between the fit of economic with political developments and country performance and development; that is, in order for a country to engage in sustainable economic development, economic growth must be accompanied by political development and vice versa – that is, for political development to be sustainable, a certain level of economic development must generally be obtained (Przeworski, 1995).

We propose operationalizing the foregoing general propositions by distinguishing economic transformation from political transformation as shown in Figure 17.1. The economic dimension is mainly a proxy for the relative openness of economy. It consists of free trade and investment, and the liberalization and deregulation of financial markets. In the political dimension, we intend to consider factors such as the structure and distribution of power within a society, the transparency of the legal environment, as well as the development of intermediary bureaucratic institutions that would regulate macroeconomic variables.

Viewed in these terms, we can describe the East Asian model of development as in Figure 17.1, that is to say, some East Asian economies are examples of totalitarian regimes that have fostered a market economy more quickly than they have political liberalization. We well understand the irony that the factors which we, in hindsight, are now suggesting should be viewed as contributing to the crisis – that is, government controls over investment and industrial policies – were the very factors

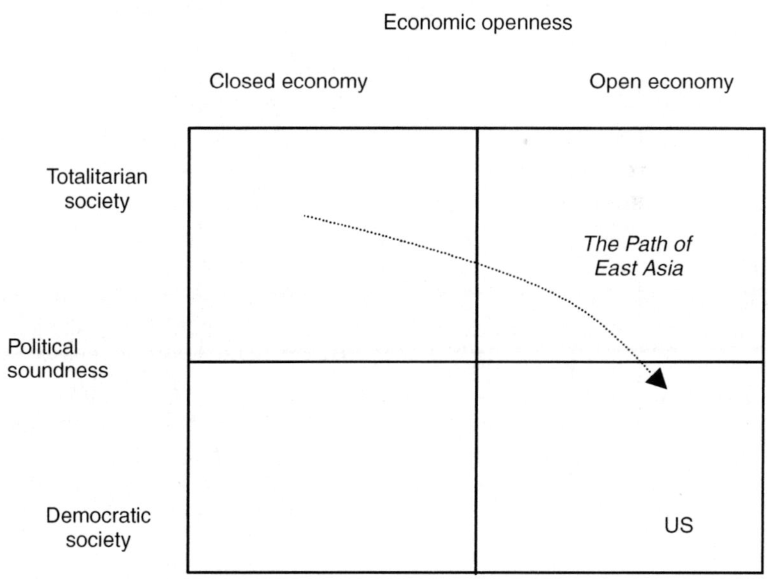

Figure 17.1 Development model

that just a few years previously were hailed as being responsible for the economic rise of East Asia. Despite enormous differences in local conditions and stages of development, East Asian economies have been shaped by a common open industrialization development strategy that was thought to be responsible for their success (Altomonte et al., 1996). Open industrialization – greater freedom of inward and outward flow of goods, services and capital as a cornerstone of their developmental strategies – enabled East Asian economies to enjoy dynamic growth and to catch up rapidly with more developed economies (Dunning and Narula, 1996).

The open industrialization policies in the development-oriented Asian economies have been, however, leavened with a large dose of central planning. East Asian governments tend to exercise significant control over investment flows within industrial sectors and often guide capital to particular companies. As the East Asian economies were achieving rapid growth from a low stage of development, the ability of autocratic central governments, unfettered by political and institutional bureaucracies, to direct capital flows was viewed by many as a positive development factor. However, after these countries reached a certain stage of development, the absence of intermediary institutions and political checks and balances proved to be a liability, as heavy-handed government involvement in the economy was often responsible for capital misallocations.

Ironically, the iron hand of these authoritarian governments has proven powerless to affect critical macroeconomic factors in an open industrialization context. It is difficult for governments of developing economies in East Asia to initiate economic reforms via macroeconomic policies because of the absence of political institutions for governing. To put it in other words, political capacity has not marched along with economic openness, resulting in the failure to build political depth, which is needed for further seamless development. The success of East Asian economies in the future will depend on the quality and speed of the process of both economic and political transformations. A pace of economic liberalization that is commensurate with the institutional and regulatory capability of the country is critical for financial stability and long-term sustainable economic development (Tan, 1999).

Conclusion

At first blush, the connection between the financial crisis and political risk might not seem apparent. The financial crisis in Asia was not precipitated by any political turmoil. On closer inspection, however, political factors did indeed play a significant though subtle role in the genesis of the crisis. Rather than focusing on political turmoil as a determinant of overall political risk factors, we suggest that greater attention be paid to the development of political institutions and systems as a whole in the East Asian region. In particular, we would suggest that a higher political risk core be assigned to countries which are experiencing rapid economic development without a corresponding development in governing institutions.

In general, we argue that although East Asian economies have been experiencing rapid economic and political transformation, in some countries, economic transition has preceded political transformation by too fast a pace and thereby put the economic development at risk. As we have seen, the government-initiated and engineered economic transition was often regarded as an enabling factor of the region's stunning economic performance. Recently, however, some countries in these economies have suffered from their relatively slow political transformation. The countries which have experienced political development – most notably South Korea and Taiwan – on the heels of economic development managed to avoid the worst ravages of the Asian financial crisis and recovered most quickly from the crisis. We do not think this was an accident. Rather, it was a reflection of the fact that sustainable political development correlates strongly with sustainable economic development.

To say that political development must proceed before economic development is clearly wrong. But so too, we have seen, is the view, often trumpeted by East Asian leaders, that economic development can and should precede political development. One way to interpret the financial crisis in East Asia and in other regions of the world in the latter half of the twentieth century is that they demonstrate the necessity of political and economic development proceeding in tandem. Any other sequencing is unstable. Countries which do not follow a simultaneous path of political and economic development must be counted as greater investment risks than those which endeavour to develop political institutions at the same pace that they develop economic institutions. The best strategy for countries to take for a sustainable economic development is to avoid the anomaly of economic and political developments. For private firms, investments in countries where political and economic development proceed at an uneven pace should be viewed as presenting a political risk. Safer investments can be had in countries where political development keeps pace with economic development. We would urge that firms begin to incorporate this tandem development concept into their country-risk assessment scores. In this manner, such scores might prove to be more reliable as early warning signals for any future economic crisis.

Acknowledgements

The authors gratefully acknowledge a research grant from the Aspen Institute's Initiative for Social Innovation through Business.

References

Altomonte, C., Bolwijn, R. J. and H. P. Gray (1996) *Outward foreign direct investment by Asian industrializing countries*, mimeo.

Barro, R. J. (1997) *Determinants of economic growth*, Cambridge, Massachusetts: The MIT Press.

Dunning, J. H. and R. Narula (ed.) (1996) *Foreign investment and governments*, London and New York: Routledge.

Euromoney (1996–98) 'Country risk ratings', various issues.

Gehani, R. R. (1999) 'Architectual concentration and the catastrophic financial crisis in the Newly Industrializing Economies of East Asia', *Global Focus: An International Journal of Business, Economics, and Social policy*, 11(2): 121–37.

Institutional Investor (1996–98) 'Country credit ratings', various issues.

Kobrin, S. J. (1979) 'Political risk: A review and reconsideration', *Journal of International Business Studies*, 10: 67–80.

Przeworski, A. (1995) *Sustainable Democracy*, Cambridge University Press.

Rahman, M. Z. (1998) 'The role of accounting disclosure in the East Asian financial crisis: Lessons learned?', *The United Nations Conference on Trade and Development*, December.

Santoro, M. A. and C. Kim (2001) 'Asynchronous political and economic development and financial crisis: preliminary empirical evidence', Rutgers Business School working paper.

Schneider, F. and B. S. Frey (1985) 'Economic and political determinants of foreign direct investment', *World Development*, 13: 161–75.

Scott, B. R. and G. C. Lodge (1985) *U.S. Competitiveness in the world economy*, Harvard Business School Press: Boston, Massachusetts.

Standard & Poor's (1996–98) 'Sovereign ratings', various issues.

Tan, K. Y. (1999) 'Financial crisis in Southeast Asia: Policy responses and lessons', *Global Focus: An International Journal of Business, Economics, and Social policy*, 11(2): 47–63.

UN Centre of Transnational Corporations (UNCTC) (1992) *The determinants of foreign direct investment: A survey of the evidence*, United Nations, New York.

World Economic Outlook (1999) 'International Monetary Fund. From Crisis to Recovery in the Emerging Market Economies', October.

18

Women, the Disabled and Ethnic Minorities in Business in Contemporary China

Beverley Kitching

Introduction

The last two decades of the twentieth century have been a period of significant organizational change within companies operating in Europe, North America and the Asia-Pacific region (Callus et al., 1991; Bamber and Lansbury, 1993; Patrickson et al., 1995; Patrickson and Obrien, 2000). Management strategies have had to be re-evaluated in order to implement the reforms necessary to enable firms to deal successfully with the factors responsible for inducing change. Those factors include trends towards:

- more international trade, increasing competition and the globalization of economic units;
- increasing technological change in both processes and products;
- deregulation and privatization;
- greater participation in decision-making by stakeholders together with a rise in the influence of non-traditional stakeholders such as women, governments or consumers;
- gender equality in career opportunities; and
- fluctuations in exchange rates, stockmarket crashes and economic recessions.

The reform trends have been from vertical to horizontal, from authoritarian to network-based, tall to flat, fat to lean, just-in-time product focused to customer/client focused. In the late 1990s the Asian economic downturn added extra stress on the international environment particularly for Japan, South Korea, Malaysia and Indonesia. Such change and stress has been traumatic for firms and individuals who have always functioned within the accepted capitalist system where market mechanisms are well established and the operations and procedures of such international bodies as the WTO are well understood. How much greater the challenge then for a country such as China emerging from a bureaucratic, state controlled, planned economy with no market structure, to open its doors to an international-business environment undergoing such change. The focus of this chapter is on the position and experiences of women, the disabled and ethnic minorities in business in the new market system developing in China.

Post Asian-crisis China

According to official sources, China 'has successfully resisted the impact of the Asian financial crisis' and its national economy 'has maintained a sustainable, rapid and healthy development' (*China Economic News*, 2000: 1). During the period of the Ninth Five-Year Plan (1996–2000), the average annual growth of the economy has been over 8 per cent and by the end of 2000 the per capita GDP was expected to exceed US$800. Many Chinese see the twenty-first century as destined to be the period marked by the rise of China. They are, however, also conscious that many problems will need to be resolved on the road to great power status. These were listed recently as population, water resources, environmental degradation, education, economic structure and sustainable development (*China Economic News*, no. 39, 2000: 2).

One impact of the Asian crisis has been to raise questions about the role of the government in managing China's market economy. The old planned economic system was completely dominated by the government and so was the initiative for reform and opening up. There has been little questioning of the view of a developing market system in which the government would play a very active role. Recently, however, there has been criticism of the chronic lack of separation between the government and the enterprises, blind spots in policy-making, inefficiency and the issue of the inadequate role played by the market in resource allocation particularly in monopoly-dominated industries such as electric power, transport and telecommunications (Guo Shuqing, 2000: 26–28). Even the SOEs which have nominally been liberalized and subject to the regulation of the market, in reality are still subject to intervention by the government in numerous areas from investment to hiring and firing of staff.

The impact of the Asian crisis can still be seen in China's rate of utilization of foreign capital. Japan, Korea and Hong Kong are primary sources of foreign capital and such investment declined in 1998–99. In the non-state-owned sector for instance, actual input capital of FDI declined by over 11 per cent in 1999, and the growth rate of that sector dropped from 10 per cent in 1998 to 6.8 per cent in 1999 (Fang Min, 2000: 3). The special study group of the Investment Research Institute of the State Commission on Development Planning argues that China's economic growth was relatively significantly affected by the financial storm and that the PRC has problems similar to those that touched off the financial crisis in Asia. They include excessive amounts of unhealthy loans made by state-owned banks, irrational areas in industrial structure and the economic inefficiency of SOEs (Zhang Changchun, 2000: 84). The group predicts that the effect of the crisis will be to force China to increase the strength of reform with regards to the financial market and enhance the quality of economic growth so that the factors which lead to financial turmoil will be gradually decreased. Opening up the financial sector will incur high risks and China lacks the managerial skills to deal with such a situation. China is still making a transition from a planned economy to a market economy. Its economic growth therefore, is not of high quality and is relatively susceptible to the emergence of all kinds of economic bubbles. The group advised necessary protectionist measures even if this means delaying entry to the WTO, rather than risk the damage to the economy from opening up the financial sector prematurely, impractically and too quickly (Zhang Changchun, 2000: 91–92).

Reform and the WTO

More important for China than the Asian crisis is the ongoing reform process and the impact of entry into the WTO. The apparent consensus among the Chinese leadership is that the opportunities and benefits of joining the WTO will far outweigh the problems. For domestic enterprises it will mean easier access to the international market and greater advantages in international competition. In the home market, however, it will mean fierce competition for industries and enterprises which have hitherto been protected from the realities of the capitalist market system. Entry to the WTO means complete opening up of the Chinese industrial, agricultural and service sectors to foreign competition.

The reform process so far has resulted in enormous unemployment, disruptive rural/urban migration, corruption and environmental degradation. There is growing disparity between rich and poor and between the cities and the countryside. China now has both millionaires and beggars. There is an acute shortage of qualified personnel in IT, finance, law, education and management. So how have the more disadvantaged groups in Chinese society fared in the reform period? Will WTO membership provide more opportunities than problems?

Research questions

Many questions can be raised about the position of women in business in China. Has the reform period given women greater opportunities to enhance their economic and social status? What proportion of new small businesses are owned by women and how does the situation in China compare with other countries? Are women involved in large businesses? Are women in managerial positions in private business? Are women as strongly motivated as men to achieve managerial positions? Do men and women in China manage businesses differently? Do men and women have different personnel management styles? What are their career options? Are women subject to discrimination and harassment in the workplace? Does the glass ceiling exist in China? Are the issues of concern for Chinese businesswomen similar to those of businesswomen elsewhere or are their experiences determined more by specifically Chinese social and economic conditions?

With respect to the disabled there are also many questions. Has private business provided opportunities for disabled entrepreneurs and workers? What is government policy with respect to equality of access to education, jobs and services? What impact will the changes brought about by membership of the WTO have on employment and opportunities?

Industries and firms producing goods used by National Minorities currently enjoy special status and access to funding. Will this continue in the much more competitive market environment now developing in the PRC? Will government policy to encourage investment in China's Western provinces and autonomous regions where most ethnic minority groups live, be successful?

The following hypotheses are being tested through literature search, questionnaire survey and structured interviews:

1 The re-emergence of the market in China has not served to provide women, the disabled or ethnic minorities with greater opportunities to enhance their economic and social status.

2 The re-emergence of private business has not decreased discrimination against women, ethnic minorities or the disabled in the workplace.
3 Issues of concern to Chinese businesswomen are not the same as those of women elsewhere.
4 Gender-based differences in business management in China are not culturally determined.

Methodology

The focus of this chapter is on the position and experiences of women, the disabled and ethnic minorities in business in the new market system developing in China based on a survey of existing literature and on data from ongoing research being conducted in Yunnan province in Southwestern China. Research has so far been conducted in the capital city of Yunnan, Kunming, in the small tourist town of Shilin located in a rural area some 80 km from Kunming, and in Xishuangbanna, a tourist destination 45 minutes by air south of Kunming near the Burmese border. Visits have been made to neighbourhood markets, banks, department stores, wholesale markets, streets of shops, factories (including one making toys for disabled children), trading companies, hotels and tourist destinations such as temples, resorts, scenic areas, the zoo and the botanic gardens. In addition to observation and casual conversations, structured open-ended interviews were conducted with women business owners, managers and employees ranging in age from 22 to 67 years in both private firms and SOEs. The sample included respondents of both Han and Minority Nationality origin. These respondents were chosen from lists provided by the local Womens' Federation and the Kunming Chamber of Commerce.

The interview protocol comprised four sets of questions. These were:

1 *Questions about the respondent's firm* – ownership, type of business, number of employees, number of women employees, number of women managers, geographical distribution and the problems facing the firm.
2 *Questions about personal details* – age, marital status, educational level and work history; husbands' jobs and contribution to the household; household responsibilities including decision-making; daily schedule in hours – travel, work, household jobs and recreation.
3 *Questions about the respondents' career experiences and expectations* – problems, reasons for success or failure, why they were working in

business, whether they would change jobs and why, how long they would continue working.

4 *Questions eliciting the respondents' opinions* – did men and women differ in management styles, in style of running a business; how did they differ; did men and women have the same opportunities in business; had the reintroduction of the market improved women's status and opportunities; what were the main problems for women in China now.

The rise of private business

Private business is a fairly new area of opportunity for both women and men in the PRC. It was virtually non-existent until the reforms of the 1980s, and it is only 12 years since an amendment to the Chinese Constitution in 1988 legalized private business activities. From the beginning of that decade private business activities were first tolerated and later encouraged because they created jobs and supplied goods and services in short supply (Lu and Tang, 1998: 17). Chinese entrepreneurs took up the new opportunities with great vigour and by the end of 1986 the Chinese media was reporting that there were 12 million licensed entrepreneurs of whom 8 million were women (*Xinhua*, 3 December 1986). By the time of the Chinese Communist Party (CCP) Plenum in 2000, the private economy was no longer merely being tolerated but was supported and guided by the party. President Jiang Zemin hopes the party will come to represent the development needs of what he termed in his February 2000 speech in Guangdong, as the advanced forces of production, which together with the forward direction of advanced culture, and the fundamental interests of the broad masses, has come to be called the Three Represents. In practice, private businesses have been told to accept party members' help and guidance in their business practices.

Problems for private business

As Lu and Tang (1998) have noted, some enterprises are more equal than others. The SOEs have had priority in receiving raw materials at below-market prices and state bank loans at low interest rates (Lu and Tang, 1998: 19). Foreign firms both wholly owned and joint ventures, are better served by their regulatory frameworks and have more security of ownership of both capital and property. Private Chinese-owned firms have least access to capital investment, are worst served by laws and regulations, and have much less access to and security for both capital and property.

Women in Chinese private business

Around the world it is estimated that firms owned by women account for between 25 and 33 per cent of all businesses (National Foundation for Women Business Owners, 1998: 2). In the USA, women-owned firms employ one out of every four company workers, and employment in women-owned firms with 100 or more employees has expanded six times faster than for all firms in the economy. In the USA and Canada, growth of women-owned firms outpaces overall business growth by around 2:1. Similar findings are reported from Australasia and parts of Asia, with more women setting up new small businesses than men and with a lower failure rate.

As the OECD Conference on Women Entrepreneurs in Small and Medium Enterprises held in Paris in April 1997 pointed out, a situation where women are discriminated against in business has negative economic, social and political consequences for any country and a lack of data on obstacles to women's entry or success in business makes policy formulation difficult (OECD, 1998). Should China follow a pattern similar to other societies during its development process with respect to greater frequencies of divorce, and with a growth in single parent families predominantly headed by women, and often living below the poverty line, the negative consequences could be severe. Concern for the welfare of women prompted the UNDP to set up a programme in China to provide funds for women to set up businesses, which seems to be meeting with some success.

From the early 1980s, Chinese women were undertaking entrepreneurial activities in astonishing numbers with extraordinary success. By 1986, two-thirds of entrepreneurial licenses countrywide had been taken out by women. In 1990, *China Women's News* announced that 4.6 million rural women were running businesses which meant that a third of all rural businesses were owned and run by women. This means that within a decade, Chinese women in rural areas had reached the world average. The All China Women's Federation lists the Top Fifty Businesswomen each year and women regularly appear in the Top 100 CEO listings. Women have become millionaires. Yet one mainland Chinese feminist has dismissed business as 'merely a side road to development for women' (Li in Gilmartin et al., 1994: 381).

The status of women

Under the terms of the 1982 Constitution of the PRC, women are guaranteed equal rights with men in all spheres of life since, as the Maoist slogan put it, women hold up half the sky. Women have the right to work outside the home and are supposed to have equal pay with men for equal work. By law they are able to inherit land and property. They can initiate divorce and claim custody of their children. They can join the CCP and stand for political office, and they are supposed to have equal access to education. Ten years later in 1992, a Law Protecting Women's Rights and Interests was adopted which was intended to ensure the protection of 'women's special rights and interests granted by law' (FBIS, 1992: 17–20). As is so often the case, the gap between rhetoric and reality is quite large.

Compared with many other societies Chinese women do have a high labour participation rate of 80 per cent, less than 20 percentage points behind men. The female/male wage ratio is 85.6 per cent which is certainly not equal but again comparatively speaking, is higher than most other developing countries (Cheng and Hsiung in Thompson, 1998: 114–119).

There are about 400 million women in China aged 15 plus years, 300 million are economically active and two-third urban and three-fourth rural women engage in work outside the home. Forty-four per cent of employees are women, and they comprise the majority of agricultural workers. There are many impediments to full participation by women in Chinese society. They are under-represented politically (in 1993 they comprised only 21 per cent of deputies to the National People's Congress or NPC), under-represented in higher managerial positions and over-represented in jobs requiring heavy labour such as farming (Joint Economic Committee of the Congress of the United States, 1997: 373). Over the last two decades fewer women have joined the CCP particularly in rural areas and fewer have been elected to office. In the current government (1997–2002) women certainly do not hold up half the sky, that is, of the 29 ministers, only two are women; of the membership of the fifteenth CPC Central Committee, only 4 per cent are female; of the membership of the Standing Committee of the Ninth NPC, only 11.94 per cent are female; of the members of the Special Committees of the Ninth NPC, only 13.59 per cent are women (*Beijing Review*, 1998: 23).

Divorce is still not common in China but the incidence has been increasing in recent decades as unemployment and economic hardship for women has increased. The majority of divorces are instigated by women. Many men refuse to pay child maintenance and it is difficult for the single mother to support her children on her own salary (*Family*, no. 5, 1991: 49; *Women of China*, no. 5, 1987: 42). Wife battering is cited as cause for divorce by many women. In 1992, the Institute of Women's

Studies of China cited 33 per cent of respondents in a survey as reporting abuse, 9 per cent frequently. Another survey in Beijing in 1994 reported a 21.3 per cent rate of abuse.

Chinese statistics in 1990 showed that women accounted for 45 per cent of professional and technical personnel (up from 38 per cent in 1982), 11 per cent of all heads of authorities and government organizations, enterprises and institutions (up from 10 per cent in 1982), 26 per cent of office and clerical staff, 47 per cent of workers in commerce, 53 per cent of labourers in agriculture, forestry, animal husbandry and fisheries, and 36 per cent of workers in industrial production and transport. The 1990 population census showed that more women than men are shop assistants, workers in poultry farms, textile workers and tailors, and machine operators. More men than women are plasterers, truck drivers, purchasing agents, furniture carpenters, teachers in secondary schools, electricians and mining workers. The ratio is nearly equal for primary school teachers, accountants and auditors, vegetable growers and office staff (Hall, 1997: 44). Secretary, interpreter, translator, businesswoman and tour guide are the top dream jobs for Chinese women (Hall, 1997: 52). Self-employment is also a dream for many Chinese women. There are 14 million self-employed people in rural areas engaging in commerce and service trades and two-thirds of them are women (Hall, 1997: 63). It is very difficult to work out how many women are purely self-employed and how many actually employ others. It is even difficult to estimate how many businesses are owned by women because often, when asked by a non-family member, they will say a firm is their husband's or is a family firm even when they have provided the whole capital and are running it themselves.

Chinese women managers

It is only since the late 1980s that studies on issues related to women in management around the world have entered the Western management literature (Adler and Israeli, 1988; 1994). Investigations of women in management in China are very few. Hildebrandt and Liu (1988) surveyed 150 Chinese women managers and concluded that compared with other Asian and US women, they had little job mobility, worked longer hours, were less well-educated and their careers were strongly influenced by central government planning and a patriarchal tradition. A brief review of Chinese women's status in organizations and management was presented by Korabik (1994), and Chen and Yu (1997) addressed the question of motivation to manage. They found that the overall managerial motivation of Chinese women was as high as that of Chinese men. Far fewer women, however, are to be found in management positions in the PRC. Despite their qualifications, a high level of commitment to their careers, and a critical shortage of professionally trained people in China, female Chinese students are pessimistic about their prospects for career advancement (McKeen and Bu, 1998: 171). Barriers cited included negative stereotypes, lack of mentors and role models, isolation and a lack of organizational policies. In a recent Chinese study, Yu and Zhu (2000) argued that female managers are less effective in time management than their male counterparts and work fewer hours. They reported that male managers spent more time than females 'presiding over and attending meetings, talking with subordinates, inspecting work, taking official trips, participating in official intercourse' (Yu and Zhu, 2000: 35). Women spent less time on leading, decision-making, controlling and handling foreign affairs, less time at work and more time on domestic duties which the authors concluded reflected traditional patriarchal values in which 'men are in charge of the outside world while women are in charge of the house' (Yu and Zhu, 2000: 38).

Of the firms in the Kunming sample, the smallest firm employed 10 people, the largest employed 2000. Of that 2000, 35 per cent were female; women managers comprised only 2 per cent of the labour force and 5 per cent of the management staff even though the CEO was a woman. Only two companies had more than 50 per cent women in their workforce, a hotel and a domestic goods retail outlet, both with 60 per cent. Female managers comprised 22 per cent of the retail firm's employees but only 1 per cent of the hotel employees.

Factors influencing women's entry into business

The introduction of the socialist market system in China has led to a variety of problems and opportunities for women in both urban and rural areas. Although most women enter business for the same entrepreneurial reasons as men, over the past two decades, women in a variety of countries including the USA and Australia, have expressed increasing frustration with their work environments. They cite the desire for greater challenge and the need for more flexibility in their work environment as reasons for moving to business ownership. The greatest reward of business ownership for women is in gaining control over their own working lives. Women report their greatest challenge in business is being taken seriously.

Urban business in China

Opportunities for women in the SOEs are declining. As Xiao-Zhou (1997–98: 24–28) points out, jobs in the urban areas are threatened by competition from rural factories set up under the new policies of economic liberalization and by the government's response to market pressures on the SOEs with the emphasis on profitability. Entry into the WTO will merely exacerbate this situation. Women are not being recruited because they bear and rear children, care for the elderly and have to do the housework, all of which makes them less productive than men according to Chinese male managers. Also the necessary welfare provisions such as maternity leave make the enterprise less profitable. Many women are forced to retire at the age of 40–45, long before the average retirement age for men, and women are a primary target for state lay-offs because industries dominated by women such as textiles are the first to go. By 1993, women accounted for 60 per cent of the urban unemployed and the rate is increasing (Joint Economic Committee of the Congress of the United States, 1997: 374). The number of laid-off female workers may be as high as 10 million and around 10 per cent are living in poverty. Even when not in abject poverty, those laid-off report a sharp drop in living standards and increasing conflicts in the family, being looked down upon by husbands and relatives. They also report feelings of disappointment, helplessness and loss of confidence (Wang Jinliang, 1991: 6–15). Organizational change in the state sector is, therefore, disadvantaging the women. One response to this is that more and more women are turning to jobs in the private sector.

In the private sector, however, women are also encountering discrimination. Large private factories, both foreign owned and joint ventures, employ large numbers of women but this female labour force consists almost exclusively of the young and unmarried, and frequently, of rural migrant workers. Management is almost exclusively male and there is considerable evidence of exploitation and harassment of women employees. Tang Can (1998: 64–71) reported that 36.8 per cent of respondents in a survey of female migrant workers claimed that they had been subjected to harassment. Only 14.8 per cent claimed never to have been subjected to it. Other problems include overwork, harmful working conditions, poor living conditions and no proper labour contracts. In 1991, 1993 and 1996 women have died when locked doors prevented escape from fires in factories or dormitories (Tan Shen, 1995: 332–342). Entry to the WTO may pressure Chinese business to conform to more stringent workplace safety regulations, but at present China lacks the institutional infrastructure to monitor and to enforce such measures.

With greater economic freedom and more role models it is likely that more and more women are going to start their own businesses, mostly on a small scale with enterprises which require little capital, for example as street vendors, or providing services such as tailoring and bicycle mending. Self-employment gives women of any age group and educational level the opportunity to control their own working lives and to have greater economic independence.

Rural business in China

In rural township or village enterprises, women are for the most part excluded from management, the few in such posts usually being politically well-connected through fathers or fathers-in-law. Judd (1994) showed that in rural villages in North China, women are still more completely excluded from the critical economic activities of sales and procurement. This work requires travel and contact with buyers and suppliers elsewhere, activities thought more suitable for men. Traditional social custom, still very strong in rural areas, decrees that women should not travel long-distances alone, have individual contact with unrelated men or go drinking. Also each job is defined as a job for a certain gender and age – men do heavy work, women do detailed work. Positions of authority are for older men, female employees have little freedom or control over the production process. There is little sign of the kind of organizational change with respect to gender equality of opportunity which is being experienced in developed Western business cultures. Entry to the WTO may expose Chinese firms to greater pressure to conform with international standards on equal opportunity.

Rural opportunities

The area where rural women have found most opportunity is in the courtyard economy and many women now take their produce to market and interact with numerous people there. Women produce and market 80–90 per cent of meat, eggs and other fowl and during the 1980s farmers' markets were dubbed Streets of Women. Although this reflects significant employment opportunities for rural females, the female workforce is still smaller than the male (Xiao-Zhou, 1997–98: 25).

In some cases, women's work in the courtyard economy involves them in negotiating loans and arranging business deals as well as marketing. On the other hand, much of the work that women undertake in activities such as weaving and handicraft production is subcontracted, and women are not involved in the business side of the work (Jacka, 1997: 153). Even where the work is not subcontracted it is more common for women not to be involved in business transactions with non-family members. Most females prefer the household economy because it is easier for them to cope with husbands or fathers than to conduct business with predominantly male, local cadres or male managers of local enterprises.

Some rural women have been able to develop the potential of the courtyard economy to the full and are running specialized households and private enterprises such as growing grain, medicinal fungi, bonsai and flowers; raising cows, pigs and chickens; food processing; running hotels; running tailoring schools and grocery shops; machine knitting jumpers and sewing. Some have become private industrialists. A 1994 survey by the Zaoyang County Women's Federation in Hubei found that women had initiated 18 600 private enterprises. It is still very difficult, however, for rural women to gain access to or to control land and resources since the patriarchal family system is still very strong.

Self-employment is difficult for women from the more patriarchal minority groups. The largest private enterprise in Xinjiang Province was set-up and run by a Uighur woman whose husband, a strong Muslim, had divorced her for making and selling children's clothes in the street when his income was insufficient to support his family (Hall, 1997: 65–66).

Problems in business for women

Although business does provide opportunities for Chinese women, those opportunities and whether women choose to take advantage of them, are constrained by their social and political environment. This is illustrated by the variety of the following responses given by women working in business in Kunming in August 1998 when asked the question: 'Why did you choose to work in business'?

- No choice, my job was allocated by the government (hotel sales manager).
- No choice, I was sent to the factory in the Cultural Revolution (CEO).
- No choice, I could not get a government job (joint-venture employee).

- My husband is in business.
- Business is a good opportunity, high job satisfaction.
- Business is a challenge.
- To make a living (millionaire).
- To make profit to benefit society (millionaire).
- My own company is better than a factory job (millionaire).

The primary concerns of businesswomen throughout the world are similar. They comprise both day-to-day management issues such as maintaining profits, finding good employees and managing cash flow, and external factors such as government policy, the state of the economy, access to technology and access to capital.

Once women have become established in business in China, what do they identify as problems? Interviews with women in Kunming, Yunnan Province, in August 1998 produced the following list of problems for their businesses (grouped in order of frequency):

1 Lack of qualified staff
2 Lack of access to capital
3 Changes in government policy
  - Personnel management
4 Economic downturn
  - Too much competition
  - Low profits
  - Bad debts
  - Lack of opportunity to expand
5 Lack of opportunity to enter export and import markets
  - Market price fluctuations
  - Communication problems between state and private business
  - Communication problems with foreign clients
  - Pirating of goods

This list is a mixture of the concerns listed by the National Foundation for Women Business Owners as being internationally the key concerns for women entrepreneurs plus some problems more specific to China. The latter are the lack of opportunity to enter export and import markets, communication problems between state and private business and pirating of goods. Private Chinese business (in contrast to SOEs and foreign firms) is still discriminated against in China with respect to access to capital and security of investment, and women entrepreneurs face more difficulties than men.

Problems as women in business

The glass ceiling seems to be operating in China. Even in enterprises where 50 per cent of the employees are female they are not equally represented at all levels. Women are clustered in the lower paid, lower status positions and only around 11 per cent of CEOs are women. In Kunming, only 10 per cent of the private firms are owned by women. Anecdotal evidence from cities such as Shanghai suggests that women travelling on business are subject to harassment with special female-only hotels being set up to protect women travellers from unwelcome attentions and even violence. Although government policy may declare equality between men and women, men have more power, *de facto* inequality still exists (Institute of Population Studies, Chinese Academy of Social Science, 1994).

Types of problems identified by Kunming women

In my research, Kunming women identified the following problems:

- I look too young to be taken seriously.
- Some men do not want to have a woman boss.
- There is not enough access to capital for women.
- Men will not help a woman manager.
- Women must depend on men in business.
- Business is stressful for women.
- Society is conservative.
- People think I am not aggressive enough to be a director.
- When a woman works with men there is gossip.
- It is difficult even as a senior manager.

When asked: 'Has being a woman disadvantaged your career?' 70 per cent of the respondents said yes. The following were some of the reasons given.

- My husband is in the same company and he is standing in the way of my career. He pushes me out of discussions with clients and is trying to push me out of decision-making.
- Education for women is lacking in technology skills.
- Men will not help women in their careers.
- Women don't have such good *guanxi* as men.
- I had to give my husband all my share in our six businesses in order to get him to agree to a divorce and let me keep the children.

- Society is less sympathetic to women's style of management.
- Big companies are not such a good environment for women. There are big problems in promotion and men set the rules. It is very difficult for women to get top jobs.
- The business world is very high pressure. Without good *guanxi* it is difficult to attract finance, and women have less good *guanxi* than men.

On being asked: 'Has being a woman helped your career?', 70 per cent said yes and gave the following reasons:

- Women are more careful and do better work than men, women have better skills in personnel management.
- Yes, in my family business I can depend on my son.
- Women think in a better way. Women are good people managers so employees helped me because I had good relationships.
- Women are more thoughtful and more careful.

Among the dissenting voices was the following comment:

- Not really. Women must have self respect and be independent and strong – this is harder for women.

I asked the women: 'Who has helped you most?', top of the list were friends, followed by fellow workers particularly other women. Then came family, particularly mothers. I also asked: 'What has helped you most?', the three most important factors were listed as ability, *guanxi* and political activities.

When asked: 'In general do you think it is more difficult for a woman to succeed in business than a man?', 80 per cent said yes. Some answers include:

- More men succeed. Kunming is conservative. Change is greater in places like Beijing and Shanghai and it is easier for women.
- There is much competition and a man with the same ability will get the job in preference to a woman.
- Men think women are weaker. Men subject women to harassment and there is no anti-harassment legislation or movement.
- Women must work harder than men. A woman must study harder.
- Society does not value women. Women's lives are very hard.

- There are double standards – if a woman is independent she is accused of being selfish. If a woman neglects her family she is blamed, a man is not. Youth acts against women and not against men.
- There is prejudice against women. Women have to be better than men to succeed.

Those women believed it was not more difficult claimed:

- The new market system gives good opportunities. Capital is not so important as ability and skills. If women do not succeed it is their own fault.

When asked: 'Do women have the same opportunities as men in business?', women responded:

- Yes. Women are not being restrained now. Women are more diligent than men and work harder. (These were the SOE, Commune Co. and factory owner. All were older women, 50 plus years in age.)
- It depends on the person. A smart person will grasp the opportunities. You need to analyse problems and use your brain. (This respondent was the youngest, unmarried one.)
- Yes and no – opportunities are there but it is more difficult for women to take advantage of them.
- Only in some areas of China, in some areas of business.
- It is hard for women to compete with men.
- No, they are held back by slow social change.
- No, fewer go into business in Yunnan. In Zhejiang it is different.
- No, men have higher prestige.

The problems faced by women can be summed up in the following comments from two of the respondents:

- 'Society needs to value women more and give them better education. The social system suppresses women and says women must have men to support them. Ability is not enough, you need background and *guanxi* and men have better advantages here. Women are not recognized by society and cannot communicate with society, men can. There is a double standard. If women work closely with men their reputations suffer but the men's don't' (36-year-old minority nationality, millionaire business owner, Kitching, interview material 1998).

- 'Chinese men do not have the same responsibilities at home and think women are subordinate. It is not socially acceptable for a woman not to marry and have children. We need a proper legal system to be equal,' (22-year-old employee of a Chinese–American joint-venture firm, Kitching, interview material 1998).

Gender-based differences in management

My research revealed that in China, women and men differ in their management styles. Men tend to be more authoritarian, aggressive, like hierarchical structures, be impatient of failure. Women are less hierarchical, may take more time over making decisions, seek more information and are more likely to look for input from employees, other business owners and experts in special areas. Women place a higher value than men on relationships, responsiveness and reputation. Women tend to listen more, are more egalitarian and cooperative, will take account of employee's problems and have better personal relations with colleagues and employees.

What came out of the work in Kunming was that women think they are better at managing people than men, have good people skills, are good at personal relations, communicate better, are more sensitive, gentler and give their employees more opportunity to develop. Men are thought to be more aggressive, do not want to discuss the personal problems of workers, order their employees to do things and shout at people when they do things wrong.

Gender-based differences in running a business

The businesswomen in Kunming certainly identified differences between the way men and women ran a business. They claimed that men take a long-term view, see the bigger picture, are more aggressive, take more risks, waste money, do not pay attention to details, ignore things and fail more often. Women are more careful, pay more attention to detail, are better with money, more practical, more decisive, quicker at solving problems and succeed more often. This fits with success and failure rates for small business in Australia and some other areas in Asia. Over the last ten years, more new, small businesses have been set up by women and they have a higher success rate than men. These behavioural differences one would expect to find reflected in such areas as organizational structures, business strategies and decision-making styles. Very little work has been done in this area in China.

Career options

Differences in career options were apparent between the older and younger women. The younger women obviously had more choice of career, changed jobs more frequently, expected to spend money on fashionable clothes, had mobile phones, had learned to drive but complained more of inequality, of being restricted, of discrimination because they were women. Those who were still employees or worked with their husbands wanted to own their own businesses in the future. Working in large companies was seen as less desirable for women, as not such a good environment. This parallels trends in the USA and Australia where women working in business (even some who have made it to the top in large corporations) have pulled out and set up their own enterprises. The woman who was CEO of the largest company in my sample (the SOE), who got awards every year for being in the top 100 businesses in the province, commented that it was very difficult for women to get to that level and still more difficult for a woman at the senior management level to do her job than for a man.

Double burden for Chinese businesswomen

A double burden appears to exist for Chinese businesswomen. Yes, all of my respondents commented that it was women who had to take on the responsibility for children and the household. All obviously worked extremely hard and in no case was any allowance made at work for family needs. The suggestion of flexible working hours was dismissed as impossible for China because it was a developing country but also because it would be impossible to educate Chinese men to understand the need. The shortest working day was ten hours with, in some cases, only 15 minutes for lunch. The single parent in the sample claimed that for several years the joint demands of earning a living and looking after the home and children meant that most nights she did not get to bed until 3.00 a.m. only to get up again at 7.00 a.m. to be at work by 7.30 a.m. Her children buy their lunch but she always cooks their dinner. Double standards were mentioned here, women being blamed for neglecting their family, men not being blamed. All the women with children expressed regret, often guilt over not spending enough time with their children.

Discrimination and harassment in the workplace

Women in China are exposed to discrimination and harassment in the workplace. Harassment was mentioned although usually as having happened to someone else and by the younger women. The woman who spoke most openly about this was a rural migrant worker who had sold cigarettes on the street for several years. This reflects other work done on migrant workers which has shown them to be by far the most exploited group. They are away from their home areas and the urban people rarely help them, as I observed only too well. In Kunming, most of the migrant rural workers I saw were men, but not all. In one incident hotel security men violently dispersed a group of rural job seekers from the front of one of the new hotels because having them there did not look good and the women were just as badly beaten as the men.

Some women petty traders who had not been able to get a license, had to earn a living somehow and were constantly on the lookout for the police. They were selling out of cases that opened into trays and could be closed quickly or just out of carrier bags. They were selling lucky flowers or other small easily-carried objects.

The impact of the reintroduction of the market

Chan et al. (in Cheng, 1998: 590) have called the post-Mao period 'an epoch of women's confusion' commenting that women have to compete with men in the market for employment, education and political participation. This is a painful experience for which the Maoist affirmative action policies did not prepare them. Forced equality brought no real understanding of equal opportunity and there is little indication that the problems preventing equal access for women are on the male-dominated political agenda in China today. In urban areas in particular, many women find the market hostile, bringing insecurity, lack of social support, unfair competition and a threat to participation in the public sphere. For others however, it represents choice, mobility, new opportunities for economic independence and increased status in the family and society.

When asked: 'Do you think the market system is improving women's status in China?', 70 per cent of Kunming respondents replied yes and gave the following kinds of reasons:

- It gives you more opportunities.
- It has raised the status of business in general, jobs in business are challenging and this will raise women's status in the future if they succeed.
- It gives you more choice in your career.
- Without the new market system we would not know how to do all sorts of things. No market, no development. Workers are now better motivated.

Again there were dissenting voices:

- No, status depends on *guanxi* not ability, and there is still too much politics. A woman who moves from her home area has no *guanxi* connections. There are opportunities but the legal system is a problem.
- Honesty and credibility are important but many people in business and society have neither.
- Women in China are equal.
- Women need intelligence, culture and character and it is family background which determines your characteristics and character.

There was less variety in the responses to the next question, the major variable being age: 'What are the major problems for women in China today?', responses from women included:

- No problems. Women are equal. (This was the response of the older women in their 50s and 60s.)
- There are fewer opportunities for women than men. Women are restricted because they have to take responsibility for family, children and the house.
- Women do not have equal status. We will never be able to educate Chinese men to understand the need to change such things as work hours to take account of family needs.
- Society needs to give more recognition to women and their value.
- Society needs to have more sympathy for women's problems and the way women do things.
- Society and the system treat women unfairly. Women are not valued.
- Society needs to value women more and give them better education.

Results

Is business, as one female Mainland scholar has dismissed it, merely a 'side road to development' for women (Li in Gilmartin et al., 1994: 381)? Certainly one can see the re-emergence of some of the worst aspects of the traditional treatment of women. The word secretary has begun to take on the connotations of concubine in firms in some areas of China. One respondent remarked that in business, women were still *neiren* and men tried to monopolize the public roles. At a lunch one day with two male business academics, a member of the provincial economic commission and two prominent businessmen, the response to hearing that I was interviewing women was derisive laughter and the observation that when they went to business meetings there were no women so why was I talking to women? They would not be able to tell me anything about Chinese business. Obviously these men did not take women in business seriously.

If one regards begging as a business, women were certainly well represented. The most degraded beggars I saw were women in a rural town stretched full length on the road inching themselves forward by fingers and toes pushing a begging bowl in front of them and dragging babies behind them. I was informed that these were girl babies and this was the reason these women had been thrown out by their husbands' families.

To return to the hypotheses:

H1 The re-emergence of the market has not served to provide women with greater opportunities to enhance their economic and social status.

From the Yunnan data so far, it would appear that some women in private business are being given access to greater opportunities to enhance their economic and social status to the extent of becoming millionaires in their own right.

H2 The re-emergence of private business has not decreased discrimination against women in the workplace.

The Yunnan research to date supports this statement, and data from elsewhere in China suggest that discrimination has actually increased.

H3 Issues of concern to Chinese businesswomen are not the same as those of women elsewhere.

The main issues of concern to businesswomen interviewed were the same as those of women elsewhere plus some issues peculiar to China.

H4 Gender-based differences in business management in China are not culturally determined.

The perceptions of Kunming respondents support this.

Obviously the problems faced by many women in China are appalling – poverty, domestic violence, sexual harassment and discrimination in the workplace, the triple burden of caring for the household, children and the aged while at the same time holding a full-time job for some, unemployment for others. China is a developing country where the traditional, patriarchal culture is still very strong and women's opportunities are constrained by both those factors. Women's issues and problems have been marginalized in this period of market reform. Change takes time. In China today, although the pace of change is phenomenal, organizational change with respect to gender equality of opportunity appears to be almost non-existent. Some Chinese women have found in ownership of, or employment in, private business the road to economic success and thereby greater independence and influence in the family. They are role models and hopefully many other women will be encouraged to follow their example.

The disabled

Since 1949, there has been much less focus on the disabled than on women although their needs were recognized. Before 1987, the only state-defined disability criteria of the PRC were those for Revolutionary Disabled Veterans drafted by the Ministry of the Interior in the early 1950s. Factories and workshops were set up to provide employment for the disabled such as the Shiwan Ceramic Arts Factory set up in 1974 in Guangdong Province. This has now become a major producer of ceramic tiles, has changed its name to Eagle Brand Holdings Ltd. and was listed on the Singapore Stock Exchange in 1999 (Leung, 1999).

Special education was formally included in the education system of the PRC in 1951. The Decision with Regards to Reforming School Systems was promulgated, and stipulated that special schools should be set up for deaf and blind people at all government levels and education was to be provided for those with physiological impairment (Xu, 1994). There were, however, many problems including lack of financial support, few specialist teachers and shortages of equipment. The first school set up for people with intellectual disability in Dalien in 1959 only lasted for four years and no further attempt to provide education for the intellectually impaired was made until 1979 (Xu, 1994).

Very little attention has been paid in Western literature to issues affecting the disabled in China. Within the PRC, this area came to prominence only after Deng Xiaoping was rehabilitated in the late 1970s. His son, Deng Pufang, had become a paraplegic during the Cultural Revolution when he leapt from a third-storey window to escape from assault by Red Guards. During the 1980s and 1990s Deng Pufang championed the cause of the disabled. On his return from medical treatment in Canada, he set up the China Disabled Person's Welfare Fund, which grew significantly during the 1980s and eventually became the Disabled Persons' Federation.

In 1987, the first epidemiological survey of disabled people ever carried out in China was completed. The sample survey of 1.5 million people reported that 4.9 per cent had a disability, which in conjunction with the results of the census of 1987, suggested a figure of 51.6 million disabled people in the PRC. This estimate had grown to around 60 million by 1999 (Kohrman, 2000: 906). A breakdown into disability groups reported 7.55 million people with physical disabilities, 17.7 million with speech and hearing difficulties, 10.17 million with intellectual disabilities, 7.55 million blind persons and 1.94 million with multiple handicaps (Xiao Fei in Ashman, 1995: 48). Around 8 million of those disabled are children (Ashman, 1995: 48) and 66 per cent of those children are intellectually impaired (Sonnander and Claesson, 1997: 180). As Sonnander and Claesson (1997) have pointed out, this means that China has more individuals with disabilities than any other country in the world.

Legislation

During the Reform and Open Door Policy decades of the 1980s and 1990s, there has been considerable development in legislation and provision of services for the physically and intellectually impaired. It is a provision of the current Constitution of the PRC that the government must guarantee that 'the disabled enjoy the same civic rights as the able-bodied' (Section 1X Guarantee of Human Rights For the Disabled, Government White Paper *Renmin Ribao*, 5 January 2000). In 1982, the Chinese government accepted the United Nations World Program of Action Concerning Disabled Persons and set up the China Organizational Committee of the United Nations Decade of Disabled Persons. In 1987, the PRC accepted the Convention Concerning Vocational Rehabilitation and Employment (Disabled Persons), which had been passed by the International Labor Conference in 1983.

In December 1990, the Law of the PRC on the Protection of Disabled Persons was adopted by the Standing Committee of the NPC. The formation of the law was said to be guided by the principles of equality, participation and co-enjoyment. Many important laws now have special provisions guaranteeing the rights and interests of the handicapped in education, political participation, inheritance, marriage, civil and criminal procedures. The Labor Law of the PRC and the Regulations for SOEs for changes in operating mechanisms include specific regulations guaranteeing the rights of the disabled to employment. Twenty-seven provinces, regions and municipalities have formulated local legislation, setting a quota for disabled employees of at least 1.5 per cent in government-run organizations. According to the Government White

Paper, 'Chinese laws prohibit discrimination, insult and injury against the handicapped or their ill-treatment and abandonment.'

Education

Since 1981, special classes for children with intellectual disability have been promoted in regular schools. By 1986, there were 36 special schools and 55 classes. By 1992, there were 235 special schools and 1235 classes (Xu, 1994; Yang and Wang, 1994). The continuing problems of funding, shortage of teachers and equipment meant that by the mid-1990s only 0.5 per cent of intellectually impaired children were attending special schools, 61 per cent were attending regular schools but 38.1 per cent were not attending school at all (Xu, 1994). In its guidelines for the 1991–95 Five Year Plan for the Chinese handicapped, the government set goals for the percentage of disabled children who should receive junior high school education at 60 per cent in developed areas and 30 per cent in moderately developed areas.

In January 2000, the government White Paper reported progress. It claimed that some 2300 community rehabilitation centres, 750 handicapped children's care centres and training classes and 1300 work-rehabilitation centres for the mentally and intellectually handicapped had been set up. Between 1997 and 2000, the number of special education schools had increased by 20 per cent per annum and special classes in regular schools had doubled. The number of children attending these classes and schools had increased by 30 per cent per annum and in 1998 and 1999 some 4700 self-taught disabled persons had won college diplomas through special examinations. Twenty-eight vocational education centres had been established. Special education divisions were being established at universities, and teacher-training institutions for special secondary education were being set up in 27 provinces, regions and municipalities. Subsidies, fees-exemption, scholarships and prizes had been instituted (Kitching in Patrickson and Obrien, 2000, in press).

Employment

There is a system of government-supported welfare enterprises in which the disabled are employed. The number of such enterprises has increased from 1022 in 1979 to 42 000 by 1990 employing a total of 750 000 people (*Renmin Ribao*, 5 January 2000). Government figures claim that 50.19 per cent of urban handicapped and 60.55 per cent of rural handicapped have employment, that is some 13 million people. Handicapped persons are also employed in regular government departments, SOEs and private business. Since instituting the disability tax-credit system in

1984, the government has been increasingly urging disabled men and women to become independent business people as a means of reducing the state's welfare burden. By 1995, there were more than 500 000 disabled entrepreneurs registered (Kohrman, 2000: 906).

The disabled face some of the same problems faced by women in a rapidly changing economic system. The welfare factories are short of investment and impeded in efforts to compete in the new market place by outdated equipment. With the loss of jobs in the state sector and both state-owned and private business emphasizing profit, unemployment is increasing. Entry into the WTO is likely to exacerbate these problems although again China may find itself under greater pressure to conform to Western views of equal opportunity. Welfare facilities designed to accommodate those who are physically and mentally incapable of working and have no legal providers or resources, are unable to meet the actual needs. The disabled are certainly to be found among the beggars especially in poorer regions of the PRC.

Social attitudes

Over the last two decades, the government and the Disabled Persons' Federation have worked hard at creating a social environment in which the disabled are respected and helped. Many activities have been sponsored such as the Young Pioneers', Helping the Handicapped Programme which has involved more than 30 million children over the last five years. There was a Humanitarian Publicity Week, a Day of the Disabled and May 19 each year is now the legal National Day for Helping the Handicapped.

The question of access is now being addressed to enable the handicapped to participate more easily in social activities. Standards for the Design of Urban Roads and Buildings for the Disableds' Convenience have been worked out and attempts are being made to implement them. Slopes and handrails are being built in shops, hotels, libraries, theatres, airports and other public places but so far only in the more developed and richer cities such as Beijing, Shenzhen, Shanghai, Tianjin, Shenyang and Guangzhou.

In 1994, the Sixth Far East and South Pacific Games for the Disabled were held in Beijing with more than 30 000 volunteers involved. The PRC sent 87 athletes to the Paralympic Games in Sydney in October 2000.

As is the case with gender issues, there is a large gap between law and policy and the realities of life for many of the disabled. Much of the traditional stigma against the disabled has survived the changes of the past century particularly for men. This becomes very apparent when comparing marriage rates of the disabled, the *can ji*, with those of the general population which emerged in the 1987 sample survey of the disabled. In the general population only 0.7 per cent of women have never married compared with 4.0 per cent of female *can ji* whereas for men the rates are 7.0 per cent and 45 per cent respectively (Di, 1987; Kohrman, 2000: 890–91). The fact that men outnumber women in China is not sufficient explanation!

In his chapter about *can ji* men, Kohrman (2000: 894) reports the comments of one elderly woman about disabled (*que*) men. 'Men need to get out of the house and be fast on their feet. They (*que* men) just don't have what it takes to be a man, to go out and do what's expected of them. That's why they have such a hard time marrying'. Families of handicapped persons try to prevent them marrying other *can ji*.

Disabled people employed in the regular workforce can face discrimination. One interpreter in a government institute visited by the author was lame and despised by fellow workers especially those with a lower educational level. They made his life difficult in a variety of ways. In one incident, the driver of the institute car deliberately drove off before the interpreter got in forcing him to try and run to catch up. The driver laughed at his efforts to do so.

There are of course dedicated individuals trying to bring about change. One elderly female business owner in Yunnan runs a factory making toys for handicapped children. She then uses the profits from this enterprise to employ teachers to train mothers how to use these toys in helping to educate their children. She particularly tries to help rural families. She had visited Australia and had been very impressed with Australian equal opportunity legislation and with the provisions to ensure that the law was put into practice. She also admired the educational and care facilities in place to help the disabled and commented 'We have a long way to go, it is not like that here' (Kitching in Patrickson and Obrien, 2000, in press).

National minorities

During the 1930s and 1940s, the CCP sought the support of ethnic minority groups some of whom, such as the Naxi of the Lijiang basin, adopted CCP policies with fervour even to the extent of carrying out land reform and class labelling twice (White, 1997: 2–3). After Liberation in 1949, autonomous minority administrative structures were set up. There are about 130 autonomous minority areas in the PRC at the level of the county, prefecture and region comprising about 60 per cent of the land area. Since most of these areas are along China's borders, particularly the politically sensitive zones in the north and west, the extent of autonomy has been limited. Factors involved here include the fear of invasion from a number of the 12 neighbouring countries bordering China to the North, West and Southwest such as the old USSR, India and Vietnam, and the fact that these regions are very sparsely populated. What resulted was a government policy which encouraged the migration of Han Chinese into minority autonomous regions such as Xinjiang, Tibet, Inner Mongolia, Yunnan and Heilonjiang. In addition to security implications, the intention also appears to have been to acculturate and assimilate – Han-ify – minority nationalities (Kormondy, 1995: 164).

The theories of Lenin and Stalin provided a view under which minority nationality is legitimized. Under this view, linguistic and cultural practices are sanctioned, there is a place for tradition and authentic cultural practices (*zhenshi de*) and cultural diversity is tolerated (White, 1997: 3301). This view led to policies which gave preferential treatment to minorities such as exemption from the one-child policy, preferential admission to higher education institutions, exemption from land taxes and state payment of primary teachers in schools run by minorities (Kormondy, 1995: 163). Such preferential treatment is the source of considerable resentment by Han Chinese especially exemption from the one-child policy.

One area in which ethnic minorities were seen to be particularly backward was in their religious beliefs and traditions often castigated as feudal superstition. Resentment of attempts to suppress religion is particularly strong amongst Islamic groups in the North and Northwest and in Lamaist Tibet.

There are currently 58 ethnic minority groups identified by the Chinese government, 55 of which are officially designated as National Minorities. They are scattered throughout the PRC but are still most strongly concentrated in autonomous regions and provinces in the border regions of the North, such as Inner Mongolia, in the Northwest, such as Xinjiang and Gansu, in the West, such as Tibet, Qinghai and Sichuan and in the Southwest, such as Yunnan. Their origins and cultural traditions are very diverse, ranging from the nomadic herders of the northern plains such as the Mongols to hunter/gatherer groups in the tropical forests of Xishuangbanna such as the Hani; from patriarchal Islamic groups such as the Uighurs of Xinjiang to the matriarchal Mosuo (labelled as Naxi by the PRC authorities) living on the Sichuan/Yunnan border. Their religious traditions are also extremely diverse and include Islam, Lamaism, Buddhism and Animism. Many groups have been in contact with and influenced by Han culture for over a thousand years. Current government policy speaks of China as having been a united multinationality country since ancient times and describes the PRC as a united multinationality state founded jointly by the peoples of all nationalities (*Beijing Review*, 1999: 16).

National Minorities comprise nearly 9 per cent of the population and have a higher growth rate than the Han Chinese because they are exempt from the one-child policy. A comparison between the 1982 census and the 1990 census showed a growth in the percentage from 6.7 per cent to 8.7 per cent and some groups appeared to be growing in excess of 4 per cent per annum (Yusuf and Byrnes, 1993: 3). An explanation for this explosion of ethnicity (Gladney, 1991) is that it would appear that people are now more ready to identify with their ethnic groups than they were in the past.

Legislation

Article four of the current Constitution states that all nationalities are equal, and discrimination against and oppression of any nationality are prohibited (*Beijing Review*, 1999: 18). Minorities are guaranteed equal rights to vote and stand for election, freedom of religious belief, the right to education, to use and to develop their own language, and have the freedom to preserve or to reform their own folkways and customs and to be assisted in economic development. This can provide a substantial challenge to government resources. For instance, 70 different languages with around 20 different scripts are in use. Only three minorities use Mandarin (SEDC, 1988; Lin in Kenichiro, 1993).

The Electoral Law of the NPC Issues for National Minorities guarantees that minority groups shall be represented by their own deputies. Of the 2979 deputies elected in 1998, 428 were from ethnic minorities accounting for over 14 per cent of the total (*Beijing Review*, 1999: 19). Among the vice-chairpersons of the Standing Committee of the NPC at present, 21 per cent are of ethnic minority origin and they comprise 9.6 per cent of vice-chairpersons of the National Committee of the Chinese People's Consultative Conference (CPCC). On State Council, one leading member and two ministers are from ethnic minority groups.

China has joined International Conventions such as the International Convention on the Elimination of All Forms of Racial Discrimination, the International Convention on the Suppression and Punishment of the Crime of Apartheid and the Convention on the Prevention and Punishment of the Crime of Genocide.

Education

In 1949, many of the minority languages had no written form. In the 1950s, National Minority Institutes were set up to study minority languages and cultures and by the late 1990s, ten ethnic groups using the 13 languages were provided with written versions. Around 100 newspapers and 73 journals are published in minority languages and more than 20 languages are used in radio broadcasts. By 1998, there were 36 publishing houses specializing in minority language publications in 23 languages.

Before 1949, there was only one university for minority students. In general the literacy rate was very low. In areas such as Tibet and Ningxia, 95 per cent of people were illiterate in 1949. The first tertiary institute in an autonomous area was set up in 1949 in Tibet. This was the School for Tibetan Issues which later became the Northwest Nationalities University. The aim of the new minority institutions was to improve tertiary industry, help economic development, and train cadres and intellectuals needed in the autonomous areas. They were also intended to 'preserve and develop the characteristics of the nationalities in the context of international cultures' (Xie in Kormondy, 1995: 165). Official figures report that in National Minority Autonomous Areas between 1952 and 1998, there was substantial growth in education (see Table 18.1) (*Beijing Review*, 1999: 16).

Since 1980 only one Minority Tertiary institution, the Central Institute for Nationalities in Beijing, has been designated as a key institution. Some other key universities have considerable minority enrolment such as Xinjiang University, but 75 per cent of key institutions are in the Southern and Eastern coastal provinces and municipalities, 22 in Beijing alone. This means that they are sited in the most developed and wealthy areas of China with, in general, fewer numbers of minority people. Since 1976, the key universities have received higher funding, attracted the best teachers and provided them with better salaries and enrolled the best students.

Table 18.1 Educational institutions in China

Type of institutions	1952	1998
Tertiary institutions	11	94
Secondary schools	531	13 466
Primary schools	59 597	90 704

The question of language has had to be addressed. Most Chinese universities teach in Mandarin which disadvantages ethnic minority students. In some areas, one-year bridging programmes have been introduced to give students whose first language is not Mandarin the level of skill needed for a tertiary course. There are also special classes offered by universities to prepare minority students for entry to particular degree programmes such as chemistry. Entry to university is by national examination and special provisions for minority students include taking a part of or sometimes the entire exam in their native language and adjusting the scores.

The major issues challenging the education system are: Firstly, that most minority nationalities are in remote and rural areas which have been well behind urban developments in education. Secondly, poor economic conditions have limited educational opportunities and development. The current goals are to train more talent and raise the standard of living by introducing science and technology and improving the quality of education described as the golden key to economic development (Wei in Kormondy, 1995: 169).

Employment and finance

In 1949, there were very few industries in minority areas and modern infrastructure was largely non-existent. Agriculture was the primary economic activity and in some areas this was of the slash-and-burn type with a few groups still not using iron tools. Over the last 20 years, the government has increased investment in minority areas in infrastructure, construction of power stations, railways, roads and airports. In 1998, 62 per cent of the total increased financial investment by the state was used in Central and Western areas of the PRC. Since the 1950s, some 1400 industrial enterprises have been set up in the major minority areas (*Beijing Review*, 1999: 25). Minority nationality people employed in SOEs face the same problems as women and the disabled as these enterprises are restructured on a profit basis. There is now a preferential policy on FDI to direct more to minority areas.

Since 1980, there has been a quota subsidy system in place for the five autonomous regions and the three provinces with the highest number of minority people, Yunnan, Guizhou and Qinghai. In 1994, China began to reform its financial management system including its tax-sharing scheme, the source of funding for the quota system. All the existing subsidies and special financial allocation policies for minority areas were retained and a transfer payment method worked out for what was seen as a transitional period. In 1998, the minority regions and provinces received 48 percent of the total transfer payment sum.

Since 1963, China has had preferential policies toward ethnic trade and guarantees the production of some 4000 items of ethnic articles in daily use. A new package of preferential policies is included in the Ninth Five Year Plan (1996–2000) which involves funding the construction of an ethnic trade network and the technological upgrading of enterprises producing basic ethnic goods. The state-owned ethnic enterprises and the grass-roots supply and marketing cooperatives are exempt from value-added tax. State policy recognizes that Western China, where most minority people live, is relatively backward compared with the coastal areas in East China. Improvement in living standards has been restricted by geographical conditions, a low social development level, poor production conditions and lack of scientific, technological and cultural knowledge (*Beijing Review*, 1999: 28).

Private business

Just as with women and the disabled, ethnic minority people have identified the opportunities presented by the changing economic system and become private entrepreneurs particularly in the new tourism industry. In cities like Kunming, capital of Yunnan Province, there are many ethnic minority restaurants, which also offer entertainment by ethnic dancers, singers and massage practitioners. Ethnic minority markets are found at many tourist sites with stalls selling food, costumes, art and artifacts.

Some minority businesspeople have become wealthy like the Uighur woman with a children's clothing business mentioned earlier. One Aini woman interviewed in Kunming (Kitching in Patrickson and Obrien, 2000, in press) had become a millionaire with a wholesale firm selling fire alarms and sprinkler systems.

Social attitudes

Although many minority nationality people are very concerned about seeing their traditions, languages, and cultural identities maintained, there are differences within and between groups as to how and to what extent this should be done. One extreme is the case of Tibet where a highly vocal expatriate community tries to influence global leaders to pressure the Chinese government to allow Tibet to become an independent country. Within the Tibet Autonomous Region there are both supporters and opponents of this view. Some Tibetans have a vested interest in maintaining the status quo including many of the Tibetans who make up 75 per cent of the cadres in the region. Many Han Chinese now live in Tibet, and during the 1990s, this group increased substantially in numbers by taking advantage of business opportunities in the region. Many Tibetans live outside Tibet in Qinghai, Southern Xinjiang and Sichuan Province. Separatist groups can also be found in Xinjiang and other areas along the northern border of China.

At the other end of the spectrum, there are individuals who see themselves as Chinese first and then as members of an ethnic group. Many young people want to be modern and up-to-date and see greater opportunities in being competent in Mandarin and, for business, English rather than in a minority language. As one young Bai nationality academic said 'I am Bai, my wife is Miao. Our children are Chinese' (Kitching in Patrickson and Obrien, 2000, in press).

Concluding remarks

China is a developing country which, over the last 20 years, has emerged from relative political and economic isolation into an international environment undergoing the trauma of rapid technological and social change. The current situation for women and other disadvantaged groups reflects a mixture of historical experience incorporating traditional value systems, political ideology and a variety of external influences. Change is constrained by economic conditions and the availability of resources. There are many problems and issues to be confronted in managing such a dynamic situation during a time of rapid economic reform accelerated by the impact of the Asian downturn and by imminent entry to the WTO.

China's entry to the WTO will offer increasing opportunities for foreign firms to move into this rapidly changing market place. They too will find problems of finding and retaining good IT and management personnel. Those firms already in China report that qualified Chinese staff are in high demand and move readily from firm to firm in search of higher salaries. Chinese firms are often unwilling to employ women in managerial positions, and foreign firms have benefited with Western executives finding they work better with Chinese women staff than with Chinese male managers.

References

Adler, N. J. and D. N. Israeli (eds) (1988) *Women in Management Worldwide*, Armonk, NY: M.E. Sharpe.

Adler, N. J. and D. N. Israeli (eds) (1994) *Competitive Frontiers: Women Managers in a Global Economy*, Cambridge: Blackwell.

Ashman, A. F. (1995) 'The education of students with an intellectual disability in the People's Republic of China: some observations', *European Journal of Special Needs Education*, 10(1): 47–57.

Bamber, G. J. and R. Lansbury (eds) (1993) *International and Comparative Industrial Relations*, 2nd edn, Sydney and London: Allen and Unwin/Routledge.

Beijing Review (1998) 'Top female officials of China', *Beijing Review*, 41(20) (March).

Beijing Review (1999) 'China's policy on minorities and its practice', 16–33, 18 October.

Callus, R., Moorehead, A., Cully, M. and J. Buchanan (1991) *Industrial Relations at Work: The Australian Workplace Industrial Relations Survey*, AGPS, Canberra.

Chen, C. C. and K. C. Yu (1997) 'Motivation to manage. A study of women in Chinese state-owned enterprises', *Journal of Applied Behavioural Science*, 33(2) (June): 160–73.

Cheng, J. Y. S. (ed.) (1998) *China in the Post-Deng Era*, Hong Kong: The Chinese University Press.

China Economic News (2000) 'Repositioning in the World', XXI(39): pp. 1–2.

Di, Y. (ed.) (1987) *National Sample Survey of Disabled persons*, Beijing: Office of the National Sample Survey of Disabled persons.

Fang, M. (2000) 'Investment made by non-state owned economies picking up', *China Economic News*, XXXI(40): 2–3.

Foreign Broadcast Information Service (1992) *Daily Report: People's Republic of China*, April 14, pp. 17–20.

Gilmartin, C. K., Hershatter, G., Rofel, L. and T. White (1994) *Engendering China. Women, Culture and the State*, Cambridge, Mass: Harvard University Press.

Gladney, D. C. (1991) *Muslim Chinese: Ethnic Nationalism in the People's Republic*, Cambridge: Harvard University Press.

Guo, S. (2000) 'The government's role in China's market economy', *The Chinese Economy*, 32(5) (September–October): 26–68.

Hall, C. (1997) *Daughters of the Dragon. Women's Lives in Contemporary China*, Scarlet Press.

Hildebrandt, H. W. and J. Liu (1998) 'Chinese women managers: a comparison with their US and Asian counterparts', *Human Resource Management*, 27(3) (Fall): 291–314.

Jacka, T. (1997) *Women's Work in Rural China Change and Continuity in an Era of Reform*, Cambridge: Cambridge University Press.

Joint Economic Committee, Congress of the United States (ed.) (1997) *China's Economic Future*, M.E. Sharpe.

Judd, E. R. (1994) *Gender and Power in Rural North China*, Stanford University Press.

Kohrman, M. (2000) 'Grooming *Aue zi*: marriage exclusion and identity formation among disabled men in contemporary China', *American Ethnologist*, 26(4): 890–909.

Korabik, K. (1994) 'Managerial women in the People's Republic of China: the long march continues', in N. J. Adler and D. N. Israeli (eds) *Competitive Frontiers Women Managers in a Global Economy*, Cambridge: Blackwell.

Kormondy, E. J. (1995) 'Observations on minority education, cultural preservation and economic development in China', *Compare*, 25(2): 161–78.

Leung, J. (1999) 'Spreading its Wings', *Asian Business*, February, pp. 12–13.

Lin, Y. (1993) 'Different social and cultural types among the Chinese National Minorities: their transition to Socialism and development towards modernisation', in H. Kenichiro (ed.) *The State and Cultural Transformation*, Tokyo: United Nations University Press.

Lu, D. and Z. Tang (1998) *State Intervention and Business in China*, Cheltenham: Edward Elgar.

McKeen, C. A. and N. Bu (1998) 'Career and life expectations of Chinese business students: the effects of gender', *Women in Management Review*, 13(5): 171–83.

National Foundation for Women Business Owners (1998) *Key Issues Affecting Women Business Owners in Argentina and Other Latin and Iber-American Countries*, April.

OECD proceedings (1998) 'Women Entrepreneurs in Small and Medium Enterprises', Paris.

Patrickson, M., Bamber, V. and G. J. Bamber (1995) *Organisational Change Strategies*, Melbourne: Longman.

Patrickson, M. and P. Obrien (eds) (2000) *Managing Diversity: An Asian and Pacific Focus*, Wiley.

Renmin Ribao (2000) 5 January.

SEDC (State Education Commission) PRC (1988) *Education in China 1978–88*, Beijing: State Education Commission.

Sonnander, K. and M. Claesson (1997) 'Classification, prevalence, prevention and rehabilitation of intellectual disability: an overview of research in the People's Republic of China', *Journal of Intellectual Disability Research*, 41(2): 180–92, April.

Tan, S. (1995) '*Zhongguo Funu zhuangkuang*' (Womens situation in China) in L. Jiang et al. (eds) *1994–5 nian Zhongguo Shehui xingshi fenxi yu yuce* (*Analysis and Prediction of the Social Situation in China 1994–5*), Beijing: Zhongguo shehui Kexue chubanshe, pp. 332–42.

Tang, C. (1998) 'Sexual harassment: the dual status of and discrimination against female migrant workers in urban Areas' – a speech delivered at the Asia University in Japan'. *Social Sciences in China*, 3, pp. 64–71.

Thompson, G. (ed.) (1998) *Economic Dynamism in the Asia Pacific*, London: Routledge.

Wang, J. (1991) 'The maimed "Half-Sky": the employment crisis of women in China', *Women, Education and Employment*, 11(25) (Spring): 6–15.

White, S. D. (1997) 'Fame and sacrifice: the gendered construction of naxi identities', *Modern China*, 23(3) July: 298–328.

Women of China (1987) No. 5, p. 42.

Xiao-Zhou, K. (1997–98) 'Women divided. The blessing and the curse of China's changing economy', *Harvard International Review*, XX(1) (Winter): 24–8.

Xinhua (1986) 3 December.

Xu, Y. (1994) 'China', in H. Winzer and G. Mazurek (eds) *Comparative Study of Special Education*, Genalland University, Washington, DC, pp. 163–78.

Yang, H. and H. Wang (1994) 'Special education in China', *Journal of Special Education*, 28: 93–105.

Yu, G. and Y. Zhu (2000) 'Gender differences of China's managers in time management', *Women in Management Review*, 15(1): 33–43.

Yusuf, F. and M. Byrnes (1993) 'Ethnic mosaic of modern China: an analysis of fertility and mortality data for twelve largest ethnic minorities', Research paper no. 374, Macquarie University School of Economic and Financial Studies, October.

Zhang, C. (2000) 'An analysis of the state of the utilization of foreign capital in our country in 1999', *The Chinese Economy*, 33(1) (January–February): 77–92.

19

Sustainable Development and Sustainable Management: Promoting Economic, Ecological and Social Sustainability in Post-crisis Asia

Hock-Beng Cheah and Melanie Cheah

Introduction

The recent economic crisis in Asia demonstrated clearly that the path towards higher levels of development is not a smooth one, and that success in the past does not assure future success in the development process. Furthermore, while some groups and countries have made significant progress in raising their living standards in the twentieth century, the President of the World Bank recently admitted that progress is too slow. Specifically, 'With 3 billion people still living under US$2 a day, with growing inequity between rich and poor, with forests being degraded at the rate of an acre a second, with 130 million children still not in school, with 1.5 billion people still not having access to clean water, and 2 billion people not having access to sewage [facilities], we cannot be complacent. More than this, we must be concerned that 80–90 million people are being added annually to our planet, mainly in the developing world. Two billion more souls must feed themselves by the year 2025, hampered by wars, with growing inequity, and with distortions of economies and politics as evidenced in crises from Indonesia to Russia and from Latin America to Africa. With the reduction in Overseas Development Assistance and current instability in the international financial markets, there is much to be concerned about' (Wolfensohn, 1999).[1]

However, it has also been contended in various circles that the difficulties lie not just in the relatively slow pace of the development process but, more significantly, in the very nature of the development model that has been adopted so far. It is a model in which excessive emphasis has been placed on the economic aspects, that has generated significant inequities, that is not meaningful for a large proportion of the world's population, and that may not be sustainable in the longer term. These concerns have provoked a critical questioning of present forms and processes of development, and have led to a search for better and more viable alternatives; for instance, alternatives flowing from the concept of sustainable development.

Sustainable development has become an increasingly important concern to governments, Non-Governmental Organizations (NGOs) and international development agencies, such as the World Bank. Increasingly, business organizations too must incorporate sustainability concerns into their planning and operational activities. Indeed, sustainable development at the level of economies and societies needs a corresponding concept of sustainable management at the level of enterprises and organizations. This also has to be related to the significant changes that are presently transforming the mass production system that has dominated many economies for most of the twentieth century. These changes lead in the direction of what may be called a diversified production system. Some of the principal outcomes of the new production system lead to outputs of goods and services that are potentially available anywhere, anytime, any kind, with no matter and at no charge. This development could contribute to a transformation of economies and societies. Enterprises will have to respond appropriately to this new environment for their long-term economic survival and success.

The post-crisis environment: economic, ecological and social dimensions

Development in Asia was focused largely on the economic realm, with trickle-down benefits to the poor. When growth rates were relatively high for two or more decades, this strategy appeared to succeed. However, there were two important shortcomings. First, while many people escaped from poverty through this process, disparities were widening. Second, when the economies were buffeted by the crisis, the social safety nets were absent or inadequate to cope with the resulting demands. Consequently, while poverty had been reduced significantly during preceding decades, the economic crisis in Asia resulted in many people sinking back into poverty (APEC, 2000a: 132–44; Hayward, 2000; Suryahadi et al., 2000).

While much blame for the economic crisis has been placed on domestic factors within the affected Asian countries, broader external factors were also involved. Dieter (1998: 24) argued that while mistakes were made in the affected countries, 'The more important causes of the crisis were the flow of "hot money" into Southeast Asia, the sudden withdrawal of capital and the speculation against the currencies . . . The world financial system . . . failed to provide both adequate warning signals as well as solutions once the Asian crisis developed'. More fundamentally, Cheah (2000: 102–8) suggested that, from a global evolutionary perspective, the so-called Asian crisis is part of a larger systemic process of relative convergence and divergence, of catching-up and slowing-down, in the development process. In this process, development does not occur in the form of continuously harmonious evolutionary change. Indeed, crises are an inherent feature of this process. They contribute to periodic major discontinuities in the development process, and lead to radical shifts towards new forms and directions.

Furthermore, efforts to promote economic development in Asia incurred significant environmental and social costs.[2] One study of the consequences of economic development in China reported, 'Unfortunately, serious environmental damage has accompanied . . . rapid growth. Many of China's waterways are close to biological death from excessive discharge of organic pollutants. In many urban areas, atmospheric concentrations of pollutants such as suspended particulates and sulfur dioxide routinely exceed WHO safety standards by very large margins. As a result, hundreds of thousands of people are dying or becoming seriously ill from pollution-related respiratory disease each year' (Dasgupta et al., 1997a: 1). Another report noted that, 'The serious environmental degradation in China is . . . a result not only of its stage in development . . . its technological level, and size of its population, but also its policies – which have focused narrowly on accelerated industrialization, coupled with inherent biases which have led to protection, subsidization and unrealistic underpricing of natural resources' (Munasinghe, 1997: 16).[3]

Even in countries that have been successful in the pursuit of economic development, attention to environmental concerns has been limited and constrained (Perry and Teng, 1999). In Asia, many enterprises continue to engage in practices that are grossly detrimental to the local and wider environment. Recent occurrences that came to public notice include the events that contributed to the explosion at the nuclear materials processing plant at Tokaimura in Japan on 30 September 1999; the extensive recurring smog created over Indonesia, Singapore and Malaysia resulting from the practice of land clearance by the use of fire in Sumatra and Kalimantan (Glover and Jessup, 1999);[4] and the problems resulting from the OK Tedi mine in Papua New Guinea (Harper and Israel, 1999) and elsewhere. The involved organizations may not be willing to change or improve their practices (Dasgupta et al., 1997b; Banks, 1999).

While all business enterprises are keenly aware of the need for economic sustainability, and the more enlightened ones are increasingly conscious of the need for ecological sustainability, very few are attuned to the importance of social sustainability in their operations. For some, corporate philanthropy[5] serves to enhance corporate image and public goodwill towards the enterprise, but the organizations' operations are not directly concerned with and consciously geared towards poverty alleviation, reduction of social inequity, tensions and conflict, or the direct enhancement of the community's social well-being (see Haley, 1991). These enterprises knowingly or unknowingly adopt the narrow philosophy that 'the business of business is business'; that the 'only social responsibility of business is to increase its profit' (Friedman, 1963: 192); and that social and other needs in the community and society are the concerns of 'others', such as the government or charitable organizations.

However, in the aftermath of the crisis, popular concern has increased over the rise in poverty, widening social disparities, corruption, foreign domination, exploitative employment and trade practices, and the sale of questionable (possibly unsafe) products. Firms that have been subjected to criticism included McDonald's (Vidal, 1998; Wong, 2000), Nike (Vietnam Labor Watch, 1997; UNITE, 2000), Rio Tinto (TRAC, 1999: 1; Watts and Holme, 1999: 10), Mitsubishi (Greer and Bruno, 1996; Barkin, 1999: 182) and Monsanto (Krebs, 1999). Criticisms have also been directed against the World Bank and, in particular, the IMF (Oxfam International, 2000).[6] During the crisis, Oxfam International (1998: 8) highlighted the 'discrepancy between the macroeconomic framework of the IMF, and the social policy framework of the World Bank. In effect, these are pulling in different directions. The World Bank is in the hapless position of erecting social safety nets which are collapsing under the weight of rising poverty and the mass unemployment resulting from IMF programmes'. This discord compounded both the economic difficulties and the social strains.

These and other concerns and dissatisfactions have led to significant public demonstrations and protests. The most notable of these occurred at the third WTO ministerial meeting at Seattle in November 1999 (see Mander and Cavanagh, 1999), followed by further demonstrations at the IMF/World Bank spring meeting at Washington, DC in April 2000, at the World Economic Forum (WEF) held in Melbourne and the IMF/World Bank annual meeting in Prague in September 2000 (Pearlstein, 2000). These protests emphasize the need for new thinking and new strategies to address the problems that have emerged.

Achieving sustainability: the twenty-first century challenge

In this regard, Robinson and Tinker (1998: 14, 22) identify the economy, the ecological system, and human society as three interconnected, overlapping and coequal prime systems, with corresponding imperatives, namely: (a) the economic imperative is to ensure and to maintain adequate material standards of living for all people; (b) the ecological imperative is to remain within planetary biophysical carrying capacity; and (c) the social imperative is to provide social structures, including systems of governance, that effectively propagate and sustain the values by which people wish to live.

Robinson and Tinker (1998) pointed out that these three imperatives are interconnected and mutually reinforcing, with direct and indirect effects on each other, such that 'any attempt to address one system in isolation not only runs the risk of intensifying problems in the other systems, but also may give rise to feedback effects from the other systems which overwhelm the effects of the first intervention' (p. 24), and 'addressing any of these issues in isolation, without considering their interacting effects, can give rise to unanticipated higher order consequences in other realms, which cause problems of their own or undercut the initial policies' (p. 12).[7] Furthermore, they claimed that 'anthropogenic stress generated on a global scale is increasing in all three prime systems' (p. 17), and that 'accurately predicting system change in response to stress . . . requires greater knowledge than we have at present. Such change often goes in counter-intuitive directions' (p. 18).

Consequently, 'addressing any one of the three imperatives in isolation virtually guarantees failure. Nevertheless, this is what current policy-making commonly does' (Robinson and Tinker, 1998: 24).[8] Specifically, 'the current tendency is to concentrate on the economic imperative combined with a post hoc attempt to reconcile this with the ecological imperative, while ignoring the social imperative and its questions of North–South and intracountry equity' (p. 35). In contrast, Robinson and Tinker see the necessity for an integrated approach that explicitly and jointly addresses all three prime systems in a complementary manner.[9]

In 1987, the World Commission on Environment and Development (1987) introduced the concept of sustainable development, which postulated that economic, ecological and social development should be placed on an equal footing. Since then, sustainable development[10] has become an increasingly important concern among researchers, governments, NGOs and development organizations (see World Bank, 1999a: 87–105). Increasingly business organizations too must participate and incorporate sustainability issues into their planning and operational activities. For business enterprises, sustainability, or the concern for long-term viability, also includes three main dimensions: (a) economic sustainability, that is, business activities must be economically profitable; (b) ecological sustainability, that is, the activities must also be ecologically friendly and not damaging to the environment; and (c) social sustainability, that is, in addition to individual or private gain, the activities must also promote community and societal well-being, for instance by reducing social divisions, inequity and conflict. In this connection, the quest for sustainable development at the national and international (macro) level requires a corresponding concept, sustainable management, at the organizational and enterprise (micro) level; that is, management directly focused on the creation and effective management of economically, ecologically and socially sustainable enterprises. The specific foci and criteria for these three dimensions are identified in Figure 19.1.

If positive synergies are generated successfully by this integrated approach, they offer the possibility of achieving a state of sustainable abundance (Q4), depicted in Figure 19.2. While this situation may already exist for some groups, the challenge is to extend it towards a universal condition. Where business enterprises had previously focused their efforts largely (or completely) on achieving competitiveness vis-à-vis their business rivals (measured by various indicators of profitability), in the future enterprises will need to adopt a broader and more balanced focus to include concerns for habitability (measured by various indicators of eco efficiency), and community (measured by various indicators of quality of life).[11] By these means, sustainable management can provide the more integrated, holistic and balanced approach necessary for creating genuinely sustainable enterprises (see Brooks, 2000; Jorgensen, 2000). Similarly, such an approach would guide sustainable development efforts in the right direction to create sustainable societies.

Dimension	**Focus**	**Corporate performance criterion**	**Societal performance criterion**	**Global performance criterion**
Economic sustainability	Competitiveness	Corporate profitability	Societal wealth[12]	Global wealth
Ecological sustainability	Habitability	Corporate ecoefficiency[13]	Societal ecoefficiency	Global ecoefficiency
Social sustainability	Community	Corporate reputation[14]	Societal quality of life[15]	Global quality of life
All dimensions	Combined foci	Sustainable management index[16]	Sustainable development index[17]	Sustainable development index

Figure 19.1 Dimensions, foci and performance criteria for sustainable management and sustainable development

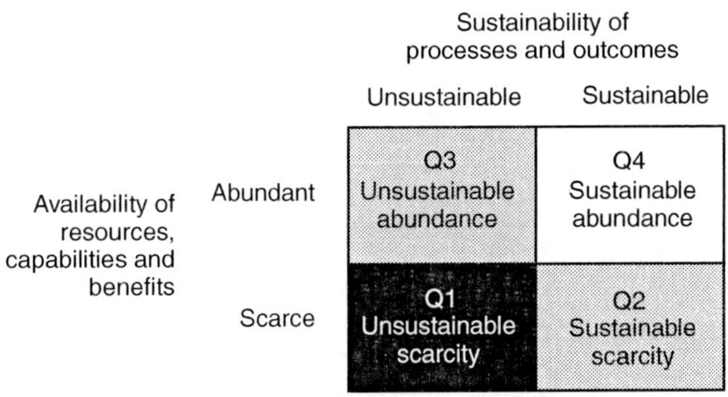

Figure 19.2 From unsustainable scarcity to sustainable abundance

Towards a diversified production system and a network economy

The growing need to address sustainability concerns occurs concomitantly with major technological and organizational changes in the mass production system that has dominated the major economies in the twentieth century. These changes have been described as flexible specialization (Piore and Sabel, 1984), lean production (Womack et al., 1990), diversified quality production (Streeck, 1991), productive diversity (Cope and Kalantzis, 1997), and mass customization (Pine, 1999).

Each of these overlapping concepts identifies certain aspects of what we may call the Diversified Production System (DPS), in contrast to the earlier Mass Production System (MPS).

The DPS refers to the emergence of a relatively new technological and organizational configuration, significantly different from the technological and organizational features of the MPS.[18] Firstly, the DPS benefits from the use of the new Information and Communication Technologies (ICT). This changes the dynamics of the production and communication process radically. According to Jain (1992: 245), it provides the capacity for decentralized production, descaling, better use of local resources and skills, reduced affluent discharges, improved energy efficiencies, and lower capital/labour ratios. Each of these benefits is significant; in combination, they have the capability to be revolutionary.

Evans and Wurster (1999) also suggest that the new technology alters the economics of information delivery, by removing the previous unavoidable trade-offs between richness (quality of information) and reach (number of recipients). This will alter the dynamics of business strategy and business operations.[19] The outcomes of this shift from the MPS to the DPS are manifested in at least six distinct dimensions: (a) location, (b) time, (c) variety, (d) material, (e) price, and (f) provider.

Location

Dramatic improvements in communication and transportation have reduced the impediment of distance. This has enabled organizations to extend the range of their operations and the number of locations where they can establish their presence. Physical barriers and national boundaries are also diminishing constraints with the emergence of a borderless world (Ohmae, 1990). Moreover, with miniaturization combined with the shift towards intangibles, distribution constraints can be reduced tremendously, such that products and services can be more easily delivered anywhere (everywhere). Furthermore, advances in ICT, the growth of the Internet, and the emergence of cyberspace and virtual worlds are significant means through which this process is being spread and intensified. Consequently, 'The meaning of "market place" is being fundamentally transformed for both the seller and the buyer' (Davis, 1987: 56).

Time

The developments described above are leading to outcomes where customers are served the product or service that they desire in the shortest possible time. Improvements in this capability lead to a tendency where the desired product or service becomes available at any time. This can be seen in the examples of home delivery of pizza in the case of products, and home-banking in the case of services. Ultimately, it generates a tendency towards immediate gratification of consumer wants, the moment they are conceived.[20] To facilitate this possibility, organizations will need to endeavour to create 'real-time structures; structures that change continually in tiny increments, not in large static quantum jumps. Each change is so minute that the overall effect is one of a structure in constant, seamless motion' (Davis, 1987: 41).

Variety

Another significant change resulting from the tremendously improved flexibility of production and distribution is the increasing range and diversity of products and services. This can be observed in the evolution from the corner grocery store to supermarkets, to shopping emporiums and shopping malls. Indeed, customers are now capable of being offered not just a range of goods and services produced in one location, but from throughout the globe.[21] This is complemented by the shift from mass production towards mass customization (see Gilmore and Pine, 2000). Ultimately, the tendency is that customers will be able to have any kind of goods or service tailored to their specific desires or specifications, anywhere and anytime. This is worlds apart from the situation when Henry Ford proclaimed that the Model T was available in any colour, so long as it was black.

Material

Miniaturization of products has led to a dramatic contraction of the space that they previously occupied. This is illustrated most vividly by the evolution from main-frame computers to palm-held portable computers, but the process is also observable in many other products; for instance, the encapsulation of the 32-volume contents of *Encyclopaedia Britannica* within two CD-ROMs. This spatial contraction has generally been accompanied by increased (not reduced) product capability, functionality, sophistication and, consequently, value. Another significant outcome is the development of products that use less (or no) material; for instance, new digital cameras that do not require film. An even more significant development in the shift away from materials is related to the rapid expansion of services in the economy. This has accelerated the shift away from tangibles such as physical resources (see Larson et al., 1986), towards intangibles (immaterials) such as information. This has the important consequence that economic activity is shifting away from resources which are potentially or actually finite, to resources (e.g., information) that are potentially or actually infinite. Indeed, the increasing importance (value added) of intangibles (no matter) attaches both to goods as well as to services. According to Davis (1987: 99), 'in the new economy, both inputs (resources) and outputs (goods and services) are increasingly intangible, and value will increasingly be attached to intangibles'.[22]

Price

There is a deflationary tendency (Shilling, 1998), leading towards a general fall in prices; and secondly, to a growing number of products and services becoming available at no charge. Software that are freely and legally available to be downloaded from the Internet provide examples of the latter.[23] This does not mean that no revenues will be available to private producers of such goods and services, only that not all aspects (parts) of the products and services that are provided in the private sector will be transacted for a price. Nevertheless, it is intriguing that it may be postulated as a general tendency that goods and services will become progressively cheaper, and that many privately produced goods and services will assume the characteristics of public ('free') goods (see Gross et al., 1995).

Provider

An increasing range of goods and services are self-made or self-serviced. That is, there is a growing capacity to shift from do (make) it for me to do (make) it yourself. Indeed, according to Kelly (1997: 188), 'The Network Economy rewards schemes that allow decentralized creation . . . An automobile maker in the Network Economy will establish a web of standards and outsourced suppliers, encouraging the web itself to invent the car, seeding the system with knowledge it gives away, engaging as many participants as broadly as possible, in order to create a virtuous loop where every member's success is shared and leveraged by all'. In this regard, it is noteworthy that, more than two decades ago, Gershuny (1978: 145–51), had perceptively predicted that in post-industrial society the household would become more important in production as well as in consumption.

These characteristics of the old vs. the new dynamics of production are summarized in Figure 19.3, which lists the six tendencies that lead ultimately to the provision of goods and services anywhere, anytime, any kind, with no matter, at no charge, and do it yourself. These developments lead towards a network economy.[24] In this regard, Kelly (1997) pointed to the widespread, relentless act of connecting everything to everything else. We are now engaged in a grand scheme to augment, to

Dimension	Old dynamics of the mass production system	New dynamics of the diversified production system
Location	The product or service is available only at specific or limited locations.	The product or service is available anywhere (everywhere).
Time	The product or service is available only at specific or limited times.	The product or service is available at any time.
Variety	The product or service is available only in specific or limited forms.	The product or service is available in multiple or customized forms.
Material	The product is tangible and bulky.	The product is miniaturized, or intangible, or available as a service.
Price	The product or service is available at a price.	The product or service is available at no charge.
Provider	The product or service is provided by others.	The product or service is self-provided.

Figure 19.3 Characteristics of the old and new dynamics of production

amplify, to enhance, and to extend the relationships and communications between all beings and all objects. That is why the Network Economy is a big deal. It is also significant because it offers possibilities for the dematerialization and the resocialization that Robinson and Tinker (1998: 24–35) advocated.

Consequently, the question that arises is: how do organizations and societies achieve sustainability while seeking to make the shift towards a diversified production system and a network economy? Conversely, how do organizational and societal responses to the challenges posed by the emergence of the DPS achieve congruence with the increasing need to achieve sustainability in that process? The answer is to consciously design (see de Bono, 1995: 110–116) organizational and societal systems that have the capability to marry flexibility and connectivity with sustainability.

The role of private enterprises

In congruence with the developments described above, private enterprises can make significant positive contributions by promoting wider access for themselves, their associates and their customers to the new ICT and, through that, greater access to a wide range of resources, services and opportunities. In this regard, Asian firms such as NEC, Acer and Creative Technology, have demonstrated that they can become significant players in the domestic as well as global economies. Furthermore, significant ICT production bases are developing in Singapore (the intelligent island), Malaysia (the multimedia supercorridor) and India (in Bangalore).[25] Such developments help to improve the foundation for promoting sustainable management and sustainable development.

For instance, Muhammed Yunus, the founder of Grameen bank in Bangladesh, is promoting the installation of cellular pay phones in all the villages in the country (Singh, 1997; Bhagat, 1998).[26] This method of extending communication facilities to the villages reduces the cost and other difficulties related to the provision of fixed-line telephone facilities. On that foundation, Yunus fosters new enterprises in the rural economy and directly promotes economic development in these poorer areas.

In fact, this development extends Yunus' earlier efforts to promote microcredit to the poor in Bangladesh through the Grameen Bank. This bank caters specifically to the poorest group in the country, particularly women (Ravallion and Wodon, 1997; Khandker, 1998; Yunus, 1999). Relatively small loans are provided without the requirement of collateral or security. Indeed, the ownership and control of the bank was designed to be owned principally by its clients, each of whom buys one share in the bank.

This is an example of how private firms can address more directly issues of economic, ecological and social sustainability, such as the problems of poverty and social inequity. The bank now serves as a model that has been replicated in several other countries, including the USA.[27] The success of its activities has led the Bank to extend its services to provide assistance for housing construction, medicare, land cultivation, fisheries and textiles. However, to achieve economic sustainability in a DPS and a network economy, enterprises will also need to develop better capabilities for managing diversity and managing responsiveness. The former will be necessary because in the DPS, firms will need to pursue a greater degree of diversity in their business strategies, production locations, scales of operation, forms of organization, composition of their workforce, and other aspects of business activity.

In relation to learning and innovation strategy, Llerena and Oltra (2000: 19) argue that 'diversity is a necessary condition and a result of technological change . . . an increase in the diversity of firms may lead to an increase in the efficiency of industrial dynamics'. In relation to workforce composition, as organizations diversify their strategies as well as the locations of their operations, management will tend to encounter greater diversity among their employees, and among their customers (Fernandez, 1993: 291).[28] The reported benefits of a diverse workforce are 'more critical strategic analysis, creativity, innovation, and high-quality decisions and solutions . . . given a creative task, heterogeneous groups adopted multiple strategies and identified more solutions than did homogeneous groups' (Fernandez, 1993: 284–85).[29] Indeed, in the DPS, pluralism is a major source of strength and competitive advantage (Cope and Kalantzis, 1997).

The reported success of Japanese companies in inculcating relatively successfully the main principles of the lean production system into a very different cultural milieu in the USA (Abo, 1994), as well as other locations in Asia (Itagaki, 1997), albeit in the form of hybrids, suggest that these companies are responding to the differences in the conditions of their foreign plants, and making numerous adaptations to their production system to suit the different composition of the workforces and other conditions abroad.[30]

In addition to achieving economic sustainability in the DPS, enterprises will need to develop better capabilities for managing responsiveness in the entrepreneurial process (see Cheah, 1998). Here, responsiveness refers to appropriate and timely changes or shifts from incremental innovations in stable or evolutionary situations (adaptivity) to radical innovations in revolutionary situations (creativity), or vice versa (see Li, 2000). In the more fluid and dynamic conditions of the DPS, capabilities for both adaptivity and creativity will be required by all firms (see Das, 2000; Haley and Haley, 2000a; Hobday, 2000). They will need to initiate and to implement not just single innovations one-at-a-time, but combinations of adaptive and creative innovations. The strategic considerations will hinge increasingly around questions of composition, balance, timing and sequencing of these combinations.

While economic viability has been a traditional concern of private firms, at present and in the future, this concern can no longer be pursued with a narrow focus (see de Bono, 1992; Harman and Porter, 1997; Prahalad, 1997; Theobald, 1999: 37–62). The private sector also has to be more concerned about the immediate environmental effects and the long-term ecological impact of its activities (see Stiglitz, 1997), for dangers to the local and global environment also generate significant direct and indirect costs and problems for private enterprise.

In the West, popular concerns, combined with the introduction of more stringent environmental regulations and new incentives have encouraged more firms to take fuller account of environmental issues in their operations (see Robertson and Jett, 1999; Browne, 2000; Wright, 2000). While the need for ecological sustainability creates greater demands on enterprises, it also provides many new entrepreneurial opportunities in pollution reduction (relating to air, water and land), resource conservation (relating to energy, water, land, fauna and flora), new waste management practices (such as recycling and vermiculture[31]), new forms of agricultural practices (Mollison, 1990), new energy sources (such as solar energy and clean fuel-cell technology, wind and geothermal technology),[32] and new economic activities, such as ecotourism (see Dowling, 1998; Haley and Haley, 2000b).

Various governments have introduced policies and incentives to encourage more ecologically friendly practices by private firms. Business associations such as the World Business Council for Sustainable Development have also helped to educate management on these issues, in particular, promoting the concept of ecoefficiency[33] (see WBCSD, 1996; 1999). Growing awareness of the environmental costs of their operations has caused some enlightened managers to change their corporate strategies. However, there is still a need for many more firms to raise their efforts to a strategic level and make the process of environmental management an essential part of doing business, not a side issue (Dechant and Altman, 1994: 7).

Private firms can also promote social sustainability by adopting socially responsible practices that deliver safer products, provide fair rewards and good working conditions, enhance social capital, reduce social inequities, tensions and conflicts, and provide support for democratic principles and practices in the society. Like the Grameen Bank, they can also try to cater to the needs of the lower-income groups in the community to a greater extent. Enterprises whose activities focus directly on serving the poor, and whose operations directly and indirectly reduce social disparities and alleviate societal tensions and conflict generate virtuous circles that expand their own market potential over time, and generate positive externalities for the society as well.

With much of the world's population beyond the reach of many of the world's business enterprises because their goods and services are not affordable by, or are simply irrelevant to the needs of that population, those enterprises that cater only to the wealthy are limited to a relatively small segment of the potential world market. Indeed, those enterprises whose operations serve to make the rich richer, and the poor poorer, are directly and indirectly narrowing their potential client base further and, consequently, eroding their own long-term sustainability in this respect. Furthermore, in cases where the deepening of such social divisions compounds ethnic, religious and other community differences, the result could be a very volatile environment that is not conducive to normal business activity and to further investment in that location. The social divisions, tensions and upheavals in Indonesia and Fiji are only the most recent experiences that highlight this point.

With the extension of the Internet, there is significant potential for affordable communication services to be provided by private enterprises even to people in relatively isolated and economically impoverished locations. With this development, affordable but good quality educational and health services could follow. As these groups are increasingly connected to the providers of goods and services that can potentially and actually be provided anywhere, anytime, and at a decreasing price or with no charge, the economic and other capabilities of these groups will improve, including their ability to raise their purchasing power. This will make them more attractive to an even wider range of private providers of goods and services. By these means, the poor can be reintegrated into the mainstream economy and society.

Local firms and multinational corporations are justifiably concerned about the climate for new or continuing investments, and this has led to growing interest in business risk assessment and risk management (Howell and Xie, 2000). In this regard, however, private enterprises also need to consider more carefully the manner in which their own behaviour and operations may pollute and damage the investment climate for their individual and collective interests.[34] When business firms aggressively pursue narrow self-interest and short-term profitability at the expense of their customers, employees and the community, they poison the atmosphere and the environment in which they operate. When consumers are hurt by unsafe products and unethical business practices, when employees are exploited through low wages and oppressive working conditions, when business enterprises encourage corrupt practices and directly and indirectly promote social inequity, tensions and conflict, private enterprises undermine the basic foundations for their sustainable operations. In reaction to this, firms now confront the emergence in various locations of a moral code that carries wider and higher standards and expectations (see Narayanan, 2000; Zeldin and di Florio, 2000). It is in this context that an emphasis on corporate reputation (based on corporate accountability, transparency and social responsibility) has re-emerged (see Kahn et al., 1999; Peters, 2000).

Thus, for business enterprises, recovery from the crisis should not mean a return to business as usual (see Hitt, 2000; Nadler and Tushman, 1999). To achieve a major reorientation of business objectives and strategies to take into account the need to manage for economic, ecological and social sustainability, firms will need to adopt a significantly broader perspective in their planning, operational and self-monitoring efforts (see Porter, 1997; Cottrell and Rankin, 2000).

In particular, these efforts should also take into account the ongoing shift from the mass production system towards what may be called a diversified production system. Indeed, the new DPS could make previously economically depressed, socially disadvantaged and geographically isolated communities more attractive to private providers of goods and services that are seeking to find new markets and to expand their potential client base. Those enterprises that capitalize on the new dynamics of the DPS are likely to see these possibilities most clearly. They would be among those who realize that economic, ecological and social sustainability can be complementary (not necessarily conflicting) objectives, and they would seek to create strong competitive advantages based on that fact. These multidimensional advantages would make such enterprises more genuinely sustainable than others that fail to perceive these possibilities and to capitalize on them. In short, the twenty-first century will be the century of the rise of the sustainable enterprise.

The role of the public sector

Contrary to the claims of the neo-liberals and economic rationalists, there is a large, important and growing role for the public sector in the development process. *Laissez-faire* is not (and never was) a serious option in the modern context, and smaller government may simply be weaker government.[35] To the problem of bad (inefficient, incompetent or corrupt) government, the economic rationalists and neo-liberals make the mistake of prescribing the wrong solution of significantly smaller (or no) government,[36] when the correct remedy is good (effective, competent and ethical) government.

The desirable alternative to the soft state (Myrdal, 1968) is not the small state of the neo-liberals, or the strong (hard) state of the authoritarian regimes, but the effective state that (independently or in collaboration with other states) establishes, observes and enforces high ethical standards of behaviour, competently promotes productive economic activities that lead to full employment and rising living standards, expands social capital, cares for the disadvantaged, protects the habitat and other public goods, within a genuinely democratic framework (see Kaul et al., 1999; UNRISD, 2000). Within this context, the most fruitful concept is not self-regulation, or no regulation, but responsive regulation (Ayres and Braithwaite, 1992). In this regard, 'it seems strange that, in spite of increasing evidence that liberalization worsens the situation for the poor and the local environment in the countries of the South, it continues to be widely adhered to (Forrester, 1999). It may be in the interest of certain sectors of business to promote liberalization, but it seems clear that many social groups, including some in the business community, are not benefiting from liberalization. On the contrary, all indications are that the economies of the South . . . are continuing to deteriorate, with the incidence of poverty spreading . . .' (Atkinson, 2000: 38.) See also Weisbrot et al. (2000).

Indeed, private enterprise too relies significantly on the benefits of a competent government and an effective public sector to provide the physical and institutional infrastucture required for a modern economy and society to function normally; to establish appropriate, clear and stable ground rules for business and other activities to be conducted effectively; and, not least, to provide support and even protection when serious problems threaten the collective interest. These conditions would apply even in the most free-market oriented countries in the world, and the clearest demonstration of these imperatives is revealed when those functions are not performed adequately or effectively, resulting in a crisis or malaise that the private sector cannot resolve by itself.[37]

Even where enlightened private enterprises act in economically, ecologically and socially responsible ways in their business activities, there are inherent limits to the extent to which these enterprises (and their sustainable management efforts) can take responsibility for ensuring improvements in the wealth, ecological health and general well-being of the broader society. More importantly, sustainable management and sustainable development are complements (not substitutes) in the development process.

Governments can promote economic sustainability by enhancing domestic productive capacity and wealth generating capability, and providing effective guidance and support for private-sector efforts to increase its competitiveness and its business opportunities (see Haley, 2000; Wei and Christodoulou, 2000: 468–69). In this regard, the DPS and the network economy provides greater scope and opportunity for governments to facilitate and to support wealth-creation activities.

However, it should also be clear to the leaders of market economies that they should be prepared for the busts as well as the booms. Indeed, Galbraith (1996: 33) pointed to '... the painful tendency of the modern economy to periods, sometimes prolonged, of recession and stagnation, accompanied, inevitably, by more unemployment. These recurrent periods, not continuous vigorous expansion, are a basic feature of the market system. So in modern times is continuing unemployment, even in periods of marked growth and well-being'.

These recurring recessions (crises), and persistence of significant levels of unemployment, cannot be attributed simply to individual and random causes; they also have structural and systemic roots. Indeed, the enhanced capabilities of the new ICT has the potential to intensify the frequency, volatility and the severity of these problems. This highlights the need for a fundamental rethinking of the methods and the processes of managing modern economies in the dual contexts of the shift towards the DPS and the network economy; as well as the imperative for a broader focus on sustainability. However, there is little evidence that this need is widely appreciated, least of all among the neo-liberals and economic rationalists.[38]

Next, governments can promote ecological sustainability, not only by formal regulation and enforcement, but also through a variety of other complementary measures. A recent report noted that the imposition of anti-pollution levies, complemented by community monitoring and other practical measures, led successfully to significant reductions in pollution levels in several countries in Asia and South America. It suggests that 'coordinated action on all three fronts – economic reform, formal regulation and informal regulation – can reduce industrial pollution significantly, even in very poor countries' (Wheeler et al., 2000: 144; see also Hanrahan, 1997). This outcome provides the basis for further efforts to formulate and to implement other innovative and collaborative measures involving government regulators, community representatives, factory managers and other stakeholders, to reduce pollution levels further.

However, to be more effective in this field, governments will need to confront and reform some key aspects of current thinking and practice. For instance, '... mainstream economists reject the very existence of the problematic of sustainability, asserting that whatever resources are exhausted or despoiled will always be replaced by substitutes ... At the level of practice ... sustainable development is promoted as a voluntary activity of all actors with little attempt to provide structures within which the various actors can work towards the same ends. Environmental ministries and agencies are universally on the margins of the development process and their capacity and remit even to regulate environmental impacts adequately... are restricted by the neo-liberal ideological and political context that puts the interests of economic actors first (Atkinson, 2000: 14)'.

Finally, governments can and should promote social sustainability more effectively. In this context, Robinson and Tinker (1998: 35) noted that, 'Sustainable development will not be achieved through technical fixes alone. A strong social dimension has to do not only with political issues, but also with values, lifestyles, social organization, and individual and collective behaviour. Both dematerialization and resocialization are needed.' These, too, will require significant reforms. For instance, a recent Asia Pacific Economic Cooperation (APEC) report noted that 'the absence of formal social safety nets in most of the [Asian] economies was a real cause of concern. Social security and pension systems, medical or health insurance and educational loan systems in these economies were observed to be weak or non-existent when the crisis broke out. In Indonesia, Thailand and the Philippines, workers have to rely on their own resources or their families as they become unemployed' (APEC Economic Committee, 2000a: 144). Moreover, even the existing limited safety nets 'have been constrained by fiscal retrenchment and associated institutional weaknesses' (p. 150). See also Mittal et al. (1998) and Tegtmeier (1999).

However, the APEC report failed to provide significant and effective advice on how to promote social sustainability in its own right. The report focused principally on how economic recovery might be achieved and, thus, provide relief to other areas of the society. In contrast, the International Labour Organisation (ILO) gave strong encouragement to the adoption of social protection measures. It emphasized that 'Alarmist rhetoric notwithstanding, social protection, even in the supposedly expensive forms to be found in most advanced countries, is affordable in the long-run. It is affordable because it is essential for people, but also because it is productive in the longer term. Societies which do not pay enough attention to security, especially the security of their weaker members, eventually suffer a destructive backlash' (Juan Somavia, in the introduction to ILO, 2000).

Beyond the measures for social protection and poverty reduction, there are significant issues relating to questions about the basis of community well-being, the preservation and expansion of social capital, and the promotion of social cohesion and social transformation (see Bessis, 1995; Durston, 1999; Social Development Department, 2000).

These issues go beyond remedial concerns, and touch on societal values and meanings. For instance, it may be asked: if a DPS and a network economy provide possibilities for substantially enhanced wealth creation, how would that wealth be distributed and what would it be used for? This would also call into question current patterns of wealth distribution and utilization.

Movement towards a DPS and a network economy also raises questions about the most likely and most appropriate form of governance in this new context. One perspective suggests that there will be a corresponding shift towards more liberal, participative and decentralized government. Tapscott and Agnew (1999: 37) postulate that 'Citizen-centered government will create new roles for citizens and new prominence for citizen engagement as governance systems re-engage the citizenry, moving beyond "broadcast" democracy to a more intimate and immediate model'. However, they also warn, 'Serious issues remain unresolved. Around the globe, people are rightfully wary of the power of the new technologies to erode their privacy. Even in countries with the highest levels of technology penetration, unacceptable gaps between digital haves and have-nots are growing, challenging both governments and businesses to address the international and domestic digital divide with substantive and meaningful solutions' (Tapscott and Agnew, 1999: 37).

At the international level, there have been several major meetings among governments, international development agencies and NGOs at various forums to try to promote more coordinated international efforts to address these and other sustainability concerns and opportunities.[39] These agencies are also increasingly aware of the importance and growing impact of the new ICT. In this regard, recently, the leaders of APEC countries committed themselves to promote universal Internet access to information and services by 2010.[40] However, serious consideration also needs to be devoted to further reforms in international trade, investment, technology transfer and related issues (see Smith, 2000, Chs. 20–3). Proposals offered by the Brandt Commission and others (see Brandt Commission, 1983; Frankman, 1996; Nef, 1999; Sagasti and Alcalde, 1999, Ch. 6; Sen 1999), also deserve attention and effective action.

Possibilities vs. realities

The propositions presented above relating to the attainable benefits flowing from sustainable management and sustainable development refer largely to possibilities. Undoubtedly, the process to convert them into reality will be a difficult one in many cases (see Lappe et al., 1998;

Mkandawire and Rodriguez, 2000; Singh, 2000). Several difficulties may be postulated.

First, the shift towards a diversified production system and a network economy, facilitated by the new ICT, will bring along negative as well as positive impacts (see Holderness, 1995; Gulledge and Haszko, 1996; Hamelink, 1997). The benefits as well as the difficulties will not be distributed evenly. Consequently, for some groups the net impact will be adverse.

Second, the incentives for firms to adopt sustainable management practices are not well appreciated, and are also weak or lacking.[41] Efforts to promote sustainable management and sustainable development lack coherence, support and continuity. Consequently, they fail to blossom and to generate dynamic ripple effects. Meanwhile, domestic and global competition has grown more intense, and there are strong pressures for firms and governments to focus on a narrow definition of the bottom line, and on short-term concerns (see Atkinson, 2000: 8–9).

Third, sustainability and unsustainability lie on a separate dimension to abundance and scarcity (see Figure 19.2). Consequently, even if sustainability were achievable, abundance would not be assured because it does not depend only on the physical quantity of a product relative to the number of people who want it. There are significant artificial and institutional barriers that block access for some individuals and groups to goods that are otherwise in abundant supply.[42]

Fourth, economic liberalization policies and the processes of globalization, despite their benefits, have left countries more exposed and vulnerable to the vagaries of market forces. This problem is particularly acute in countries where the social safety nets are weak or lacking. The public sector has been weakened significantly by cost-cutting, downsizing and privatization. Consequently, it is less capable of promoting or supporting sustainable development and sustainable management efforts, as well as the shift from the MPS to the DPS.

Fifth, the needs of poorer groups continue to be neglected because they are not backed by effective purchasing power, or by political influence. Indeed, there are strong forces of polarization that favour the rich, the powerful and the more technologically advanced groups and countries. The shift from the MPS to the DPS will make the rich richer, and the technologically advanced more powerful and more dominant. Economic, social and political crises also lead to a shift from the rule of law to rule by the strong and the corrupt, or to the deeper entrenchment of the latter. More fundamentally, it has been argued that, 'The only feasible answer to ever-increasing underdevelopment is a response to basic needs that is planned as a long-range goal for areas which will always have a different capital structure' (Illich, 1973: 365). See also Douthwaite (1999) and Schumacher (1974).

Sixth, the current international environment is less supportive. The more developed countries are less willing to provide (a) substantial financial and other forms of assistance to developing countries; and (b) market access to developing-country exports on a scale large enough to reverse fully the adverse effects of the economic crisis, and to support a sustained recovery leading to substantially higher levels of employment and improvements in living standards. If successful, recent international trade liberalization efforts will benefit the more developed countries just as much as (or more than) the less developed countries.

Finally, the problem lies with a system that is fundamentally crisis-prone.[43] With the failure of previous efforts to promote a New International Economic Order (NIEO), there are currently no significant efforts being undertaken to correct the structural and systemic problems that exist at the international level.

For these and other reasons, there are grounds for pessimism (even cynicism) about the prospects for betterment in the living conditions of the poor. From this perspective, in the absence of more fundamental reforms, sustainable abundance may be only another mirage that the poor and the less-developed countries face. Indeed, the contradiction between the possibilities and the realities will itself generate significant tensions and stresses. These will intensify as the possibilities flowing from the DPS and the network economy become more profuse and more obvious.

Conclusion: towards sustainable abundance in a network economy?

At present, most of the world's population inhabits the space between the horrors of unsustainable scarcity and the prospect of sustainable abundance, while the forces that have been unleashed by global competition and intensified by the recent economic crisis are generating pressures for organizations to respond to the new dynamics of production. At the same time, organizations and governments will need to broaden their focus and devote greater emphasis to the management of economic, ecological and social sustainability. In this context, there are optimists who perceive a very bright future for humankind,[44] and who seem to dismiss present concerns and difficulties as temporary or insignificant. However, the pessimists (Meadows et al., 1992; Leakey and

Lewin, 1995; Rifkin, 1995) foresee a compounding of the difficulties to the point where it is beyond human control. These opposed perspectives represent the two sides of the sustainability challenge. Between the sights of the optimists and the pessimists lie both the threats to and the opportunities for a better life for a much greater proportion of the world's population.

The twenty-first century is still divided markedly between the rich minority and the poor majority. This is not a morally desirable situation. It is arguably also not sustainable in practice. At the same time, environmental and ecological problems are also threatening the viability of present development processes in the world. Furthermore, there is the real possibility that major economic crises will recur (see Galbraith, 1999). Moreover, while the DPS and the network economy provide significant possibilities for creation of greater wealth, reduction of disparities, and higher levels of participation, these may not be realized if the opportunities are not widely distributed and effectively utilized. In such situations, the haves could gain significantly more, while the have-nots could fall even further behind (see Castells, 1998: 75–165).

This situation raises fundamental questions at both the micro and macro levels about the processes of creation and distribution of wealth and resources, and about the possibilities for a satisfactory quality of life for the world's population. How can we generate and equitably share an abundance of wealth and other resources in a sustainable way? Specifically, how do we manage the processes of innovation and organizational, societal and global change so as to transform this situation into a state of sustainable abundance? While the possibilities exist for this transformation to occur, in reality there are many obstacles and difficulties. This presents both an intellectual challenge (to formulate appropriate concepts, analytical frameworks and diagnostic techniques), as well as practical challenges (to create, for instance, more effective organizational strategies, decision-making processes, and reward systems). In short, the challenge is to formulate clear concepts, identify appropriate goals, and develop effective means to achieve them.

Notes

1 Singh (2000: 34–5) also noted that 'in the light of current macroeconomic trends in both advanced and developing countries, the short-term prospects for reducing poverty and achieving full employment are far from encouraging... the present regime of liberalization and globalization... is sub-optimal for both developing and developed countries'.

2 See, among others, Bello and Rosenfeld, 1990; Kurien, 1991; Brookfield and Byron, 1993, Chaps. 13–15; Howard, 1993; You, 1995; Barraclough and Finger-Stich, 1996; Zhang, 1996; Intal, 1998: 239–44.
3 See http://www.worldbank.org/nipr/china/video/index.htm
4 Harrison (1997) reported, 'The fires in Southeast Asia are a world disaster caused by indifference to pollution, powerful multinationals, lack of law enforcement and official corruption. Fuelling it is unfathomable greed'. He cited the involvement of companies from the USA, Japan, Korea, Malaysia and Indonesia.
5 Brooks (2000) cites philanthropy as only stage two in a five-stage process beginning with profit focus, followed by philanthropy, community affairs, community investment and sustainable business.
6 See also Bello et al., 1982; Danaher, 1994; Chossudovsky, 1997; Joint Economic Committee, 1998; Krugman, 1998; Tobin and Ranis, 1998; Boafo-Arthur, 1999; The Development Gap, 1999; Hansen-Kuhn et al., 1999; Chomthongdi, 2000; Hellinger, 2000; Smith, 2000, Chaps. 10–12; Stiglitz, 2000; and Woodroffe and Ellis-Jones, 2000. Stiglitz asked: 'To what extent did the IMF and the Treasury Department push policies that actually contributed to the increased global economic volatility?... Most importantly, did America – and the IMF – push policies because we... believed the policies would help East Asia or because we believed they would benefit financial interests in the United States and the advanced industrial world? And, if we believed our policies were helping East Asia, where was the evidence? As a participant in these debates, I got to see the evidence. There was none'.
7 They provide the example that 'raising energy prices significantly to reduce energy emissions will disproportionately affect poorer citizens, thus increasing income disparities and contributing to social unsustainability' (Robinson and Tinker, 1998: 12).
8 In this regard, Oxfam International (1998: 8) emphasized that 'it is crucial that the artificial separation of social and economic policy be ended. Human development and poverty considerations should be integral parts of the macroeconomic policy framework, which is currently dominated by narrow – and deeply flawed – financial targets. Second, an institutional framework must be created within which the IMF and the World Bank can provide a more integrated response to financial crisis. The alternative is for the World Bank to continue its present policy of arriving after the event in a largely futile effort to counteract the negative consequences of IMF prescriptions'.
9 They suggest that this integrated approach should incorporate two sets of policy measures that aim to promote 'dematerialization' of the economy and 'resocialization' of the society. The former involves the uncoupling of (a) economic growth and improvements in living standards (consumption of goods and services) from (b) increased consumption of energy and materials (for instance, by further development and greater utilization of more environmentally benign technologies). The latter involves the uncoupling of (c) human well-being from (a), for instance, by greater participation in the informal economy.
10 The concept of sustainable development has been broadly defined as development that 'meets the needs of the present without compromising the ability of future generations to meet their own needs... Sustainable

development is not a fixed state of harmony, but rather a process of change in which the exploitation of resources, the direction of investments, the orientation of technological development, and institutional change are made consistent with the future as well as present needs' (World Commission on Environment and Development, 1987).

11 From this perspective, there has been an excessive dominance of Economics and the profession of economists in the public policy arena, as well as the excessive emphasis on competitiveness by Business Schools and the management profession in the corporate arena.

12 An improved version of the orthodox Gross National Product (GNP) may be formulated for the Societal Wealth Indicator (SWI).

13 See WBCSD (1999).

14 See Fombrun (1986); Kahn et al. (1999).

15 This should take into account the 'human poverty index' (UNDP, 2000). Another relevant concept is the 'index of social progress' (Estes, 1992). See also Department of Community Services (1998), and Hirschhorn (2000).

16 See the latest sustainability reporting guidelines presented by GRI (2000), and the concept of 'the triple bottom line'. For one organization's attempt to apply such standards, see Shell (2000).

17 Existing relevant concepts include the 'human development index' (UNDP, 2000) and the 'genuine progress indicator' (Cobb et al., 1999). Another intriguing concept in this regard is the 'gross national happiness', used in Bhutan. See http://community.expo2000.de/forum/exhibits/ex_322/queen. html. Similarly, for Galbraith, the goal is to reach an achievable 'good society': 'In the good society all of its citizens must have personal liberty, basic well-being, racial and ethnic equality, the opportunity for a rewarding life' (Galbraith, 1996: 4).

18 The observation by Schonberger (1996: 115) that mass customization is 'the first derivative of mass production' is noteworthy. Indeed, the DPS does not constitute a complete rejection of MPS methods. Instead, it involves the incorporation and revolutionary extension of those methods within a broader framework of the production process, and based on significantly superior capabilities (relating to aspects such as flexibility, quality, speed, design, coordination, etc.) that were unfeasible or inapplicable in the MPS phase of the evolution of the production process. To use an analogy, if the DPS is the butterfly (adult), the MPS is the caterpillar (infant).

19 'When everyone can exchange rich information without constraints on reach, the channel choices for marketers, the inefficiencies of consumer search, the hierarchical structure of supply chains, the organizational pyramid, asymmetries of information, and the boundaries of the corporation itself will all be thrown into question. The competitive advantages that depended on them will be challenged. The business structures that had been shaped by them will fall apart' (Evans and Wurster, 1999: 37).

20 In this regard, it is significant that Bill Gates' (2000) recent book is titled, *Business @ the Speed of Thought*.

21 For an account of how water, bottled in Fiji, is exported to the USA to compete against 600 versions of this product, see Cossar (2000: 20, 22).

22 Ayres (1996) and Robinson and Tinker (1998) suggest that dematerialization is a positive development that promotes sustainability. Indeed, Itami

(1987: 1) argued that 'invisible assets are often a firm's only real source of competitive edge that can be sustained over time'.

23 In addition to software such as Netscape Communicator and Internet Explorer that are offered without charge by commercial firms, open-source software, provided by programmers who volunteer to develop software for public distribution, is also becoming more significant (see Wegberg and Berends, 2000).

24 There are several other concepts in the literature that have an overlapping meaning or focus. They include: new economy, information economy, knowledge economy, internet economy, digital economy, weightless economy, attention economy and e-economy.

25 Wetzler (2000) provides an account of developments in Bangalore that is both inspiring and depressing.

26 For examples of other efforts to introduce new ICT to poor and remote populations in Asia, see Wheeler (1996) and Long (1996).

27 For some criticisms of the operations of the Grameen Bank and other micro-credit schemes, see Mayoux (1995) and Chowdhury (2000).

28 From this perspective, 'Managing diversity is a corporate strategy directly tied into the business strategy for managing organizational change and improving productivity in the 1990s and beyond . . . As today's work forces and customer bases in Japan, the United States, and the EC countries continue to evolve and become more diverse in terms of race, gender, age, sexual orientation, culture, language, religion, disabilities, and other characteristics, it is necessary for corporations to shift their emphasis from homogeneity to diversity in their approach to managing people and courting different customer markets' (Fernandez, 1993: 291–92). While marketing departments have long realized the importance of taking into account differences in customer tastes and preferences, it is only relatively recently that managers have been alerted to the importance of managing effectively the ethnic, cultural and other significant experiential differences among their employees (see Kossek and Lobel, 1996).

29 These results flow partly from the combination of the strengths of different cognitive styles contained in heterogeneous groups (Kirton and de Ciantis, 1989: 95–6).

30 See also Steffensen (2000). Remarks by some Japanese researchers demonstrate their appreciation of the need for a new form of management and production that would be capable of effectively accommodating national differences: 'We believe that the future belongs to companies that can take the best of the East and the West and start building a universal model to create new knowledge within their organizations. Nationalities will be of no relevance . . . Managers in the East and the West need to build and manage multiple conversions, spirals, and syntheses' (Nonaka and Takeuchi, 1995: 245).

31 See the efforts of Vermitech to apply the use of earthworms on a large scale for waste management, and to derive valuable soil-enriching by-products from this process at: http://www.vermitech.com.au

32 See Flavin (1996), Leslie (1997), and Chawii (2000). A study of the introduction in India of renewable energy technology, in particular, wind energy, found that there were benefits as well as various planning, administrative and implementation difficulties (Iyer, 1999).

33 'Ecoefficiency is reached by the delivery of competitively priced goods and services that satisfy human needs and bring quality of life, while progressively reducing ecological impact and resource intensity throughout the life cycle, to a level at least in line with the earth's estimated carrying capacity' (WBCSD, 1996: 11).

34 One study noted that, 'In most East Asian economies wealth is concentrated in the hands of a few families. Legal and regulatory developments may have been impeded by the concentration of corporate wealth . . . Whether structural reforms can fully take hold without changes in ownership is an open question' (Claessens et al., 2000: 36–37).

35 Atkinson (2000: iii) contends that, 'neo-liberal policies undermine development efforts by weakening government responsibility in key areas of public concern. In addition, free-market reforms lack environmental sensitivity and encourage deep splits with communities, as income gaps grow larger'.

36 Fisher (2000) describes a bleak scenario resulting from the absence of government. See also the meagre and questionable results of privatization experience in Africa (Makalou, 1999). Whether China, in its efforts to reduce the size of its government (see Zhang and Li, 2000), can gain the expected benefits and avoid the negative experiences encountered elsewhere, will have to be assessed in the future.

37 The recent (and continuing) economic crisis in various Asian countries provides one example.

38 An analogy may be drawn to the practice of conducting present-day elections based on nineteenth-century voting methods and vote-counting practices. The capacity of news networks to disseminate the results of the voting, far exceeding the capacity of the machinery to collect and count the votes comprehensively, accurately and expeditiously, can lead to dubious and problematic outcomes, as illustrated by the recent American presidential elections.

39 At the United Nations Conference on Environment and Development (UNCED), held in Rio de Janeiro in June 1992. The outcome was *Agenda 21: the Rio Declaration on Environment and Development.* It embraced the concept of sustainable development, and formulated a framework for its promotion. This was followed by the World Summit for Social Development at Copenhagen in March 1995. It issued the *Copenhagen Declaration on Social Development.* In 1997, a meeting to confer on the problem of climate change produced the *Kyoto Protocol.* A follow-up to the Copenhagen meeting was held in June 2000, and its report was titled, *Visible Hands: Taking Responsibility for Social Development.* The United Nations also hosted the Millennium Forum in May 2000. Its report was titled *We the Peoples: the Role of the United Nations in the 21st Century.* Atkinson (2000: 2–5) provided a critical assessment of such events.

40 Specifically, Point 15 in the APEC Leaders Declaration issued on 16 November 2000, stated: 'Our vision is to prepare each of our economies and all of our people to use the technology revolution as a passport to the fruits of globalization . . . We commit to develop and implement a policy framework which will enable the people of urban, provincial and rural communities in every economy to have individual or community-based access to information and services offered via the Internet by 2010. As a first step toward

this goal we aim to triple the number of people within the region with individual and community-based access by 2005'. See also APEC Economic Committee (2000b).

41 Utting (2000: vi) noted that, 'While [various factors] may encourage corporations to be more responsive to environmental and social concerns . . . the process of change is likely to remain fairly fragmented, spread unevenly in terms of companies, countries and sectors, and, from the perspective of sustainable development, fraught with contradictions. What amounts to a fairly minimalist and uneven agenda is not simply a reflection of the fact that the process of change is of recent origin; it also derives from the way in which companies choose to respond – responses that often involve imagery, public relations and relatively minor adjustments in management systems and practices, as opposed to significant changes in the social and environmental impact of a company's activities'.

42 This situation has been noted by Lappe et al. (1998) in relation to the continuation of hunger and famine in the midst of an overall abundance in the world's food supply.

43 'When a single car has an accident on a bend in the highway, one might infer something about the driver or his car. But when, at the same bend, there are accidents day in and day out, the presumption changes – there is probably something wrong with the road. The fact that such a large number of countries have been affected by this crisis and required large official bailouts suggests some fundamental systemic weaknesses' (Joseph Stiglitz, in World Bank, 1999b: xii).

44 Zey (1994: 45) claimed boldly that 'Humanity is about to overcome scarcity, biological restrictions, and nature itself'. Furthermore, 'In the final analysis, humanity does not have to choose between progress and the health of the environment. Not only are these two not in conflict, they are very much interdependent. As the Macroindustrial Era evolves, society will simultaneously tap the potential of its own inventions and utilize technology to improve the environment'. See also Penzias (1995), and Schwartz and Leyden (1997).

References

Abo, T. (ed.) (1994) *Hybrid Factory: the Japanese Production System in the United States*, Oxford: Oxford University Press.

APEC Economic Committee (2000a), *Building the Future of APEC Economies*, APEC, Tokyo.

APEC Economic Committee (2000b), *Towards Knowledge-based Economies in APEC*, APEC, Tokyo.

Atkinson, A. (2000) 'Promoting sustainable human development in cities of the South: a Southeast Asian Perspective', *Geneva 2000* Occasional Paper no. 6, UNRISD, Geneva.

Ayres, R. (1996) 'Technology, progress and economic growth', *European Management Journal*, 14(6): 562–75.

Ayres, I. and J. Braithwaite (1992) *Responsive Regulation: Transcending the Deregulation Debate*, Oxford: Oxford University Press.

Banks, G. (1999) 'Keeping an eye on the beast: social monitoring of large scale mines in New Guinea', Resource Management in Asia-Pacific, Working Paper 1999/21, Australian National University, Canberra.
Barkin, D. (1999) 'The greening of business in Mexico', UNRISD Discussion Paper no. 10, Geneva.
Barraclough, S. and A. Finger-Stich (1996) 'Some ecological and social implications of commercial shrimp farming in Asia', UNRISD Discussion Paper no. 74, UNRISD, Geneva.
Bello, W., Kinley, D. and E. Elinson (1982) *Development Debacle: the World Bank in the Philippines*, Institute for Food and Development Policy, San Francisco.
Bello, W. and S. Rosenfeld (1990) *Dragons in Distress: Asia's Miracle Economies in Crisis*, Harmondsworth: Penguin.
Bessis, S. (1995) 'From social exclusion to social cohesion: towards a policy agenda', MOST-UNESCO Policy Paper no. 2, UNESCO, Paris.
Bhagat, R. (1998) 'Cell-phones a big hit in Bangladesh villages', *Business Line*, 16 April.
Boafo-Arthur, K. (1999) 'Structural adjustment programs (SAPs) in Ghana: interrogating PNDC's Implementation', *West Africa Review*, 1(1).
Brandt Commission (1983) *Common Crisis North-South: Co-operation for World Recovery*, London: Pan.
Brookfield, H. and Y. Byron (1993) *Southeast Asia's Environmental Future: The Search for Sustainability*, New York: United Nations University Press.
Brooks, J. (2000) 'Sustainability: the new bottom line', *'Re: Business*, PricewaterhouseCoopers, June.
Browne, J. (2000) 'Sustainability: what will it cost?', *Re: Business*, PricewaterhouseCoopers, August.
Castells, M. (1998) *End of Millennium*, Oxford: Blackwell.
Chawii, L. (2000) 'The Future of Clean Energy', *Down to Earth*, 9(5).
Cheah, H. B. (1998) 'Entrepreneurial development: understanding and managing change in the entrepreneurial process', *Journal of Enterprising Culture*, 6(1): 25–47.
Cheah, H. B. (2000) 'The Asian economic crisis: three perspectives on the unfolding problems in the global economy', in F.-J. Richter (ed.) *The East Asian Development Model: Economic Growth, Institutional Failure and the Aftermath of the Crisis*, London: Macmillan.
Chomthongdi, J. (2000) 'The IMF's Asian legacy', *Focus on Trade*, September.
Chossudovsky, M. (1997) *The Globalisation of Poverty: Impacts of IMF and World Bank Reforms*, London: Zed Books.
Chowdhury, A. (2000) 'Macro story of micro credit', *Himal South Asian*, March.
Claessens, S., Djankov, S. and L. Lang (2000) 'East Asian corporations: heroes or villains?', World Bank Discussion Paper no. 409, World Bank, Washington, DC.
Cobb, C., Goodman, G. and M. Wackernagel (1999) *Why Bigger Isn't Better: The Genuine Progress Indicator 1 – 1999 Update*, San Francisco: Redefining Progress.
Cope, B. and M. Kalantzis (1997) *Productive Diversity: a New Australian Model for Work and Management*, Annandale: Pluto Press.
Cossar, L. (2000) 'Paradise potion', *The Qantas Club*, Winter, pp. 20, 22.
Cottrell, G. and L. Rankin (2000) *Creating Business Value through Corporate Sustainability*, Sydney: PricewaterhouseCoopers.

Danaher, K. (ed.) (1994) *50 Years is Enough: The Case against the World Bank and the International Monetary Fund*, Cambridge: South End Press.

Das, R. (2000) 'Defending against multinational corporation offensives: strategy of the large domestic firm in a newly liberalising economy', in U. C. V. Haley (ed.) *Strategic Management in the Asia Pacific*, Oxford: Butterworth-Heinemann.

Dasgupta, S., Wang, H. and D. Wheeler (1997a) 'Surviving success: policy reform and the future of industrial pollution in China', World Bank Development Research Group Working Paper, World Bank, Washington, DC.

Dasgupta, S., Wang, H. and D. Wheeler (1997b) 'Bending the rules: discretionary pollution control in China', World Bank Development Research Group Working Paper no. 1761, World Bank, Washington, DC.

Davis, S. (1987) *Future Perfect*, Reading, Mass: Addison-Wesley.

de Bono, E. (1992) *Sur/petition: Going Beyond Competition*, London: Fontana.

de Bono, E. (1995) *Parallel Thinking*, Harmondsworth: Penguin.

Dechant, K. and B. Altman (1994) 'Environmental leadership: from compliance to competitive advantage', *Academy of Management Executive*, 8(3): 7–27.

Department of Community Services (1998) *Pierce County Quality of Life Benchmarks: Annual Report*, 3rd edn., Tacoma: Pierce County.

Development Gap, The (1999) *The All-too-visible Hand: A Five Country Look at the Long and Destructive Reach of the IMF*, The Development Group for Alternative Policies, Washington, DC.

Dieter, H. (1998) 'Crises in Asia or crisis of globalisation?', Centre for the Study of Globalisation and Regionalisation Working Paper no. 15/98, CSGR, Coventry.

Douthwaite, R. (1999) *The Growth Illusion: How Economic Growth has Enriched the Few, Impoverished the Many and Endangered the Planet*, Gabriola Island: New Society Publishers.

Dowling, R. (1998) 'Ecotourism in Southeast Asia: appropriate tourism or environmental appropriation?', *Asia Pacific Journal of Tourism Research*, July.

Durston, J. (1999) 'Building community: social capital', CEPAL Review, no. 69, pp. 103–18.

Estes, R. (1992) *At the Crossroads: Dilemmas in Social Development toward the Year 2000 and Beyond*, New York: Praeger.

Evans, P. and T. Wurster (1999) *Blown to Bits: How the New Economics of Information Transforms Strategy*, Boston: Harvard Business School Press.

Fernandez, J. (1993) *The Diversity Advantage: How American Business Can Outperform Japanese and European Companies in the Global Marketplace*, New York: Lexington.

Fisher, I. (2000) 'Somali Businesses Stunted by Too-free Enterprise', *Mogadishu Journal*, 7 August.

Flavin, C. (1996) 'Power Shock: the Next Energy Revolution', *BWZ*, No. 5.

Fombrun, C. (1986) *Realising Value from the Corporate Image*, Boston: Harvard University Press.

Forrester, V. (ed.) (1999) *The Economic Horror*, Cambridge: Polity Press.

Frankman, M. (1996) 'International taxation: the trajectory of an idea from Lorimaer to Brandt', *World Development*, 24: 807–20.

Friedman, M. (1963) *Capitalism and Freedom*, Chicago: University of Chicago Press.

Galbraith, J. K. (1996) *The Good Society: the Humane Agenda*, Boston: Houghton Mifflin.

Galbraith, J. K. (1999) 'Challenges of the New Millennium', *Finance and Development*, 36(4): 2–5.

Gates, B. (2000) *Business @ the Speed of Thought: Succeeding in the Digital Economy*, New York: Warner.

Gershuny, J. (1978) *After Industrial Society? The Emerging Self-service Economy*, London: Macmillan.

Gilmore, J. H. and B. J. Pine, II (eds) (2000) *Markets of One: Creating Customer-unique Value through Mass Customisation*, Boston: Harvard Business School Press.

Glover, D. and T. Jessup (eds) (1999) *Indonesia's Fires and Haze: the Cost of Catastrophe*, International Development Research Centre, Ottawa.

Greer, J. and K. Bruno (1996) *Greenwash: The Reality behind Corporate Environmentalism*, Third World Network, Penang.

GRI (2000) *Sustainability Reporting Guidelines on Economic, Environmental and Social Performance*, Global Reporting Initiative, Boston.

Gross, N., Coy, P. and O. Port (1995) 'The technology paradox: how companies can thrive as prices dive', *Business Week*, 6 March, pp. 36–44.

Gulledge and R. Haszko (1996) 'The Information Technology enabled organisation: a major social transformation in the USA', MOST Discussion Paper no. 14, UNESCO, Paris.

Haley, U. C. V. (1991) 'Corporate contributions as managerial masques: reframing corporate contributions as strategies to influence society', *Journal of Management Studies*, 28(5): 485–509.

Haley, U. C. V. (2000) 'Virtual Singapores: shaping international competitive environments through business–government partnerships', in U. C. V. Haley (ed.) *Strategic Management in the Asia Pacific*, Oxford: Butterworth-Heinemann.

Haley, U. C. V. and G. T. Haley (2000a) 'Boxing with shadows: competing effectively with the overseas Chinese and overseas Indian business networks in the Asian arena', in U. C. V. Haley (ed.) *Strategic Management in the Asia Pacific*, Oxford: Butterworth-Heinemann.

Haley, U. C. V. and G. T. Haley (2000b) 'When the tourists flew in: strategic implications of foreign direct investment in Vietnam's tourism industry', in U. C. V. Haley (ed.) *Strategic Management in the Asia Pacific*, Oxford: Butterworth-Heinemann.

Hamelink, C. (1997) 'New information and communication technologies, social development and cultural change', UNRISD Discussion Paper no. 86, UNRISD, Geneva.

Hanrahan, D. (1997) 'Persuasion and incentives: new ways to achieve a cleaner world', *Environment Matters*, Winter/Spring.

Hansen-Kuhn, S., Hansen-Kuhn, K. and D. Hellinger (1999) 'Conditioning debt relief on adjustment: creating the conditions for more indebtedness', The Development Group for Alternative Policies, Washington, DC.

Harman, W. and M. Porter (eds) (1997) *The New Business of Business: Sharing Responsibility for a Positive Global Future*, London: Berrett-Koehler Pub.

Harper, A. and M. Israel (1999) 'The killing of the fly: state-corporate Victimisation in Papua New Guinea', Resource Management in Asia-Pacific, Working Paper 1999/22, Australian National University, Canberra.

Harrison, D. (1997) 'Greed fuels disaster of world-wide proportions', *The Observer*, 7 October.

Hayward, H. (2000) *Costing the Casino: The Real Impact of Currency Speculation in the 1990s*, London: War on Want.

Hellinger, S. (2000) 'World Bank ignores own failure', *The Financial Times*, 23 June.

Hirschhorn, J. (2000) *Growing Pains: Quality of Life in the New Economy*, National Governors Association, Washington, DC.

Hitt, M. (2000) 'The new frontier: transformation of management for the new millennium', *Organizational Dynamics*, 28(3): 6–17.

Hobday, M. (2000) 'Innovation in Southeast Asia: lessons for Europe', in U. C. V. Haley (ed.) *Strategic Management in the Asia Pacific*, Oxford: Butterworth-Heinemann.

Holderness, M. (1995) 'The Internet and the South: superhighway or dirt-track?', Panos Media Briefing no. 16, October. See http://www.panos.org.uk/briefing/internet.htm

Howard, M. (1993) *Asia's Environmental Crisis*, Boulder: Westview Press.

Howell, L. and D. Xie (2000) 'Asia at risk: the impact of methodology in forecasting', in U. C. V. Haley (ed.) *Strategic Management in the Asia Pacific*, Oxford: Butterworth-Heinemann.

Illich, I. (1973) 'Outwitting the "Developed" Countries', in H. Bernstein (ed.) *Underdevelopment and Development*, Harmondsworth: Penguin.

ILO (2000) *World Labour Report 2000: Income Security and Social Protection in a Changing World*, ILO, Geneva.

Intal, P. (1998) 'Integrated research and policies in East Asia', in J. Schurr and S. Holtz (eds) *The Cornerstone of Development: Integrating Environmental, Social and Economic policies*, London: Lewis Publishers.

Itagaki, H. (1997) 'Basic characteristics of the Japanese production and the hybrid evaluation system', in H. Itagaki (ed.) *The Japanese Production System: Hybrid Factories in East Asia*, London: Macmillan.

Itami, H. (1987) *Mobilizing Invisible Assets*, Cambridge, Mass.: Harvard University Press.

Iyer, M. (1999) 'Can renewable energy herald a transition to sustainable societies? A case study of wind energy in India', Institute of Advanced Studies Working Paper no. 62, United Nations University, Tokyo.

Jain, A. (1992) 'Social diversity and technology for sustainable development', in S. Ito and Y. Yasuda (eds) *Nature and Humankind in the Age of Environmental Crisis*, Industrial Research Center for Japanese Studies, Kyoto.

Joint Economic Committee (1998) 'IMF financing: a review of the issues', US Congress, Washington DC. See http://www.house.gov/jec/imf/imf.htm

Jorgensen, H. (2000) 'Sustainability reporting', *Re: Business*, PricewaterhouseCoopers, September.

Kahn, H., Peters, G. and L. Ponemon (1999) 'Reputation assurance: the value of a good name', *Re: Business*, PricewaterhouseCoopers, February.

Kaul, I., Grunberg, I. and M. Stern (1999) *Global Public Goods: International Cooperation in the 21st Century*, Oxford: Oxford University Press.

Kelly, K. (1997) 'New rules for the new economy', *Wired*, September, pp. 140ff.

Khandker, S. (1998) *Fighting Poverty with Microcredit: Experience in Bangladesh*, Oxford: Oxford University Press.

Kirton, M. J. and S. de Ciantis (1989) 'Cognitive style in organisational climate', in M. J. Kirton (ed.) *Adaptors and Innovators: Styles of Creativity and Problem Solving*, London: Routledge, pp. 79–96.

Kossek, E. and S. Lobel (eds) (1996) *Managing Diversity: Human Resource Strategies for Transforming the Workplace*, Oxford: Blackwell.

Krebs, A. (1999) 'Monsanto: food, health, hope', *Backgrounder*, 5(2), Institute for Food and Development Policy.

Krugman, P. (1998) 'The confidence game: how washington worsened Asia's crash', *The New Republic*, 5 October.

Kurien, J. (1991) 'Ruining the commons and responses of the commoners: coastal overfishing and fishermen's actions in Kerala State, India', UNRISD Discussion Paper no. 2, UNRISD, Geneva.

Lappe, F., Collins, J. and P. Rosset (1998) *World Hunger: Twelve Myths*, 2nd edn., Grove Press.

Larson, E., Ross, M. and R. Williams (1986) 'Beyond the Era of Materials', *Scientific American*, June, pp. 24–31.

Leakey, R. and R. Lewin (1995) *The Sixth Extinction: Patterns of Life and the Future of Humankind*, New York: Doubleday.

Leslie, J. (1997) 'Dawn of the hydrogen age', *Wired*, 5(10).

Li, P. (2000) 'The evolution of multinational firms from Asia: a longitudinal study of Taiwan's Acer Group', in U. C. V. Haley (ed.) *Strategic Management in the Asia Pacific*, Oxford: Butterworth-Heinemann.

Llerena, P. and V. Oltra (2000) 'Diversity of innovative strategy as a source of technological performance', DRUID Working Paper no. 00–1, Danish Research Unit for Industrial Dynamics, Aalborg.

Long, G. (1996) 'The PAN Mongolia Experience', *IDRC Reports*, 6 December.

Makalou, O. (1999) 'Privatisation in Africa: a critical analysis', A paper presented at the 9th International Anti-Corruption Conference, 10–15 October, Durban, South Africa.

Mander, J. and J. Cavanagh (1999) 'WTO feeds Corporate greed', *USA Today*, 2 December.

Mayoux, L. (1995) 'From vicious to virtuous circles? gender and micro-enterprise development', Occasional Paper no. 3, UNRISD, Geneva.

Meadows, D. H., Meadows, D. L. and J. Randers (1992) *Beyond the Limits: Confronting Global Collapse, Envisioning a Sustainable Future*, Post Mills: Chelsea Green Pub. Co.

Mittal, A., Rosset, P. and M. Borchardt (1998) 'Shredding the safety net: welfare reform as we know it', *Institue for Food and Development Policy Backgrounder*, 5(4).

Mkandawire, T. and V. Rodriguez (2000) 'Globalisation and social development after copenhagen: premises, promises and policies', Geneva 2000 Occasional Paper no. 10, UNRISD, Geneva.

Mollison, B. (1990) *Permaculture: A Practical Guide for a Sustainable Future*, Washington, DC: Island Press.

Munasinghe, M. (1997) 'Economic growth and environmental sustainability: concepts and issues with Relevance for China', Institute of Advanced Studies Working Paper no. 32, United Nations University, Tokyo.

Myrdal, G. (1968) *Asian Drama: An Inquiry into the Poverty of Nations*, Harmondsworth: Penguin.

Nadler, D. and M. Tushman (1999) 'The organization of the future: strategic imperatives and core competencies for the 21st Century', *Organizational Dynamics*, 28(1): 45–60.

Narayanan, D. (2000) 'Corporates' turn to play the good samaritan', *FT Asia Intelligence Wire*, 21 September.

Nef, J. (1999) *Human Security and Mutual Vulnerability: The Global Political Economy of Development and Underdevelopment*, 2nd edn., IDRC, Ottawa.

Nonaka, I. and H. Takeuchi (1995) *The Knowledge-creating Company: How Japanese Companies Create the Dynamics of Innovation*, Oxford: Oxford University Press.

Ohmae, K. (1990) *The Borderless World: Power and Strategy in the Interlinked Economy*, London: Collins.

Oxfam International (1997) 'Poor country debt relief: false dawn or new hope for poverty reduction?'.

Oxfam International (1998) 'East Asian "recovery" leaves the poor sinking', Oxfam International Briefing, October.

Oxfam International (2000) 'Debt relief and poverty reduction: failing to deliver', Oxfam International Briefing, April.

Pearlstein, S. (2000) 'A new politics born of globalisation', *Washington Post*, 1 October.

Penzias, A. (1995) *Harmony: Business, Technology and Life after Paperwork*, New York: Harper Business.

Perry, M. and T. S. Teng (1999) 'An overview of trends related to environmental reporting in Singapore', *Environment Management and Health*, 10(5): 310–20.

Peters, G. (2000) 'Reputation management: why nice guys finish first', *Financial Times*, see http://www.ft.com/specials/sp41da.htm

Pine, B. J. (1999) *Mass Customization: The New Frontier in Business Competition*, Boston: Harvard Business School Press.

Piore, M. and C. Sabel (1984) *The Second Industrial Divide: Possibilities for Prosperity*, New York: Basic Books.

Porter, M. (1997) 'Creating tomorrow's advantages', in R. Gibson(ed.) *Rethinking the Future*, London: Nicholas Brealey, pp. 48–61.

Prahalad, C. K. (1997) 'Strategies for growth', in R. Gibson (ed.) *Rethinking the Future*, London: Nicholas Brealey, pp. 62–75.

Ravallion, M. and Q. Wodon (1997) 'Banking on the poor: branch placement and non-farm rural development in Bangladesh', Working Paper no. 1858, World Bank, Washington, DC.

Rifkin, J. (1995) *The End of Work: The Decline of the Global Labour Force and the Dawn of the Post-market Era*, New York: Putnam-Tarcher.

Robertson, C. and T. Jett (1999) 'The environmental and industrial benefits of project XL at Merck & Co., Inc.', *Organizational Dynamics*, 28(2): 81–8.

Robinson, J. and J. Tinker (1998) 'Reconciling ecological, economic and social imperatives: towards an analytical framework', in J. Schurr and S. Holtz (eds) *The Cornerstone of Development: Integrating Environmental, Social and Economic Policies*, London: Lewis Publishers.

Sagasti, F. and G. Alcalde (1999) *Development Cooperation in a Fractured Global Order: An Arduous Transition*, IDRC, Ottawa.

Schonberger, R. (1996) *World Class Manufacturing: The Next Decade*, New York: The Free Press.

Schumacher, E. F. (1974) *Small is Beautiful: A Study of Economics as if People Mattered*, London: Abacus.

Schwartz, P. and P. Leyden (1997) 'The long boom: a history of the future, 1980–2020', *Wired*, 5 July.

Sen, A. (1999) *Development as Freedom*, New York: Alfred A. Knopf.

Shell (2000) *How Do We Stand? People, Planet and Profits: The Shell Report 2000*, London: Royal Dutch/Shell.

Shilling, G. (1998) *Deflation*, Short Hills: Lakeview Pub. Co.

Singh, S. J. (1997) 'It makes a village', *tele.com*, December. See http://teledotcom.com/1297/features/tdc1297bang.html

Singh, A. (2000) 'Global economic trends and social development', *Geneva 2000 Occasional Paper* no. 9, Geneva: UNRISD.

Smith, J. W. (2000) *Economic Democracy: The Political Struggle of the 21st Century*, New York: M.E. Sharpe.

Social Development Department (2000) *New Paths to Social Development: Community and Global Networks in Action*, World Bank, Washington, DC.

Steffensen, S. (2000) 'Informational network industrialisation and Japanese business management', in U. C. V. Haley (ed.) *Strategic Management in the Asia Pacific*, Oxford: Butterworth-Heinemann.

Stiglitz, J. (1997) 'Stepping toward Balance: addressing global climate change', Remarks by the Chief Economist of the World Bank to the *Conference on Environmentally and Socially Sustainable Development*, 6 October, Washington, DC. See http://www.worldbank.org/html/extdr/extme/jssp100697.htm

Stiglitz, J. (2000) 'The insider: what I learned at the world economic crisis', *The New Republic*, 17 April.

Streeck, W. (1991) 'On the institutional conditions of diversified quality production', in E. Matzner and W. Streeck (eds) *Beyond Keynesianism: The Socio-economics of Production and Full Employment*, London: Edward Elgar.

Suryahadi, A., Sumarto, S., Suharso, Y. and L. Pritchett (2000) 'The evolution of poverty during the crisis in Indonesia, 1996 to 1999', *Work Bank Working Paper* no. 2435, World Bank, Washington, DC.

Tapscott, D. and D. Agnew (1999) 'Governance in the digital economy', *Finance and Development*, December, pp. 34–7.

Tegtmeier, W. (1999) 'Social security: an obstacle to full employment?', *Employment and Training Papers* no. 14, ILO, Geneva.

Theobald, R. (1999) *We Do have Future Choices: Strategies for Fundamentally Changing the 21st Century*, Lismore: Southern Cross University Press.

Tobin, J. and G. Ranis (1998) 'Flawed fund: the IMF's misplaced priorities', *The New Republic*, 9 March.

TRAC (1999) *A Perilous Partnership: the United Nations Development Programme's Flirtation with Corporate Collaboration*, Transnational Resource and Action Center, San Francisco.

UNCED (1992) *Agenda 21: Report of the United Nations Conference on Environment and Development*, Rio de Janeiro, 3–14 June, United Nations, New York.

UNDP (2000) *Human Development Report 2000*, UNDP, New York.

UNITE (2000) 'Sweatshops behind the swoosh', Union of Needletrades, Industrial and Textile Employees, New York.

UNRISD (2000) *Visible Hands: Taking Responsibility for Social Development*, UNRISD, Geneva.

Utting, P. (2000) 'Business responsibility for sustainable development', *Geneva 2000 Occasional Paper* no. 2, UNRISD, Geneva.

Vidal, J. (1998) *McLibel: Burger Culture on Trial*, New Press, New York.

Vietnam Labor Watch (1997) *Nike Labour Practices in Vietnam*, VLW, New York.

Watts, P. and L. Holme (1999) *Corporate Social Responsibility: Meeting Changing Expectations*, Geneva: WBCSD, Geneva.

WBCSD (1996) *Environmental Assessment: A Business Perspective*, WBCSD, Geneva.

WBCSD (1999) *Eco-efficiency Indicators and Reporting*, WBCSD, Geneva.

Wegberg, M. and P. Berends (2000) 'Competing communities of users and developers of computer software: competition between open source software and commercial software', *NIBOR Working Paper* no. nib00001, Maastricht: University of Maastricht.

Wei, H. and C. Christodoulou (2000) 'An examination of strategic foreign direct investment decision process: the case of Taiwanese manufacturing small- and medium-sized enterprises', in U. C. V. Haley (ed.) *Strategic Management in the Asia Pacific*, Oxford: Butterworth-Heinemann.

Weisbrot, M., Naiman, R. and J. Kim (2000) 'The emperor has no growth: declining economic growth rates in the era of globalisation', *CEPR Briefing Paper*, Center for Economic and Policy Research, Washington, DC.

Wetzler, B. (2000) 'Boomgalore', *Wired*, March.

Wheeler, C. (1996) 'Moving Asia from grassroots to cyberspace', *IDRC Reports*, 22 January.

Wheeler, D. et al., (2000) *Greening Industry: New Roles for Communities, Markets and Governments*, World Bank, Washington, DC.

Wolfensohn, J. (1999) 'A proposal for a comprehensive development framework', A statement to the *Board, Management and Staff of the World Bank group*, 21 January. See http://www.worldbank.org/cdf/cdf-text.htm

Womack, J., Jones, D. and D. Roos (1990) *The Machine that Changed the World*, New York: Harper.

Wong, M. (2000) 'Children toil in sweatshop', *South China Morning Post*, 27 August.

Woodroffe, J. and M. Ellis-Jones (2000) 'States of unrest: resistance to IMF policies in poor countries', *World Development Movement Report*, September.

World Bank (1999a) *Entering the 21st Century: World Development Report 1999/2000*, New York: Oxford University Press.

World Bank (1999b) *Global Economic Prospects and the Developing Countries 1998/99: Beyond Financial Crisis*, World Bank, Washington, DC.

World Commission on Environment and Development (1987) *Our Common Future: From one Earth to one World*, Oxford: Oxford University Press.

Wright, D. (2000) 'Sustainability and profitability', *Re: Business*, Pricewaterhouse-Coopers, July.

You, J. (1995) 'The Korean model of development and its environmental implications', in V. Bhaskar and A. Glyn (eds) *The North, The South and the Environment: Ecological Constraints and the Global Economy*, Tokyo: United Nations Press.

Yunus, M. (1999) *Banker to the Poor: Micro-lending and the Battle against World poverty*, New York: Public Affairs.

Zeldin, M. and C. di Florio (2000) 'Business ethics and corruption risk management', *Re: Business*, PricewaterhouseCoopers, May.

Zey, M. (1994) *Seizing the Future: How the Coming Revolution in Science, Technology, and Industry will Expand the Frontiers of Human Potential and Reshape the Planet*, New York: Simon and Schuster.

Zhang, K. (1996) 'Industrial hazards raging in China', *October Review*, 29 February, 23(1).

Zhang, N. and H. Li (2000) 'China scraps 9 state bureaus, cutting government meddling of business', Chinadaily.com.cn, 18 September.

Part 6
Epilogue

20
Afterword

Frank-Jürgen Richter

September 11, 2001 will change the world. The impact of the terrorist attacks is particularly severe in Asia. Even before September 11, Asia was experiencing an imprecedented economic downturn. Now, Asia is in recession.

One of the factors that caused the Asian economic crisis in 1997 may have been the deceleration in export growth suffered by East Asian economies. Four years after the crisis erupted, a similar pattern emerges, but this time the hit comes from the slowdown of the US economy which absorbed more than a fourth of Asia's exports during the last two years of the outgoing century. Since the 1997 Asian crisis, buoyant US demand has kept many companies in Asia afloat, helping them finance their working capital needs.

As our book has shown (see Chapter 1), East Asia's export-dependent economies are starting to lose momentum as the decline of the US economy hits the region. And, as US demand weakens, Japanese demand wanes, which further deepens the decline in Asian exports. There is certainly a correlation between US investment in IT and computers, and Asian exports, especially for countries such as Japan, South Korea, Taiwan, Singapore and Malaysia that have large electronics sectors.

Despite Asia's strong rebound in 1999 and 2000, it continued to be plagued by excess capacity while restructuring in the corporate and banking sector of some countries had probably not been deep enough to ensure financial strength and sustainable growth. Authors in this book have argued (see Chapters 11–14) that the ills of the corporate and banking sectors have not been fully fixed. While many businesses have strengthened their governance and renewed competitiveness, concerns linger over the sustainability of institutional reform in a number of countries. And it is interesting to observe that voters have been turning against governments who preside over slowing economies but at the same time try to pursue restructuring (see Chapters 8–10 for analyses of the effects of governmental policy).

There will hopefully not be another Asian crisis, but the export slowdown could not have come at a worse timing for Asia. It coincides with a period of weak domestic activity in Asia because many of the region's banks continue to be plagued by non-performing loans; and naturally their managers are unwilling to lend to local companies. As the corporate sector is unlikely to be able to refocus on domestic growth, they create further instability in the banking system. It is clear that Asia is suffering from an investment crisis creating anxiety since money is no longer plentiful, even for worthy investments (see Chapter 1 for an analysis of investment hesitation).

In April 2001, many governments across the region announced packages to offset the impact of the US slowdown. This stimulation of local firms maybe a useful maneouvre – steeper reliance on domestic markets followed by diversified exports make for sustainable growth, at least on the short-term. But a dependence on a few goods (or sectors) puts economies at greater risk due to external factors (i.e., the US slowdown). Therefore, Asia cannot merely target its exports to grow out of the crisis, as it did in the years after 1997.

Most importantly, if the region is to avoid a repeat of the devastating turmoil experienced in 1997, Asia's economic as well as its political leaders have to focus their attention on reforming the non-performing aspects of their political, social, corporate, and financial institutions. Of course, it is too simplistic to put the blame on the US economic slowdown. The crisis of 1997 and the crisis of 2001 are not the mere result of slowing exports and macroeconomic mismanagement, but the result of certain deep-rooted institutional deficiencies that have created moral hazard among enterprises, leading finally to inefficient corporate management. This book, with its coverage of actors and policies, has aimed to foster understanding of these deficiencies, and to develop the concepts of corporate and governmental strategies that should lead to sustainable competitive advantage in Asia.

We can hope that real reform, and the creation of competitive advantages aiming on sustainable growth, is now on the agenda. Asia may also have to focus on higher value added services industries rather than manufacturing to achieve adequate growth. This has the advantage that services are generally less capital intensive – but they also demand better education. The latter has been in some decline since the mid-1990s in many Asian countries as they concentrated their efforts on their apparent burgeoning economies. This book has argued that for the future, Asian post-crisis management has to include all sectors and stakeholders of society – including NGOs and the voice of the underprivileged (see Chapters 15–19 for wide-ranging discussions and analyses of various stakeholders' interests and goals). Once we have an open exchange of opinions in which each party is treated with respect, we will most probably see sustainable solutions – in Asia, as in other parts of the world. Let's hope that Asia will be back on the growth path soon again. And let us hope that the world will soon be a peaceful planet to live on.

Index